Migration Law in Hungary

Migration Law in Hungary

Second Edition

Judit Tóth

This book was originally published as a monograph in the International Encyclopaedia of Laws/Migration Law.

General Editors: Roger Blanpain, Frank Hendrickx
Volume Editor: Dirk Vanheule

Wolters Kluwer

Published by:
Kluwer Law International B.V.
PO Box 316
2400 AH Alphen aan den Rijn
The Netherlands
Website: www.wklawbusiness.com

Sold and distributed in North, Central and South America by:
Wolters Kluwer Legal & Regulatory U.S.
7201 McKinney Circle
Frederick, MD 21704
United States of America
Email: customer.service@wolterskluwer.com

Sold and distributed in all other countries by:
Turpin Distribution Services Ltd.
Stratton Business Park
Pegasus Drive, Biggleswade
Bedfordshire SG18 8TQ
United Kingdom
Email: kluwerlaw@turpin-distribution.com

Printed on acid-free paper

ISBN 978-90-411-8266-1

This title is available on www.kluwerlawonline.com

Printed and Bound by CPI Group (UK) Ltd, Croydon, CR0 4YY.

The Author

Tóth, Judit, PhD, Dr jur. (1962), is a lawyer and an associate professor of constitutional law (Department of Constitutional law, Faculty of Law – Szeged University) and has been a senior research fellow in the Centre for Migration & Refugee Studies (1991–2000) and Minority Studies since 2000 (Hungarian Academy of Sciences). She has her own courses on citizenship law, minority and migration rights, and rules on non-profit sector at the University, and she is the leader of the Legal Clinic in Szeged. Tóth has published more than a hundred articles and books on refugee law, the migration policy of contemporary Hungary, European Union (EU) enlargement as well as on Diaspora in legal regulation and policy. She has worked in international research teams on migration and Human Rights (HR) issues since 1991, and recently in the EU 6th Framework Programme 'Challenge – The Changing Landscape of the European Security and Liberty' (2004–2009). Tóth has been involved in legislative preparatory work as adviser since 1986 (Ministry of Environment, Ministry of Social Affairs, Ministry of the Interior, Parliamentary Committee on Constitutional Reform, Prime Minister's Office, Ministry of Justice, Ombudsman Office). She represented Hungary in the expert committee for refugees and stateless persons (CAHAR) in the Council of Europe in 1990–1996, and is the founder of the Hungarian Association for Migrants (1995) and curator of the International Fund for Comparative Research (1991).

Her recent publications include:

Tóth, Judit. 'Czech and Hungarian Roma Exodus to Canada – How to Distinguish Between Unbearable Destitution and Unbearable Persecution'. In: *Foreigners, Refugees or Minorities? Rethinking People in the Context of Border Controls and Visas*, Edited by Bigo D., Guild, E. and Carrera, S. Ashgate, 2013, pp. 39–54.

Tóth, Judit. 'Entre politique étrangere et politique intérieure – La « Politique de Diaspora » de la Hongrie'. In: *Loin des yeux, prés du coeur. Les États et leurs expatriés,* Sous la direction de S. Dufoix, C. Guerrassimoff, A. De Tinguy. Presses de Sciences-Po, Paris, 2010, pp. 221–237.

The Author

Tóth, Judit. *The Incomprehensible Flow of Roma Asylum-seekers from the Czech Republic and Hungary to Canada.* CEPS *'Liberty and Security in Europe'* publication series, Brussels, November 2010 pp.42 ISBN 978-94-6138-063-0.

Table of Contents

Table of Contents

List of Abbreviations

Act on Accession	Act XXX of 2004 on Accession of Hungary to the European Union
AdminA	Act CXL of 2004 on Administrative Procedural and Public Service Code
AMF	Asylum and Migration Fund
AsylA	Act LXXX of 2007 on Asylum
AsylD	Government Decree No. 301 of 2007, 9 November on implementation of the rules of the Act LXXX of 2007 on asylum
BordA	Act LXXXIX of 2007 on the Borders of the State
Civil Code	Act V of 2013 on Civil Code
CivPA	Act III of 1952 on Civil Law-suit Procedural Code
Constitution	Act XX of 1949 on the Constitution of Hungary modified by the Act XXXI of 1989. It is replaced by the Fundamental Law (25 April 2011) on 1st January 2012
CrimPA	Act XIX of 1998 on Criminal Procedural Code
DeptD	Decree of the Minister of Justice and Law Enforcement No.26 of 2007, 31 May on Implementation of Deportation Order
DetD	Decree of the Minister of Justice and Law Enforcement No.27 of 2007, 31 May on Detention of Foreigners
EU	European Union
ECJ	European Court of the Justice (Luxemburg)
EEA	European Economic Area
EEKH	Office of Health Authorization and Administrative Procedures
ECHR	European Convention of Human Rights (1950, Rome)

List of Abbreviations

EkhoA	Act CXX of 2005 on Simplified Contribution to Public Revenues
EqualA	Act CXXV of 2003 on Equal Treatment and Promotion of Equal Opportunities
ETA	Equal Treatment Authority
EUCJ	European Union Court of Justice
ExD	Government Decree No.355 of 2007, 23 December on Free Employment of EEA Nationals and Temporary Provisions in Hungary
FeeD	Ministerial Decree of Justice and Law Enforcement No. 28 of 2007, 31 May on Fees of Procedures in ambit the Act I of 2007 and Act II of 2007
FreeA	Act I of 2007 on Free Movement and Right to Residence
FreeD	Government Decree No. 113 of 2007, 24 May on Implementation of the Act I of 2007
FreeLA	Act LXXX of 2003 on Free Legal Aid
HEIC	Hungarian Equivalence and Information Centre
HealthD	Decree of Minister of Healthcare No. 32 of 2007, 27 June on diseases endangering the public health in connection with residence of persons in ambit of the Act I of 2007 and Act II of 2007
HighA	Act CCIV of 2011 on the High-level Education]
LabInA	Act LXXV of 1996 on Labour Inspection
Labour Code	Act I of 2012 on Labour Code
LandA	Act CXXII of 2013 on Acquisition of Arable Land and Forest
LandD	Government Decree No. 7 of 1996, January 18 on Acquisition of Real Estate by Foreign Nationals
LisbonA	Act CLXVIII of 2007 on publishing the Lisbon Treaty modifying the Treaties on the European Union and the European Community
MinD	Ministerial Decree of Justice and Law Enforcement No. 25 of 2007, 31 May on executive rules to the Act I of 2007 and Act II of 2007
MinofA	Act II of 2012 on Minor Offences and Procedure
MinofD	Ministerial Decree No.22 of 2012, April 13 on Executive of Minor Offences
NAV	National Tax and Customs Office (Authority)
NATO	North Atlantic Treaty Organization

NSO	National Security Office
OECD	Organisation for Economic Cooperation and Development
OIN	Office for Immigration and Nationality Affairs
PassA	Act XII of 1998 on Travelling Abroad
PassD	Government Decree No.101 of 1998, 22 May on the Implementing Provisions of the Act XII of 1998 on Travelling Abroad
Penal Code	Act C of 2012 on Criminal Code
PensionA	Act CXVII of 2007 on Pension scheme for Employee and its Institutions
PermitD	Government Decree No.445 of 2013, November 28 on Work Permits Issued to Third-Country Nationals in Hungary
PolA	Act XXXIV of 1994 on Police
PrivA	Act CXV of 2009 on Private Entrepreneurs and Sole Proprietorship
PuboA	Act CXCIX of 2011 on Public Officials
QualA	Act C of 2001 on Recognition of Foreign Diplomas and Qualifications
ResD	Government Decree No.181 of 2007, 6 July on Accreditation of Scientific Institutes Receiving Researchers who are Third-Country Nationals and on the Receiving Contract
RegA	Act LXVI of 1992 on Registration of Personal Data and Address
SecA	Act CXXV of 1995 on National Security Services
SeTax	Act XLIII of 2002 on Simplified Entrepreneurial Tax
SocialA	Act III of 1993 on Social Administration and Social Benefits
SocInA	Act LXXX of 1997 on Eligible for Social Insurance Benefits and Private Pension Scheme and their Cover
TaxA	Act CXVII of 1995 on Personal Income Tax
TaxPA	Act XCII of 2003 on Taxation Procedural Rules
TCN	Third-Country National
ThirdA	Act II of 2007 on Entry and Residence of Third-Country Nationals

List of Abbreviations

ThirdD	Government Decree No. 114 of 2007, 24 May on the Implementation of Act II of 2007
UNCCPR	United Nations Covenants on Civil and Political Rights
UNHCR	United Nations High Commissioner for Refugees
UnemplA	Act IV of 1991 on Job Assistance and Unemployment Benefits
UNHRC	UN Human Rights Council
VAT	Value-Added Tax
VolA	Act LXXXVIII of 2005 on Volunteer's Activity for Public Utility

Preface

The readers may agree with the general statement by Roscoe Pound in the *Introduction to the Philosophy of Law* that '*the law must be stable, but it must not stand still*'. While writing this book my main challenge was the unfounded and frequent changes in the legislation on migration law allowing time neither for public debates on needs, necessities of society or economy, nor for law practitioners to assess the applicability of rules. The major lesson from this monograph is how a country in a transition period has to protect the perception of the legal system from degradation due to hit-or-miss amendments, mechanical transposition of the EU law, a simplified replication of the international commitments and the waste of human capital in public administration.

This book is based on the interpretative description of the migration law in force, and some components from the legal practice, if available. However, both are limited: since the constitutional reform in Hungary (1989), we have been witnessing the birth of the fourth generation of migration rules (1993, 2001, 2007 and after 2010), so a crystallized system and principles have not yet been developed. As regards the judicial and administrative legal practice, it is not accessible as most of the migration case law has remained in non-litigation procedural files without being entered into public databases. While training for judges on asylum law I feel their vivid interest in judgments, and apart from certain exceptions a motivation to learn from one's own mistakes.

The reluctance of the migration policy makers is clear because they shift publicly the position of a sending country to a receiving or destination country but only for a kin-minority. The quick accession of Hungary to the Council of Europe, the Organisation of Economic Cooperation and Development, the North Atlantic Treaty Organisation and the European Union has assisted the postponement of the vital public discussions on international migratory movements. At the same time, the law makers have to regulate this complex issue and practitioners have to implement these provisions without confirmation on finality. For this reason, this book in eight substantial parts illustrates the structure of the regulation and the division of competence in administration, in the reception of a migrant, though a deeper assessment of the legal impacts will be prepared in future.

General Introduction

§1. Immigration History and Statistical Information

1. The entire history of the Hungarian nation and state may be *articulated on the grounds of migratory movements.* The state was established in the great wave of peoples in the tenth–eleventh century by the Hungarian tribes coming from the neighbourhood of China and Mongolia, wandering through the steppe and Ural environment. 862 AD is the earliest date referred to in sources, regarding Hungarians fighting in the Carpathian Basin (Zsoldos, 2004). The Carpathian Basin has been the homeland for Hungarians since King (Saint) Stephen I established the Hungarian Kingdom, receiving and sending away thousands of migrants. The history of the conquest and unification of the Carpathian Basin meant certain forms of forced migration for people living there at that time, including battles for power, alliance, Christianity and plunders. The best known part of the regulation of Saint Stephen is not his 56 laws in the Corpus Juris Hungarici issued during his reign (997–1034) but his political testament given to his son, Prince Imre, on how diversity in society and culture would be respected while receiving foreigners into the country, together with their own traditions. During the troubled centuries of the Middle Ages, the forced migration and forcible subjugation was decisive such as the invasion of Tartars-Mongolians (thirteenth century), domination of the Ottoman Empire (sixteenth–seventeenth century), the Habsburg Empire in Hungary (seventeenth–nineteenth century) together with numerous fights of Hungarians for independence, liberty and recovery of the ancient privileges of nobles. The Confederation Agreement (1867) establishing the Austro-Hungarian Monarchy provided public stability for economic prosperity together with immigration of investors, industrialists, skilled labour and merchants while approximately 1 million poor ploughmen and menial workers without an opportunity to have any means of subsistence and property left the rural areas and migrated overseas[1] due to the postponement of land reforms. This loss of working force, defence and demography was addressed in the public policy requiring control on emigration (Rácz, 1980). While the first Act on Emigration was adopted in 1881 defining how carriers were to be operated and how the emigrants were to be registered and allowed to apply for passports in a liberal manner, the immigration to Hungary was totally unregulated and free. This migration model and scale of migration was common in this

1. According to the statistics in European harbours the total number of emigrants between 1871 and 1913 from Hungary was 2,038,360 (Rácz, 1980:215).

Central-Eastern European region,[2] and until the adoption of the Quota Acts in the US the foreign labourers could have been considered as 'birds of passage' to a great extent (Puskás, 1990). Their emigration and return was dependent on the need for workforce and the need to accumulate sufficient capital for family existence in Hungary. After the dissolution of the Austro-Hungarian Monarchy (1918) and the Peace Treaty after the First World War, the Hungarian state borders were shifted, in the process losing territories inhabited by millions of ethnic Hungarians who now came under the sovereignty of the newborn nation states in the neighbourhood (Czechoslovakia, Yugoslavia, Romania, Ukraine and Austria). While the labour emigration was prevalent to a smaller extent in the interwar period (1918–1940) from Hungary, the forced migration owing to racial laws and to escape from the Holocaust was growing. During the same period, the mass immigration meant the inflow of almost half a million ethnic Hungarians from the adjacent states (Szarka, 2004). The Diaspora or/and kin-state policy is rooted in mass emigration in 1870–1956 and the changing of borders in 1920, 1941–1945 and the Peace Treaty after the Second World War that altogether formed a virtual community comprising 3–5 million ethnic Hungarians and/or citizens in Europe and other continents. Whereas, during the Second World War Hungary received many escaped Polish citizens (Jews, soldiers, students and family members) providing a temporary shelter, forged documents and schooling for them, the Jews and Roma citizens numbering approximately half a million living in Hungary's countryside were deported in by the Hungarian authorities in cooperation with the German troops, and were killed in German concentration camps. During the Cold War period, Hungary received thousands of refugees from the Greek civil war in 1947–1950, from Chile after the failure of the Salvador Allende regime in 1973, transit migrants from the Republic of Eastern Germany (DDR) in 1989 marching to the German re-unification, refugees from the Romanian anti-democratic regime and inter-ethnic clashes in 1988–1990 (Tóth, 2008c) and victims of the Balkan war, ethnic cleansing and ethnic disturbances since the 1990s. Although the waves of migration and immigration maintained the emotional sensitivity to human tragedies in public opinion, the loss and frustration in relation to migratory movements cannot forcibly set up a comprehensive reception system and integration policy, or at least legal safeguards for immigrants of the last two decades. (Adelman et al., 1994; Tóth, 2004a)

2. Since the Constitutional Reform in 1989 and democratic elections in 1990, the net migration has been positive although the precise figures of emigrated Hungarian citizens are missing due to the right to free travel abroad, introduced in January 1988. Since its introduction, the citizens are required to register at the people's registry office their address abroad or consular office if they reside outside Hungary for more than three months. In the absence of sanction, it is not known how many Hungarian citizens left the country permanently within the traditional meaning of

2. Fifty-five million people left Europe and travelled overseas in the hundred years preceding the First World War, thirty-three of them heading for the US. Small wonder, then, that the matter of the 'ethnic roots' is a personal issue to a great many people who never dream of actually visiting the land of their forebearers. The ethnic composition of the 'peasant exodus' by Polish, Croats, Slovaks, Jews, Czechs, Russians, Slovenians or Hungarians inspired passions in the region at that time, at turn of the century (see the articles in the book edited by Puskás, 1990).

emigration. After the accession of Hungary to the European Union, the migration statistics were challenged by new categories of persons by law, necessitating a restructure of the estimation, which is pending (Table 1).

Table 1 Net Migration in Hungary (1990–2009)

Year	*Immigrants*	*Returned Expatriated*[3]	*Left Citizens*	*Left Immigrants*	*Difference in Migration*
1990	37,242	397	1,054	11,271	25,314
1995	14,008	1,427	772	2,401	12,262
1998	16,052	1,217	716	2,343	14,210
2000	20,184	1,542	332	2,208	19,186
2003	19,365	1,962	569	2,553	18,205
2004	22,164	2,134	354	3,466	20,478
2006	23,569	2,163	358	3,956	21,418
2007	22,607	1,775	392	4,133	19,857
2008	35,547	1,974	580	4,241	32,700
2009	25,552	2,112	553	5,600	21,511

Source: Database of the Demographic Yearbooks (Hungarian Statistical Office, Budapest).

However, the oscillating trend of residing and registered migrants is visible alongside the limited scale of transit migration. Moreover, the balance of migratory movements has been positive, but it cannot compensate for the high mortality of the population which causes a severe loss and a disproportional age component. Nevertheless, the total population is slightly below 10 million, possibly due to the immigrants. The census in November 2011 registered 9.9 million residents while the minimal estimation of emigrated citizens (workers, students) was 0.4 million, who have left the country since 2010.

3. The other characteristic feature of the migratory movements has been the circular migration of *ethnic Hungarians living in adjacent states*. While they are legally and sociologically foreign migrants, their cultural proximity may raise the question of whether they need integration services, legal preferences and naturalization in Hungary, in particular when they are also EU citizens or family members. Only a reluctant public policy has hindered for decades the whole reception and integration policy towards them in Hungary. Every year, there are millions of visitors, commuting workers and employees (not necessary lawfully), petty traders, domestic workers, students, medical treatment users, service providers and business partners belonging to the kin-minorities present in Hungary. Not all of them are included in the proper statistics on admission procedures, tax and social insurance

3. It covers the birth of nationals abroad and registered.

contributors. The economy and the society in transition have benefited from the migrants' role in the shadow economy, privatization, reduction of regional labour shortages, gasoline and tobacco tourism (ordinary smuggling of these products to avoid paying the inland revenues and/or higher Value-Added Tax (VAT)) particularly in isolated border zones without formal employment.

The Constitution/Fundamental Law has legitimized the preferential policy towards the kin-minority and diaspora living all over the world, laying down a state obligation to take care of ethnic Hungarians' preferred contact with Hungary, their well-being and fate. This political statement has penetrated the migration law and legal practice on migration authorization on entry, visa, residence, settlement and naturalization issues. This may explain why knowledge of the Hungarian language by migrants is presumed in all procedures, with the exception of the format introduced by the EU law, and why cultural and social integration as well as legal safeguards of residence have been consequently neglected in the law and in practice. The 'typical migrant' is an ethnic Hungarian who can communicate well and who, culturally speaking, is not a stranger, so he/she can find work, schooling, housing easily or by the assistance of family members and friends, without municipal and Government support. The equal treatment for European Economic Area (EEA) nationals and family members residing in Hungary, and minimal requirements of reception and integration services to other foreigners according to the EU law means that this 'in-group and out-group' policy must alter in favour of non-Hungarians and exclude those ethnic Hungarians who are third-country nationals by European Community (EC) law in parallel (ethnic Hungarians in Serbia and Ukraine) (Tóth & Sik, 2003). Due to the recent amendment of the nationality law the total number of naturalized persons based on ethnic preference without requirement of residence in Hungary was over 450,000 in early 2014. They are dual citizens.[4]

4. Taking into account the available data on immigration, either Hungary's attractiveness to potential immigrants has slightly diminished, or the trend of immigration is stable. The asylum seekers can hardly enter with visas, so they are entering illegally with supports of smugglers in human beings or alone across the green border thus they are apprehended in the border zone. Moreover, applicants' detention that was introduced in 2013 increases figures (Table 2).

Table 2 Asylum Seekers in Hungary (2003–2013)

Year	*Number of Applicants*	*From Europe %*	*Illegal Arrival %*
2003	2,401	27.5	76.8
2004	1,600	31.4	71.6
2005	1,609	36.3	64.6

4. Honosított Magyar állampolgárok, Statisztikai Tükör 2014/35, p. 2. KSH, Budapest (www.ksh.hu/docs/hun/xftp/stattukor/honositas12.pdf).

Year	*Number of Applicants*	*From Europe %*	*Illegal Arrival %*
2006	2,117	40.0	69.5
2007	3,419	33.9	82.5
2008	3,118	57.2	92.3
2009	4,672	56.0	96.7
2010	2,104	27.0	97.0
2012	2,157	14.1	96.0
2013	18,900	34.2	98.3

Source: data on the base of the OIN (http://www.bmbah.hu).

The Common Area for Asylum in the European Union means that the geographical position of Member States has an influence on asylum statistics (and procedural burdens), because the peripheral Member States receive more applicants in accordance with the pre-screening method under the Dublin rules than they can send to another state for a substantial procedure. The 'applicants in orbit' having to pass through the Member States on the grounds of the many requirements for entry, visa, family relations, prior residence or prior application is inhuman, expensive and unequal. The Hungarian statistic proves its extent (Table 3).

Table 3 Reception and Surrender of Asylum Seekers under the Dublin Procedure (2005–2013)

Year	*Received by Hungary from other Member States*	*Admission from Hungary by other Member States*
2005	159	n.d.
2006	273	n.d.
2007	239	15
2008	334	63
2009	934	84
2010	742	177
2012	335	126
2013	850	32
	From Austria, Germany, France, Poland, Switzerland	To Romania, Austria, Germany, Greece, Bulgaria

Source: database of the OIN <www.bmbah.hu>.

5. The 'myth of transit country' associated with Hungary is supported not only by ethnic circular migration but also by asylum applicants' disappearance prior

to the final decision. Considering the low recognition rate (e.g., in 2013 below 2%), the further migration of applicants may be explained in another way as well (Table 4).

Table 4 Recognized Refugees in Hungary (2003–2013)

Year	*Persons*	*1st Group by Nationality*	*2nd Group by Nationality*	*3rd Group by Nationality*
2003	178	Iraq	Afghanistan	Serbia-Montenegro
2004	149	Afghanistan	Serbia-Montenegro	Iraq
2005	97	Iran	Afghanistan	Serbia-Montenegro
2006	99	Iraq	Iran	Afghanistan
2007	169	Iraq	Somalia	Iran
2008	160	Somalia	Iraq	Afghanistan
2009	177	Somalia	Iraq	West-Bank + Gaza
2010	83	Somalia	Afghanistan	Iraq
2012	87	Syria	Afghanistan	Somalia
2013	173	Syria	Afghanistan	Georgia

Source: database of the OIN <www.bmbah.hu>.

Similar to refugees, the number of other persons in need of international protection (alternative status for protection, tolerated migrants) is minimal (Table 5). However, the prospects of refugees and non-expelled migrants have to be improved in the future in Hungary to prevent the waste of human capital.

Table 5 Protected Persons Living in Hungary (2009–2013)

Status	*31 December 2009*	*31 December 2013*
Recognized refugees (on the grounds of 1951 Geneva Convention)	1714	1513
Recognized alternative protection (on the grounds of EC law)	150	927
Tolerated migrants (on the grounds of prohibition of removal in HR)	217	98
Total	**2,081**	**2,538**

Source: statistics of the OIN <www.bmbah.hu>.

6. The data on migrants residing longer than a simple visitor or tourist in the country is perhaps the other important indicator of the general feeling of a migrant living in Hungary. The stock data of migrants implies that their ratio in the total population remains marginal: since 1998 it has been below 2%. However, their importance is partly determined by their ethnic origin, not only by the absolute number of that mass. There are no available statistics on the ethnic origin of migrants but the nationality indirectly corroborates the conclusion on proximity. China, Russia or Germany belong to the 'out-group', while citizens of neighbouring countries or the US (Hungarian Diaspora) would be considered as members of the 'in-group' (Table 6).

Table 6 Foreign Residents in Hungary on 31 December 2008 and 2013 (Stock Data)

Entitlement	*Permit Holders 2008*	*Permit Holders 2013*	*1st Group by Nationality*	*2nd Group by Nationality*	*3rd Group by Nationality*
Immigration permit (issued before the ThirdA entered into force)	47,205	38,505	Romania	Ex-Yugoslavia	Ukraine
Settlement permit (issued before the ThirdA entered into force)	28,522	4,376	Romania	Ukraine	China
Residence permit for TCN	15,304	33,585	China	Ukraine	Serbia
EEA residence permit (issued before FreeA entered into force)	30,579	7	Germany	Slovakia	Romania
Registration certificate for EEA nationals	48,527	113,507	Romania	Germany	Slovakia
Permanent residence card for EEA nationals	6,560	17,344	Romania	Germany	Slovakia
Family member of Hungarian national who is a third-country national (residence card)	4,733	3,530	Ukraine	Serbia	Russia

Entitlement	*Permit Holders 2008*	*Permit Holders 2013*	*1st Group by Nationality*	*2nd Group by Nationality*	*3rd Group by Nationality*
Family member of the EEA national who is a third-country national (residence card)	322	273	Ukraine	USA	Serbia
EC permanent residence permit	242	478	n.d.	n.d.	n.d.
National permanent residence permit	2,568	6,672	China	Ukraine	Serbia
Interim permanent residence permit	6	5	n.d.	n.d.	n.d.
Total	**184,568**	**218,282**			

Source: data on the base of the OIN <www.bmbah.hu>.

7. However, the attractiveness of Hungary as a destination (or transit) country can be illustrated better with flow data. According to the available data, the number of persons who want to come to Hungary, who are able to come and who do arrive is harmonized. In the absence of goodwill, it can be said that screening, the method of approval of the letter of invitation, visa authorization or work permission is intimidating enough for potential migrants (and their families) not to submit a claim at the competent migration authority (Váradi, 2006). In other words, the reputation of the migration procedure is the main selection power that only persons with a high probability of success may request authorization. As the figures in Tables 7, 8, and 9 prove, the number of potential migrants is standard while the rate of refusal is relatively low among approvals of letters of invitation as well as in visa authorization.

Table 7 Registered Flow of Migrants' Mainstream (2009–2013)

Entitlement	*Applicants in 2009*	*Issued Permission in 2009*	*Applicants in 2013*	*Issued Permission in 2013*
Residence permit for TCN	32,252	n.d.	37,547	31,218
Registration certificate for EEA national	20,794	20,464	13,583	12,565
Permanent residence card for EEA national	4,656	1,527	2,639	2,235

Entitlement	*Applicants in 2009*	*Issued Permission in 2009*	*Applicants in 2013*	*Issued Permission in 2013*
Family member of Hungarian national who is a third-country national (residence card)	2,110	565	1,628	1,113
Family member of the EEA national who is a third-country national (residence card)	166	28	178	133
EC permanent residence permit for TCN	2,209	n.d.	232	182.
National permanent residence permit for TCN	2,083	n.d.	2,558	1,839
Temporary permanent residence permit for TCN	123	n.d.	0	0
Visa (C+D)	281,562	n.d.	345,510	~310,000.
Total applicants	**341,299**		**403,875**	

Source: data on the base of the OIN <www.bmbah.hu>.

Table 8 Authorization of the Letter of Invitation By the Migration Authority (2005–2013)

Year	*Approval of the Invitation*	*Refusal of the Authorization*
2005	11,365	682
2006	9,563	652
2007	7,654	403
2008	10,607	490
2009	9,428	616
2010	10,512	148
2013	8,834	185

Source: database of the OIN <www.bmbah.hu>.

This ratio of the successful visa applicants is also significantly high. It can be explained by the flexibility of applicants, consular offices and supporters, the kin-state policy, and the less experienced staff in the administration or a combination of these. The management of migration is a business (Váradi, 2005), so corruption would also shadow some cases.

The official numbers of visas issued were as follows: 264,000 in 2002, 425,000 in 2003, 757,000 in 2004, 695,000 in 2005, 640,000 in 2006, and 502,000 in 2007.

In 2008, the total number of issued short-term visas was 317,519. The accession to the Schengen regime immediately influenced the visa statistics in 2008. The 'top three countries' where Hungary issues the highest numbers of visas are Serbia, Ukraine and Russia. The recent decline may be due to several reasons: already issued Schengen visas allow multiple entries (valid for one year or more); due to the principle of main destination, visas are applied for in another country (transiting people are unaccounted); special cards for relatives and also because fees have been raised. From 2008, the decline has been accelerating due to the newly functioning Schengen visa system in Hungary. As for Hungary, the rejection rate of 'A', 'B' and 'C' types of visas (short-term visas) applied for at consulates across the world was 1.8% in 2007, while the rejection rate of 'C' type visas applied for at consulates across the world was 1.9%. The overall value was 2.4% in 2007. According to visa data in 2008, the rejection rate of 'C' type visas applied for at consulates was 3.6% (Illés & Melegh, 2009).

Table 9 presents the purpose of travel and number of applications in a gradually liberalized entry system due to the EU common visa policy (e.g., visa-free travel has been provided for Serbian nationals since 2010).

Table 9 All Visa Applications Submitted to the Consular Offices (2008–2010)

By Main Purpose of Entry	*Applications in 2008*	*Applications in 2009*	*Applications in 2010*
Tourism	182,971	142,648	98,987
Business	47,589	47,536	28,606
Visit	29,759	35,110	30,475
Other	88,095	46,281	38,187
Total	348,414	271,575	196,255
Recognition rate of applications	94.1%	80.9%	89.4%

Source: database of the OIN <www.bmbah.hu>.

8. Although the migrant status ends with the acquisition of Hungarian citizenship, the pattern of low rate of refusal and high probability of success of the application is evident in the statistics. It is obvious that these applicants are well-integrated enough to establish this agreeable scoreboard, taking into account the fact that the procedure of acquisition takes years, but in visa and naturalization procedures there is no reasoning on the part of the proceedings authority. Thus the presumption of a probable winner being a good migrant is not rebutted (Tóth, 2009). Table 10 illustrates the same. However, the recent ethnic-preference amendment of Act LV of 1993 on Hungarian Nationality[5] in May 2010, which entered into force

5. Article 4 of the Act, see the consolidated text in its English translation at <www.allampolgarsag.gov.hu/images/Act_LV_of_1993_on_Hungarian_Citizenship.pdf>.

in January 2011, will multiply the number of applicants and naturalized persons in comparison with the annual average since 1993[6] (Sárosi, 2011). For instance, in the first six months of 2011, the number of applications was over 100,000 while the number of accelerated, benefiting naturalized persons was close to 10,000.[7]

Table 10 Applications for Acquisition of Hungarian Citizenship and Re/naturalized Persons (2004–2010)

Entitlement	*2004*	*2005*	*2006*	*2007*	*2008*	*2009*	*2010*
Applications for re/naturalization	5,761	3,898	9,127	5,437	4,143	4,921	3,257
For other acquisition	6,129	5,618	4,225	4,361	5,026	71	36
Naturalized persons	5,667	9,981	6,564	9,398	8132	5,959	5,513
Refused persons	502	482	424	552	628	600	488

Source: database of the OIN <www.bmbah.hu>.

9. The Government adopted a migration strategy (2014–2020) required by the European Union for the planning of and acess to national allocations of the future Asylum and Migration Fund (AMF). This document,[8] adopted in October 2013 has not been discussed in the political arena nor influenced the governmental practice yet. The United Nations High Commissioner for Refugees (UNHCR) and some NGOs (for instance, the Hungarian Helsinki Committee) made numerous comments on the draft with limited success. The strategy defines some principles, aims and instruments in visa policy, lawful migration, free movement of Union citizens and international protection while the security control and combating illegal migration are in details. The strategy has three main points of reference: the national-building (ethno)policy as determined by the Parliament up to 2020; the Internal Security Fund of the EU and the National Program on combating human trafficking (2013–2016).[9] The context of these documents is the management of the international migratory movements in harmony with the EU policy and the national security principles. In brief, the country has neither an explicit nor an implicit migration policy (Tóth & Sik, 2014), and it intends to become merely a fairly operating Member State in the EU, adhering as much as possible to the common immigration,

6. N = 123,324 persons re/naturalised in 1993–2008, hence its annual average is 8,222.
7. See the announcement of the deputy prime-minister (27 Jun. 2011) <www.allampolgarsag.gov.hu/index.php?option=com_content&view=article&id=197:hirek20110628&catid=1:friss-hirek&Itemid=50>.
8. Government Resolution No. 1698 of 2013, October 4.
9. Government Resolution No.1351 of 2013, June 9.

defence, security, external and asylum policies. Instead of pro-migration measures and a national migration profile on the reception and integration of migrants, these documents reflect a derivative, consecutive, additional and subsequent policy subordinated by the security phenomena. As a result, the migration management has to be in complete harmony with the advanced combat against international terrorism and organized crime related to migration, and the investigation of clandestine human trafficking networks.

10. The National Program on combating human trafficking is mandated by the European Union. It describes what preventive and law enforcement, health, social measures and actions have to be taken in this field. In accordance with this, Hungary being a transit country between Ukraine, Moldova, Russia and Austria, Germany or overseas for networks of prostitution, smuggling and human trafficking, the latency is high. Admitting that actual trends are not known – there are about 20 disclosed criminal cases of human trafficking yearly – the regulative and administrative instruments are determined to research the facts and ramifications. It is an example of how impact assessment of regulation and administrative measures cannot be done when government decisions on legislative content are acted upon without sufficient information and impact assessment.

11. The data of the preceding years on measures taken by the migration authority against unlawful residence and migration do not require more stringent instruments. Table 11 indicates a decrease in expulsion measures.

Table 11 Expulsion Order Issued by the Migration Authority and the Court (2004–2013)

Nationality of	*2004*	*2005*	*2006*	*2007*	*2008*	*2009*	*2013*
By the migration authority							
Romania	2,310	2,398	1,750	0	0	n.d.	n.d.
Ukraine	410	623	165	43	59	n.d.	25
Moldova	62	34	32	32	74	41	n.d.
Serbia-Montenegro	42	54	123	349	106	153	40
Kosovo	0	0	0	0	262	294	508
Other	430	233	259	103	242	472	393
Total	**3,254**	**3,342**	**2,329**	**527**	**743**	**960**	**966**
By the court in penal procedure							
Romania	259	340	274	168	102	58	n.d.
Ukraine	224	332	147	164	156	142	65
Moldova	81	33	32	27	26	30	n.d.
Serbia-Montenegro	55	66	67	77	90	90	122
Slovakia	29	32	22	13	9	n.d.	n.d.

Nationality of	*2004*	*2005*	*2006*	*2007*	*2008*	*2009*	*2013*
Other	256	200	161	119	123	125	199
Total	**904**	**1,003**	**703**	**568**	**506**	**484**	**386**

Source: statistics of the OIN <www.bmbah.hu>.

The Accession of Romania to the European Union rewrites the migration statistics in Hungary because Romanians almost disappear from the data on detention while the number of people from Kosovo is significant. It has to be added that changes in regulation and capacity building of enforcement better explain the growth of figures than the quantity of illegal movements. Table 12 and Table 13 illustrate it.

Table 12 Detention Ordered By the Migration Authority (2004–2013)

Nationality of	*2004*	*2005*	*2006*	*2007*	*2008*	*2009*	*2013*
Romania	155	125	56	7	3	n.d.	n.d.
Moldova	68	14	24	27	52	43	4
Turkey	45	22	15	9	23	31	13
China	38	8	22	6	20	n.d.	n.d.
Serbia-Montenegro	26	30	123	318	115	91	54
Kosovo	0	0	0	0	229	231	459
Other	239	175	129	76	124	216	219
Total	**571**	**374**	**369**	**443**	**566**	**612**	**749**

Source: statistics of the OIN <www.bmbah.hu>.

Deportation implies that the expulsion order is executed with escorted travel to the country of origin for security reasons. As Table 13 indicates, the number of substantially risk-laden migrants in the preceding years was strongly dropping, and the growing diversity of (legal and illegal) migrants is a prominent feature. Hence, the statistical sub-group of 'others' has been upgraded in all tables.

Table 13 Deportation Ordered by the Migration Authority (2004–2013)

Nationality of	*2004*	*2005*	*2006*	*2007*	*2008*	*2009*	*2013*
Romania	353	383	432	30	51	44	n.d.
Moldova	79	27	22	37	61	42	n.d.
Serbia-Montenegro	67	51	119	295	127	207	92
Ukraine	67	162	93	23	46	27	n.d.

Nationality of	*2004*	*2005*	*2006*	*2007*	*2008*	*2009*	*2013*
Turkey	50	15	12	5	11	n.d.	13
China	31	6	14	4	5	n.d.	n.d.
Other	218	81	56	87	172	314	494
Total	**865**	**725**	**748**	**481**	**473**	**634**	**599**

Source: statistics of the OIN <www.bmbah.hu>.

According to the last presented data on the frequency of the confinement of migrants, the number is increasing slightly, but in the case of approximately a hundred persons under this order, direct contact of unlawful migrants with international terrorism or organized crime cannot be proved. Figures in Table 14, as in the earlier tables, maintain a distance from the anti-migration rhetoric.

Table 14 Residence in Compulsory Designated Place by the Migration Authority (2004–2012)

Nationality of	*2004*	*2005*	*2006*	*2007*	*2008*	*2009*	*2012*
Serbia-Montenegro	46	15	48	115	92	217	n.d.
China	25	12	15	15	20	14	n.d.
Ukraine	18	8	8	2	1	n.d.	n.d.
Iraq	16	14	11	17	18	12	n.d.
Afghanistan	13	16	17	10	25	91	65
Other	187	146	191	183	223	375	243[10]
Total	**305**	**211**	**290**	**342**	**379**	**709**	**308**

Source: statistics of the OIN <www.irm.gov.hu>.

§2. Overview of National Legal Instruments

I. Historical Overview

12. The Constitution adopted in 1949 contained the fundamental rights together with citizens' duties, as the socialist canon required the same from a basic law on the ground of the ruling power of the workers' class. The right to free movement was useless beyond the hermetically closed borders, and a simple provision on asylum was inserted. It was available for freedom fighters persecuted for socialist and democratic behaviour, liberation of the people and the nation. There was no act or implementation rule regarding this right, and the political bureau of the Communist

10. Including 81 persons from Kosovo, 37 from Pakistan, 17 from Syria, 16 from Algeria.

Party decided on the reception and the Ministry of Health was responsible to care for him/her. The local councils provided housing, schooling for Greeks and Chileans in the capital and in the countryside. The other form of migration was shortly regulated in law-decree and decree of the Ministry of the Interior. The Alien Police authorized the entry, residence and settlement of citizens of other communist states between 1965 and 1989. Western migrants (particularly emigrants) visiting the country were strictly screened by consular and police services, and their entry was refused for years. The Border Guard and Security Services were directed by the Ministry of the Interior as well, and to them migrants were suspicious troublemakers, spies, subversive agents of capitalism – while among them were numerous ethnic Hungarians who wanted to see the family members left behind on this side of the border. The emigration was lawful by the deprivation of citizenship, social insurance, property compensating for it with a passport. It was both a privilege and a punishment for political and ideological enemies. The dissidents could not use the lawful channel: they had illegally left the Iron Curtain by air, by boat or by other clandestine manner, seeking asylum in Austria at first. Otherwise, regulated tourism inside the communist states was gradually allowed from 1976 on the grounds of bilateral agreements. The entitlement of the border guard to use coercive measures for the prevention of illegal entry and exit from the country was not in confrontation with the Iron Curtain.

13. This 'frozen migratory regulation' was shifted by the introduction of the right to a passport on 1 January 1988. Beyond the growing but covert economic crisis, the Helsinki Process and the dialogue between Eastern Europe and Western Europe strongly supported the Constitutional Reform in 1972 and the ratification of the United Nations Covenants on Civil and Political Rights (UNCCPR) and of Social, Economic and Cultural Rights (1966) after a delay of ten years in Hungary. The wave of refugees from the oppressive Romanian regime between 1988 and 1989 urged a new epoch in administration and regulation. The party state leaders legalized the spontaneous supportive movements of civil and charity organizations in favour of Romanian (irregular) migrants, setting up a mixed body on co-ordination at a central and a mezzanine level. These bodies governed the management of reception, while the country prepared for the democratic elections, privatization and liberal institutions with the consent a peaceful regime change. Hungary ratified the Geneva Convention 1951 in March 1989 whereas implementation rules were ready six months later. During this interval, refugee camps were set up for Romanian refugees by the Ministry of the Interior and temporary shelters were set up by the Red Cross for the DDR transit migrants whose surrender to the Stasi (secret police) for overstaying and attempted border-crossing on the grounds of bilateral agreements was over in June 1989. The government decree on asylum procedure and applicant's documents, and the Decree of the Presidium (Law-Decree) on the status of recognized refugees were passed as the first generation of refugee legislation in modern Hungary.

14. The Constitutional Reform in 1989–1990 ensured the right to free travel, citizens' return to Hungary, prohibited the deprivation of citizenship, the right to claim asylum and the right to be expelled from Hungary as per a lawful decision.

All of these rights relevant to migration shall be regulated by law and adopted by a qualified majority of votes. Due to this guarantee, the Parliament adopted the Alien Act (1993) and its revised version (2001) inspiring a complexity of prohibitions and control over the entry, residence and permanent stay of non-nationals together with governmental and ministerial decrees. The labour authorization was incorporated in the Act on Employment (1991), delegating the entire regulation on foreign labour migration to the ministry of labour. The Parliament adopted the second generation of asylum (1997) in close cooperation with the Alien Police in the spirit of restrictions. Furthermore, the geographical reservation made to the Geneva Convention 1951 was deleted and as a consequence, Hungary has received, from March 1998 onward, asylum applications from non-European regions. The UNHCR office established in Hungary in 1990–1998 could not escape the daily procedure concerning the non-European applicants. Furthermore, the UNHCR contributed to administrative and supported the capacity building of Hungary, but the reception conditions and accession to the substantial protection procedure were developed gradually. The main inadequacy has been the linkage of the refugee migration authority to 3,200 municipals (settlements, towns, cities, counties, the capital and its districts) in the reception and integration of migrants, the provision of public services on equal basis for all, together with specifications. The Act on Local Self-Governments (1990) ensures autonomy in the regulation, administration and the provision of public service for local inhabitants and budgeting for 3,200 units without hierarchy between them. The Constitution/Fundamental Law also requires a qualified majority in votes concerning this Act, which shields them from formal responsibility for migrants for two decades. For this reason, the central authority and some Non-Governmental Organizations (NGOs) are working in direct migration-relevant services. The reform period included the split of the social insurance fund into the health care fund and the pension scheme. While the Act on Health Care (1997) ensures certain supplies on the grounds of legal status (citizenship, student and minor) the acts regarding insurance funds are based on contributory services. In the absence of the individual's contribution, the municipal or state budget (e.g., from the sub-item on refugees, unaccompanied minors and victims of human trafficking) is required to repay the costs of services.

All these factors doubled and/or tripled the quantity of the regulations on migrants in comparison with the year 1989. The rule-of-law requirement inspires more and more modifications which do not impact the assessment and critical monitoring of the implementation. This vortex of insufficient legislation cannot be stopped, while there is a growing inconsistency among the legal provisions. The total number of legal sources adopted by the Parliament, the Government and the ministers is over 10,000 and the number of the municipals' decrees is over 70,000. The EC law minus agricultural provisions amounts to approximately 10,000 binding laws.

15. Since 1989, the other stream of migration law has been connected to the extended international relations of the country and newly, the commitments regarding human rights. Although the participation in United Nations (UN), the Helsinki Process and professional organizations had begun earlier, the democratic Hungary was invited to the Council of Europe (1990), to the Partnership in Peace of the North Atlantic Treaty Organization (NATO) (1994) and to the OECD (1998). The European Agreement (1994) with the EC projected a ten-year preparatory period of accession. These events also forced a tight reflex and adaptation in the legislative and public administrative institutions within a short period. For instance, the Alien Act and implementation decrees had to be modified more often in favour of the NATO-staff and EU-supported project personnel. Whereas, the newly regained sovereignty of the state – in the absence of economic independence and with high state debts – guided a rather symbolic (foreign) policy. For instance, Hungary terminated the bilateral agreements with (ex-)communist states that excluded the dual citizenship in 1990–1993. Thus a diaspora and kin-minority policy could effectively operate where migrating ethnic Hungarians and expatriates acquired their lost nationality while preserving another. The Act on Hungarian Nationality (1993) can further develop the principle of ethnic preferences and multiple citizenships.

II. Current Applicable Legislation

16. Without repetition of the substantial chapters, it shall be emphasized that legislation must be compatible with international customary law as respected by the international community and the international commitments in treaties (Article Q of the Fundamental Law). As a member in the European Union, the transposition of EU law and respect for the EU Treaties in national legal acts as well, and the implementation of the same, determines the legislative work.

The following constitutional principles are important:

(a) certain issues and rights shall be regulated in an act adopted by a qualified (two-third) majority of votes as determined in the Fundamental Law, for instance the acquisition of Hungarian nationality, arable land, operation of security services, or personal data protection;
(b) the regulation in all migration-relevant issues is multi-level (international treaty, EU law, domestic law, decree of the Government and/or decree of the minister in charge, municipal decree);
(c) legal sources are determined in the Fundamental Law[11] together with the main competences in the regulation with the exception of the EU law that shall be directly implemented with the exception of transposable provisions and sources;
(d) international agreements and treaties shall be promulgated and published after ratification in the form of law or government decree; the direct reference to international law and its formally issued interpretation (e.g., by the UN, specific organizations or the International Court of Justice) is required if the

11. These sources: Constitution and its amendments, statutory law, Law-decree until annulment and its amendment by statutory law, government decree, decree of the National Bank, Prime Minister decree, decree of National Media Authority, decree of Energy Inspectors Authority, ministerial decree, municipal decree. In the event of an emergency, the state president and the National Defence Council are entitled to adopt temporary decrees.

international commitments avoid mediating the provisions of domestic law (e.g., international convention on bill of exchange);

(e) the constitutional consistency of the legal system is controlled by the Constitutional Court that has the authority to annul any legal source which contradicts the Fundamental Law[12] (and by virtue of its Article Q, and T any legal provisions) upon the initiative of some entitled authorities or in the event of incompatibility with international commitments or omission of legislation ex officio. The Constitutional Court has not been active in narrow migration law issues since 1990 but its interpretative efforts in passing binding judgments on constitutional rights are relevant in migration procedures (e.g., the substance of the right to effective remedy);

(f) the Ombudsman in charge of fundamental rights has also developed migration law in certain segments (e.g., equality of refugees in family benefits, unaccompanied minors' right to child protection, right to population registry of the migrant with unconfirmed identity, stateless persons' right to travel).

17. An exhaustive list of legal sources on migration does not exist because the speed of legislation is high and due to the complexity of the migrant's life. Furthermore, public supplies are regulated and provided partly by local self-governments (municipals) in 3,200 settlements; and a comprehensive database of municipals' decrees does not exist. Finally, the judgments of courts and the judicial legal practice are available only partially (e.g., the case law of local courts and the decisions in non-litigation process are not published).[13] Researchers in legal and judicial issues must be detached, with a focus on national-level legislation and available high court practice. The main components of regulation are as follows:

(a) Act on persons enjoying the right to free movement provides guarantees (hereinafter FreeA) while the Act on non-preferential non-nationals including stateless persons are referred to as '*third-country nationals*' in a mirror-translation from the EU law. The FreeA, the Act on third-country national (hereinafter ThirdA) together with executive rules in government and ministerial decrees together form the skeleton of the migration law derogating certain guarantees in procedural codes;

(b) Act on asylum (hereinafter AsylA) and seekers of other forms of protection and the status of migrants under any form of protection, government decree on supports and benefits for applicants and status holders;

(c) Act on passport (hereinafter PassA) that determines how resident migrants can obtain travelling documents;

(d) Labour Code and Act on unemployment and benefits for job-seekers (hereinafter UnemplA), ministerial decree on foreign labour authorization; reception of working volunteers in the civil sector coming from abroad as well;

12. The exceptions are determined in the amendment of the Constitution, see Act CXIX of 2010 entered into force on 1 Nov. 2010, and the 4th Amendment of the Fundamental Law in Arts 24 and 37 entered into force on 1 Apr. 2013.

13. See the electronic database of judgments at <www.birosag.hu/engine.aspx?page=anonim>.

(e) Acts on health care and pension insurance, obligatory entry to the contribution-paying system and the services, benefits and allowances to be provided to workers, self-employed persons, minors and pensioners (regardless of nationality);
(f) Acts on child-protection, allowances and family benefits, child's rights and guardianship;
(g) Acts on public education and higher education, vocational training, how non-national students and pupils can join public education and may access education while in the schooling age (five to sixteen years of age); reception of non-national researchers, students and scholarships ;
(h) Self-employment and Act on private entrepreneurs and sole proprietorship (hereinafter PrivA) is a segment pertaining to self-employed foreigners and freelance professionals;
(i) Penal Code, rules on penal procedure and minor offences in certain geographical areas relate to international migration, including the legal aids, cooperation between the judiciary and the administration in criminal matters on the grounds of universal conventions, regional conventions and bilateral agreements;
(j) Law-decree on international private law regulates the marital and personal status of residing migrants (e.g., specifying the law on which the migrant has an ability to act, family law and rules on references to applicable law (renvoi);
(k) The Code on public administration procedure (hereinafter AdminA) and the Act on civil law procedure (hereinafter CivPA) are both applicable in migration authorization and legal disputes.

The substantive chapters contain a description of these provisions and a linkage between them using abbreviations in the further parts of the monograph.

18. The dualistic legal system is accompanied by the maintaining of a distance from case law. This tradition is strong in legal practice (e.g., at court, legal representatives may win with reference to the decree on refugee procedure rather than with reference to documents of the UNHCR, the European Union Court of Justice (EUCJ) or the European Court of Human Rights (ECHR)). The continental law tradition together with legal positivism has been alienating judges and other law practitioners from analogy, equity and interpretation of closures, abstract entitlements or bans. The role of case law as a source of law implies the following:

(a) The Constitutional Court is entitled to issue *erga omnes*, universally binding decisions interpreting a constitutional provision, annulling unconstitutional legal source/provisions, determining liability of legislation for absence of regulation or annulling a domestic rule infringing the stipulated international treaty. These are published in the Official Gazette. It has to be added that the Constitutional Court's activity in migration law has been limited, for example, the interpretation of 'registered partner' in the context of family unification or detention of migrants may represent its efforts. However, the requirements of fair procedure and the right to effective legal remedy developed by the Court in the preceding decades have not been neglected in legal practice even in cases involving migrants.

(b) The Supreme Court is entitled to issue mandatory decisions for courts that are published in the Official Gazette to unify the judicial practice regarding certain legal provisions wherein there are diverse judgments by courts.[14] Similarly, the Chief Public Prosecutor is responsible for the unequivocal legal practice of Public Prosecutor Offices, so he is allowed to pass orders (normative instructions) pertaining to the common interpretation of prosecutors' competence (e.g., how the legality of migrants' detention can be controlled). It is published in the Prosecutors' Gazette.
(c) The high courts can publish their principal and explanatory decisions providing guidelines for lower courts. Their applicability is optional.
(d) The case law of the European Court of Justice (ECJ), the European Court of Human Rights and UN treaty organs are sporadically translated into Hungarian and published along with proper references to the domestic law and legal terminology used in the administration of justice. Some legal periodicals[15] or certain kinds of training imparted to judges[16] attempt to incorporate the non-national case into their future practice. Hence, the law practitioners in the field of international migration, human rights and humanitarian law are not very familiar with international legal developments.

III. Administrative and Judicial Authorities

19. The migration authority has strong ties with the police, law enforcement subordinated by the Ministry of the Interior. It is a heritage from the communist past operating in a militant hierarchy on the grounds of unit leaders' actual orders instead of abstract norms of national and international law. In the past, it was understood that security and the total control of migration were two sides of the same coin, but since 1989 this law enforcement approach has been anachronistic. This rationale of national security hardly suits the needs of the labour force, social policy, human rights and the individual's conditions in authorization.

(a) The Office for Immigration and Nationality Issues (hereinafter OIN) with seven regional directorates is the central player, while its own units are named Refugee Authority, and the Nationality Directorate located in the OIN is also considered as part of law enforcement or alien policing. Furthermore, the reception centres under the subordination of the OIN shall be considered as part of the law enforcement accommodating applicants and recognized refugees. Finally, the registration and the residence card administration also belong to the OIN

14. Also for unification of the judicial practice the Supreme Court may issue Guidelines for lower courts, e.g., On the Criteria of Safe Third Country No. 2 of 2012, December 10 published on the SC homepage http://www.lb.hu/hu/kollvel/22012-xii10-kmk-velemeny-biztonsagos-harmadik-orszag-megitelesenek-egyes-kerdeseirol/.
15. For instance, Acta Humana, JeMa, Közjogi Szemle, Föld-rész.
16. Before accession those were financed by the EU, Academy for Judges, UNHCR or the responsible ministry.

system. In brief, FreeA, ThirdA and AsylA as the main areas of migration law are within the competence of the OIN and its directorates.

(b) The Police as part of law enforcement is the other actor in migration authorization controlling the borders, conducting in-country checks and implementing coercive measures against migrants including detention, expulsion and deportation.

(c) The consular offices have more competence due to the Schengen acquis, while all important decisions on visa authorization are decided in the OIN or in the Ministry of Foreign Affairs.

(d) The Labour Service at county level approves or provides work permits to third-country nationals with exceptions determined in the UnemplA and international treaties. Also, the labour authority maintains a register of employment, while the Labour Inspector Office at county level imposes fines for illegal jobs or violations of the Labour Code.

(e) The employed (self-employed) or residing migrants must make a monetary contribution to the National Health Insurance as mandatory members of the health care (and the pension scheme) system. Similar to public revenues, these contributions are also levied by the taxation and duty offices.

(f) Immigrants including protection seekers, visa applicants, applicants for long-term migrant status and for naturalization shall be checked for potential security risks. The Act on national security services (hereinafter SecA) determines how the law enforcement is to cooperate with the National Security Office (hereinafter NSO) in this context. Their public health screening is obligatory in order to acquire long-term residence admission or within the protection-seeking procedure. This task belongs to the sanitary authority at county level.

(g) The lawful address, identity and travelling documents are issued for migrants by the local registrar office within the local (district) unit of the governmental office. Upon request by the immigrant and payment of the fee, these documents are available immediately or within some days.

20. In the Appendix, a list of competences may assist to make an overview of the authorization system in the immigration. It suffices here to state that the Ministry of the Interior has been in charge of migration and integration policy, legislation and administration since 1988. The EU supports (integration fund, support to return, border management and refugee fund) are also governed by this Ministry. It is no wonder that this Ministry's approach is in line with public order, security, regulative order and centralization.

21. The judicial system is independent from the executive power. The self-governance of judges was established in 1997 with the inclusion of three representatives of the Parliament and the government into its leading body (National Council of Administration of Justice, with fifteen members). This criticized body led by the president of the Supreme Court includes the representatives of the Public Prosecutor Office and the Bar of Association (chamber of attorneys) and nine judges elected by their own colleagues, was terminated in 2011. The grade of courts is as follows:

(a) The Supreme Court its president elected by the Parliament.
(b) The five superior courts adjudicating on the challenged judgments of the nineteen county courts and the Capital Court.
(c) The power of judicial review of refused protection, long-term migrant status and expulsion orders belongs to the Capital Court and to the county courts. The registry court, the labour and the administrative court are located in the central region of each county.
(d) The local courts (approximately 140 in number) are neglected in migration law with the exception of the review of decisions relating to migrants' detention, minor offences or private disputes.

The list in the Appendix covers the judicial system with the legal remedies.

22. The Constitution/Fundamental Law, in accordance with the UNCCPR[17] and the ECHR[18] and its supplementary Protocol,[19] provides the right to the effective legal remedy of all acts, decisions or measures adopted by powerful public authorities. Moreover, domestic law ensures this right for a wider circle than these international agreements (Halmai and Tóth, 2003) do, because of the following:

(a) the said right shall be provided to all whose legitimate interests or rights are attached in the given dispute or decision of public power (Court, public administration or other authority);
(b) the concrete names and forms of legal remedy are changing (appeal, complaint, objection, request for review, etc.) and are defined in procedural law codes (CrimPA, AdminA, CivPA) and other acts providing this right to all public power procedure;
(c) actors in each procedure are separate, and shall be included within the generalized term 'all', which includes natural persons, unincorporated companies or legal personalities that are determined in procedural codes.

23. Whereas, the right to legal remedy as a fundamental right can be limited when three related preconditions are met: a limitation (e.g., excluding appeal or the other regular methods of remedy) shall be defined in the act adopted by a qualified majority of votes (two-third) in legislation; it shall be pertain to resolving the legal dispute within a reasonable deadline; and the limitation shall be proportionate to that aim.

24. The effective legal remedy is not clarified in the Constitution/Fundamental Law, but its interpretation is based on how the Constitutional Court outlines the criteria of legal remedy, as follows:[20]

---

17. Article 2(3), published in Law-Decree No. 6 of 1976.
18. Article 13, published in Act XXXI of 1993.
19. Article 2(2) in 7th Supplementary Protocol to the ECHR, published in Act XXXI of 1993.
20. See the following Constitutional Court decisions: No. 24/1999, 6 October; No. 21/1997, 26 March, No. 5/1992, 30 January, No. 1350/B/1992, No. 22/1995, 31 March, No. 799/E/1998, No. 60/2003, 26 November, No. 26/2004, 7 July, No. 57/1991, 8 November, No.46/1994, 21 October.

(a) legal remedy shall be ensured on all substantial decisions (not including procedural measures) that shall be judged in a contextual analysis;
(b) remedy shall be decided by an organ that is higher or separate from the decision-making authority in question (e.g., in a hierarchical or horizontal division of competences);
(c) remedy does not imply more instances of review, and that a system with two instances of proceedings is lawful;
(d) no legal remedy on an enforceable judicial decision is also constitutional (e.g., instead of appeal inside the administration, a judicial review of the decision in question without further remedy);
(e) remedy shall not imply the entitlement for discretionary power or equity of the reviewing authority;
(f) right to the judicial route for a violated fundamental right shall be implemented through the various procedural rules or codes, and it does not imply an exclusive reference to the Constitution or the Constitutional Court.

In sum, the right to legal remedy in the Hungarian constitutional system basically depends on the quality of legislation, because the regular courts dislike comparing procedural rules to the constitutional criteria in the context of respect for fundamental rights. If a collision is visible, they pass the responsibility to the Constitutional Court, or – as in almost all cases – they mechanically implement the most specific rules relating to the dispute in question.

25. The AdminA is a general codex with about 180 sections that determines the entire procedure in public administration. It provides the right to remedy in all substantial decisions and important procedural measures, either upon request or ex officio. However, this codex shall be implemented as a secondary set of rules in all procedures that belong to the ThreeA, FreeA and AsylA. It means that numerous provisions which are beneficial to the clients, determined in the AdminA, are derogated by these laws together with their implementing decrees including special restrictions. Thus AdminA is applicable if these specific acts silent as regards certain procedural momentum. Furthermore, the ThreeA, The FreeA and the AsylA contain many entitlements of the proceeding authority for discretionary power. The most relevant rules from this secondary (substitute) codex are, briefly, as follows:

(a) The following remedies may be submitted by the clients: appeal, judicial review of the administrative decision and the renewal of the administrative procedure. From these, the appeal is the most frequent. In accordance with this, within fifteen days of providing notice of the substantial decision to the client, an appeal may be submitted to the higher administrative organ of the authority conducting the proceedings. The appeal has a prerogative effect unless the execution of the issued decision has to be immediately ordered on the grounds of public policy, protection of life, property or national security. Regardless of the reasons for the appeal, the second instance of the administrative procedure involves checking the legality, formality and functionality of the first instance decision, and finally it may modify, supplement, annul or confirm the first decision;

(b) Whereas, other legal entitlements for remedy (revision of its own decision by the authority in proceedings, supervision of decision by the higher grade of authority, review by the Constitutional Court, public prosecutor control) are launched ex officio or within the proceeding authorities without the clients' initiative;
(c) With reference to nullity, the issued decision shall be abrogated if it is incompatible with international self-executive obligations or the EC law that is directly applicable (direct effect), if the competence of another authority was not respected in the administrative procedure, if an expert opinion was totally neglected in the decision, if the decision-making process was influenced by a proved offence (e.g., corruption of the responsible official), if the required rate of votes or the quorum of the decision-making body was not met, or if a severe procedural or substantive requirement was violated. However, the administrative decision shall not be annulled if it violates any bona fide right(s) of the client and if at least three years have elapsed since its issuance and entering into force, or at least five years have elapsed since the disadvantaged decision entered into force.

26. The final administrative decision – after the appeal or in the absence of appeal by law – may be reviewed at the County/Capital Labour and Administrative Court exclusively on the ground of a violation of law that shall be indicated by the client. The CivPA has a special chapter (Chapter XX) regulating review and law suits against administrative decisions. The most common provisions are as follows:

(a) The Court of first instance, if the case is highly complex, may consist of three professional judges (judges in council). If a council is set up, a single judge cannot proceed alone with the case.
(b) That the county Court is competent in the review of a decision concerning the accession and the residence of foreigners which is located in the same county as the first instance authority in the administrative proceeding, and the Capital Court is competent if a reviewable decision has been made by a national authority; the Capital Regional Court is competent in all appealed county/capital Court judgments passed in the administrative procedural review.
(c) The statement of claim shall be submitted, addressing the administrative authority of the Court of first instance, within thirty days of the date of providing notice of the decision to the client. All documents are required to be attached to the statement of claim, and the entire set of documents is required to be forwarded, together with its own legal opinion, to the Court within fifteen days. If the statement of claim requests for suspension of the administrative decision by the Court, this forwarding period is shorter.
(d) An excuse may be submitted for a failure to meet the deadline in the judicial review submission to the administrative authority of the court of first instance, addressing it to the Court.
(e) Facts that are relevant to the case shall be proved and clarified by the administrative authority at a Court procedure, and if the facts are based (in part) on the expert opinion of another authority, the latter cannot refuse to be involved in a judicial review.

(f) The hearing and the negotiation shall be conducted at the Court procedure if the relevant facts in the reviewed case are not clarified. Otherwise, a non-litigation procedure is allowed in the judicial review (procedure by documents).
(g) An unlawful administrative decision may be abrogated, and if necessary – a new (repetitive) administrative procedure may be ordered. The Court may modify the final decision of the administrative authority if the law allows it (e.g., in asylum determination).
(h) The Court's judgment is final, with some exceptions, for example, when the judicial review of an administrative decision in which the appeal to the higher administrative authority is excluded, and the Court is entitled to modify the final administrative decision. The Supreme Court is entitled to review the judgment of the county Court if its legality is seriously violated.

27. The migrants, like everybody under the jurisdiction of Hungarian courts, are entitled to submit complaints to the independent non-judicial organizations and to the international fora. From those, the most relevant ones are as follows:

(a) The Ombudsman is responsible for remedy in the cases of maladministration or abusive behaviour violating the fundamental rights, which are committed also by the Police or the immigration authority.[21] In accordance with the Fundamental Law (Article 30), a complaint – if an ex officio procedure has not been launched by the Ombudsman – may be submitted to him/her within a year since the maladministration or the abuse (final administrative decision entering into force), unless the judicial procedure is being carried out. He/she can scrutinize the finding of the facts and propose an individual and general remedy, modification of rules, solution and prevention of any further maladministration to the administrative authority first instance. In the event of its refusal and in the absence of a voluntary correction of a wrong/unlawful measure or practice adopted in time, the Ombudsman shall propose the proper measures to the higher administrative organ and to the government or to the parliament in legislative issues. The annual report to the Parliament contains numerous complaints on asylum, refugee, international protection, visa, residence, reception and settlement authorization.
(b) The Public Prosecutor's Office in accordance with the Fundamental Law (Article 29), and as a hierarchical organization (local, county, capital, regional and supreme directorates), is responsible for the control of the legality of actions, measures in the public administration authorities, deprivation of liberty by law enforcement and it is the office for prosecution.[22] In the context of migration, the public prosecutors have a legal right to protest in all administrative proceedings to stop ex officio or upon complaints of their unlawful operation, measures or actions. Thus they control legality of detention or deportation

21. Act LIX of 1993 on the parliamentary commissioner's competence and its legal status. It was replaced by the Act CXI of 2011 that entered into force on 1 Jan. 2012, in accordance with the Fundamental Law that simplifies the ombudsman system as it was established in 1995.
22. Act CLXIII of 2011 on public prosecutors.

of (illegal) migrants and they may submit to the Court charging for committed criminal act or offence by migrants or other offenders (e.g., human traffickers).

(c) The Equal Treatment Body (hereinafter ETA) since 2004 has been authorized to receive complaints against discriminatory measures by public administration, municipal and state-financed public suppliers (e.g., schools, hospitals, universities, public transport companies regardless of property), and all employers and owners of public businesses (e.g., shops, banks regardless of property). Act CXXV of 2003 (hereinafter EqualA) provides an optional procedure for the discriminated person on the grounds of most frequent discriminatory behaviour (gender, age, health condition, race, etc.) instead of formal appeal, if the unlawful behaviour is within the ambit of AdminA (see Table 15). The ETA can impose fines or implement other sanctions (prohibition of further discrimination, publicity of the case) or determine proper compensatory measures or mediate the conflict. The ETA is subordinated by the responsible minister, so the requirement of independence (see the Paris Principles[23]) is not fulfilled.

(d) The Independent Complaints Body of Law Enforcement was set up in 2008 by the Parliament to receive complaints against abusive and discriminatory measures adopted by the police.[24] According to a few experiences, the migrants have not recognized this forum with the exception of street demonstrators claiming fair scrutiny on policemen who were misusing their power. It may propose the correction of measures and practices of the police to the headquarters. This body would serve a public and political control on police than redress in individual cases.

(e) The rules on detention, arrest, custody and imprisonment ensure a non-hindered communication (by sending letters) to the international organizations dealing with the control of human rights, in particular the prohibition of torture, inhuman or degrading treatment or refoulement. The inmates can send complaints to bodies such as the UN Committee against torture (CAT),[25] the UNHCR, the Committee for Prevention of Torture (CPT) and the ECtHR. Often, the first step is to establish contact with the Hungarian Helsinki Committee that assists in making the complaints complete, attaches the relevant documents to them and undertakes the legal representation of the inmates. It has concluded an agreement with the Headquarters of Penology Law Enforcement, the OIN and the Headquarters of the Police to provide free entry to closed institutes purely for the accomplishment of this legal protection and the information sharing role since 1995 (Mink, 2005).

23. The Paris Principles were defined at the first International Workshop on National Institutions for the Promotion and Protection of Human Rights held in Paris on 7–9 Oct. 1991. They were adopted by the UN Human Rights Commission as Resolution 1992/54 of 1992 and Resolution 48/134 of 1993. The Paris Principles relate to the status and functioning of national institutions for the protection and promotion of human rights.

24. Act XXXIV of 1994 on Police (in a consolidated version).

25. The Optional Protocol of the CAT was ratified by Hungary setting up a proper national mechanism for prevention of torture, inhuman and degrading treatment. The national controlling mechanism belongs to the competence of the Ombudsman, see the Act CXLIII of 2011 entering into force in late 2014.

In sum, the system of legal remedy and safeguards forms is complex in Hungary and has some shortcomings. The applicable legal sources and the institutional procedures overlap one another even in migration law, so the access to a fair procedure and legal protection strongly depend on fortune and the counselling capacities of the NGOs – at least in the short run.

28. The general ban on discrimination (Article XV of the Fundamental Law) and the EqualA transposed from the anti-discrimination EC law provide a variety of organs and authorities dealing with equal treatment. Table 15 summarizes the various applicable fora available for requesting the proper measures to combat discrimination, mainly on the grounds of race, age, health and gender in the labour market or against non-equal treatment by public suppliers and police brutality. Furthermore, there is no comprehensive, independent and analytical (data-collecting and monitoring) institute of human rights in Hungary.

Table 15 Anti-discrimination Forum Shopping in Hungary

Universal competence	Civil Court Equal Treatment Authority and its county agents (its decision may be reviewed at the court) Ombudsman
Law enforcement issues	Independent Complaint Body in Law Enforcement (in the Parliament) Public Prosecutor Office
Labour issues	Labour Court (at county/capital level) Labour Control and Inspector Office
Education issues	Public Education Office Ministerial Representative of Education Rights
Health-care issues	Public Health and Sanitary Office and its regional institutes Centre for Protection of Patients', Inmates and Child Rights (OBDK)
Consumers' rights	National Consumers' Protection Authority and its county inspectorates Inspector Office of Financial Institutions inside the National Bank
International organizations	The cross-border forum for consumers' complaints in the EU (SOLVIT, European Consumer Centres' Network) European Court of Human Rights UN organs
NGOs	Roma Rights Centre Hungarian Helsinki Committee

§3. Overview of International Legal Instruments Applicable in Hungary

29. EU law has its own identity and structure, including migration law (Peers & Rogers, 2006), so it cannot be intertwined with traditional international law. In brief, under the Hungarian public law system, the conclusion of international treaties and agreements under various names, is completely reserved for the Parliament, and for the president of the state only by prior approval by the Parliament and for the government with the exclusion of ratification by the Parliament in all topics that belong to legislative and foreign policy. As a result, the parliamentary, dualistic legal system and the Unitarian state construction prevents ministers, municipalities and state agents from undertaking international public law commitments. This raises problems in cross-border cooperation. Furthermore, the authentic translations and monitoring of the implementation of international agreements have not been ensured.

30. Hungary is a party to all the important conventions on human rights concluded under the aegis of the UN and the Council of Europe. Without providing a comprehensive list, the cornerstones in the context of migration may be indicated as follows:

(a) humanitarian law and suppression of war crimes and crimes against humanity,
(b) combating terrorism and international organized crime, cooperation in criminal matters, extradition and penal procedural guarantees;
(c) right to fair procedure and effective remedy, autonomy and independence of courts, local self-governments;
(d) combating discrimination and promoting equality;
(e) protection of children; social, economic and cultural rights for all;
(f) protection of refugees and stateless persons;
(g) a universal consular convention and numerous bilateral treaties providing legal counselling and legal aid for migrating nationals;
(h) recognition of diplomas and certificates;
(i) and general conditions in labour, employment, as well as prevention of dual taxation.

The regional harmonization of law through agreements prepared by the European Economic Community (EEC), EC and EU on private law and on the interoperability and exchange of law enforcement data (of passengers, genetic identification, etc.) are also relevant in the free movement and residence of persons in the European Union.

31. International treaties in the Hungarian dualistic legal system shall be promulgated and published but their regular monitoring, follow-up and the data collection on implementation has not been institutionalized. The recent Universal Periodic Report to the UN Human Rights Council (UNHRC) by Hungary (May 2011) would develop, at least, the regular cooperation among the academic, governmental and civil organizations dealing with human rights (Haász & Szappanyos, 2011). It is urgent because the groups of binding documents are growing and fluid.

32. Three kinds of inadequacies can be seen. The migrants' specific social rights and the labour migration conventions adopted in the UN and in the Council of Europe are absent in the list. During the mass emigration, it was a political taboo in Hungary, and becoming a destination country its recognition for its own advantages was delayed.[26] Second, the ratification of the Statute of the International Criminal Court (Rome) has been delayed for ten years although it would be relevant to the implementation with regard to protection seekers and lawful exclusion from the international status (Varga, 2006). Third, the new, popular forms of migration, such as those involving transnational operations of volunteers, au pairs, gap year travellers or posted workers, researchers, returning expatriates have neither been internally regulated in details nor stipulated at the international stage by Hungary.

26. Some Member States in the UN proposed to become party to International Convention on the Protection of the Rights of All Migrant Workers and Members of their Families, ICRMW (1990) in the Universal Periodic Report system to the Human Rights Council of the UN (May 2011, Geneva). The refusal of the Hungarian government is based on the absence of national legislative competence in this issue because the third-country nationals' rights belong to the EU regulative competence. (July 2011) <www.kormany.hu>.

Part I. Border Control and Entrance

Chapter 1. Organization of Border Control

33. The *border of the state* is crucial to *sovereignty*, so this domain traditionally belongs to the constitutions. The Fundamental Law also regulates the issue of the state border in the following three aspects:

(a) The Hungarian legal system accepts the international customary law as generally respected by the international community, and the harmony of the national law with the international commitments shall be ensured (Article Q). Due to the fact that the delimitation of the state borders is under the purview of international law, whereas the demarcation depends on the cooperation of the actors under international law, this article establishes the Hungarian approach to the international instruments either in the form of treaties, or in the form of customary international norms. Furthermore, the Hungarian legal system is dualistic in the context of the formal international treaties[27] and commitments[28] while being monistic in the context of the international customary law[29] that without further transformation is an organic part of the Hungarian legal system. For instance, it took a longer time for Hungary to conclude on state borders (delimitation of state borders, management of the border signs, communication between the responsible organs) with new successors in adjacent states after the disintegration of Yugoslavia, Czechoslovakia and the Soviet Union in the early 1990s. During this interval with Serbia, Slovenia, Croatia, Slovakia and Ukraine the binding legal principle of respecting sovereignty, peaceful coexistence and good neighbourhood was the primary policy of Hungary towards these new-born adjacent states. In other words, delimitation and demarcation of the border shall be considered as binding international actions with the consent of the international community.

(b) On the grounds of the Hungarian parliamentary system, the conclusion of the most important and outstanding international undertakings and commitments shall be made by the Parliament (Article 1 (2) d). In this way, all treaties on the

27. Law-Decree No. 12 of 1987 on publication of the UN Convention on International Treaties (Vienna, 23 May 1969).
28. Act LV of 2005 on the procedure of conclusion of international treaties. It determines not only how to implement the Vienna Convention in Hungary by the public power but also the legal position of the UN Security Council's binding decisions (they shall be published as laws, incorporating them into the legal system).
29. Constitutional Court's decision No. 53 of 1993, 13 October.

territory of the state, borders and their control belong to the competence of the highest representative organ, either as concluding actor, or as legislator. Whereas, accession to the European Union derogates this competence, dividing it with other legislative and decision-making powers (Article E (2)) even regarding the topics of the order at state borders. However, the transposition of the EC law to the Hungarian legal system is based on the constitutional division of power and competence. Thus, the parliament shall adopt all basic rules through laws relating to the border and border protection or control.

(c) The border control and protection of the order at borders belong to the competence of the police (law enforcement) (Article 46 (1)).

34. Apart from the international treaties concluded by Hungary with each of its seven bordering states including its executive documents (demarcation map, protocols on changes, exchange of territories),[30] the BordA regulates the most *decisive legal institutions in connection with the state border.* In addition, in 2007 the BordA was not to repeat the provisions of the Schengen Border Code[31] which determined the rules on crossing the external borders of the European Union and deleted control at internal borders. Taking into account these references, the relevant institutions of the BordA are as follows:

(a) state borders shall be determined by international agreements that shall be promulgated and published in law;
(b) state borders on land shall be marked with border signs that belong to the state property and the right to use the territory occupied by the border signs shall belong to the state as determined by the law on ground-survey and map-making activities;
(c) the border lines after demarcation may be altered in the natural environment, so their correction shall be made by the replacement of border signs along with the appointed representatives of Hungarian[32] authorities and neighbouring state authorities maintaining joint records and protocols on it, made by properly nominated representatives of the party states appointed by the minister; after signature, the minister responsible for migration must publish the border issue protocol in ministerial decrees. These documents shall be archived in an original copy by the Ministry of Foreign Affairs;
(d) the border signs shall be protected, their disturbance, unlawful replacement, manipulation or destruction is a minor offence that shall be punished according

30. For instance, between Austria and Hungary Act XXV of 1997 on publication of the agreement on how to use a small road between the two Austrian villages using the territory of Hungary in the border zone (Mörbisch – Siegendorf), Act CIII of 1999 on publication of the agreement how to use the railways connecting the industrial park in Szentgotthárd to Vienna, or Act XXXIV of 1993 on publication of the modified agreement on visibility of the border signals and rectified the borderline due to the Lapincs river's movement.
31. Regulation of the European Parliament and the Council 562/2006/EC.
32. The modified Government Decree No. 338 of 2006, 23 December delegates the documentation of border demarcation and its archive, storage and recording changes of border lines to the agriculture authority while representatives of border management are appointed by the county police captains.

to the Act II of 2012 on minor offences (hereinafter MinofA) including fine and arrest of the apprehended perpetrator during the procedure (Articles 177, 205);

(e) the visibility of the border signs shall be ensured; protection and integrity of signs and borders must be provided during economic activities in the border zone (e.g., building, hunting, trafficking on border roads, fishing in frontier waters), so the property owner in the border zones shall notify the competent authority before starting certain activities unless the laws require permission from the municipal or other authorities to carry out the given activities; however, the rules of conduct on border roads and border waters are regulated in the international agreements;

(f) The 'internal' and 'external' borders are not defined but there are references to the terms in the Schengen Borders Code (Articles 2.1. and 2.2), although Hungary has no sea frontiers. Moreover, there are no provisions regarding how the control operates in the non-Schengen Romanian-Hungarian border. Due to the scattered areas of the Schengen zone,[33] EU Member States and EEA states[34] (with a specific agreement with the EU Member States) the answer is vague in other parts of Europe.

35. Border crossing points at the border as determined in the Schengen Border Code (Article 2.8) may be established, closed, pending in operation or may change its profile (e.g., opening for lorries or only for passengers) as well to set up a temporary crossing point (for instance, during a festival or a tourist event), only in accordance with international treaties. All other decisions in connection with border-crossing including the implementation of international agreements belong to the competence of the government. The headquarters of the police is entitled to suspend the operation of a crossing point for a maximum of forty-eight hours if an emergency case or any troubles in border control cannot be avoided otherwise. The criteria of setting up a crossing point depend on whether it is a temporary or permanent crossing point, and the kind of border that will be crossed.[35] For instance, the international airports (crossing points in air traffic) shall separate personal and cargo traffic physically, ensure entry and departure movement, ensure that passengers move across the external and internal borders by different corridors, and also

---

33. Schengen State means any Member State of the European Union applying in full the Schengen acquis defined in Art. 1 of the Protocol integrating the Schengen acquis into the framework of the European Union annexed to the Treaty on the European Union, to the Treaty establishing the European Community and to the Treaty establishing the European Atomic Energy Community (Schengen Protocol) and in Council Decision 1999/435/EC, as well as the measures adopted by the institutions of the European Union in these fields, and any other State that is in association with the implementation, application and development of the Schengen acquis by virtue of Art. 6 of the Schengen Protocol within the meaning of the Agreement concluded with the Council of the European Union. As of July 2011 the Schengen countries are as follows: Austria, Belgium, Czech Republic, Denmark, Estonia, Finland, France, Germany, Greece, Hungary, Iceland, Italy, Latvia, Lithuania, Luxemburg, Malta, Netherlands, Norway, Poland, Portugal, Slovakia, Slovenia, Spain, Sweden and Switzerland.
34. Party state in Agreement on the European Economic Area.
35. Government Decree No. 332 of 2007, 13 December on opening border crossing point, temporary crossing point and their operation conditions.

ensure designated premises for staying of refused persons until departure in the transit area. In a crossing point at the railways, proper illumination, service cabins for custom officers, cameras to monitor the place and premises for the checking and staying of refused passengers are also required. Upon establishing a crossing point on international waters, the operator shall provide a separate control for passenger vessels and freighters, entry and departure of passengers, an enclosed space for checking, and premises for staying the refused passengers. From the commercial point of view, setting up and operating a regular border crossing point is rather disappointing, because 'the owner of the real estate on which the border crossing point is established shall provide free of charge the infrastructure and equipment for the authority responsible for the border and the passengers' checking. The other costs of operation and its sharing may conclude a civil contract with the responsible authority' (Article 15). In the event that a permanent crossing point is opened, it has to be done in accordance with the county police station and the neighbouring state authority's consent for sport, tourism, cultural, religious, municipal, business purposes or for international commitment. Only the fee of the custom officers and police checking services are defined,[36] but the other payments of opening and operation are to be determined in a civil law contract (e.g., a municipal body and local NGOs intend to organize a border-zone holiday along with the twin town across the border but all costs of management are to be decided, shared and paid on the basis of a civil law accord). The authorization of opening a temporary crossing point belongs to the county police station. The crossing points at the land border shall be furnished with state and EU symbols, the name of the place in English and in the language of the adjacent state, the time of operation and possible restrictions in English and in German as well. At all other crossing points, the time of operation and certain restrictions in crossing shall be clearly mentioned on the signs.

36. The BordA in compliance with the Schengen Borders Code regulates the *border control* and the requirements of crossing the external border. The former provides rules regarding checking the border traffic, including the permission of entry, and border surveillance between the crossing points outside the fixed opening hours. The main purpose of guarding the border is to impede illegal border crossing, to combat crime across the borders and to take measures against illegal border crossing. This military language is in harmony with the structure of the border guarding authority that has strong traditions in the Hungarian law enforcement. It explains the weak accountability, transparency and strategic thinking of law enforcement as well as laser parliamentary scrutiny and public control on law enforcement (Finszter, 2007). Due to the detailed rules provided in the Schengen Borders Code, the BordA contains neither interpretative provisions nor institutional connections of the EU law to the Hungarian public administration, to other law enforcement organs, or to division of competence in border control.

36. The fee per Police and customs officer employed during the operation of the temporary crossing point is hourly EUR 10 on working days, EUR 15 in the evening and at night and EUR 20 on weekends and non-working days.

37. The *external border crossing can be suspended* for up to thirty days in a given part of the state border in order to limit the entry and exit of passengers, vehicles or transport, by the Ministry of the Interior in case of emergency (Article 12 of BordA). This suspension of movement is lawful if it is based on national security reasons, or is done for the prevention of epidemics or pandemonium – upon the initiative of the responsible minister implementing the rules of sanitation and the World Health Organization (WHO). The minister shall inform the responsible parliamentary commission regarding the ordered suspension.

38. Also, the BordA regulates the conditions of entry (see below) and delegates the regulatory power to the government in numerous issues. The temporary *re-introduction of border control at internal borders* is defined in the decree,[37] although it may strongly limit the free movement and human rights, which are under the purview of the legislative power (Article I of the Fundamental Law). The government may order the border control at internal borders to implement Article 23(1) of the Schengen Borders Code, upon the initiative of the Ministry of the Interior alone, or together with the minister of public health and of agriculture (in the event of severely endangered sanitation) or together with the minister in charge of the security and intelligence services (in the event of gross internal threat to public security). Furthermore, this minister is required to notify the EU and the neighbouring states regarding the re-introduction and its duration, and also to inform the public. This technical decree contains no clear definitions of the closures stated in the Schengen Borders Code, for instance, the notion of 'public health danger' (Article 2.19) refers to illness that – inter alia – comes under the purview of the national sanitary measures. According to a survey on the legal rules, two different decrees can be applicable to this bogus provision (on checking migrants' health and on sanitary measures preventing epidemics). In sum, the BordA and implementing decrees were adopted in order to formally transpose the EC law but a genuine applicability of transposed norms was not the goal.

39. The border control comes under the purview of the *tasks of the Police*, since the Border Guard was integrated to that category in January 2008 on the eve of the enlargement of the Schengen area. This institutional unification ceased the existence of a homogenized unit and the border control domain moved to the overworked, militant police. The staff[38] was selectively absorbed by the police but loss of human capital was high.[39] According to the PolA, the protection of public security and order, border control, checking the border traffic and keeping up the order

37. Government Decree No. 333 of 2007, 13 December on interim re-introduction of the border control at internal borders refers back to the Schengen Border Code, Art. 23 (1).

38. The number of staff in the border guards was 10,000 and in the police it was 34,000. After the integration of two law enforcement organization the new police staff numbered 40,000. However, under the preferential retirement system the most experienced persons after twenty-five years in duty left the law enforcement with good pensions and started a new business activity in the private security sector.

39. The planned rationalization rate of the staff in integration was officially 20%. See: Piros Attila 'Fragmentumok a rendészeti integráció folyamatából' Pécsi Határőr Tudományos Közlemények Pécs, 2007:32.

at the border imply that the main functions of the Police would be crime prevention, criminal investigation, public administrative and law enforcement entitlements (Article 1 (1),(2)) This amalgam of tasks and competences – inter alia – includes the following:

(a) safeguard the border, impede, prevent and investigate the illegal border crossing by passengers or by vehicles;
(b) controlling persons and vehicles, granting their entry and maintaining the order at border crossing points; checking the travelling documents, identity and conditions of passengers during entry, scrutinizing the passenger cars and vehicles, controlling the legality of residence in transit areas, and refusing the entry of migrants in the absence of the fulfilment of required conditions (Article 35/A);
(c) directing the scrutiny of border events;
(d) supervising the maintenance and reconstruction work on border signs;
(e) administering the mass influx of migrants or aggressive mass events at the borders, in violation of the order therein.

40. The Police as a centralized law enforcement organization led by the Chief Captain of the Headquarters of the Police are subordinated by the Ministry of the Interior transmitting the governmental policy towards the organization. The minister is entitled to adopt decrees on the operation and tasks of the Police within the framework of laws and international cooperation, he is responsible politically for lawful, effective, professional and economic activity of the Police, giving general instructions to the Chief Captain without derogation to his/her competence.

(a) The Headquarters of the Police are directed by the Chief Captain appointed by the Prime Minister upon the initiative of the minister and after the nominee's hearing in the parliamentary committee in charge of public security and law enforcement. The Captain is entitled to issue regulatory orders to all Police units on operation and profession, human resources and finance. The Headquarters of the Police has centrally directed units such as an emergency unit in mass demonstrations or an air-controlling security unit of the Police at the international airport. These units are trained, controlled and financed by the Headquarters. The Directorate of Counter-terrorism and the Directorate of Internal Checking (anti-corruption unit) cooperate horizontally with the Headquarters.
(b) The county and the capital Police stations (twenty in number) are subordinated by the Headquarters of the Police. These have formal contacts with the county municipal assembly through an annual report on the general development of the public order and security challenges in the given territory.
(c) The Police stations operate in cities, towns and capital districts (approximately 250) in subordination to the county/capital police station and Headquarters of the Police. At this level, there is clear contact with municipality: police station concludes contract with municipality that contributes to the police resources to the local order and maintaining security. The joint committee on the public order and the exchange of views is part of the practice in many places.
(d) The local representative in the other three thousand settlements of the country is hardly provided. There is a network of police agents in bigger villages and

border controlling units in external border zones and at crossing points as directed by the county police stations.

(e) The Police Code of Conduct was approved by the top management of the Police as an ethical requirement.[40] The legally binding rules on activities are regulated in the ministerial decree (Rules on Duty Conduct)[41] in a detailed manner. Furthermore, the main components of law enforcement are defined in a separate act on officers[42] that is applicable to customs, police, prison institutions, fire brigade officers and members of the security services. It provides them with more privileges in comparison to the legal position of public officials, compensating them for the tight hierarchical order, militant operation and/or daily risks in duty. The police officers are remunerated on the grounds of their ranks, the relevance of their experience. The place of duty and individual abilities are secondary, and the rank basically depends on the formal qualification acquired through the schooling system and secondarily on personal assessment.

41. The Police, as a law enforcement organization, have wide international cooperation with the neighbouring countries in implementing bilateral agreements and the EC law on crime prevention, and combating illegal migration. It includes the implementation of readmission agreements (giving back to the country of origin or transit the illegally entered migrants, escorting them to the border, transferring the apprehended persons, safeguarding the returned migrants). The police are entitled to use coercive measures (firearm, scuff, tear-gas, truncheon, dog, physical force, etc.) and limit liberty in the transit area as well (Chapter V in PolA). Whereas the member of another Member State authority and fast reacting unit also has the right to apply coercive instruments and measures in the territory of Hungary[43] as follows:

(a) physical force, handcuff and truncheon may be implemented by the non-national staff of the law enforcement unit if the said instruments and implementation are officially standardized at the Police in Hungary;
(b) the duty firearm may be kept and may be applied only in self defence in emergency situations;
(c) he/she may apprehend the illegally residing person and shall surrender him/her to the Police (Article 62/A).

42. The National Tax and Customs Office (hereinafter NAV) is responsible for implementing the national law and the EC customs rules[44] controlling the entry and residence of third-country nationals, vehicles and means of transport. The regional and county airport and investigation units of customs offices under the subordination

40. See <www.Police.hu>.
41. Decree of the Minister of Justice and Law Enforcement No. 62 of 2007, 23 December.
42. Act XLIII of 1996 on professional officers' duties and rights in law enforcement employment.
43. In compliance with the European Parliament and Council Regulation 863/2007/EC.
44. Regulation 2913/92/EEC on Community Customs Codex.

of the NAV are regulated in a separate act together with an executive decree.[45] In accordance with this, the NAV is governed by the Ministry of Economy. The customs offices are law enforcement and public administrative authorities entitled to use coercive measures, including firearms. The NAV maintains its own forensic laboratory, risk analysis centre, and national criminal investigation unit. Before the accession to the EU, the budget income from customs was very high (the second biggest after the VAT) but after enlargement its role in the economy has changed while the legal position of the organization has remained privileged. The director of the NAV is appointed by the Prime Minister and his duties include being the Chief Commander of Customs appointed by the director of NAV. The customs officers are within the scope of the act on law enforcement officers.

43. This hierarchical organization's task is manifold, and it can be said that its distinct role is to become the centre of Hungarian protection of economic and financial interests, combating falsification and smuggling of productions, abusive manner in inland revenues (in alcohol, mineral oil and cigarette), dangerous material (radioactive materials, guns, technological developments in civil and defence/security industry) as well as prevention of certain frauds in community supports contact with the agency of the EU combating fraud and abusive economic actions (OLAF). In accordance with this,

(a) the customs offices are entitled to criminal investigation in an operative, covert and non-covert ways according to the Penal Code (Act C of 2012) and Act XIX of 1998 on Criminal Procedural Code (hereinafter CrimPA), customs controlling competence and public administrative authority (in minor offences relating to the inland revenues and customs by the MinofA, registration in customs storage); the internal hierarchy means that the appealed decision by the court of first instance shall be decided by the higher customs office and the final decisions may be reviewed at the county/capital court according to the CivPA;
(b) its mobile units participate in the in-country checks on the third-country nationals and suspicious migrants in the entire territory of the country together with the Police, labour inspectors and environment protection guards;
(c) it operates the crossing points on roads, and
(d) the customs officer is entitled to control the passengers, vehicles and cargo moving across the external borders in order to implement the Community Customs Code. The controlled persons may submit within eight days a complaint against the officer's measure or decision, addressing it to the higher directorate (level) that shall decide, with reasoning, the complaint within fifteen days unless the decision by the court of first instance is modified or withdrawn in agreement with the complaint. The decision may be contested by claiming a judicial review at the court.
(e) the customs offices processing numerous personal and non-personal data contacting the European Customs Database, the Europol, the OLAF, criminal record authority and Police, inter alia.

45. Act CXXII of 2010 on National Tax and Customs Office and the Government Decree No. 273 of 2010, 9 December.

44. In the border controlling task, the PolA sets up a patrolling and a passport controlling duty, while the Rules on Duty Conduct determine some further details in migration control.

(a) A travel document and vehicle scrutiny aim to control the conditions of entry and residence not extending to the customs. At the moment of entry, the police shall control the personal data and parameters of the travelling and vehicle documentation using the database (Schengen Information System, other the PolA established database) for identifying and screening out persons for whom an alert, a European Arrest Warrant and/or Interpol requests have been made; without derogation of the customs officers' competence a stricter scrutiny of the vehicle shall be made together with the customs officers with the exception of urgent measures due to suspicion of an offence (smuggling, human trafficking and other severe crimes);
(b) the passport controller shall stamp and record the date of entry, place, take measures for any irregularity in the travelling document and its attached documents pertaining to the third-country national. However, the result of the controlled entry and the residence conditions shall be recorded in an in-country check issuing a format decision;[46]
(c) the Policemen, in collaboration with other authorities outside the border zone, are entitled to investigate any illegally residing migrants and may conduct an in-country check in the entire territory of the country using numerous technical equipment's, stopping vehicles, checking persons or monitoring the space. It shall be separate from border traffic control; the in-country check is managed by mobile units and patrolling units;
(d) the operation rules of crossing points shall be approved by the county captain of the Police upon request of the leader at the border crossing unit. It shall be posted in Hungarian, in the official language of the bordering state and in English at a clearly visible place at each border crossing point determining the premises or designated places for control, method of refused entry, designated or safeguarded place for refused and apprehended persons waiting for return, parking places, place for hygienic measures of vehicles or cargo, and method of prevention of accident;
(e) the police are entitled to arrest third-country nationals in order to take the proper measures on the grounds of the ThirdA for a maximum of twelve hours;
(f) passport controller, security and passenger safety police officers are entitled to wear firearms at work at the international airport for controlling the travellers, staff of traffic companies, baggage, air cargo and catering; prevention of terror or public security threats in the closed and open parts of transit area.

46. See Appendix VIII in the Reg. 562/2006/EC.

Chapter 2. Right to Enter the Country

§1. Conditions for the Right to Enter

45. The annual number of persons moving across the borders into Hungary has been four to five times the number of the total population for many years. As a result, the quick yet precise identification of those entering lawfully and those who are irregular/illegal migrants requires a practical compromise. The BordA defines the major criteria of entry into the territory of Hungary. They are as follows:

(a) the state border may be crossed at a publicly opened crossing point on the road, railways, water or air harbours, unless international agreement or directly applicable EC law regulates otherwise (e.g., at the internal border between the two neighbouring Schengen states the land or water frontiers may be crossed without crossing points in order to encourage neighbourhood contacts);
(b) the border crossing shall be controlled, unless international agreement or directly applicable EC law regulates otherwise (e.g., at the internal border, the control was temporarily re-introduced during the Football Championship or the G-8 summit meeting, perceiving a security risk);
(c) the crossing points at external borders are not closed. The minister in charge of migration is entitled to order a temporary close-down for a maximum of thirty days (see above);
(d) the passenger has to meet all requirements as determined in the Schengen Border Code.

46. Hungarian nationals have to be identified with identity cards, passports or nationality certificates issued by the Hungarian authority; due to the fundamental right pertaining to the *law of return and entry*, it cannot depend on whether the document is void if the holder's identity can be verified by an emergency travel document issued the consular office of another Member State or through a database in which the Police can control the identity of the passenger.[47] It has to be added that the number of persons who have dual citizenship is high, so all passengers presenting documents issued by the non-Hungarian authorities – with the exception of the emergency travelling document – shall be considered as citizens of that state of which the identification document is used.

47. The right to entry and short-term residence for *EEA nationals and their family members who are third-country nationals* can hardly be separated, taking into account the Act on the Accession and the agreement with Switzerland.[48] The FreeA

47. For instance, lawful identification is allowed with expired national passport or address card due to the on-line connection of the Police to the governmental data bases.
48. Act CXXV of 2006 publishing the agreement concluded on 21 Jun. 1999 and its additional protocol due to the enlargement of the EU between the European Community, its Member States and with Switzerland on free movement of persons.

defines who is subject to the EU law and, consequently, enjoys the right to free movement in Hungary.[49]

(a) Hungary shall ensure this right, with the exception of Hungarian citizens, to nationals of any Member State of the EU and states who are parties to the Agreement on the EEA, and to persons enjoying the same treatment as nationals of the states who are parties to the Agreement on the EEA by virtue of an agreement between the EC, its Member States, and a State that is not a party to the Agreement on the EEA with respect to the right to free movement and residence (hereinafter EEA nationals);
(b) It is provided to the family members of the EEA nationals (see details in Part III).

48. The persons who are entitled to the *right to free movement* (the EEA nationals, their family members who are third-country nationals under the ambit of the FreeA) are each identified with a valid identity card, a national passport and/or in case of family member a residence card and a permanent residence card issued in another Member State. Their free movement and conditions are defined in the FreeA and FreeD transposing the Directive 2004/38/EC and making the Schengen Borders Code applicable by the Hungarian authority.

49. Third-country nationals accompanying an EEA national or a Hungarian citizen, or joining an EEA national or a Hungarian citizen who resides in Hungary, who are family members, may enter the country with a valid travel document and – unless otherwise prescribed by any directly applicable EC legislation or an international agreement – with a *valid visa.* The said family members may enter the territory of Hungary without a visa, provided they hold a document evidencing right of residence, or a residence card issued by another EEA state to the family members of EEA nationals who are third-country nationals. The material cover on residence as determined in the MinD shall be presumed. The family member who is a third-country national may enter into possession of a valid local border traffic permit (See paragraph 68) at the external borders of Hungary. The provisions set out in the Schengen Borders Code on the rules governing the movement of persons across borders shall also apply to the admissions (as per visa requirement).

50. According to the ThirdA, the following persons shall be treated as *third-country nationals*: any person who uses a valid travel document issued by a non-EEA country to verify his/her nationality, unless proven to the contrary; or any person who is unable to show proof of having the right to free movement and

49. The FreeA contains regulations that may be transposed the Directive 2004/38/EC of the European Parliament and of the Council of 29 Apr. 2004 on the right of citizens of the Union and their family members to move and reside freely within the territory of the Member States amending Regulation (EEC) No. 1612/68 and repealing Directives 64/221/EEC, 68/360/EEC, 72/194/EEC, 73/148/EEC, 75/34/EEC, 75/35/EEC, 90/364/EEC, 90/365/EEC and 93/96/EEC, and regulations for the implementation of Arts 5 and 13 of the Schengen Borders Code together with the FreeD.

residence by the FreeA. Persons with travelling documentation of stateless persons, recognized refugees also belong to this group.

51. The third-country nationals are not entitled to the right to entry. They have to face a highly *selective or conditional authorization of entry*, although the majority of them can easily meet the requirements. In fact, the complex selection system can be used in an effective way to screen out the minimal number of dangerous passengers if the target groups are clearly designated, the officials are well-trained and would work in good conditions. In the partial absence of these preconditions, the visa and external border checking is more a collective inconvenience for all travellers than an impossibility for a meagre minority. The components of the conditionality or requirements of entry are as follows:

(a) Third-country nationals may enter the territory of Hungary and stay for up to three months within a period of six months from the time of first entry under the conditions set out in the Schengen Borders Code. At first entry, the valid and accepted travelling document (passport) shall be presented. The Police checking the passengers or the consular office may assess whether the presented document is in conformity with the list of acceptable foreign passports issued by non-EEA states.[50]
(b) The passenger is not on the list on persons who have been expelled or excluded from Hungary or by any Schengen state displaying his/her name to alert others through the Schengen Information System.
(c) Absence of a threat to public policy, national security or the international relations of any of the Schengen States. If there is information on such a migrant prior to his/her entry, his/her name is included in the list of undesirable persons. If not, the border controlling authority has to decide ad hoc whether the traveller or a cargo shall be refused in order to protect, for instance, the sanitary interests. However, the ad hoc refusal – without prior indication – or 'expected' migrants on the grounds of prior information are apprehended and/or arrested for a criminal procedure or minor offence proceedings because the combating of crime and illegal migration requires ex officio measures at first and the 'non-action' such as refusal at the border is applicable only in the event of minor negligence and/or misbehaviour of migrants.
(d) The traveller has to present a valid visa compatible to the stated purpose of visit unless otherwise prescribed by any directly applicable EC legislation or an international agreement. The EC law[51] contains a negative list, which is a list of countries whose citizens must have a visa (Annex I: approximately 130 states) and a positive list, which is a list of countries whose citizens are exempt from the requirement to have a visa (Annex II: approximately 40 states). According to the latter, entry without visa and a maximum of three months residence shall be granted to refugees and stateless persons for whom the travel documents are

50. Government Decree No. 328 of 2007, 11 December on determination of travelling documents issued by third-country nationals for recognition in entry to Hungary.
51. Council Regulation 539/2001/EC of 15 Mar. 2001, the right of entry for the purpose of residence not exceeding three months without a visa.

issued by the states listed in Annex II of Council Regulation. Furthermore, the following may enter without a visa: the third-country nationals who are the crew members of an air transport vehicle participating in aid or rescue operations in natural disasters and other and similar events, and third-country nationals participating in such rescue operations, as well as third-country nationals holding a travel document issued by the UN, Council of Europe or the International Court of Justice. The right of entry and residence not exceeding three months without a visa shall be granted to third-country nationals holding a transit visa that is also valid for the territory of Hungary, a short-stay visa or a long-stay visa issued under the requirements set out by the general requirements (Article 5) of the Schengen Borders Code. The requirement to obtain an airport transit visa shall not apply to the third-country nationals holding a diplomatic, service or other official passport; who are crew members of an aircraft, provided they are nationals of either of the countries who have signed the Convention on International Civil Aviation (Chicago, 1944); or a residence permit[52] issued by an EEA Member State – with some exceptions – by Andorra, Japan, Canada, Monaco, San Marino, Switzerland or the United States of America. Perhaps it is better to determine which nationals are required to obtain an airport transit visa: nationals of Philippines, Guinea, Cameroon, Lebanon, Liberia, Rwanda, Sierra Leone, Senegal, Syria and Sudan (Appendix of the ThirdD).

(e) Although the passenger presents a visa for a validity period not exceeding three months, it shall be considered void under the following circumstances: it is no longer valid for entry into Hungary and residence in the territory of the Republic of Hungary in light of its validity period and/or the number of days and the number of entries authorized; the visa for a validity period not exceeding three months was withdrawn; the third-country national was issued a new visa in proceedings for the exchange or replacement of the visa or for the extension of his/her visa's validity period; the data and information it contains are no longer legible; it contains false or untrue information or has been forged; the holder is granted a visa for a validity period of longer than three months, interim permanent residence permit or a document evidencing the right of free movement and residence; or the holder has died.

(f) The passenger is not suffering from illness or is not in a pathogenic state that exclude him/her from the entry and residence according to the HealthD. Although the list of illnesses is general, in the majority of crossing points there are no human sanitary controlling equipment's or staffs, with sporadic exceptions at the international airport owing to the fear of the H1N1 flu.

(g) The third-country national has a local border traffic permit that provides a visa-free entry (See paragraph 68 .).

(h) The purpose of travel and sufficient means of support is ensured and clarified. An authorized letter of invitation may properly certify the sufficient material cover of residence and accommodation. In other cases, the general rule in the

---

52. It means (Art. 2.15 of the Schengen Border Code) that the residence permit is compatible to the format as determined in the Council Regulation 1030/2002/EC or to other document issued by any Member State that grants entry and return to that country, not including the documents issued to the applicants for residence permit or asylum.

MinD is applicable (Article 25): for third-country nationals including family members of the EEA national, the minimal *financial cover* is EUR 4 per capita. This anachronistic provision has been retained for the kin-minority policy compensating for the Schengen visa fee, visa requirements and harsh social inequalities. This simplified regulation contradicts, for instance, the accuracy of provisions on the calculation of the costs of expulsion (fee of the escort, nutrition, fare of the travel) as well as the manner of their reimbursement to the authority by the migrant, or the sponsor, the hosting organization or the research receiving institution.

§2. Administrative Procedures and Documents

52. The *letter of invitation* facilitates the procedure of the entry, visa and residence authorization. Here, its importance in admission is relevant. The letter of invitation may be approved by the OIN regional directorate after a scrutiny of the inviting party in this unilateral undertaking. The inviting party could be any natural or legal person, or unincorporated company without legal personality who undertakes a commitment in a letter of invitation – with an official certificate affixed – to provide room and board and financial support for the invited third-country national during his stay in Hungary, and, unless an international treaty provides otherwise, to cover the costs of medical care and the costs of exit of such third-country national. For instance, the ThirdA requires a letter of invitation from the visitor: 'the residence permit may be issued for the purpose of visit to third-country nationals holding a letter of invitation. The validity period of a residence permit issued for the purpose of visit shall correspond to the duration of the commitment fixed in the letter of invitation, not to exceed one year, and it may not be extended for the purpose of visit' (Article 25). The person/institution inviting a foreigner shall be held liable for damages they cause to others resulting from any infringement of their obligations (Article 72). It means that an authorized letter substitutes the other documents of the visitor as proof of his/her provided subsistence, health care insurance, accommodation and travel ticket to return home.

53. A request for *approval of the letter of invitation* may be submitted by a Hungarian citizen, a third-country national with an immigrant or permanent resident status, or a recognized refugee, a long-term visa or a residence permit holder, persons under the ambit of the FreeA, and legal persons or unincorporated companies without legal personality registered and seated in Hungary. Organs of public power[53] are eligible to invite foreign visitor(s) without authorization. However, the invited person and the inviting party must be aware that a letter of invitation shall not, in itself, constitute authorization for the third-country national to enter the country (e.g., if

53. They are as follows: the Parliament, the President of the Republic, the Government, their public administration body of the Government, the State Audit Office, the Ombudsman, the Constitutional Court, the ministries, central administration authorities, the courts and the public prosecutors' offices, the public administration body of the Government at counties, minority self-governments, and the Hungarian Academy of Science.

after the approval, the passport expires or an order on exclusion of the visitor is adopted). The approval means as follows:

(a) A request shall be submitted on a standard form defined in the MinD, at the competent Regional Directorate to the requesting person's permanent or temporary residence or place of accommodation, or the registered office of a legal person.
(b) It must decide on the request within fifteen days, or seven days if the entry and stay of the invited third-country national is desired on the grounds of substantial national interest of the state in the field of economics, culture, science or sports.
(c) The person requesting a letter of invitation must be able to verify his/her compliance with the conditions to satisfy the commitments (e.g., proving his/her monthly income, property of place for accommodation).
(d) If the regional directorate approves the letter, it shall grant consent for invitation and issue an authorization closure into the letter in a form with defined content. The validity period of a letter of invitation shall be specified in days, determined with regard to all prevailing circumstances. The maximum validity period of a letter of invitation is 365 days. The responsibility to send the letter of invitation to the invited third-country national lies with the inviting party.
(e) The fee of the authorization is EUR 15, and its appeal fee costs EUR 20.
(f) The migration authority shall process the following data of the inviting party and the invited third-country national: the identification data, address or registered office of inviting party, the duration of commitment and reasons of refusal. The migration authority shall process these data for five years following the expiration of the commitment.
(g) A request for a letter of invitation shall be refused if the requesting person is unable to satisfy the conditions for the performance of the commitment; has failed to perform his commitments associated with a previous letter of invitation; has supplied false or untrue information in his/her request. An appeal against refusal may be submitted to the OIN in accordance with the standard rules in the AdminA.

54. Nobody has the right to obtain a visa, and its authorization covers its issuance and also its withdrawal or invalidation. In this context, the migration authority shall consult with the central authorities of the Schengen States requesting consultation prior to granting consent for the issue of a visa for a validity period not exceeding three months.[54] Family members, who are third-country nationals holding a valid visa shall have the right to multiple entry within a period of three months from the date of issue of the visa. The right of entry exercised upon a visa shall terminate when the requirements of the Schengen Borders Code are no longer met. Furthermore, his/her visa shall be considered void if the data and information it contains are no longer legible; it contains false or untrue information or has been

54. Ministerial Decree issued by the Minister of justice and law enforcement, foreign affairs and minister without portfolio No. 29 of 2010, 12 May on obligatory co-ordination in short-term visa authorization.

forged; the holder was issued a document evidencing the right to free movement and residence; the holder is granted Hungarian citizenship or citizenship in a country whose nationals are not required to obtain a visa for entry into the territory of Hungary by virtue of any directly applicable EC legislation or an international agreement; or the holder has died. Where a visa authority learns of any reason during its proceedings due to which the visa has to be invalidated, it shall be withdrawn, and it is necessary to provide for a replacement. Where a visa issued by another Schengen State is withdrawn, the issuing Schengen State shall be notified without delay.

55. The decision for the *withdrawal of a visa* for a validity period not exceeding three months from the third-country national before his/her entry into Hungary lies with the visa authority that learns of any reason, during its proceedings, due to which the visa has to be invalidated. The decision for the withdrawal of the short-stay visa held by a third-country national who resides in Hungary lies with the competent Regional Directorate of the OIN to the place where the residence of the third-country national is located. Where a transit visa or a short-stay visa issued by another Schengen State is withdrawn, the issuing Schengen State shall be notified without delay, at the most within hours. The visa cancellation of the issued visa may be contested, according to the ThirdD.

56. As an exception, a visa may be issued at road, air and water border crossing points of the state to the *family member of the EEA national who is a third-country national*, provided that he/she is able to satisfy the requirements of entry and residence otherwise, and he/she makes it probable that he/she was prevented from obtaining a visa in advance. According to the FreeD (section 7), the Policeman shall forward visa applications submitted at border crossing points by electronic means without delay to the OIN. It shall promptly adopt a decision concerning the aforesaid applications, within three hours, and shall notify the applicant of its decision – via the police – electronically. The OIN operates a non-stop customer service department to ensure the continuity of visa services. If the application is approved, the visa shall be issued to the applicant by the Police.

Chapter 3. Refusal of Entry

57. Nationals – including the dual citizens – have a *fundamental right to return* to and enter the territory of Hungary (Article XIV (1) of the Fundamental Law). As is obvious, he/she must prove his/her Hungarian citizenship with a passport, identity card or citizenship certificate issued by the OIN. The expired document is not constitutional basis for refusal but procedure is simplified with valid documents. It has to be added that a national passport with the most advanced biometrical identification sign is available in consular offices within a standard deadline, hence an expired passport is renewed abroad without urgency.

58. During the *refusal, the non-refoulement* shall be taken into account. This means that the migrant shall not be sent back or expelled to the territory of a country that fails to meet the criteria of 'safe country of origin' or 'safe third country' regarding the person in question, in particular where he/she is likely to be subjected to persecution on the grounds of his race, religion, nationality, social affiliation or political conviction, nor to the territory or the frontier of a country where there is substantial reason to believe that the expelled foreign national is likely to be subjected to torture or any other form of cruel, inhuman or degrading treatment or capital punishment. In the event that there is any doubt as to whether or not the principle of non-refoulement applies in the ordering and the execution of refusal, the Police shall request the opinion of the refugee authority. The refugee authority shall comply with the above request, without delay, as per the ThirdD. Furthermore, any non-national whose application for asylum is pending may be forced to go back or expelled only if his/her application is refused by the final and executable decision of the refugee authority. If there is no safe third country receiving the third-country national, because refusal and sending back is not an option, or expulsion is prohibited, the Regional Directorate of the OIN shall grant a 'tolerant migrant' status to him/her, and shall take measures to issue a humanitarian residence permit in accordance with the ThirdA provisions. When the grounds for tolerant migrant status cease to apply, the Regional Directorate shall withdraw the said status.

59. The non-nationals under the personal scope of the ThirdA may be *rejected at the border*, and its substantial provisions are determined in the Schengen Borders Code (Article 13) referring back to the general conditions of entry (Article 5). The Police shall refuse the entry of the third-country national seeking admission for a stay not exceeding three months according to the provisions of the Schengen Borders Code, and shall return such person – in due observation of its interests towards the country of origin of the third-country national in question; to the country that is liable to accept him/her; to the country where his/her the customary residence is located; or to any third country that is ready to accept him/her. If the entry is refused because the third-country national is under exclusion, the visa issued in accordance with the ThirdA shall be void. However, the ThirdA and the ThirdD contain some additional procedural rules, as follows:

(a) The decision to refuse entry may not be appealed by the ThirdA. However, the Schengen Borders Code (Article 13) does not only require the implementation of the format on refusal (Appendix V/B) to be delivered to the migrant but also a legal remedy against the reasoning decision on refusal. The legal remedy shall be executed according to the national law. It would be also necessary to provide the address of national contact points to him/her from where he/she can obtain information on legal representatives who can represent his/her claim to remedy. Finally, if the refusal was unlawful by the legal review, all records on refusal made by the migration authority shall be deleted. From these provisions there is only a slight, hardly controllable guarantee in the ThirdA: if refusal is not pursued within 72 hours, expulsion measure shall be ordered (Article 41 (2)), and legal remedy is available for expulsion. Furthermore, the non-refoulement requirement shall be investigated either in case of refusal or in expulsion according to the ThirdD. If foreigner is not refused/expelled, a tolerant migrant status is ensured for him (section 124).

(b) A third-country national whose entry was refused and is sent back shall remain, for a maximum period of eighty hours, on the means of transport that is scheduled to depart to the point of origin or another destination of transit; or remain in a designated place located in the frontier zone for a maximum period of seventy-two hours, or if having arrived by means of air transport, in a designated place of the airport for a maximum period of eight days; or transfer onto another means of transport of the carrier that is liable to provide return transport.

(c) If the return procedure cannot be carried out within seventy hours, the third-country national shall be expelled following his/her admission. If the expulsion is ordered for reasons other than international commitment or the decision of the Council of the European Union, or whose entry and residence represents a threat to national security, public security or public policy, the third-country national in question may not be excluded.

(d) If the Police confines a third-country national to a designated area of the frontier zone or the airport, the place set up in the airport transit zone or in the frontier zone shall support him/her (nutrition, accommodation, emergency health care).

(e) If the entry was allowed for humanitarian (exceptional) reasons in absence of all conditions of entry, the Police shall transport him/her to the competent Regional Directorate of the OIN for the place of entry, and it shall examine immediately as to whether the expulsion measure applies.

60. Refusal of entry of the persons enjoying right to free movement means a severe limitation that shall be in compliance with the human rights and limitation of the EC law including the case law of the ECJ. From this point of view, the guarantees in the FreeA (Articles 36–37) and the FreeD for the migrant are important although those shall be respected by the officials and the officers. The right to free movement and residence of the persons under the ambit of the FreeA may be restricted in compliance with the principle of proportionality and based exclusively on the personal conduct of the individual concerned, where such personal conduct represents a genuine, present and sufficiently serious threat affecting public policy, public security or public health.

(a) The Police may refuse the entry of an EEA national or his/her family member who does not fulfil all the entry conditions, or if having been excluded (prohibition of entry and residence has been ordered against him/her) from the territory of Hungary. The refused EEA national or his/her family member shall be returned to the country of origin; to the country that is liable to accept him/her; to the country where his/her customary residence is located; or to a third country that is ready to accept him/her.

(b) If the entry is refused due to the absence of the conditions of entry – and not due to the exclusion order – the Police shall – upon request – provide the EEA national or his/her family member the opportunity to obtain the necessary documents within seventy-two hours from the time of the decision to refuse, or to provide other means of evidence for his/her right of entry. It shall be applied to any person who is able to provide proof of his/her identity and of being an EEA national within seventy-two hours.

(c) Refusal shall be ordered by a substantiated decision indicating the reasons. It shall take effect immediately – or after the lapsed seventy-two hours – and there is no appeal against refusal.

(d) The refused person must remain on the means of transport that is scheduled to depart, or to transfer onto another means of transport of the carrier that is liable to provide return transport for the person in question. However, until departure but for a maximum of seventy-two hours, he/she shall remain in a designated place located in the frontier zone if the return procedure cannot be carried out in accordance with staying on the means of transport, or he/she requested a seventy-two hour deadline to obtain the missing documents for entry. If he/she is able to produce the necessary documents or proof regarding right of entry within this deadline, the decision on refusal and return becomes void.

(e) If the return procedure cannot be carried out within the time limit defined above, the Police may order the expulsion of the migrant. However, his refusal or expulsion may be ordered only to a safe country (Article 34 of ThirdA).

Part II. Right of Residence: General Provisions

Chapter 1. Short Stay

§1. Conditions for Short Stay

61. This chapter describes what legal requirements shall be met by the non-preferential migrant groups within the category of third-country nationals. The conditions determined for specific migrant groups are available in Part III, including the EEA nationals, their family members and protected persons under the international law.

62. A *third-country national* may enter with a *visa-free residence* for a short period on the grounds of an international commitment or the directly applicable EC law, transposed national rules, or in possession of a valid visa. However, such a person will have to reside in the country for up to three months within a period of six months if he/she meets the conditions of the Schengen Borders Code. In other words, the third-country nationals who satisfy the conditions set out in the Schengen Borders Code on entry shall be authorized to stay in the country for a period not exceeding three months. Exceptions may be made on the grounds of urgent humanitarian or national reasons or of international commitments. Hence, if the expiry date of the traveller's passport is less than one month away the police may exempt him/her from this general condition (section 3 of ThirdD). Furthermore, a visa-free entry and stay not exceeding three months is provided for the following:

(a) recognized refugees and stateless persons if their travelling document is issued by the state whose nationals are eligible for visa-free travel;[55]
(b) crew members and other staff of emergency relief or vehicle if they are third-country nationals on duty;
(c) each third-country national in possession of a travelling document issued by the UN, Council of Europe or the International Criminal Court;
(d) regular crew members of vessels, seafarers or air companies.

55. See Appendix II of Reg. 539/2001/EC.

63. The Visa Code[56] which entered into force in October 2009 determines how to issue the *visa for each third-country national under the ambit of the joint list of visa obligations*[57] including the airport transit visa requirements and the procedure of visa authorization. The ThirdA together with its executive rules contains only additional, procedural provisions belonging to the national competence.

64. A Schengen visa comes in several *Schengen visa categories* based on the purpose of travel or stay. A Schengen visa can belong to one of the following categories:

(a) The airport transit visa (Category A) is required by a few nationals[58] while passing through the international transit area of airports during a stop-over or transfer between two sections of an international flight.
(b) The transit visa (Category B) is required by nationals who are not allowed to travel visa-free while travelling from one non-Schengen country to another non-Schengen country. It allows travellers who are going from one non-Schengen country to another non-Schengen country to pass through the territories of the Schengen country. This visa may be issued for one, two or, as an exception, several transits, provided that the duration of each transit does not exceed five days.
(c) The short-term visa (Category C) is the most common Schengen visa issued for reasons other than immigration. It entitles travellers, subject to the visa requirement, to enter the territories of the twenty-five Schengen countries to pay a continuous visit or several visits, the duration of which does not exceed three months (ninety days) in any half-year from the date of first entry in the Schengen area. *The single-entry visa* allows one uninterrupted stay whose duration does not exceed the number of days indicated on the visa, ninety days being the maximum number of days which may be granted. In the example below, the duration of the stay authorized by the visa is thirty days. A period of grace of fifteen days of validity of the visa is normally added to the number of days of authorized stay, should the visa holder wish to postpone his or her departure. *The multiple-entry visa* allows several stays on the territory of one or several Schengen countries, provided that the total length of the visits does not exceed ninety days in any half-year from the date of first entry. The stay may be continuous or spread over several periods within the validity of the visa. The multiple-entry visa may be valid for one year, and in some cases, for more than a year, with a maximum of five years, for travellers providing sufficient guarantees. It is known as a travel visa.
(d) The national visa (Category D) can be issued by Hungary in accordance with ThirdA, allowing a stay longer than three months.
(e) The combination of Category D+C is intended for long-term stay within the Schengen Member States that issued it, and also to travel in the Schengen area

56. Regulation 810/2009/EC, 13 Jul. 2009 published in the OJ L 243, 15 Sep. 2009.
57. Regulation 539/2001/EC, 15 Mar. 2001.
58. The visa is required from the nationals of Afghanistan, Bangladesh, DR of Congo, Eritrea, Ethiopia, Ghana, Iran, Iraq, Nigeria, Pakistan, Somalia, Sri Lanka.

similar to a holder of a category C visa. The visa category D+C is for those who live and work in a Schengen state.

65. Visas with entitlement for a period not exceeding three months for third-country nationals are applicable for a maximum five years. Visa for a validity period not exceeding three months shall not be issued, or if already issued shall be *withdrawn* from the following third-country nationals: those who fail to comply with either of the general requirements set out in the Schengen Borders Code (Article 5(1)(a),(c) – and (e) if it is not issued by another Schengen Member State); those who had disclosed false information or untrue facts to the competent authority in the interest of obtaining the right of residence; or those who had attempted to mislead the competent authority as to the purpose of entry and stay.

66. Transit or *short-term visa with geographical limitation* (inside the Schengen area only to Hungary and to another Schengen country) may be exceptionally issued for the third-country national in the following cases:

(a) In the absence of the general conditions, the visa with a validity period not exceeding three months may be granted – as an exceptional – on humanitarian grounds, on the grounds of national interest, or because of international obligations to the third-country national;
(b) In the absence of the consent of other central authority of the requesting Schengen state – the OIN, as an exception, may issue the visa;
(c) The visa applicant has already used the short-term visa within the six month period since entry, but he/she has an acceptable reason for a further short-term visa; or
(d) The travelling document of the visa applicant not recognized by another Schengen state may grant a visa only to Hungary.

The Schengen Information System shall be notified when a visa with limited territorial validity is issued.

67. The *short-term visa may in extraordinary cases be extended* for humanitarian reasons, even in relation to employment or earning money or for other acceptable personal reasons, wherein the applicant meets all other requirements of residence in accordance with the Schengen Border Code, the facts substantiating the extension have appeared after the visa had been issued and the purpose of entry and residence have not changed. The maximum duration of the extended visa's validity shall not exceed ten days (transit visa) or three months.

68. The *local border traffic permit*[59] is also applicable for the short-term residence of the family member of the EEA national who is a third-country national.

59. Under the Regulation (EC) No. 1931/2006 of the European Parliament and of the Council of 20 Dec. 2006 laying down rules on local border traffic at the external land borders of the Member States and amending the provisions of the Schengen Convention as specified in the relevant international agreement.

A local border traffic permit must be refused, or an existing local border traffic permit shall be withdrawn if the applicant or the holder of the local border traffic permit fails to comply with the requirements for the issue of a local border traffic permit; has supplied false or untrue information in his/her application for a local border traffic permit; has made an attempt to mislead the competent authority as far as the purpose of entry and residence is concerned. The issued permit is void if it is withdrawn by final decision; the data and information that it contains are no longer legible; it contains false or untrue information or has been forged; or the holder has died.

69. The *local border traffic permit is available for third-country nationals* under the above mentioned Regulation and bilateral agreements. In the event of fulfilment of the requirements in the Schengen Border Code, and if the border resident is not considered a threat to public policy, internal security, public health or the international relations of the states of Hungary, and in particular are not subject to any expulsion or ban on entry or stay on the same grounds, the permit holder is entitled to multiple entry and for a continuous stay of a maximum of three months within six months in the border area. The holder may enter and reside in particular for social, cultural or family reasons, or substantiated economic reasons that are not to be considered as a gainful activity according to the national regulations. An application for a local border traffic permit must be refused, or an existing permit shall be withdrawn if the applicant or the holder fails to comply with the requirements for the issue of a local border traffic permit; has supplied false or untrue information in his/her application, he/she has made an attempt to mislead the competent authority as far as the purpose of entry and residence is concerned. The permission may be withdrawn if the third-country national leaves the border area defined in the relevant international agreement without authorization. The permit is void *ex lege* if the local border traffic permit was withdrawn by a final decision; the data and information that it contains are no longer legible; it contains false or untrue information or has been forged; or its holder has died.

§2. Administrative Procedures and Documents

70. In the cases defined by the Ministry of the Interior, the minister of foreign affairs and minister in charge of supervising the national security services, for reasons of public or national security, visas for a validity period not exceeding three months may only be granted upon the *prior consent of the central visa authority* (OIN). The central visa authority shall *consult with the central authorities of the Schengen States* requesting consultation prior to granting consent for the issue of a visa for a validity period not exceeding three months.[60] In accordance with this, the negotiation with the OIN in visa authorization[61] shall be requested if is well founded

60. The reasons and process of checking third-country national applicants is regulated in Reg. 767/2008/EC, 9 Jul. 2008 on Visa Information System and exchange of data on visa applicants for short-term visa among the member states of the EU (VIS Regulation).

61. Ministerial Decree issued by the Minister of justice and law enforcement, foreign affairs and minister without portfolio No. 29 of 2010, 12 May on obligatory co-ordination in short-term visa authorization.

that the security threats posed by the applicant – taking into account his/her origin, nationality, habitual residence or personal conditions – require scrutiny in order to prevent terrorism, illegal arm, human trafficking, falsification of travelling documents or other security threats.

71. Under international agreement, the diplomatic or *consular missions of other Schengen states* with proper entitlement may also issue visas for a validity period not exceeding three months in the name of and on behalf of Hungary; and Hungary is also entitled by international agreement to receive visa requests and issue visas on behalf of other Schengen states. For instance, on behalf of Latvia, the Hungarian consular office issues the Schengen visa in Vietnam, or in Albania it issues visas on behalf of Estonia, Latvia and Slovenia. Due to the absence of consular offices in numerous states,[62] this cooperation is important for travellers.

72. The *short-term visa procedure* for migrants under the scope of the ThirdA is regulated in detail in the ThirdD. The most relevant provisions are as follows:

(a) the visa applications may be submitted to any consulate office of Hungary, or to the foreign mission of any nation that is authorized to accept visa applications in the name of and on behalf of Hungary or any other place authorized to accept such applications among the Member States of the Union (e.g., if the applicant is able to verify a reasonable cause to submit his/her application in a country other than where his/her permanent or temporary residence is located);
(b) the consulate office is competent in the visa application if the applicant's final destination is Hungary, or the applicant wishes to enter Hungary to gain admission into the territory of the Schengen states, provided that the country of final destination cannot be determined;
(c) the minister of foreign affairs is competent for visa applications by diplomats and other persons enjoying privileges or immunities under international law or for external relations interests;
(d) the application for a visa shall be submitted on a standard form within three months prior to the planned date of travel, presenting the applicant's valid travel document;
(e) the validity period of the travel document – with certain exceptions for humanitarian reasons, national interest or international obligations – must exceed the planned date of exit from Hungary by at least three months, and must have at least one empty page where the visa can be affixed;
(f) one photograph of the face; documents to verify the purpose and duration of stay; the availability of the financial means necessary for the entire duration of stay, or for the return or continued travel; documentation with regard to appropriate accommodation shall be attached to the application; a document shall be attached in proof of having a travel insurance up to EUR 30,000 at least covering emergency medical care for the entire duration of stay and for all

62. Hungary operates embassies and consular offices in fifty non-EEA states in worldwide. <www.mfa.gov.hu>.

Schengen states, and covering the insurance holder's transport costs in returning home for health reasons (with the exception of third-country nationals holding a diplomatic, service or other official passport, or if it cannot be obtained as determined under local consular cooperation);

(g) where it is necessary to clarify the relevant facts concerning the applicant's stay, the competent consulate officer may request him/her to produce further documents;

(h) the costs of language services (translation, interpretation of a sign language, etc.) shall be borne by the applicant.

73. The visa authority shall record in the applicant's travel document – with some exceptions – the fact of application (date and place, the code of the visa requested, and the name of the authority receiving the application). The competent consulate officer shall adopt a decision as follows:

(a) within fifteen days from the time of receipt (regular deadline that may be extended up to sixty days in complicated cases);

(b) immediately or within a maximum of ten days the application of a minor and his/her accompanying legal guardian shall be decided upon, if the substantiated purpose of travel is medical treatment for the minor; visa application of a guardian of an unaccompanied minor who is arriving to escort the minor home; or if the entry and stay of the applicant is desired on the grounds of the substantial national interest of Hungary in the field of economics, culture, science or sports;

(c) the Minister in charge of foreign policies, and the competent consulate officer in cases falling within his competence, as well as the central visa authority in Schengen visa consultation (OIN) may request the opinion of the NSO or the anti-terrorist unit of the Police concerning applications for visas. They shall provide the aforementioned opinion within six to ten days – within the period of the regular deadline.

74. Also, in exceptional cases, visas with a validity period not exceeding three months may be issued for the third-country national at road, air and water border crossing points in due compliance with the Schengen Borders Code. The Police shall forward applications for visas with a validity period not exceeding three months submitted *at border crossing points* – by way of electronic means – without delay to the Western Regional Directorate of OIN. It shall promptly adopt a decision concerning the aforesaid applications, within three hours, and shall notify the applicant of its decision via the Police. The application for legal remedy for refusal may be submitted within three days, and the OIN shall decide on the appeal within five days.

75. The favourable decision adopted in relation to applications for visas with a validity period not exceeding three months may not be contested. If the visa application is refused, or in the event of annulment, revocation and renewal of visas, legal remedy is available as follows:

(a) appeal may be submitted within eight days to the proceeding consulate office, and it shall be decided by the minister of foreign affairs within fifteen days involving the OIN in the procedure with a right to veto. There is no further legal remedy available;
(b) appeal may be submitted within three days to the proceeding authority (Police, Regional Directorate of OIN or consular office in the event of annulment, revocation and renewal of visas), and it shall be decided by the minister of foreign affairs or the Headquarters of the Police or the OIN within five days. If the appeal is accepted, a new visa shall be issued to the third-country national. The consultation with NSO and the counter-terror unit of the Police is provided even in the legal remedy procedure relating to visa authorization;
(c) refused appeal may be reviewed by the Capital Administration Court. The claim shall be submitted within three days to the Court that decides on visa within eight days in a non-litigation procedure.

76. The *extension of short-term visas* belongs to the competence of the Regional Directorate of the OIN by reference to the place where the third-country national's accommodation is located. The application shall be submitted on a standard form defined in the MinD on the last day of validity of the visa while presenting the valid travel document. The validity period of the travel document must exceed the planned date of exit from the territory of the Schengen states. It is required to enclose one photograph of the face and documentary evidence verifying compliance with the requirements of entry and residence. The Regional Directorate shall adopt a decision immediately. The fee of the procedure is EUR 18. If the decision is in favour of the application, a new visa shall be issued. If Hungary cannot recognize the travel document of the applicant, or if the travel document does not have any empty page for affixing the visa, the visa shall be issued on a separate sheet. The territorial validity of renewed visas with a validity period not exceeding three months shall cover the same Schengen states to which the original visa applied. In case of refusal, the appeal may be submitted within three days to the Regional Directorate of the OIN, which shall forward it to the OIN. The OIN decides it within three days.

77. Applications for *local border traffic permits* shall be submitted on a standard form as prescribed in the MinD to the consular office of Hungary. When lodging it, the applicant shall present his/her valid travel document. The validity period of the travel document must not be less than one year from the date of submission of the application, plus thirty days, and must have at least one empty page where the local border traffic permit can be affixed. The applicant shall enclose one photograph of the face and a document in proof of lawful residence in a border area as defined in the relevant international agreement. The decision for the withdrawal of the local border traffic permit lies with the authority that has issued the local border traffic permit, or if held by a third-country national who resides in Hungary, with the competent Regional Directorate of the OIN to the place where the residence of the third-country national is located. The appeal against refusal of permission can be submitted to the consular office, which will forward it to the Ministry of Foreign Affairs. The minister is entitled to decide on appeal by the ThirdD.

78. The FeeD and EU law regulates the *fee in visa authorization*. In accordance with this, the fee shall be transmitted to the bank account as per the following:

(a) the fee of category B and C is EUR 35;
(b) the fee of visa in which the submission of required documents is made only three days before the planned entry is EUR 70;
(c) airport and transit visa and visa issued by non-resident third-country national to the consulate office is EUR 60;
(d) the seasonal labour visa procedure costs 40 EU;
(e) the fee of appealing against refusal, withdrawal or annulment of visa is EUR 30, and the fee of appeal against refusal of local border traffic permit is EUR 10.

§3. Legal Position in the Event of Short Stay

79. Third-country nationals with lawful short residence may enjoy human rights and fundamental rights though they have to be registered and he/she may be checked by the Police in the streets or in public places. The third-country national shall be required to register his/her place of accommodation and shall simultaneously disclose the following information to the immigration authority: his/her natural identification data, particulars of the travel document, address of place of accommodation; date of arrival to and estimated departure from the place of accommodation; date and place of entering the country. Operators of commercial lodgings and other hotel establishments of legal persons shall keep records (guest books), on a prescribed form, of the information of those of their guests who are third-country nationals. Furthermore, the short-term visa holder shall report the birth of a child in the territory of Hungary and shall simultaneously supply the following information to the Regional Directorate of the OIN: the natural identification data of the child, particulars of the child's travel document; address of the child's place of accommodation or home address.

80. The Police and custom officers are entitled to control compliance with and enforce the provisions of the ThirdA. Upon request for checks, the third-country national shall produce and surrender his/her travel document, authority to reside and other personal identification documents. In the event that any travel document is found in the possession of a third-country national that is issued to another person, and is held illegally by the third-country national, it shall be confiscated and – if no criminal charges are filed – sent to the foreign mission of the issuing State, or failing this, it shall be returned to the issuing agency via the minister of foreign affairs. Any third-country national who is unable to verify his/her lawful residence in Hungary or is unable to produce credible evidence of his/her identity, or who violates the provisions of the ThirdA shall be apprehended and taken into custody by the immigration authority. If the grounds for his/her residence or the identity cannot be established, the custody may be extended for up to maximum of twelve hours. A complaint may be submitted against this action in accordance with the PolA, on which the higher county captain will decide.

81. Third-country nationals with short-term visas, as well as nationals from certain states determined in Appendix II of the Regulation 539/2001/EC,[63] if staying lawfully in the territory of Hungary are eligible to be employed or participate in a remunerative work (Article 7/A of the ThirdA). The UnemplA can define exceptions.

§4. Position of Family Members

82. Although the term 'family member' is different as compared to the EEA nationals, Hungarian citizens and third-country nationals, their common factor is that they shall be self-subsistent, without causing any (unreasonable) social and/or security-related burden to the Hungarian public policy. The '*family member of a third-country national*' implies any of the following: the spouse of a third-country national; the minor child (including adopted children) of a third-country national and his/her spouse; the minor child, including adopted and foster children, of a third-country national, where this third-country national has parental custody and the children are dependent on him/her; the minor child, including adopted and foster children, of the spouse of a third-country national where the spouse has parental custody and the children are dependent on him/her as per the ThirdA. This family tie shall be documented in visa applications with a proper authentic document.

83. For the purposes of short-term residence and applications for visa, family status is a lawful reason for entry, visit and residence without further specific rights or positions beyond the human rights and fundamental rights. However, the letter of invitation issued by a resident migrant would contribute towards proving the ensured subsistence by the sponsor or inviting partner in the entry, visa and residence authorization.

63. They are as follows: Albania, the US, Andorra, Antigua & Barbuda, Argentina, Australia, Bahamas, Barbados, Bosnia-Herzegovina, Brasilia, Brunei Darussalam, Bulgaria, Chile, Costa Rica, South-Korea, Guatemala, Honduras, Croatia, Israel, Japan, Canada, Macedonia of ex-FRY, Malaysia, Mauritius, Mexico, Monaco, Montenegro, Nicaragua, Panama, Paraguay, Romania, Saint Kitts & Nevis, Salvador, San Marino, Seychelles Islands, Holy Sea, Serbia (with exception of passport issued by *Koordinaciona uprava*), Singapore, New-Zeeland, Uruguay, Venezuela, Hong Kong, Macao, Taiwan and Overseas British citizens.

Chapter 2. Residence More than Three Months

§1. Conditions for Residence

84. Taking into account the general provision, the criteria of crossing the external borders and residing for shorter or longer period are the same (Article 5 of the Schengen Borders Code). In accordance with this, there are *five main requirements* (Article 13 of ThirdA) as follows:

(a) possession of valid documents determined as necessary to cross the border and return or continue to travel;
(b) if applicable, submission of documents substantiating the purpose of the visit;
(c) sufficient means of support including the costs of subsistence, health insurance and accommodations or a place of residence in the territory of Hungary for the duration of the intended stay and for the return to their country of origin or transit to a third country. This precondition can be ensured also with valid travel tickets or means of transport that are in the legitimate use of the foreigner, with adequate insurance coverage. The requirement regarding proper accommodation is considered to have been fulfilled if the foreigner is the owner of the residential property registered in the real estate register as a detached house or a residential suite, or if entitled to use such property under any title, and the residential property has at least six square metres of living space per inhabitant unless the Regional Directorate of OIN makes an exception;
(d) absence from the list of persons banned from entry set up within the Schengen Information System (SIS); and
(e) absence of a threat to public policy, national security or the international relations of any of the Schengen states.

85. In the event of non-compliance with these requirements, the entry and stay of third-country nationals shall be authorized only on humanitarian grounds, on grounds of national interest or because of international obligations. Whereas, the aforementioned rules are transposed to the ThirdA defining each requirement under the following *legal entitlements for residence of third-country nationals*:

(a) visa with validity more than three months;
(b) residence permit (including permanent residence permit, interim permanent residence permit, national permanent residence permit, EC permanent residence permit);
(c) immigration permit;
(d) Blue Card, or
(e) temporary residence certificate issued mainly in order to respect international human right commitments.

86. Visas for a validity period of longer than three months are as follows:

(a) the visa to access the residence permit including the national permanent residence permit (for a single entry, and stays in Hungary for a period of thirty days within which he/she can obtain the issued residence permit for a longer stay);
(b) seasonal employment visa (for single or multiple entry and for employment for a maximum period of six months);
(c) national visa (for single or multiple entry and for stays in Hungary for a period of longer than three months under international agreement).

The issued visa is applicable for one year and in the national visa for five years. Unless otherwise regulated, these visas may be granted to third-country nationals who satisfy the general requirements of entry and residence. As a result, the application shall be refused, or if already issued shall be withdrawn from third-country nationals who fail to comply with either of the said requirements; who have disclosed false information or untrue facts to the competent authority in the interest of obtaining the right of residence; or whose issued residence permit has been withdrawn, or wherein its withdrawal is required.

87. Visas for entitlement to receive a residence permit may be granted to third-country nationals who have been authorized to receive a residence permit. This visa shall be cancelled if the underlying residence permit had been or is required to be withdrawn.

88. The *Blue Card* is an approved EU-wide work permit[64] allowing highly skilled non-EU citizens to work and live in any country within the European Union, excluding Denmark, Ireland and the UK as these are not subject to the proposal. The Blue Card system aims to facilitate the admission of qualified workers – excluding persons under the international protection, seasonal workers, trans-border service providers, posting workers, researchers with hosting contracts and long-term migrants – by harmonizing entry and residence conditions throughout the EU; to simplify admission procedures and to improve the legal status of those already in the EU. Since the transposition date (June 2011),[65] this 'one stop shop' admission without a pro-migration scheme and explicit (labour) migration policy has a marginal relevance. Thus its success remains questionable (Lukács, 2007), only ten permits were issued in 2011–2014. The applicant must produce the following:

(a) a work contract with a lawful minimal salary that will be regulated by the responsible minister (it would be at least 120%-150% of the average gross annual salary paid in Hungary[66]) in the given sector unless employment is

64. In accordance with the Council Directive 2009/50/EC, 25 May on the conditions of entry and residence of third-country nationals for the purposes of highly qualified employment.
65. The transposition was ensured by the Act CV of 2011 entering into force on 26 Jun. 2011.
66. The National Economy Ministerial Decree No. 44 of 2011, 16 December allows the lower salary threshold (120%) for employment of Blue Card holders in health care sector.

prohibited for third-country nationals and he/she will exceed the annual quota in the given profession as determined by the minister responsible;
(b) preconditions of residence longer than three months including the registered address in Hungary. If a third-country national has had a Blue Card and a residence permit issued by another Member State of the EU having spent at least eighteen months there, he/she is eligible to obtain the new Blue Card in Hungary;
(c) proof of sickness insurance;
(d) for regulated professions, documents establishing that he/she meets the legal requirements, and for unregulated professions, the documents establishing the relevant higher professional qualifications; and
(e) proof of absence of threat to public security.

The Blue Card shall be issued for at least one year and for a maximum of four years but it has to correspond to the validity of the labour contract with an additional three months. The extension up to a further four years shall be denied or issued. The Blue Card shall be withdrawn under the following circumstances:

(a) the holder cannot meet the requirements of issuance, including self-subsistence;
(b) the holder cannot prove the proper qualification;
(c) the holder has provided false, incorrect data or documents to the authority in order to acquire the permission;
(d) the holder's residence does not comply with the goals of the Blue Card;
(e) the holder has been unemployed for at least three consecutive months;
(f) the holder's employment has been terminated at least twice within the period of the Card's validity,
(g) the holder has been employed in different positions and sectors without permission, which are different from what is determined in the Blue Card within two years of its issuance.

89. The residence permit for third-country nationals in possession of valid visas shall be authorized unless the ThirdA provides otherwise. A residence permit provides a lawful residence in the country for a limited duration of not more than two years, but it may be extended for two additional years. With certain exceptions, the application for a residence permit or for the extension of the permit shall be refused, or if already issued, shall be withdrawn from the following third-country nationals:

(a) who fail to comply with either of the requirements of entry and residence;
(b) who have disclosed false information or untrue facts to the competent authority in the interest of obtaining the right of residence;
(c) who suffer from any disease that is considered to constitute a threat to public health (see in HealthD), and who refuse to submit to the appropriate compulsory medical treatment, or who fail to abide by the Hungarian health regulations while staying in Hungary; or
(d) who established the family relationship for the purpose of obtaining a residence permit on the grounds of family reunification.

The exception implies that the residence permit may be granted or maintained if it is necessary for international commitments, urgent humanitarian reasons or on the grounds of national interest if the third-country national is excluded due to the Schengen Information System (SIS) alert.

90. Beyond these general preconditions, the ThirdA contains some *special further requests depending on the purpose of residence.*

(a) A residence permit may be issued for the purpose of a *gainful employment* to third-country nationals whose purpose of stay is to perform work for others under a contract of employment for remuneration, which constitutes subordinate and superior positions; to lawfully perform work in a self-employed capacity for remuneration; to engage in any gainful activity in the capacity of being the owner or director of a business association, cooperative or some other legal entity formed to engage in gainful employment, or is a member of the executive, representative or supervisory board of such an entity. Furthermore, the third-country national, taking into account the relevant labour rules, may engage in a gainful employment who has a seasonal employment visa, a Blue Card, a residence permit granted on humanitarian grounds, a residence permit for the purpose of family reunification, or has a residence permit in order to pursue studies. The third-country national with a residence permit issued on grounds of pursuit of studies may engage in gainful employment during their term-time for a maximum of twenty-four hours per week, and outside their term-time, or for a maximum period of ninety days or sixty-six working days. The validity period of a residence permit granted for the purpose of gainful employment shall be three years at the most, and it may be extended by three additional years at a time. The period of validity of this residence permit of the holder who is subject to work permit shall correspond to the duration of the work permit. Third-country national may submit application for residence and work permit in a unified procedure (section 72/H of ThirdD). The one-stop-shop procedure shall be finished within sixty days by the Regional Directorate of OIN together with the competent county labour authority.[67]

(b) A residence permit may be issued on the grounds of the *pursuit of studies* to third-country nationals accepted by an establishment of the secondary or higher education accredited in Hungary and admitted to Hungary to pursue as his/her main activity a full-time course of study, or to attend a course in an establishment of higher education, which may cover a preparatory course prior to such education, if they are able to verify the linguistic knowledge required for the pursuit of studies. The validity period of a residence permit shall correspond to the duration of the training if it is less than two years, or shall be at least one year or a maximum of two years if the duration of the training is two years or more, and it may be extended by at least one or at the most by two additional years at a time. However, the validity period of a residence permit issued on

67. Due to the transposition of the European Parliament – Council Directive No.2011/98/EU (13 Dec. 2011) it entered into force in Hungary in 2014.

grounds of the pursuit of studies may not exceed the validity period of the applicant's travel document. The repeated extension of the residence permit requires extra administration for many students in non-divided studies (e.g., medical doctor, dentist) which take five–six years.[68]

(c) A residence permit may be issued for the purpose of carrying out a *scientific research* to third-country nationals arriving for the purposes of carrying out a research project under a hosting contract concluded with a research organization accredited under a specific separate legislation; and the research organization provides a written commitment for reimbursing the costs of the expulsion in the event that the researcher overstays, and the researcher does not have the financial means necessary. The validity period of this residence permit shall correspond to the duration of the hosting contract, not exceeding five years, and it may be extended by a duration corresponding to any extension of the contract, not exceeding a further five years.

(d) A residence permit may be issued for the *official duty* to the third-country national enjoying any special privileges and immunities under diplomatic relations or international law, and their family members; who are members of official delegations of foreign states or foreign government bodies, or international organizations; who are journalists; arriving within the framework of an international agreement, international cooperation, or an inter-governmental aid program in the field of education, science or culture or participating in or continuing a professional training; who are staff members of scientific, educational and cultural institutions operating in Hungary under an international agreement and to persons seeking admission in connection with the activities of such institutions. The validity period of this residence permit shall correspond to the duration of the training or continuance of a professional training, not exceeding three years, and it may be extended by the duration corresponding to any extension of the training or continuance of professional training, not exceeding an additional three years.

(e) A residence permit may be issued for the purpose of *medical treatment* to a third-country national receiving medical treatment in Hungary; or accompanying his/her minor children or family member in need of support for receiving medical treatment in Hungary.[69] The validity period of this residence permit shall correspond to the duration of treatment, not exceeding two years, and it

68. Pharmacists, doctors, dentists are studying in English and German language and recruiting students abroad, these foreign language curricula have been pursued for decades in Szeged, Budapest, Debrecen and Pécs at universities. For instance, the University of SOTE has a program leading to the Doctor of Medicine degree, consisting of six years: two years of general medical studies, three years of clinical studies and one year of a rotating internship. The applicants to the program must pass an examination in Biology, Chemistry and English. The university practices a rolling admission policy. Entrance examinations are arranged at several locations in Europe, Israel, North America, Asia and Africa. <www.studyhungary.hu/index.php?show=men&mid=63>.

69. For instance, the International Pető Institute has been receiving thousands of young clients together with parents from all continents. Professor Pető set up his 'institute' in a Budapest basement immediately after World War II, in 1945. The Hungarian government officially established today's 'Pető Institute' in the 1950s. The 'Pető Institute for Conductive Education of the Motor Disabled and Conductors' College' is the centre of the conductive educational network operating in various countries of the world. Conductive education is based on the idea that despite the damage, the nervous system

may be extended by the duration corresponding to any extension of the treatment, not exceeding two further years.

(f) A residence permit may be issued for the purpose of *visit* to a third-country national holding a letter of invitation specified in a specific separate legislation. The validity period of this residence permit shall correspond to the duration of the commitment fixed in the letter of invitation, not exceeding one year, and it may not be extended for the purpose of visit.

(g) A residence permit may be issued for the purpose of *voluntary service* activities to a third-country national arriving under a voluntary service contract concluded with the receiving organization specified in the VolA for providing voluntary services in public interest. The validity period of this residence permit shall correspond to the duration of the voluntary services provided in public interest, not exceeding one year, and it may not be extended.

(h) A *national visa and national residence permit* may be issued under international agreement to the third-country national seeking admission into the territory of Hungary to engage in activities to preserve and maintain the Hungarian language, cultural and ethnic identity; for the purpose of learning and participating in a course outside the schooling (secondary or higher education) system; or for the purpose of furthering family ties, other than family reunification. The validity period of this residence permit shall be five years at the most, and it may be extended by five additional years at a time.

(i) In the event of non-compliance with the requirements of entry and residence, the entry and stay of third-country nationals shall be authorized only on *humanitarian grounds,* on grounds of national interest or because of international obligations.

(j) Since 2013 temporary residence permit may be issued for tourists that are at casual work in accordance with the international agreement on working holiday scheme.[70] The validity period of this temporary permit shall be one year at most (section 72/D of ThidD)

(k) Since 2013 residence permit may be obtained for investor if s/he purchases Treasury Bonds at least for 250,000 EUR from entitled foreign agencies. The validity period of this 'state-dept reduction permit' shall be five years when the stock expires[71] (Article 28 (4)-(11) of ThirdA)

(l) Residence permit may be issued for a purpose of stay other than those listed above. The validity period of this residence permit shall be five years at most, and it may be extended by a maximum of five additional years at a time.

(m) The civilian staff and their relatives (civilian personnel) under the ambit of the Agreement on the status of the staff in NATO forces (NATO-SOFA)[72]

---

still possesses the capacity to form new neural connections. http://www.peto.hu/start/en/services/first-assessment/.

70. For citizens of New Zealand and South Korea on the ground of bilateral agreements promulgated in the Act LIV of 2012 and Act LXIV of 2013.

71. Within one year 434 permits were issued, mainly for Chinese citizens (423) according to OIN statistics.

72. Paragraph (b) of Art. I of the Convention between the Parties to the North Atlantic Treaty on the Status of their Forces, signed in London on 19 Jun. 1951 promulgated by Act CXVII of 1999.

enjoy exceptions from the general rules of entry and residence regarding proving their status.

91. Among the reasons for residence permission on the grounds of humanitarian commitments the personal conditions of third-country nationals or stateless migrants are assessed (See more details in paragraph 187).

92. A *certificate of temporary residence* shall be issued to any third-country national:

(a) who has filed an application for a residence permit, and whose national visa or previous residence permit has already expired before the issuance of the permit, or the residence permit shall be granted for those applicants who are no longer under the ambit of the FreeA. During the time of parallel application for labour permission, he/she can be employed;
(b) who has submitted an application for an interim permanent residence permit;
(c) who remained in the territory of Hungary beyond the duration of the lawful residence due to humanitarian reasons or reasons in connection with his/her gainful employment, or for personal reasons beyond his/her control;
(d) who was born in Hungary and whose parent is a third-country national lawfully residing, if his/her lawful residence cannot be ensured by any other permission;
(e) who is a victim of human trafficking, if initiated by the victim support authority, for the reflection period;
(f) whose entry is authorized on humanitarian grounds;
(g) whose travel document had been withheld, and he/she does not have any form of authorization to reside in Hungary;
(h) who is subject to any pending proceeding for unlawful entry and residence;
(i) who has applied for the status of 'stateless person', for the duration of such proceedings, if he/she does not have any form of authorization to reside in the country;
(j) who is subject to an order of compulsory residence designated by the migration authority;
(k) prior Blue Card holder whose Card has expired or been withdrawn, but has submitted a new application and he/she returns to Hungary during the time of unemployment benefit.

The validity period of a certificate of temporary residence is one to six months (the certificate issued for the reflection period or the period of unemployment benefit may not be extended). That may be extended by an additional three to six months. However, a certificate may not be extended, or shall be withdrawn, if any requirement for the issuance is no longer satisfied. Certificate holders cannot exit and re-enter with it, and it shall become void upon the third-country national's departure, when it shall be surrendered. The surrendered certificate shall be returned to the issuing authority.

93. The HealthD defines which diseases, including contagious parasitic diseases of the migrants, endanger public health in Hungary that are required to be taken into account in the authorization procedure of entry, residence or expulsion according to the FreeA and the ThirdA. The regional institute of the sanitary authority at the location of the migrant's residence shall notify the Regional Directorate of OIN the following infectious diseases of the migrants:

(a) Tuberculosis;
(b) Human immunodeficiency virus (HIV) infection;
(c) Lues;
(d) Typhoid and para-typhoid state;
(e) Hepatitis B.

§2. Administrative Procedures and Documents

94. The third-country national has to prove through numerous documents in the visa and residence authorization that all requirements defined in the ThirdA are met. The procedure is regulated in the ThirdD, the formats in the MinD and the fees in the FeeD. However, it is a common requirement that the client must submit the application for visa and residence permit in person, and he/she is not authorized to communicate with the authority by electronic means but the request for appointment or for additional information from the authority may be made by phone or by e-mail.

95. The applicant's *accommodation* is proved by a certificate on property from the real estate register issued within thirty days; rental contract on the apartment, an authorized letter of invitation, documentary evidence to verify the reservation of the accommodation/hotel and the payment; an authentic statement made by a family member with the right of residence in Hungary as holding a long-term visa or a residence permit, with immigrant or permanent resident status, holding a residence card or a permanent residence card in accordance with a specific separate legislation, or with refugee status, promising a place of abode to the applicant.

96. The *sufficient resources* to cover the applicant's subsistence including living expenses, accommodation, return travel, and if necessary, health-care may be proved in particular by the possession of the national currency of Hungary, or the national currency of any other country that may be converted at a Hungarian financial institution (its amount is not defined); a bank account contract, a deposit book, cash substituting payment instruments which are accepted in commercial circulation in Hungary (cheque, credit card, etc.) and a statement from the financial institution to certify the availability of funds; an authorized letter of invitation, an authentic document in proof of the applicant's financial assets (tangible or intangible) whereby to ensure subsistence in Hungary; document on income from lawful gainful employment, regular income received from abroad; or an authentic statement made by a family member with the right of residence in Hungary promising support to the applicant. The coverage by a comprehensive sickness insurance and health-care services can be proved by a social insurance card, or with reference to status directly insured by an international agreement or on a contract concluded with the National Health Insurance Fund or another established insurance company (e.g., in case of accident).

97. Third-country nationals may apply for an *entry visa for entitlement to obtain the residence permit* before admission to the country in the application for residence permit, without having to lodge a separate application. If the decision of the Regional Directorate of the OIN is in favour of the application for residence permit, it shall constitute approval and inform the competent consulate office that will issue the visa.

98. The *applications for visas* are decided by the Regional Directorate in the case of visas for entitlement to obtain a residence permit, by the OIN in the case of national visas; and by the competent consulate officer in the case of seasonal employment visas.

(a) The applications for visas may be submitted in a format to any consulate officer of Hungary, or at any other place authorized to accept such applications located in the country where the applicant's permanent or temporary residence is located, or in the applicant's country of origin. When lodging the application, the applicant shall present his/her valid travel document. The validity period of the travel document – with certain exceptions, for instance on humanitarian grounds – must exceed the planned date of exit from the country. In connection with the applications for visas, the visa authority shall record in the applicant's passport – with some exceptions – the fact of application, the date and place when and where it was submitted and the name of the authority receiving the application.
(b) The visa and migration authorities shall request the opinion of the counter-terrorism unit of the Police and the NSO, concerning applications for long-term visas and residence permission for reasons of public security and national security. They shall provide the opinion within ten days.
(c) The visa authority shall adopt a decision concerning seasonal employment visas and national visas within fifteen days from the time of receipt.
(d) A visa with a validity period of longer than three months shall be considered void if the visa is no longer valid for entry and residence in the territory of Hungary; the visa was withdrawn or replaced; the data and information it contains are no longer legible; it contains false or untrue information or has been forged; the holder is granted a residence permit, a document evidencing permanent resident status or a document evidencing the right to free movement and residence; the holder has died or he/she was granted Hungarian citizenship.
(e) The decision adopted in connection with the applications for a seasonal employment visa, a national visa as well as the cancellation of the issued visa may not be appealed.

99. The Regional Directorate of OIN is competent in the decision of a *residence permit* and its extension.

(a) With certain exceptions, the applications for residence permits may be submitted at any consulate officer of Hungary, or any other agency authorized to accept such applications for residence permit in the country where the permanent or temporary residence of the applicant is located or in the country of the applicant's nationality. A third-country national residing in Hungary may lodge the application for a residence permit at the Regional Directorate of OIN to their place of accommodation if there are special circumstances to justify submission of the application in Hungary, such as on the grounds of family reunification or medical treatment; the purpose of residence for a period of longer than three months in research; lawfully residing in Hungary as nationals of the states listed in Annex II of Council Regulation 539/2001/EC, or together with such third-country national in the capacity of a family member.
(b) When lodging the application for a residence permit the applicant shall present his/her valid travel document.
(c) The application for a residence permit shall contain a statement from the applicant as to whether or not he/she suffers from a disease or disorder specified in the HealthD, or is suffering from a contagious or pathogenic condition, or if he/she receives compulsory and regular treatment for any disease that constitutes a potential threat to public health, or for a contagious or pathogenic condition. In accordance with this, the Regional Directorate of OIN shall notify the regional institute of the sanitary authority inside the county governmental office that may compel him/her to attend the necessary medical examinations or to present an official medical report issued by the competent authority of his/her country of origin. If the institute finds that his/her disease constitutes a potential threat to public health, and he/she is in violation of the rules of conduct, official resolutions and legal regulations concerning medical treatment or therapy, it shall notify the Regional Directorate without delay. If this fact is neglected in a residence permission or extension, the county unit of the sanitary authority shall be directed to take the necessary disease control measures.[73]
(d) The Regional Directorate of the OIN may issue a residence permit on humanitarian grounds to a third-country national for whom an alert has been issued in the SIS for the purposes of refusing entry and residence, or may renew the residence permit of such third-country national only upon a consultation held, before adopting a decision, with the competent authority of the Schengen State that has issued the alert through the national contact point to the Schengen Information System (SIRENE Office). This consultation assists in evaluating whether the affected third-country national represents any threat to public policy or public security in the Schengen state in question, and the duration of the alert. The Regional Directorate shall inform the competent authority of the affected Schengen state via the SIRENE Office.
(e) The Regional Directorate shall adopt a decision on applications for residence permits within twenty-one days from the time of the receipt. However, the following applications shall be evaluated immediately or within a maximum of eight days of receipt: applications of a minor and his/her accompanying legal

73. For instance, as defined in the Decree of the Minister for Welfare No. 18 of 1998, 3 June on preventive sanitary measures against infections and epidemics.

guardian for a residence permit, if the substantiated purpose of travel is medical treatment for the minor; application for a residence permit of a person with parental custody of an unaccompanied minor who is arriving to escort the minor home; application for a residence permit, if the entry and stay of the applicant is desired on the grounds of a substantial national interest in the field of economics, culture, science or sports. The deadline is fifteen days if the purpose of staying is the pursuit of studies; or research. A humanitarian residence permit shall be issued to a third-country national requesting asylum, or any subsidiary form of protection or temporary protection from the refugee authority within three days from the date when the request is submitted. If a security check of applicant is reasonable, duration of the expert opinion giving by the NSO or Police unit is not included (eight to twenty days) into this deadline (section 50 of ThirdD).

(f) The authority shall determine the validity period of residence permits on the basis of the documents enclosed with the application, the verifiable purpose and the planned duration of residence, and on the basis of all other available information regarding the personal and other circumstances of residence. The authorized duration of residence shall respect the third-country national's travel document that has to be valid for at least three more months when the authorized duration of residence expires but an exception from this requirement may be made.

(g) The residence permit is issued in the format defined in the ThirdD. A residence permit shall be considered void if the authorized duration of residence has expired; the residence permit was withdrawn by final decision; a new or replaced residence permit was issued, the data and information it contains are no longer legible; it contains false or untrue information, or has been forged; the holder is granted a document evidencing permanent resident status or a document evidencing the right to free movement and residence; or the holder has died.

(h) The certificate of temporary residence is issued ex officio by the Regional Directorate or the Police, and it shall be cancelled when the third-country national is granted a long-term visa, a residence permit or an interim permanent residence permit upon the conclusion of the proceedings on the basis of which the certificate of temporary residence was awarded. The residence permit on humanitarian reasons also issued ex officio by the Regional Directorate of OIN.

(i) The applications for the extension of a residence permit and for the issue of a national residence permit shall be submitted on a standard form prescribed in the MinD within thirty days prior to the expiry of the residence permit or national visa underlying the application for a residence permit.

(j) An appeal against a resolution for the refusal of an application for a residence permit or for the withdrawal of a residence permit shall be lodged within five working days following delivery of the resolution. The OIN shall decide it within twenty-one days (section 55 of ThirdD).

100. The fee of the visa within whose validity a foreigner may obtain residence permit and also the residence permission is EUR 60. The fee in appealing procedure for refused residence permission or visa within whose validity a foreigner may obtain residence permit is EUR 20 if the appeal is submitted at a consulate. The fee for residence permission in Hungary is EUR 60 while its prolongation or renewal costs EUR 33. The fee for supplementary residence permit (in the event of a demolished or lost document) is also EUR 33. The equivalent of EUR may be paid in Hungarian Forint (HUF) within the country on the basis of the National Bank's daily currency rate. According to the FeeD, full or partial exemption may be granted upon request of a foreigner on the grounds of reciprocity, international agreement, in the interest of sport, science, culture, arts or studies in Hungary (section 5).

§3. Legal Position of Residents

101. Third-country nationals with longer duration visas and residence permits enjoy human rights and fundamental rights while they are required to be registered in the registry of residents' address at the district unit of the governmental office and he/she may be checked by the police in streets or in public places. In order to control foreign students, each educational institute shall notify the Regional Directorate of OIN within eight working days if any foreign student starts, terminates, suspends studies or he/she is enrolled or has missed enrolling at the institution. Furthermore, in possession of a residence permit, the third-country national may sign a letter of invitation, attend schools and/or may obtain a single travelling document to return.

102. Third-country nationals must comply with the following:

(a) They shall promptly notify the Regional Directorate of OIN if their travel document or residence permit is lost, stolen or destroyed. The immigration authority shall confirm the receipt of such a notification in writing that will certify his/her lawful exit while crossing the border in the absence of (valid or expired) travelling document. If the lost document is found, the holder must promptly notify the same to the immigration authority. Otherwise, the third-country national must obtain a new travelling document in accordance with an international treaty.
(b) When holding a visa for a validity period of longer than three months, a residence permit shall report the birth of a child in the territory of Hungary and shall simultaneously supply the natural identification data of the child, particulars of the child's travel document; and address of the child's place of accommodation or home address. A birth registration document is issued at the municipal registrar office.
(c) As Blue Card holders, they must report the termination and establishment of any new employment to the Regional Directorate of OIN within five days of this event.

§4. Position of Family Members

103. The *family member of a third-country national* requesting long-term visa or residence permit must *prove the family ties*. Where the purpose of the entry and residence is the respect for family life, the third-country nationals may verify the family relations[74] in particular with the birth certificate, the marriage certificate or the adoption document issued in Hungary or in another state. The proper material sources, subsistence and accommodation of family members shall be documented, in particular, with a notarized statement made by a family member who has the right of residence in Hungary by holding a long-term visa or residence permit, with immigrant or permanent resident status, promising support to the applicant, along with a document in proof of the family member's ability to provide such support.

104. The *family member of a third-country national* residing lawfully in Hungary has a fragile position (Gyeney, 2014) despite Article 8 of the ECHR respecting family life or the Family Reunification Directive.[75] The spirit of 'minimalism' is visible, for instance, the registered but unmarried couple is not treated equally, and there are no bilateral agreements or regional conventions concluded by Hungary concerning migrants' social rights, and there are no national provisions to ensure a more favourable legal status to them. 'How low can minimum standards go? In this Directive, they went very low indeed.[and] there is a serious risk that Member States will move towards the very low floor established by the Directive.' (Peers & Rogers, 2006: 598)

(a) With certain exceptions, the application for a residence permit or for the extension of the permit shall be refused, or if already issued shall be withdrawn from third-country nationals who established the family relationship solely for the purpose of obtaining a residence permit on the grounds of family reunification. Perhaps the dominant public order approach may be illustrated with this provision.
(b) A residence permit may be issued on the grounds of family reunification to a third-country national who is a relative of a third-country national who is in possession of a long-term visa, a residence permit, immigration permit, permanent residence permit, interim permanent residence permit, a national or EC permanent residence permit, or is in possession of a residence card or a permanent residence card (sponsor).[76] The following persons may be granted a residence permit on the grounds of family reunification: a family member of a person with refugee status, and the parent of an unaccompanied minor with refugee status, or his/her legally appointed guardian.
(c) The following relatives of the sponsors, the spouses of the sponsors or persons with a refugee status may be granted a residence permit on the grounds of family reunification: their parents who are dependants; their brothers and sisters, if they are unable to provide for themselves due to health reasons. The spouse of a sponsor may not be issued a residence permit if the other spouse of the

74. DNA test is stressed as evidence for family member of internationally protected person (section 57 of ThirdD).
75. Council Directive 2003/86/EC on the right to family reunification that is transposed by the ThirdA and ThirdD.
76. Article 3(3) of the Directive excludes the implementation on family member of Union citizen deferring from the family unification purview as defined upper in the ThirdA.

sponsor has a long-term visa or residence permit that was issued on the grounds of family reunification.

(d) The children of third-country nationals with a national visa or a residence permit born in the territory of Hungary shall be issued a residence permit on the grounds of family reunification. Any third-country national who received long-term visa or residence permit for reasons of family reunification shall be required to report to the competent Regional Directorate of the OIN to the place of residence if his/her marriage is dissolved or in the event of the death of his/her spouse within thirty days following the spouse's death or the final court ruling for the dissolution of the marriage, with the relevant documents attached. The restrictive definition of family requires a joint life with the sponsor in the same household (Article 35 of ThirdA).

(e) The validity period for a residence permit granted for the purpose of family reunification shall be three to five years, and it may be extended by three years at a time. However, its validity period may not exceed the validity period of the sponsor's residence permit.

(f) Family members – unless they have obtained the right of residence on any other grounds – shall be authorized to extend his/her right of residence after five years from the date of issuance of his/her first residence permit, or upon the death of the spouse, and if other requirements for further residence are ensured.

(g) The applications for the extension of a residence permit and for the issue of a national residence permit shall be submitted on a standard form prescribed in the MinD within thirty days prior to the expiry of the residence permit or the national residence permit underlying the application for a residence permit.

105. The Constitutional Court evaluated whether the difference between the marriage and the registered partnership in family unification as the ThirdA regulates was compatible with the Constitution or not, taking into account the general prohibition of discrimination (Article 70/A).[77] The body said that weaker protection of registered partnership was not arbitrary because, as was reasonable and objectively argued, the partners together bringing up the descendant made the difference to the notion of joint life in registered partnership, and consequently the provision of family unification in ThirdA was in compliance with the Constitution. However, one judge, in his special opinion, explained why the majority decision was wrong: the family is a social phenomenon in fact that is protected by law regardless of the existing marriage or other ties of the couple, and in the context of residence of non-nationals representing a diversity of habits, cultures and traditions, the Hungarian restrictive rules shall not exclude from the protection all families outside of marriage. From this discussion, it appears that a registered unmarried couple does not benefit from family reunification and 'their joint living in Hungary is possible on the grounds of residence permit issued for other purposes'.[78]The Fundamental Law (Article L) openly defines that family tie shall be based on a hetero-marriage or a parent-child relation.[79]

77. Constitutional Court decision 68/E/2004. AB határozat.
78. Explanatory Report to the Bill (ThirdA).
79. 4th amendment of the Fundamental Law entered into force on 1 Apr. 2013.

Chapter 3. Long-Term Residence

§1. Conditions for Long-Term Right of Residence

106. The ThirdA enlists the *criteria and names of the permanent resident* permissions for third-country nationals, while their legal status has been substantially convergent. Naturally, the EC law forced some changes, transposing with delay the Directive on Long-term Residents[80] while the position of the existing permanent residents had to be preserved without mass exchange of documents and permissions. The third-country nationals in possession of the following permits shall be considered residents: a permanent residence permit issued before the ThirdA entered into force; an interim permanent residence permit; a national permanent residence permit and an EC permanent residence permit. A third-country national applying for an interim permanent residence permit, a national permanent residence permit or an EC permanent residence permit according to the ThirdA, has to satisfy the following common conditions:

(a) s/he has a place of abode and subsistence secured in Hungary;
(b) s/he has full health care insurance or sufficient financial resources for health care services;
(c) s/he has no prior criminal record, until relieved from the detrimental legal consequences related to his/her criminal record;
(d) s/he has not disclosed false information or untrue facts in the authorization procedure in order to obtain the permit;
(e) his/her residence in Hungary does not constitute a threat to national security; and
(f) s/he is not subject to the SIS alert, expulsion or exclusion from Hungary.

107. The third-country national holding an *EC permanent residence permit* certifies a long-term residence status that is granted by the Directive 2003/109/EC. The EC permanent residence permit may be issued for a long-term residence in Hungary to the third-country national having lawfully resided in the country continuously for at least the preceding five years before the application was submitted. The Blue Card holder may obtain it in the third year of residence in Hungary if s/he was previously staying five years in another Member State of the EU. It may not be issued to third-country nationals residing in Hungary: in order to pursue studies in an institution of higher education or vocational training; for the purpose of a seasonal employment or voluntary service activities; under diplomatic or other personal immunity; applicant for asylum or other form of protection from the refugee authority or tolerant migrant. In the event of application of students, half of his/her prior residence in Hungary may be considered. The residing period of volunteers, seasonal workers and diplomats shall be omitted, while the entire period of residence

80. Council Directive 2003/109/EC concerning the status of third-country nationals who are long-term residents. Its transposing deadline was 23 Jan. 2006 (Art. 26) but Hungary adopted the ThirdA in early 2007 and its provisions together with implementing ThirdD entered into force on 1 Jul. 2007. Fir this delay the European Commission launched an infringement procedure against Hungary.

prior to submission of applications by the recognized refugees, subsidiary and temporarily protected persons shall be taken into account if it is longer than eighteen months. The temporary absence from Hungary for less than six consecutive months shall not be deemed as discontinuity of residence, if the combined duration of absence does not exceed three hundred days over a period of five years. If a third-country national has a long-term residence permit issued by another Member State of the EU, the migration authority shall notify the Member State affected concerning the issue of an EC permanent residence permit.

108. The EC permanent residence permit shall *be withdrawn* if the permit holder was absent from the territory of the EC for a period exceeding twelve months or the Blue Card holder for a period exceeding twenty-four months; he/she was granted a long-term resident status in another Member State; he/she was absent from Hungary for a period exceeding six years; he/she disclosed false information or untrue facts to the immigration authority in the interest of obtaining the permit; or he/she is expelled or excluded. After his/her return to Hungary in the event of any of the first three situations, he/she shall be granted a new EC permanent residence permit when re-applying, regardless of the common conditions of permission. The EC permanent residence permit may be withdrawn if the permit holder's refugee or internationally protected status is terminated.

109. The *national permanent residence permit* – together with the previously issued immigration and settlement permits – belongs to the kin-state policy providing preferential migration for ethnic Hungarians and their family members hailing from the adjacent states. Due to the partial accession of Hungarians to the European Union,[81] these non-EC-law-compatible rules are considered as a continuation of this kin-minority policy. The national permanent residence permits may be issued to third-country nationals holding a residence permit or an interim permanent residence permit for establishing residence in Hungary, if any of the following conditions are met:

(a) having lawfully resided in Hungary continuously for at least the preceding three years before the application was submitted but this period is only six months for the (Treasury bonds buyer) investor in possession of residence permit;
(b) a family member of dependent direct relatives in the ascending line – other than the spouse – of a third-country national with immigrant or permanent resident status or who has been granted asylum, and living in the same household for at least the preceding one year before the application was submitted;
(c) the spouse of a third-country national with immigrant or permanent resident status or who has been granted asylum, provided that the marriage was contracted at least two years before the application was submitted;

81. Due to the non-accession of Serbia and Ukraine in which the Hungarian minority lives, this preferential category has been developed.

(d) the applicant was formerly a Hungarian citizen and whose citizenship was ceased, or whose ascendant is or was a Hungarian citizen;[82]
(e) the applicant is a minor of a long-term migrant or a recognized refugee, or the applicant is a recognized refugee even in the absence of a long-term visa or residence permit; or
(f) the minister in charge of migration, as an exception, grants the permission in the absence of all general conditions taking into account the applicant's particular circumstances, family relations and health condition as special and equitable considerations, as well as the public interest. The minister in charge of kin-state policy issues expert opinion in each claim within five days (section 106/A of ThirdD). Only for these exceptional reasons, the minister's decision may not be contested by legal remedy.

Temporary absence from the country of less than four consecutive months shall not be deemed as discontinuity of residence, if the combined duration of absence does not exceed 270 days during the preceding three years before the application was submitted. However, the Regional Directorate of the OIN may grant the permission in the event of a longer absence from Hungary, if the residence was discontinued for an acceptable reason, such as a medical treatment or foreign assignment of the third-country national in connection with his/her gainful employment.

110. The migration authority may *withdraw any settlement, immigration or national permanent residence permits* if:

(a) the circumstances based on which they were issued have changed to an extent that the criteria for authorization are no longer satisfied, and if a period of five years has not elapsed from the date of issue of the permit;
(b) it was issued on the grounds of family reunification, and the marriage was dissolved within three years from receipt of the permit for reasons other than the spouse's death, or if the third-country national no longer has parental custody, unless the third-country national in question has resided in Hungary for at least four years under permanent resident or immigrant status;
(c) the third-country national has departed from Hungary and remained absent for a period of over six months.

Without individual assessment, the migration authority shall withdraw the permit if:

(a) the third-country national in question has disclosed false information or untrue facts to the competent authority in the interest of obtaining the permit;
(b) the migration authority has withdrawn the authority to reside in Hungary of the third-country national exercising parental custody over a minor child who is

82. The amended rules on preferential, accelerated naturalisation without requirement of applicant's residence in Hungary makes this provision needless (Act XLIV of 2010 and Act CCVII of 2012).

also a third-country national, and the continued residence of the minor with the other parent with parental custody is not ensured in Hungary;

(c) it was granted to a third-country national on the grounds of family reunification and his/her spouse with Hungarian citizenship has departed from Hungary with a view to establish residence elsewhere, or the lawful residence of the spouse of the third-country national in Hungary has been terminated; or

(d) the third-country national to whom it was issued is expelled or excluded.

111. An *interim permanent residence permit* shall be issued to a third-country national holding an EC residence permit issued in another Member State if seeking admission into the territory of Hungary for the purpose of gainful employment, with the exception of seasonal employment; for the pursuit of studies or for the purpose of vocational training; or for other justified reasons. The validity period of the permit shall be five years at the most, and it may be extended by five additional years at a time. The permit may be withdrawn if the third-country national no longer satisfies the requirements defined for applicants, and it shall be withdrawn from a third-country national who has been expelled or excluded. The migration authority shall notify the Member State of the European Union concerning the issue of an interim permanent residence permit, and also, if withdrawn, with the reasons indicated, wherein the EC residence permit certifying long-term residence status was issued for the third-country national.

§2. Administrative Procedures and Documents

112. Obtaining the permanent resident status for a third-country national means a long and bureaucratic procedure and its substance follows the scrutiny in long-term visa and residence permission. When lodging an application for an interim permanent residence permit, national permanent residence permit, or EC permanent residence permit to the Regional Directorate of the OIN, the applicant shall present his/her valid travel document and shall enclose with the application his/her birth certificate, and also the marriage certificate if the applicant is married and the certificate of divorce if the marriage was terminated; furthermore, in the case of minors, documentary evidence from the competent authority of the country of origin stating that there is no legal impediment for the minor person in question who is a third-country national to seek a permanent residence abroad; a certificate of clean criminal record issued within six months to date by the competent authority of the country where the applicant's permanent or temporary residence was located before his/her entry to Hungary; documentary proof of the applicant's abode and subsistence in Hungary; and documentary evidence of insurance coverage. However, an exemption from supplying the documents of marital status and a clean criminal record may be granted if they cannot be obtained for reasons beyond the third-country national's control, or if obtaining the same would entail unreasonable difficulties. In such cases, the applicant's statement shall be accepted as a substitute to these documents. If the applicant tells a lie, a refusal or withdrawal of the permit will be the legal consequence. Throughout the entire procedure, the applicant shall notify the migration authority and the district unit of the governmental office of any change of address and personal identification data.

113. In order to determine whether the residence of a third-country national is considered to constitute a *threat to the national security* of the state, the NSO, the county police and the counter-terrorism unit of the Police is involved in the scrutiny, providing an expert opinion. In connection with the first issue of a permanent resident status, these agencies are entitled to request data on the applicant from other databases, and the competent Regional Directorate of the OIN shall allow access to the documents enclosed with such applications, or shall make copies of them. They shall complete their official assessment within twenty to forty-five days, and send it to the competent Regional Directorate in writing. The responsible minister in charge of security services and the Headquarters of the Police issues expert opinions in appealing process within fifteen to twenty days (section 97 and 97/A of ThirdD).

114. The third-country national may submit an application for an interim permanent residence permit on or before the last day of his/her lawful residence for a period not exceeding three months, or thirty days before the expiry of his/her right of residence for a period of longer than three months. He/she has to present his EC residence permit issued under Directive 2003/109/EC. The period of validity of an interim permanent residence permit shall be determined in consideration of the planned duration of stay, as stated by the applicant, and the contents of the documents supplied in support of the purpose of residence. Following the authorization, the competent Regional Directorate shall issue the residence document specified in the ThirdD containing the interim permanent residence permit.

115. The competent Regional Directorate of OIN shall process the applications for a permanent residence permit within 90 to 120 days in the first instance. The appeals against the resolution in the first instance shall be adjudged by the OIN within sixty days on the basis of documents (the applicant does not have the right to a hearing). The final decision may be reviewed at the court according to the AdminA and the CivPA without suspensive effect. Following the authorization, the competent Regional Directorate shall issue the residence document specified in the ThirdD, containing the permit. The validity period of the document shall be five years, which may be extended for an additional five years upon the third-country national's request submitted on the standard form, a model of which is contained in the MinD.

116. Following authorization, a permanent resident permit shall be issued as a document made out in the form and with the contents specified in Council Regulation 1030/2002/EC of 13 June 2002 laying down a uniform format for residence permits for third-country nationals. The format of the document is a sticker, with reference on the type of titles (immigration permit, permanent residence permit, interim permanent residence permit, national permanent residence permit, or an EC permanent residence permit).

117. Fee of the permanent, interim permanent authorization, extension of the permit, its replacement and exchange is EUR 35 as per the FeeD. It is marginal as compared to the high prices of official translation of required and attached documents and authentic statements made at the public notary. The former belongs to the monopoly of Translation Office under the aegis of the Ministry of Justice and Public Administration that is entitled to issue alone an authentic translation, while the standard prices are legally defined at public notary offices.

118. The following shall be treated as *significant changes* in the circumstances underlying the authorization of long-term residence: when the third-country national with a permanent resident status is no longer able to support him/herself and his/her dependent family members, nor is able to provide a place of abode; is receiving social welfare benefits and support in spite of having a full capacity to work; is no longer provided support or a place of abode by the family member who has previously agreed to provide them. According to the conclusion of this assessment, a withdrawal of the status is possible.

119. An immigration permit, permanent residence permit and national permanent residence permits shall be *considered void* if their validity period has expired; the permit was withdrawn by a final decision; a new document in a proceedings for the exchange or replacement of the document or for the extension of the document's validity period was provided; the data and information it contains are no longer legible; it contains false or untrue information or has been forged; the holder is granted an EC permanent residence permit or document evidencing the right of free movement and residence, or Hungarian citizenship; or the holder has died. When the document containing the permanent residence permit expires, or if the document has to be replaced, or if the person with immigrant status was issued a new travel document, upon the third-country national's request submitted on the standard form – a model of which is contained in the MinD – the Regional Directorate of the OIN to the place where the third-country national's residence is located shall issue the document specified in the ThirdD. The competent Regional Directorate shall send an official copy of the final decision for the withdrawal of the permit to the central body operating the register of the personal data and addresses of citizens by the RegA within five working days, and shall confiscate the personal identification document, the personal identification number and the official address card of the third-country national affected at the municipal registrar office.

§3. Legal Position of Long-Term Residents

120. The *legal position of the third-country national* as a settled, permanent resident is regulated in various legal sources, such as in the Fundamental Law, the PrivA, the QualA, the SocialA, the HighA and numerous decrees providing them quasi-national status. The principle of 'as much similar to national treatment as possible' has been stable since 1989 based on the ethnic proximity. For this reason, the impact of the Directive on long-term residents[83] is marginal (Tóth, 2004b). It means that neither the public debates why refugees and subsidiary protected persons are omitted from the scope of the Directive that was a reason of disappointment in many Member States (Peers & Rogers, 2006), nor is a severe harmonization work done. Due to the majority of these permanent residents who hail from the adjacent states and kin-minority, the wide spectrum of their rights has been supported by the policy and public opinion. In this way, Hungary does not fulfil the entitlement for introduction in a direct manner such as a 'proof of the appropriate language proficiency for access to the university' (Article 11(3)), while their integration to the labour market, social, political and cultural life has not been enhanced through public services because they are considered 'almost integrated' to society owing to the equal treatment. As it can be seen, there are three new entitlements by the ThirdA (national, interim permanent residence permit, EC permanent residence permission) and two old (settlement permission, immigrant permission) by the prior alien act (2001), and these are coexisting and providing almost the same rights. According to the ThirdA, 'the immigration permits and permanent residence permits issued before the time of this Act entering into force shall constitute the right of stay contained therein within their period of validity' (Article 110(2)). Furthermore, there is no a coherent integration policy in Hungary implementing the minimal rules of the Directive, the bilateral and multilateral agreements on long-term migrants and their family members, for instance in the right to family and private life (Gyeney, 2014), migrant workers, social security, child's rights or public education.

121. The most important *components* of this permanent resident status are as follows:

(a) Persons with permanent resident status – other than those with temporary resident status – are authorized to reside in the territory of Hungary for an indefinite period of time (open-ended residence).
(b) The EC permanent residence permit holders are entitled to free entry and residence for a short term in another Member State of the EU, whereas the national permanent (immigration, settlement) permit holders are not because their permissions are not based on the Directive on long-term residents (e.g., the residence period prior to the submission of the application was/has been less than five years).
(c) The permanent resident is better protected against removal because any third-country national who resides in Hungary under immigrant or permanent resident status; or is bound to a third-country national residing in Hungary under immigrant or permanent resident status by marriage or is living in the same household as a family member, and has a residence permit, may be expelled only if his/her continued residence represents a serious threat to national security, public security or public policy.

83. Council Directive 2003/109/EC concerning the status of third-country nationals who are long-term residents.

(d) Maintaining family and friendly contacts, permanent residents may sign a letter of invitation for third-country nationals that is applicable in the entry, the visa and residence authorization procedures.

(e) The permanent residents' personal data and address are kept in the population registry and its contact units are in the municipal registrar offices that are regulated in RegA. As nationals (and internationally protected persons), the permanent resident status holders are obliged to obtain an identity card issued within twenty days by the district governmental offices.[84] This identity card is readable by machine and contains safety marks, personal data of the holder (names, birth date and place, maiden name of his/her mother and gender), its validity, as well as his/her signature and digitalized photo. While this plastic card is bright blue for nationals, it is yellow for non-nationals. The period of validity of the identity card for permanent residents is the same as the duration of their permission, and *ex lege* it becomes void if the permanent resident status is terminated or withdrawn. The application for an identity card shall be submitted in person, and with the migration authority's permission, and – if the birth and marriage of the applicant was registered in Hungary, the documents pertaining to them – shall be attached, and his/her passport shall be presented. Whereas, the permanent resident shall register his/her address in Hungary requesting an address card also in the district governmental office by the RegA. The permanent residence permit holder may request to issue the identity card (and the permanent residence permit) to his/her forename in a Hungarian version.

(f) The permanent resident may obtain a travelling document if his/her national passport cannot be replaced or extended by his/her consular office. On one hand, the foreign representative of Hungary shall issue a single-entry travel document to a third-country national with an immigrant or permanent resident status, if his/her travel document was lost or destroyed abroad and it cannot be replaced abroad or it would entail unreasonable difficulties, and thus s/he is unable to return to Hungary. On the other hand, the ThirdA, the PassA and the PassD regulate that the migration authority shall issue a travel document for the purpose of travelling abroad, permitting the re-entry to Hungary upon request, if he/she does not have a valid travel document from his/her country of origin and if such cannot be replaced for reasons beyond his/her control. It is valid for one year from the date of issuance. However, the eligibility to the travelling document is limited for persons under the charge of offence accompanied with penal procedure measures (e.g., confinement, arrest, detention at home, restricted in leaving the country) or imprisoned as the PassA defines for all inhabitants. Against the refusal of the competent Regional Directorate, a claim for the judicial review on the rejection of the travelling document may be submitted to the County (Administrative) Court according to the CivPA. The fee of issuance or the replacement of the destroyed travelling document is EUR 17 at the Regional Directorate, and the permanent resident has to pay EUR 20 for a single-entry travel document at the consular office.

84. Government Decree No.168 of 1999, 24 November on identity card and its registration.

122. Furthermore, they are eligible for free entry to the labour market without a permission –except for jobs and positions that are maintained exclusively for Hungarian citizens in the public sector – for social benefits, housing loans, scholarships in public and higher education and supports for handicapped persons as well. For the sake of their political integration, they have voting rights to municipal representatives and mayors, local referendum and plebiscite. However, the Fundamental Law excludes them from being elected as mayor or president of the county municipal assembly. While social and cultural rights are vital in practice, the participation in the local and county-level public life of the permanent residents has not been actually implemented for two decades (Tóth, 2004b). A third-country national in possession of a permanent resident status may submit an application for naturalization, and the duration of residence prior to submission (zero to eight years) depends on preferential and non-preferential cases. Due to the recent amendments of nationality act[85] passed in 2005, the ethnic Hungarians enjoy preferences (naturalization without waiting period, exemption from examination on constitutional basics if the applicant has attended public school in the Hungarian language). Since 2011, resident status in Hungary is not required for the naturalization of ethnic Hungarians, so the long-term migrant status as well as non-preferential naturalization is relevant only for non-ethnic migrants while the (social, cultural and political) integration services have been underdeveloped (Kováts, 2011).

§4. Position of Family Members

123. Without having to reiterate how the *family ties and contacts* are taken into account as well as the required self-subsistence, abode, accommodation and health-care insurance, some further points of reference may be underlined. Namely, that there are neither demographic nor social/cultural/economic integration principles inserted to the regulation. Minor, dependant, elderly, unhealthy family members are designated, but there are no preferences for highly skilled, polyglot or inactive aged persons, for instance. Whereas, permanent migrants are not forced or supported to study Hungarian or to be employed, to be self-employed paying high taxes or to invest in the local economy – so the observed public order and non-infectious health conditions are central to the regulation, while these permanent residents would become, in the near future, the new naturalized Hungarian citizens.

124. There are some illustrations on the family members' derivative position, as follows:

(a) If a third-country national with a resident or immigrant status has a child born in the territory of Hungary, who is considered a third-country national, the birth of such child shall be registered, and an interim permanent residence permit shall be issued for him/her if the parent has an interim permanent residence permit; a national permanent residence permit shall be issued to him/her if the

85. Act LV of 1993 on the Hungarian Citizenship.

parent has an immigration permit, a permanent residence permit, national permanent residence permit or an EC permanent residence permit.

(b) Any third-country national who received his/her permanent residence permit or national permanent residence permit on the grounds of family relations shall be required to report to the competent Regional Directorate of the OIN to the place where the residence of the third-country national is located if his/her marriage is dissolved or in the event of the death of his/her spouse within sixty days following the spouse's death or the final Court ruling for the dissolution of the marriage, with the relevant documents attached.

(c) Third-country nationals shall promptly notify the competent Regional Directorate of the OIN if their travel document or residence permit is lost, stolen or destroyed. The authority shall confirm the receipt of such a notification in writing, and it may issue a warrant to locate the travel document or residence permit if the whereabouts of such document are unknown. Unless otherwise stipulated by an international agreement, the third-country national whose travel document is lost, stolen, destroyed or has expired shall obtain a replacement travel document. Such third-country nationals shall be allowed to leave the country only in possession of the new travel document and a certificate of the notification, or in possession of the expired travel document.

(d) The above-mentioned derivative position implies that the applicant's family members, from third countries, applying together for an interim permanent residence permit, or later arrived family members of third-country nationals holding an interim permanent residence permit obtain the interim permanent residence permit if their family relationship already existed in the Member State of the EU where the EC residence permit certifying long-term residence status was issued. The period of validity of the permit of a family member shall correspond to the duration of the third-country national's interim permanent residence permit. The permit issued to a family member shall be withdrawn if the breadwinner's permit was withdrawn; the family relationship no longer exists, unless the family member in question satisfies alone the common conditions of residence following the third-country national's death.

Part III. Right of Residence for Specific Categories of Persons

Chapter 1. Nationals with Preferential Treatment

§1. EU Citizens

I. Short-Term Residence

125. EEA nationals may enter the territory of Hungary with a valid travel document or a personal identification document. The *free movement* of the EEA national includes the right of residence not exceeding three months from the date of entry for as long as the beneficiaries of the right of residence do not become an unreasonable burden on the social assistance system of Hungary. The third-country family member of the EEA national or the Hungarian national also enjoys the right of entry and short-term residence in possession of a valid travel document and a valid visa – if he/she is not exempted by nationality or he/she has no document (residence card) evidencing the right of his/her residence, or a residence card issued by another party state to the Agreement on the EEA.

126. The term 'family member of EEA national' in the FreeA is wider than in the ThirdA. In accordance with this, the right to free entry and residence is provided to a third-country national of a family member of an EEA national or a Hungarian national accompanying or joining him/her, and to any persons accompanying or joining an EEA national or a Hungarian citizen, who are dependants or members of the household of a Hungarian citizen for a period of at least one year, or who require the personal care of a Hungarian citizen due to serious health reasons; who had been dependants or members of the household of an EEA national in the country from which they are arriving, or who require the personal care of an EEA national due to serious health reasons, and whose entry and residence has been authorized by the authority on grounds of family reunification. *The family member* shall mean the following:

(a) the spouse of an EEA national or a Hungarian national;
(b) the direct descendants of an EEA national or a Hungarian national and those of the spouse of an EEA national or Hungarian national who are under the age of twenty-one or are dependants;

(c) unless otherwise prescribed in the FreeA – the dependent direct relatives in the ascending line of an EEA or Hungarian national and those of the spouse of an EEA or a Hungarian national;
(d) the person who has parental custody of a minor child who is a Hungarian citizen;
(e) any person whose entry and residence has been authorized by the competent authority on grounds of family reunification; and
(f) registered partner[86] of an EEA national or a Hungarian national, if their partnership has been registered by another Member State authority or by the Hungarian authority.

The household shall mean, as per the FreeD, the community of persons living with an EEA national or a Hungarian citizen under the same roof, and using this address as the registered permanent or customary residence.

127. An *entry and short-term visa may be granted to any family member* who is a third-country national, and who satisfies the general requirements of entry and residence as defined in the Schengen Borders Code and Visa Code.[87] This holder of this visa shall have the right to multiple entry within a period of six months from the date of the first entry. The right of entry and residence exercised upon a visa shall terminate when the requirements are no longer met. The issued visa is valid in the entire Schengen area unless the authority in one of the party states has disagreement of issuance to this applicant in visa-negotiation. In such a situation, the visa is issued with a limitation that is applicable only in the territory of Hungary.

128. The *visa procedure for a family member* within the ambit of the FreeA is based on the following main steps:

(a) Visa on the grounds of family reunification is available to those who are dependants or members of the household of a Hungarian citizen for a period of at least one year, or those who require the personal care of a Hungarian citizen due to serious health reasons; or had been dependants or members of the household of an EEA national in the country from which they are arriving, or who require the personal care of an EEA national due to serious health reasons.
(b) In the cases defined by the ministers of the interior and foreign affairs for reasons of public security and national security, visas with a validity period not exceeding three months may only be granted upon the prior consent of the OIN that shall consult with the central authorities of the Schengen States requesting consent for the issue of a visa.

86. Public notary is entitled to issue a document on hetero-partnership while homo-partnership is registered by the local registrar at municipal. These kinds of partnership are out of the notion (and rights) of 'family' in the Hungarian law that is based on a hetero-marriage (Fundamental Law, Article L).
87. Article 5(1)(a)-(e) of Regulation (EC) No. 562/2006 of the European Parliament and of the Council of 15 Mar. 2006 establishing a Community Code on the rules governing the movement of persons across borders (Schengen Borders Code) and Regulation 810/2009/EC, 13 Jul. 2010 (Visa Code).

(c) If the consular office refuses to recognize the travel document[88] of a third-country national's family member who is subject to a visa requirement, or the passport has an empty page for affixing the visa, but otherwise he/she meets the general requirements, a visa shall be issued in a separate sheet as defined in the FreeD.[89]
(d) The visa authority shall check the authenticity of family ties, based on the available documents and the findings of an on-site inspection, on interviewing the client and the family member, and on the examination of witnesses and experts. If the applicant established the family relationship solely for the purpose of gaining entry, the benefits specified in the FreeA and in the FreeD shall not apply to the applicant, so a visa may be issued only if the applicant is able to satisfy the entry conditions set out in the Visa Code relating to third-country nationals for the issue of visas for other purposes.
(e) The visa application may be submitted at land, air or water border crossing points or at the Police that shall forward it by way of electronic means – without delay to the OIN. It shall promptly adopt a decision and issue a visa via the Police. Refusal may be appealed within three days following delivery of the decision, submitted at the border crossing point, the OIN or to the Ministry of the Interior. The Ministry shall render a decision within five days.
(f) The competent consulate officer shall adopt a decision concerning visa applications within fifteen days. An appeal against refusal may be submitted to the competent consulate officer within eight days, and it shall be decided by the minister of foreign affairs within fifteen days taking into account the opinion of the OIN, the NSO and the counter-terrorism unit of the Police.
(g) The decision for the annulment or revocation of a visa before entry lies with the visa authority that learns of any reason during its proceedings under which the visa has to be annulled or revoked. In other cases, the regional directorate of the OIN or the Police is entitled to annul or withdraw the issued visa. An appeal against any such decision may be submitted within three days to the competent consulate officer or to the Police or to the regional directorate of the OIN, and the minister of foreign affairs or the Headquarters of the Police or the OIN shall issue the final decision within five days.
(h) Since July 2013 the final administrative refusal or annulment or revocation of a visa may be contested at the Capital Administrative Court within three days. The court shall decide it in a non-litigation procedure within eight days (Article 20 of FeeA).

129. When lodging an application for a *local border traffic permit*, the applicant shall present his/her valid travel document, and its validity must not be less than one year from the date of submission of the application, plus thirty days, and must have

88. Government Decree No. 328 of 2007, 11 December on determination of travelling documents issued by third-country nationals for recognition in entry to Hungary.
89. Visa document is made out in the form and with the contents specified in Council Regulation (EC) No. 1683/95 of 29 May 1995 laying down a uniform format for visas, and form for affixing a visa is made out in the form and with the contents specified in Council Regulation (EC) No. 333/2002 of 18 Feb. 2002 on a uniform format for forms for affixing the visa issued by Member States to persons holding travel documents not recognized by the Member State drawing up the form.

at least one suitable page where the local border traffic permit can be affixed. Applications for local border traffic permit must have enclosed a document in proof of lawful residence in a border area as defined in the relevant international agreement. The local border traffic permit falls within the competence of the consular officer as specified in the international agreement. It shall be made in card format.[90] An appeal against refusal may be submitted to the competent consulate officer, and it shall be decided by the minister of foreign affairs.

130. The EEA national has the right to residence for *a period of longer than three months* if the following conditions are met:

(a) s/he intends to engage in some form of gainful employment. According to the FreeA, gainful employment means any work performed for others under the contract of employment – as governed by law – for remuneration, which constitutes subordinate and superior positions; any work performed for remuneration in a self-employed capacity in accordance with the relevant statutory provisions, if such self-employed person provides for his own health insurance and pension insurance coverage in accordance with the relevant legal regulations; or any person other than those defined, who is engaged in any gainful activity in the capacity of being the owner or director of a business association, cooperative or some other legal entity formed to engage in gainful employment, or is a member of the executive, representative or supervisory board of such entity; the genuine (registered) job-seeker also belongs to the (potential) gainful employment;
(b) s/he has sufficient resources for himself/herself and family members not to become a burden on the social assistance system of Hungary during their period of residence, and has comprehensive sickness insurance (as an employed person or as an individual contracting party) cover for full health care services; or
(c) s/he is enrolled at an educational institution governed by the Act on Public Education or the HighA, for the principal purpose of following a course of study, including vocational training and adult education if offering an accredited curriculum, and he/she has sufficient resources for himself/herself and family members not to become a burden on the social assistance system of Hungary during their entire period of residence, and has comprehensive sickness insurance cover for health care services as prescribed in a specific separate legislation, or if he/she proves that he/she has sufficient resources for himself/herself and family members for such services as required by statutory provisions.

131. An EEA national who is no longer engaged in any gainful employment shall retain his/her right of residence if the following conditions are met:

90. In accordance with Regulation (EC) No. 1030/2002 of 13 Jun. 2002 laying down a uniform format for residence permits for third-country nationals and Council Regulation (EC) No. 380/2008 of 18 Apr. 2008 amending Regulation (EC) No. 1030/2002 laying down a uniform format for residence permits for third-country nationals.

(a) s/he is temporarily unable to work as the result of an illness or accident requiring medical treatment;
(b) s/he has registered as a job-seeker by the UnemplA following termination of his/her gainful employment during the period of unemployment benefit but up to six months or for an unlimited period, if the duration of their gainful employment exceeded one year; or
(c) s/he embarks on vocational training with a view to improve his/her professional aptitude, provided that he/she obtained the experience prescribed for vocational training in connection with his/her gainful employment.

132. The *family member of a third-country national has the right of residence for a period of longer than three months* if the following conditions are met:

(a) s/he is a family member of an EEA national in gainful employment;
(b) s/he is a family member of an EEA national with sufficient resources for him/herself and family members not to become a burden on the social assistance system of Hungary during their period of residence, and has comprehensive sickness insurance (as an employed person or as an individual contracting party) cover for full health-care services or;
(c) the spouse and dependent children of any EEA national who are enrolled at an educational institution satisfy the above requirements.

133. The right of residence for a period of longer than three months may be granted until the relationship exists, as follows:

(a) to a person who exercises parental custody of a minor child who is a Hungarian citizen, in the absence of sufficient resources and comprehensive sickness insurance;
(b) to dependant or member of the household of a Hungarian citizen for a period of at least one year, or who require the personal care of a Hungarian citizen due to serious health reasons;
(c) to a person who had been a dependant or a member of the household of an EEA national in the country from which they are arriving, or who require the personal care of an EEA national due to serious health reasons, if the EEA national has a right to residence in Hungary.

134. The *right of residence of a third-country national that is a family member of an EEA national or a Hungarian citizen shall be retained* despite of the death of the EEA national or Hungarian citizen if any of the following conditions are met:

(a) s/he is engaged in gainful employment;
(b) s/he has sufficient resources for his/her own self and family members not to become a burden on the social assistance system of Hungary during their period of residence, and they have comprehensive sickness insurance cover for health care services, or

(c) s/he exercises the right of residence as a family member of a person who has right to residence in Hungary.

135. Despite divorce or annulment of marriage, the right of residence of a spouse who is a third-country national shall *be retained* if the above requirements are met, and any of the following conditions are met:

(a) prior to the divorce or annulment of marriage, the marriage has lasted for at least two years, and the former spouse has resided for at least one year in Hungary during the marriage as a family member of the EEA national or Hungarian citizen;
(b) by court order the former spouse has custody of the child of an EEA national who resides in the country, or by agreement between the spouses has the right of access to a minor child;
(c) this is warranted by particularly difficult circumstances, such as having been a victim of any intentional criminal conduct by the spouse who is an EEA national or a Hungarian citizen while the marriage was subsisting, or if having the right of permanent residence prior to marriage; or
(d) by agreement between the spouses or by court order, the former spouse has the right of access to a minor child, provided that the court has ruled that such access must be in Hungary.

136. However, the right of residence of a spouse of a Hungarian citizen who is a third-country national shall be retained unconditionally if the spouse has the custody of the child who was born during their marriage. Moreover, in the event of the EEA national's departure from Hungary, the right of residence of his/her child shall be retained – irrespective of age – for the period of the pursuit of studies, if already and continuously engaged in such studies. The right of residence of the other parent who has custody of the child shall be retained for the period of studies of the minor child.

137. The *EEA national is required to register* if he/she wishes to exercise his/her right of residence for more than three months, within ninety-three days from the time of entry by communicating their personal data. The Regional Directorate of the OIN shall decide whether the registered EEA national meets the requirements prescribed for residence. The main factors are the following:

(a) The presented and enclosed documents may be accepted without compliance with the AdminA (e.g., a document issued abroad, with no authentic translation attached); the purpose of stay is to engage in a gainful employment, which can be proved in particular with a document verifying the commencement of a relationship for the performance of work; a valid contract or an official copy of the company records, a certificate of incorporation or a company certificate to verify that the applicant is engaged in any gainful activity in the capacity of being the owner or the director of a business association, cooperative or some other legal entity formed to engage in gainful employment, or is a member of the executive, representative or supervisory board of such entity; a valid private entrepreneur's certificate/authorization issued by a competent authority in Hungary or another Member State; for persons seeking a job, documents to evidence that he/she is actively seeking employment, and there is a probability of entering into a gainful employment;

(b) The sufficient resources shall mean if the per capita monthly income in the applicant's household reaches at least the prevailing minimum old-age social security pension. A person shall be considered to lack the sufficient resources if drawing social welfare for the elderly, regular social aid including any periods of suspension and reinstatement of the payment of regular social aid, or attendance allowance under the SocialA for any period of more than three months (*unreasonable burden*). If the per capita monthly income in the applicant's household is below this prevailing minimum, the competent authority shall check the applicant's income and financial position to determine whether the applicant has the sufficient resources for himself/herself and his/her family members not to become an unreasonable burden on the social assistance system during their period of residence. This examination shall cover, in particular, the following criteria: number of family members of the household with any income or assets; number of dependant persons living in the household; whether the applicant is the owner, beneficial owner or user of the real estate property in which they reside. The attached documents would relate to assets or regular income (e.g., payments from the social security or social assistance system of any EEA Member State; income from funds or benefit plans financed by payment of membership dues or other regular contributions; income from a deposit account or contract registered in any EEA Member State or any other bank or investment asset, a bank guarantee provided by a credit institution established in any EEA Member State or that is guaranteed by a legal person established in any EEA Member State; income from maintenance or alimony by contract or declaration). However, the assets may not comprise the articles of everyday use and household equipment, any property serving as the residence of the EEA national and his dependant family members; the vehicle of handicapped persons; and any assets which are required for the EEA national's gainful activity. The amount of monthly income shall be calculated as the monthly average of the sums received during the three-month period prior to the registration of residence for regular income; or received during the twelve-month period prior to the registration of residence for non-regular income.

(c) The entitlement to a comprehensive sickness insurance and health care services can be proved by an insurance card, or with reference to directly applicable community legislation or an international agreement or to a contract concluded with the National Health Insurance Fund or another established insurance company.

(d) Wherein the purpose of residence is the pursuit of studies the applicant shall supply a certificate of admission from an educational institution governed by the Act on Public Education or the HighA; or a document to verify his/her student status.

(e) Upon receipt of any information concerning the termination of a gainful employment, in particular from the employer, the EEA national affected shall provide proof for the right of further residence when so requested by the competent Regional Directorate of the OIN presenting, in particular, a diagnosis provided by a body of medical experts concerning the loss of capacity to work, or a document supported by the assessment of a body of medical experts providing guidance to determine the degree of incapacity; a certificate issued by the relevant employment centre concerning the job-seeking assistance and its duration; or enrolment to the training/retraining course.

(f) The EEA national shall supply a statement as to whether he/she suffers from any infectious disease or contagious parasitic disease as specified in the HealthD and considered to constitute a threat to public health, or if he/she receives compulsory and regular treatment with regard to the said diseases. In the existence of a threat, the Regional Directorate shall notify the city/town institute of the sanitary authority inside the county governmental office that may compel the EEA national to undergo the necessary medical examinations, to respect rules of conduct or medical treatment or therapy. Finally, the expulsion of the persons under the FreeA may be initiated.

Upon registration, the Regional Directorate of OIN shall issue a *certificate for the registration* of residence immediately. The registration certificate shall attest the registration and the date of the registration. It shall be cancelled when the right of residence is terminated. However, the validity of this registration document is undefined.

138. An *EEA family member* who is a third-country national residing for longer than three months requires a *residence card*. The application in a format defined in MinD shall be submitted within ninety-three days from the time of entry or from the date of initiation of the fact underlying the right of residence. The documents to certify compliance with the requirements of residence shall be presented or enclosed with the application. The rationale is the same as for the EEA nationals, so some specifications shall be underlined.

(b) The family members shall prove the family relationship in particular with the birth certificate; the marriage certificate; or the adoption document issued either in Hungary or abroad.

(c) The EEA national and the Hungarian citizen shall declare his/her commitment to support the family members using the standard form described in the MinD, however, declaration of support is not required if the EEA national or the Hungarian citizen is engaged in gainful employment. It shall be enclosed with the application of family members who are third-country nationals for a residence card.

(d) Where a dependant family member is applying for authorization to reside in Hungary, he/she shall provide documentary evidence of being supported by a Hungarian citizen under a maintenance or life annuity contract, or an obligation of support described in a specific separate legislation, or a declaration of support, or if an EEA national is required to support him/her in accordance with statutory provisions or under contract; a statement of his/her doctor to verify his/her health condition due to which nursing by the EEA national or Hungarian citizen in question is required; attach documentary evidence, where applicable, in the form of an official certificate issued by the competent authority of having been members of the household of an EEA national or a Hungarian national in the country from which they are arriving, for a period of at least one year.

(e) A spouse who is a third-country national may verify his/her right of residence retained under family status with a marriage certificate to verify that their marriage has continued for at least two years; by a Court decision awarding custody or an understanding fixed in an authentic document between the spouses for sharing parental custody; by providing reliable proof concerning any particularly difficult circumstances; by a court decision or an understanding fixed in an authentic document between the spouses for the right of access to a minor child, or by a statement on being a victim of any intentional criminal conduct by the former spouse.

(f) If the child of an EEA national retains the right of residence, the child or his/her legal representative shall supply a certificate (enrolment, student card) from the relevant educational institution twice in any academic year verifying that the child is continuing his/her studies, also indicating the projected date of completion.

The competent Regional Directorate shall immediately issue a certificate of the application for the residence card to verify the right of residence of the family member who is a third-country national. This certificate is applicable during the procedure that takes three months because the authority shall decide on application within this period. The residence card shall attest the right of residence of its holder during its period of validity that follows the EEA national's residence but it is a maximum of five years. The residence card shall be cancelled in the event of the holder's departure from Hungary giving up this right, or if the right of residence is terminated.

139. In a court case[91] of *registered partnership* between a Hungarian national and his partner from Vietnam, the Regional Directorate of OIN refused the application for registration card despite of proven family life, common household for years (2004–2008) saying that the one year of life together as a minimal criterion (Article 8(1) in the FreeA to the entitlement for 'family member' status for a Third-Country National (TCN)) was not documented from the address and the alien police registration. Hence, the woman was directed to depart from the country within ninety days (in December 2008). The Capital Court annulled the OIN decision requiring a repetitive administrative procedure in which the OIN regional unit was obliged to implement Article 3(2) of Dir.2004/38/EC evaluating all personal conditions and available evidences. The OIN argued that partnership (marriage), by definition, means the existence of a common and registered, documented address, place of residence of the couple for at least one year – and other evidences belong to the margin of appreciation of the authority. The Article 8(1)(a) of the FreeA entitles the OIN to provide residence permission to a family member of a Hungarian national if he/she is dependent on him/her or they have been living under the same roof in a common household for at least one year. According to section 1(d) and

91. EBH 2010/2196. Supreme Court Decisions, 2010/1.

27(1) of the FreeD, living together in a common household is not enough, and this shall be proved by the address registration. The Capital Court accepted these arguments, and added that dependence would be proved by sponsorship declaration approved by the public notary or medical doctoral documents of the couple in caring or an officially documented shared life in a common household for at least one year before the arrival of the family member from another state in which they were living together. The Supreme Court stated that the Capital Court's fact-finding was correct but its legal conclusion was wrong. The living together in a common household is one component to permission but its other component of documented address registration is a statutory, connecting requirement. Article 3(2) of the Directive concerning the individualization of cases – for example, in the issue of 'genuine household' – is in harmony with the requirement of documentation. Hence, the OIN'S order to depart had to be executed. Combating the untrue, formal family ties such as false marriage/registered partnership, marriage of convenience and unfounded paternity declaration has inspired legislation (modified Article 14(2) of FreeA; new Article 355 of the Penal Code) and legal practice analysis in Hungary. The Supreme Court stresses that joint address, living in the same household for a certain period for a couple, and existing social, emotional contact between the partners/parent and minor, as well as DNA test shall be integrated into the individual fact-finding and evaluation of conditions.[92]

II. Long-Term Residence

140. The EEA national and family member who are third-country nationals are eligible to the right to *permanent resident status* in accordance with Directive 2004/38/EC. Permanent residence status shall be granted to the following:

(a) the EEA nationals who have resided legally and continuously in Hungary for five years;
(b) the EEA national who, having resided in Hungary continuously for more than three years from the time of entry and at the time of termination of his gainful employment, has reached the age laid down by law for entitlement to an old-age pension, or has ceased his gainful employment in order to take early retirement, provided that such person has been working in Hungary for at least the preceding twelve months before going into retirement with old-age pension or before taking early retirement;
(c) the EEA national who, having resided in Hungary for the purpose of gainful employment continuously for more than two years from the time of entry, has stopped working due to incapacity to work as the result of an illness or accident requiring medical treatment;

92. European Commission's Communication (COM (2009) 313 final) was a point of reference in the Supreme Court's analysis on the legal practice of judicial review in immigration cases (23 Sep. 2013) www.lb.hu/sites/default/files/joggyak/idegenrendeszeti_osszefoglalo_velemeny_kuria.pdf.

(d) the EEA national whose incapacity to work is the result of an accident at work or an occupational disease entitling the person concerned to a benefit specified in a specific separate legislation;
(e) the EEA national after three years of continuous employment and residence in Hungary, taking up gainful employment in another EEA State, while retaining his/her place of residence in Hungary;
(f) an EEA national with a Hungarian citizen spouse residing in Hungary for the purpose of gainful employment regardless its duration if eligible for old-age pension or early retirement; or he/she is no longer engaged in gainful employment due to incapacity to work as the result of an illness or accident requiring medical treatment;
(g) the family members who have retained the right of residence in connection with their relationship to an EEA national or a Hungarian citizen, and who have resided legally and continuously in Hungary for five years; including family members of EEA nationals who have acquired the right of permanent residence if their family members hold the right of residence;
(h) the spouse of an EEA national residing in Hungary for the purpose of gainful employment if eligible for old-age pension or early retirement; or he/she is no longer engaged in gainful employment due to incapacity to work as the result of an illness or accident requiring medical treatment;
(i) family member of EEA national who is engaged in gainful employment in Hungary but dies before acquiring permanent residence status, and his/her family members who are residing with him/her, if the EEA national had, at the time of death, resided continuously in Hungary for the previous two years; or the EEA national's death resulted from an accident at work or an occupational disease.
(j) the children of a parent who has the right of permanent residence in Hungary;
(k) the family members of Hungarian citizens – except the spouse – who have resided continuously in the country in the household of a Hungarian citizen for a period of at least one year; and
(l) the spouse of a Hungarian citizen if their marriage was contracted at least two years prior to the date when the application was submitted and they share the same household since then.

141. As regards the *calculation of residing/working time* required for the permanent residence status, some conditions shall be taken into consideration, as follows:

(a) In the absence of proof to the contrary, the first day of continuous residence in Hungary shall be deemed the date of registration of residence (registration certificate) or the date of submission of the application for the residence card.
(b) The EEA national's gainful employment shall also include the following periods: when the EEA national has registered as a job-seeker as prescribed in UnemplA; when the EEA national did not work due to an illness or accident; when the EEA national did not work due to reasons beyond his/her control; and the period of gainful employment in the territory of other EEA state.
(c) The following shall not be deemed as discontinuity of residence: temporary absences from Hungary not exceeding six months in a year; absences for

compulsory military service; one absence of a maximum of twelve consecutive months for important reasons such as pregnancy and childbirth, serious illness, study or vocational training, or a posting.

(d) The departure of an EEA national or his/her family members from Hungary shall be treated as discontinuity of residence.

(e) Where an EEA national or his/her family member has abandoned to exercise his/her right of residence in Hungary, and returned to Hungary for a period of over three months, the duration required for the right of permanent residence shall start over from this time.

142. EEA nationals and their family members shall submit their *application for a permanent residence card* at the Regional Directorate of the OIN to their place of residence.

(a) They have to present their travel document or personal identification document, and shall enclose the authentic documents specified in the FreeD. The Regional Directorate, before issuing the permanent residence card, shall check the legal background, duration and continuity of residence.

(b) The family member who is a third-country national shall submit the application for a permanent residence card before his/her residence card expires. Any applicant who submits the application after his/her residence card has expired, if unable to offer a plausible explanation for doing so, shall be required to show that his/her right of permanent residence still exists. The competent authority shall immediately issue a certificate of submitted application for the permanent residence card to verify the right of residence of the family member who is a third-country national during the procedure. The FreeD determines for instance, that the family relation and birth of the child in Hungary shall be verified by the birth certificate. Furthermore, the Regional Directorate shall consult the register of personal data and address records to verify the permanent or temporary residence of Hungarian citizens and their family members for compliance with the requirements set out in the FreeA regarding family relationship. The spouse of a Hungarian citizen shall supply a marriage certificate to verify that their marriage was contracted at least two years prior to the date when the application was submitted.

(c) Upon receipt of an application for a permanent residence card, the competent authority shall issue the permanent residence card or shall reject the application by way of a resolution. In the proceedings for the issue of a permanent residence card, the competent authority shall adopt its decision within three months. The competent Regional Directorate shall automatically renew the permanent residence card after ten years. The permanent residence card shall be invalid in the event that the right of permanent residence has terminated.

(d) The fee of the registration certificate is EUR 4, the fee of the application for permanent residence card, its replacement or exchange is EUR 5, and the fee of the residence card for the Hungarian national's family member, its renewal or replacement is EUR 34, while the fee for the residence card for an EEA national's family member, its renewal or replacement is only EUR 5 by the FeeD.

143. Moreover, the right of permanent residence may be verified by the following means: a copy of the resolution establishing old-age pension or early retirement, and an authentic instrument or other document to verify engagement in gainful employment in Hungary for at least the preceding twelve months before lodging the application for retirement with old-age pension or early retirement; a diagnosis provided by a body of medical experts concerning incapacity to work as the result of an illness or accident requiring medical treatment, or a document supported by the assessment of a body of medical experts providing guidance to determine the degree of incapacity; a copy of a decision on awarding accident-related disability benefits due to incapacity to work as the result of an accident at work or an occupational disease; a copy of an authentic instrument or other document to verify previous engagement in gainful employment in an EEA Member State; or a copy of the occupational accident report on the circumstances of the death of the EEA national.

III. Legal Position

144. The Act on Accession to the EU was a final alert to transpose and make applicable primary and secondary EU law on free movement of EU citizens and their family members regardless of their nationality. After a delay of some months, the FreeA on free movement and right to residence transposed Directive 2004/38/EC into the national law. The FreeA clearly regulates that Hungary guarantees the right to free movement and the right of residence to EEA nationals (also Swiss nationals) and that this right is also provided to the family members of Hungarian nationals irrespective of their nationality. Family members are included in the term 'persons being entitled to free movement and right to residence'. It changed the personal scope of several very important acts upon its entry into force. Usually these acts refer to 'persons being entitled to free movement and right to residence' in their personal scope meaning that family members are covered by this term. In sum, the wording of the personal scope of the FreeA and its extensive verbatim citation in other areas of law shifted family members into the category of migrant workers – with some exceptions of course. This act refers to the Schengen Borders Code and visa requirements providing certain remaining components of the Schengen acquis transposition into the Hungarian regulation. These legislative steps generally contributed to the enhanced rights of union citizens and family members in Hungary, creating a separate group of subjects in migration law. However, the family member of a Hungarian citizen enjoys preferential position comparing to other residing family members. For instance, a person entitled with parental custody on a minor with Hungarian citizenship is eligible to the right to free movement, or permanent residence card shall be provided within a shorter period of joint residence in Hungary (zero to two years) to the family member of a Hungarian national than of EEA national.

145. The competent authority shall – upon the guardian authority's request – ex officio grant the *right of residence to a minor child* who is a dependant or member of the household of a Hungarian citizen, if the child was born in Hungary, his/her nationality is unknown and there is no parent who has parental custody over the child in question.

146. According to the FreeA, the permanent resident is better protected against expulsion because the migration authority is not entitled to order expulsion against persons under the ambit of the FreeA if they have resided for more than ten years lawfully in Hungary. It means that only the Penal Court may order expulsion as punishment for severe violation of public security or order as determined by the Penal Code.

147. There is no legal difference between the lawfully residing EEA nationals and the family members in the shorter or longer term with the exception of holding the registration certificate and the residence card. In the spirit of the FreeA and the EqualA, there is an equal treatment in labour market, social, cultural and political rights within the above-mentioned frames.

The requirements of *notification* by the EEA national and family members are as follows:

(a) EEA nationals and their family members shall notify their first residence in Hungary during the proceedings for the issue of the registration certificate or residence card. According to these personal data and the address forwarded to the municipal registrar office, it shall issue an address card that is required in the daily operation of all inhabitants in Hungary. It means that the registered EEA nationals and family members have a record in the register of the personal data and addresses of citizens according to the RegA. The competent authority shall notify the central body operating the register of the personal data and addresses of citizens concerning the invalidation of any registration certificate and residence card.
(b) The EEA nationals and their family members, whose travel document, personal identification document, or residence card is lost, stolen, destroyed or has expired shall report it to the Regional Directorate of the OIN or the Police, as well as if any such document that was presumed lost and reported as such is found subsequently. The competent authority may issue a warrant to locate a document if the whereabouts of such document are unknown.
(c) Unless otherwise stipulated by an international agreement, a family member who is a third-country national whose travelling document is lost, stolen, destroyed or has expired shall obtain a replacement travel document. Such a family member shall be allowed to leave the country only in possession of the new travel document and a certificate of this notification.
(d) EEA nationals shall be required to obtain a replacement travel document that was lost, stolen, destroyed or has expired, if they do not have a valid personal identification document.
(e) EEA nationals and their family members exercising the right of residence for a period of longer than three months shall report, by communicating the personal data: the death of a family member in their household; any change of name if the death or change of name occurred outside the territory of Hungary.

(f) EEA nationals and their family members shall notify the Regional Directorate of the OIN, when they no longer wish to practice their right of residence in Hungary.
(g) The family member shall notify any changes in his/her title of residence, and shall provide proof for the right of further residence. Also, the family member shall notify the termination of his/her relationship underlying his/her right of residence.
(h) EEA nationals and their family members shall present their documents evidencing the right of residence when so requested by the authority vested with the powers to check their identity and their right of residence. Apart from the registration certificate and the residence card, the EEA nationals and their family members may use other credible means to verify their right of residence.

148. The permanent resident persons under the scope of the FreeA have no coherent, specific legal status because of the transposed Directive 2004/38/EC incorporated into about fifty different laws and decrees providing for equal treatment of all persons entitled to the right to free movement and residence. However, it is possible that certain rights – for instance, accession to social advantages – may be exercised after certain years of residence in municipal decrees. An example may illustrate how at the local level, the nationality is the decisive factor, instead of status or length of residence. The saga of the German national Mr G began in 2005. To recall the facts of the case: Mr G worked for seven years in Hungary, lived (and still lives) continuously in Harkány (where one of the most well-known spas of Hungary is situated) and wanted to use the benefits provided to the local inhabitants of Harkány when accessing the spa. According to the rules of admittance at the spa, Hungarian nationals living officially and permanently in Harkány are entitled to a reduction of 50% on the basis of a special card. Mr G's application for the card embodying the reduction was refused by the Harkány self-government (municipal), and as a result, he was forced to pay the full price when using the services of the spa.[93] He submitted an appeal to the Equal Treatment Authority (ETA) claiming that his rights to equal treatment had been breached. The ETA passed its decision on the 15 May 2006 stating that the admittance rules of the spa and related practices are contrary to the principle of equal treatment and obliged the Harkány self-government to make an end to this conduct. However, the self-government appealed against the decision at the Capital Court of Budapest. The Court[94] laid down in its final decision that the Harkány self-government had not breached the Hungarian law and set aside the decision of the ETA. The Court analysed the legal situation and stated that the application of Mr G was rejected not because he was a German national but because he was not permanently residing in Harkány. Albeit Mr G possessed a residence permit with a five-year validity and was registered in Harkány pursuant to the RegA, the Court did not equate his situation with a Hungarian national having been living for a long time in Harkány. The Court emphasized that Mr G was permanently living in Leipzig (Germany), and it is impossible to have two permanent addresses at the same time. The Court concluded that the principle

93. <http://index.hu/politika/belfold/harkany0612/?print>.
94. Fővárosi Bíróság, 8 K 33.297/2006/5.

of equal treatment had not been breached, and thereby repealed the decision of the ETA. On legal grounds, the regular appeal against this decision was excluded. A repeated complaint to the ETA on the basis of nationality confirms that the preferential price of the Harkány spa is available only for resident pensioners with Hungarian citizenship.[95] Despite a prior binding decision of the ETA imposing a fine in 2007 and the judgment of the Capital Court in 2008 to stop discrimination – upon the claim of a residing German pensioner – the spa owned by the local municipal has continued the discriminatory practice since 2004. The case was also examined in the European Parliament session. Its representative referred to 'narrow preference' because the equal treatment for Union citizens '*would extremely open* [sic] *this benefit for non-national retired persons'*. The ETA again imposed a fine (EUR 5600) and ordered to equalize the entry price within ninety days, and to publish the entire decision on the homepage of the ETA's official website. However, this case draws attention to the weak implementation of the EqualA and the ECJ references by the ETA. Moreover, there is a discrepancy in the applicability of residence card/ registration certificate of an EU citizen/family member because these terms are absent in numerous laws, such as in the RegA.

149. The preferential naturalization is provided for EU citizens although this introduction has been totally unknown according to public opinion. It was wrapped into a technical provision of the Act, modified just before accession to the EU.[96] For the purposes of the Act on Hungarian Citizenship,[97] the 'resident' shall mean a foreigner who resides in Hungary and has been granted a long-term immigrant or refugee status or as a national of another Member State of the EU who has an EEA residence permit. Moreover, since July 2007, due to the FreeA all persons within the ambit of the FreeA who implement their right to free movement and residence in Hungary with a registered address in Hungary shall be considered non-national residents (Article 23), as one of the requirements to submit the application for naturalization (the other non-national applicants have to obtain the long-term migrant status or refugee status). This interpretative regulation opened the door for EU citizens to naturalize faster than it did for third-country nationals. In practice, Hungarian citizenship is attractive as a second citizenship for ethnic Hungarians from another Member State of the EU – such as expatriates, emigrants, expelled Hungarian nationals, or 'honourable Hungarians' living with a Hungarian spouse or family members. However, since 2011 the resident status has not been required for the most preferential naturalization for ethnic Hungarians, and the easier acquisition of nationality would be relevant only for non-ethnic EU citizens.

95. EBH case 1054/2010, < http://www.egyenlobanasmod.hu/article/view/1054_2010>.
96. Article 4 of the Act LVI of 2003, and it entered into force with the Act promulgating the Treaty on the Accession of the Hungarian Republic to the European Union.
97. Consolidated Act LV of 1993.

Chapter 2. Students

150. Without repeating the admission rules for third-country nationals and the EEA national's right to residence as a student (see paragraphs 17, 90, 101, 104, 107, 123, 130, 137 and 138), some other relevant aspects will be discussed here.

151. Regardless of the nationality of residing minors, they are obliged to attend elementary and secondary school from age five to sixteen. The Act on Public Education[98] regulates this duty if migrant children are staying lawfully in Hungary longer than three months (with a registration certificate, residence card or other residence permission) and registered address in the country on equal foot as nationals. The elementary and secondary schools run by the state or churches obtain per capita subsidies from the state budget on the number of enrolled pupils. The other minors (e.g., visitors) may attend public schools upon request of the parents paying a tutorial fee for repetitive courses.[99] The adult migrants may enter the vocational training and/or tertiary education as determined by the HighA, in general, if they meet the requirements for studies (e.g., maturity exam, knowledge of the Hungarian language) and each educational institute's defined specifications (e.g., Hungarian nationality for military and law enforcement colleges, sport or artistic talent). State-financed tertiary and vocational education is available for union citizens, settled migrants and refugees, and ministerial scholarships may be provided to ethnic Hungarians and students who are third-country nationals, on the grounds of cultural and scientific interstate cooperation as per the annual quota.

152. In the absence of an explicit immigration policy or a pro-migration policy, the migrant pupils are not 'desired children' in our public education. Public schools have neither been prepared for cultural and linguistic diversity nor for political socialization, to inculcate civil society values. As many critics have stated for decades: the Hungarian public education system cannot contribute to social cohesion, reduce social and cultural distances between school children, but does just the opposite, and hence segregation and intolerant attitudes[100] are growing in a society in transition. As a result, non native children are restricted in the absence of special skilled teachers and multicultural programmes (Feischmidt & Nyíri, 2006). Non-native family members of union citizens and long-term migrants, internationally protected and stateless students attending public education may receive a special pedagogical programme for a year in order to catch up with the Hungarian language curricula. The ministerial decree[101] provides financial contribution to this programme per capita upon the schools' request. It amounts to an annual EUR 150

98. Act CXC of 2011 on Public Education, Art. 90.
99. Governmental Decree No. 229 of 2012, August 28 on executive rules of the Act on Public Education.
100. Szilassy, Eszter: 'Én nem vagyok rasszista, csak utálom a kínaiakat meg a négereket' – a külföldiekhez való viszony magyar serdülők beszédében 'I am not racist, I only hate Chinese and Niggers' – Relations to migrants in the speech of teenagers] In: Feischmidt Margit – Nyíri Pél (szerk.) Nem kívánt gyerekek. Külföldi gyerekek magyar iskolákban. MTA Kisebbségkutató Intézet, Budapest, 2006. 97–127.
101. Decree of the Minister of Culture and Education No. 17 of 2010, 30 March OKM rendelet.

up to 300 per student. However, this amount would provide a limited incentive for additional work by teachers, unless the number of non-native students is high in a given school. The Ombudsman reading the low score of the education of migrants in Hungary in the third wave of the Migrant Integration Policy Index (MIPEX),[102] contacted the leader of the complaint officials in the responsible ministry. The MIPEX in the public education stream proves that multicultural education and language training for migrants' children (including kids of migrant workers from the EU 26) are not available in public schools. Hence the Ombudsman and the representative of the responsible Ministry decided on a joint investigation to identify the shortcomings and what needed to be done in favour of non-national, non-native pupils in 2011.[103]

153. The Hungarian Student Card is automatically accorded to persons who are students of public schools or a high school that is accredited or recognized in Hungary, irrespective of their nationality.[104] The *Student Card* proves the holder's identity and enrolment to the on-going school/academic year, attending a designated education institute (its name and address). There are two daily functions for holders, as follows:

(a) Benefits in public transport: As regards the advantages in the public transport, the Government[105] determines a list of persons who are eligible for benefits in public transport, and among them the students are mentioned. There are travel fare exemptions or reductions for long-distance and local travel facilities including seasonal ticket fares. Transport exemptions or reductions (50-90%) are, as a main rule, attached to the status of the person and not to his/her nationality. For instance, Student Card holders are entitled to the advantages irrespective of whether they are Hungarian, EEA or third-country nationals if they are regular residents. It contains an exception to this rule, rather as a positive discrimination in content: students who qualify as 'entitled person' in terms of the FreeA – consequently having the nationality of an EEA state (including Hungary), being family members of those EEA nationals or of Hungarian nationals – and who are full-time students in an EEA state or in Switzerland, can avail of the same benefits as students studying in Hungary. This means that if a German student of the Humboldt University comes to Hungary as a tourist, he/she is to enjoy the benefits. Likewise, if a Hungarian national studies in Paris, when he/she is at home, he/she can avail of these benefits as well. Act LXXXVII of 2003 on consumer price-supplement adds a complementary element to the system, by regulating how the state subsidizes the service providers for the loss of income resulting from the fare benefits.

102. Huddleston, Thomas and Niessen, Jan 'Migrant Integration Policy Index III' MPG – British Council, Brussels, 2011 <www.mipex.hu>.
103. Statement by dr.Aáry-Tamás, Lajos, on MIPEX conference (14 Apr. 2011 Central European University, Budapest).
104. Government Decree No. 362 of 2011, 30 December on the Cards in Public Education.
105. Government Decree No. 85 of 2007, 25 April on advantages in public passenger transport.

(b) Benefits in museums: Entry tickets to the permanent exhibitions in museums subsided by the state budget are provided as a benefit for an EEA national (including Hungarian national) youngster under the age of twenty-six [106] However, the museum officials may provide other benefits to Student Card holders and student groups.

154. Taking into consideration the studies of third-country nationals, the FeeD provides the visa free of cost and residence permission for applicant if his/her purpose of entry is education – on the grounds of international treaty, bilateral cooperation or reciprocity – or he/she has obtained ministerial scholarship for studies (state-financed student status). The ThirdA provides for the completion of studies or at least of the school year in the removal procedure (Article 42). If the child who is in the parental custody of an expelled third-country national pursues studies in an public education institution, the immigration authority may – upon request or on its motion – extend the period for voluntary departure by a period extending till the end of the current semester. Extension of the time limit for voluntary departure shall be ordered by way of a ruling.

155. Scholarships are partly available for migrants as follows:

(a) Students attending the vocational school *(15-18-21)* are eligible for scholarship regardless of their nationality or legal status if they participate in the study of a disappearing craft. The list of crafts, occupations in shortage is determined by Government and the county vocational training and development committee after consultation with chambers and employment agencies. According to the rules,[107] the scholarship is financed from the Labour Force Fund through the administration of the county labour authority. The monthly sum of EUR 33–100 is available for each student whose study results in an average which reaches 2.52 from his/her enrolment up to the time of the first designated professional examination. The cited rules provide the grant to the student independent from any other financial support that he/she obtained.
(b) The Government regulates[108] scholarship possibilities for students and their tutors, who are qualified as being severely disadvantaged or live in a child protection institution. There are scholarships for primary schools, secondary schools, vocational training schools and also high-level educational establishments. The personal scope of the Decree encompasses both Hungarian and foreign nationals including resident third-country nationals as well, without discrimination based on citizenship. However, the half of supported students shall be Roma taking into account the affirmative actions. Furthermore, scholarships for disadvantaged students in tertiary education are available in practice only for the local (national) students.

---

106. Government Decree No.194 of 2000, 24 November on benefits for museum visitors.
107. Government Decree No. 328 of 2009, 29 December on scholarship for students in vocational training.
108. Government Decree No. 152 of 2005, 2 August on the Scholarships for Promoting the Equal Opportunities of Disadvantaged Groups.

(c) The other grants financed by ministries, municipals, NGOs or churches aim to support PhD students, segregated but busy, talented students, religious students, kin-minority youngsters or Roma pupils/students. Their common trait is that the nationality and residence condition is directly or indirectly required (for instance Bursa Hungarica scholarship for poor but talent students from the region attending the tertiary education).[109]

156. A special loan system aims at providing long-term and subsidized *study loan* construction for students in high-level education. The Study Loan Centre[110] is responsible for granting the loan to the student who meets the requirements laid down in the Decree. The following categories form the personal scope: Hungarian nationals, refugees, third-country nationals with permanent residence permits, and EEA nationals who exercise an economic activity are entitled to apply for the study loan. Furthermore, family members of EEA nationals who exercise an economic activity can also apply. Finally, persons who are entitled to permanent residence in terms of the FreeA can apply. Enrolment to the high-education institution (student's relationship with the institution) and residing at a registered address in Hungary are the main preconditions under the personal scope of the Decree. The student loan is available for a maximum of ten semesters up to his/her age of forty years, up to EUR 170 per month or up to the total study fee as determined in the tertiary education institute per semester. In brief, the Hungarian rule is in compliance with Article 24(2) of Directive 2004/38/EC. The loan shall begin to be repaid in monthly instalments after termination of the student's relationship with the institution on the basis of his/her monthly income (approximately 8% of it) and in case of unemployment, the reimbursement amount will be equal to the lowest lawful salary. The rate of interest is low (2-5%) due to the state subvention and the prudent operation of the Study Loan Centre. The loan is portable to the higher education institute in another EU Member State if the enrolled student is a Hungarian national.

157. The rights of migrant workers (Blue Card and labour permit holders), internationally protected persons, EEA nationals, kin-minority members from adjacent states and long-term migrants to enter the tertiary education are regulated in the HighA (Article 39). The high-level education encompasses universities and colleges founded or recognized by the state in the territory of Hungary, the list of which can be found in Annex 1 of the HighA. Hungarian high-level education institutions shall be registered and approved by the Education Office and recognized by the Hungarian Parliament, while the foreign high-level education establishments can be operational in Hungary if they are registered. Only recognized/registered high-level educational institutions are entitled to normative financing from the state – among others – on the basis of the number of students who are qualified as 'students taking part in the education financed by the state'. Private Hungarian institutions enter into an agreement with the state on the number of their 'students taking part in the education financed by the state'. Foreign institutions can be entitled to normative financing only on the basis of an international agreement. Full-time students are

109. Government Decree No.51 of 2007, 26 March on Supports for Students in Tertiary Education.
110. Government Decree No. 86 of 2006, 12 April on study loans and on the Study Loan Centre.

entitled to use the services of the institution (library, laboratory, etc.), and only students in state financed courses may apply for scholarships, college accommodation, social maintenance payments, contribution to the costs of their books, to their accommodation and further benefits enumerated in the statutes of the institutions. Students, as a main rule, pay attendance fees and other costs. There are special provisions on benefits for non-Hungarian national students determined in bilateral agreements (e.g., scholarship provided by the ministry of the education). Pursuant to the HighA, EEA nationals and their family members as well as migrant workers are entitled to enter into the state financed courses under the same conditions as Hungarian nationals but in practice their chance to it is minimal due to different curricula and language competences. Thus they have to pay all fees while they are excluded from numerous benefits as majority of Hungarian students since 2012.[111] Study grants are provided for kin-minority students from adjacent states in a yearly quota.

111. Government Decree No. 248 of 2012, 31 August amending the Government Decree No. 51 of 2007, 26 March.

Chapter 3. Researchers

158. The participation of non-nationals in academic research belongs to the issue of *admission and labour permission of third-country nationals* (See paragraphs 51, 81, 90, 99, 166, 176, 414) and the *free movement of EEA workers* (See in particular paragraph129.). Without repeating these rules, here are the further aspects:

159. The academic circle cannot attract foreign nationals although there are neither exclusionary rules nor prohibitively high competitive conditions in academic research institutes and at universities (Illés & Lukács, 2007). The HighA and the public education rules do not stipulate a certain nationality as a criterion for scholars, researchers, teachers, and ensure equality of working conditions, payment and dismissal and branches of social security, too. Due to the low salaries and the non-existence of a pro-migration policy in Hungary, the outflow of qualified young researchers, PhD students and experienced academics is not compensated by returnees, newcomers from the third countries and EEA academics. In the centre-periphery relation, the fundamental change was when the centres did not attract only the young any longer, but retained all age groups, and not only temporarily, but permanently. It takes a longer period – so we need further efforts towards the researchers' mobility. Furthermore, the inflow of highly skilled foreign managers to the Hungarian labour market as another economy in transition has been observed. A survey within the framework of the EU Brain Drain Project in 2000 and repeated in 2005 (Inzelt, 2008) was gathering information on how flow of brain was improving the economic management level at companies. The majority of the delegated migrants from stable (EU-15) economies and the relocation of the staff inside the multinational companies were closely related to direct investment. Whereas, there has not been much good practice on how knowledge-based regular cooperation among academics, multinational companies and regional research and development (R&D) actors who are highly skilled and innovative upgrades industrial development in this region (Hoványi, 2008).

160. Although the legislation made efforts to transpose the EC law on the reception of researchers from the non-EU states, the dichotomy of the science administration policy has hindered the cumulative effects of the otherwise limited human and financial resources. The scientific research is governed by the Ministry of Resources, the Hungarian Academy of Sciences and the National Office of Innovation. The first regulates the universities within the framework of the HighA, the second has its own network consisting of approximately thirty research institutes, and the third administers and supports the for-profit and industrial research units. Without a substantial co-ordination among these, administrative and governmental power, the regulation on the reception of third-country nationals into research projects is delegated to the government.[112]

112. Act CXXXIV of 2004 on research, development and the technological innovation.

161. According to the aforementioned government decree (hereinafter ResD) the National Office for Innovation is entitled to issue an accreditation certificate for all applicant institutes that undertake to *employ researchers who are third-country nationals in a scientific project on the basis of a hosting contract.*[113] The rules regarding these are as follows:

(a) A legal personality or an incorporated company may submit an application for accreditation that shall be issued if the institute is within the ambit of the HighA as a scientific and R&D organization; or other organization established at least three years before the submission, and at least 10% of its annual budget has been spent on R&D in any year prior to the submission, or at least 10% of its full-time employees are working in R&D.
(b) The certificate is valid for five years and it may be extended by five years per occasion.
(c) If the hosting contract was concluded with the researchers in a negligent or abusive manner, the accreditation certificate shall be withdrawn.
(d) In case of a rejected claim for extension of the accreditation certificate, or in the event of withdrawal of the organization, it will be excluded for the next five years from the date of accreditation permission.
(e) The National Office of Innovation maintains a public register of existing certificate holders.[114] However, the number of researchers received on the grounds of the ResD is only sixty-six within a period of four years although the yearly number of applicants for visa and residence permit on the grounds of research activities is about five hundred in OIN statistics. It means that researching activities are pursued in many legal titles (as PhD student, visiting professor, project worker, etc.) not only in the frame of the hosting contract.

162. The accreditation certificate holder institute is entitled to contract on hosting with a researcher *who is a third-country national.* It shall contain not only the most relevant information on the project (topics and timing), the validity period of reception, the duties and rights of the parties, but also information on undertakings of the receiving institute to cover all costs in connection with expulsion measures of researchers. The text of the hosting contract shall also be submitted in Hungarian and in the original language that is applicable in the research project. If the contract contains a duty regarding the teaching activity of the researcher, it shall not exceed one-fifth of his/her working time. These rules on the hosting contract shall be implemented in the event of exchange of researchers, who are third-country nationals, between the EU Member States, if the residing period of the researchers is to exceed three months in Hungary. The hosting contract becomes void *ex lege* if the visa and residence permit application of the researcher in question are refused in a final decision, or the employment (working) relation is ceased between the institute and the researcher. The third-country national researcher who is employed within the ambit of the hosting contract by an accredited institute is exempted from the labour

113. Government Decree No.181 of 2007, 6 July on accreditation of institutes receiving on the contractual basis researchers who are third-country nationals.
114. <www.nih.gov.hu/tanacsadas/akkreditalt/akkreditalt>.

permission. Furthermore, his/her additional teaching activity is exempted from the assessment of the labour market need in labour permission procedure by the PermitD.

163. The ThirdA and the ThirdD contain some specific provisions on received researchers providing transposition of the EC law, as follows:[115]

(a) The residence permit may be issued for the purpose of carrying out a scientific research to third-country nationals seeking residence in Hungary for the purposes of carrying out a research project under a hosting contract concluded with an accredited research organization; and it provides a written commitment for reimbursing the costs of expulsion in cases wherein the researcher remains in Hungary past the period authorized – if the researcher does not have the financial means necessary. The validity period of a residence permit granted for the purpose of carrying out a scientific research shall correspond to the duration of the receiving contract, not exceeding five years, and it may be extended by the duration of the receiving contract, but no more than a further five years. In the possession of a residence permit, a receiving contract and an employment (working) contract, a labour permission is not required.
(b) The application for residence permits may be submitted at any consulate officer of Hungary, or any other agency authorized to accept such applications for residence permit in the country where the permanent or temporary residence of the applicant is located or in the country of the applicant's nationality. However, the third-country national residing in Hungary may lodge his/her application at the Regional Directorate of the OIN to his/her place of accommodation if the purpose of residence for a period of longer than three months is research.
(c) If the purpose of entry and residence is to carry out a research project, the applicant third-country national may verify the compliance with the requirement by presenting a receiving contract concluded with the relevant research organization. The format of the application that shall be completed is defined in the MinD.
(d) The applications for a residence permit of third-country nationals shall be decided within fifteen days if the purpose of residence is research. Furthermore, the validity period of his/her travel document shall cover only the authorized duration of residence.
(e) Wherein the expulsion measure cannot be carried out, because neither the person being expelled nor his/her host has the financial means necessary, the competent authority shall pay the costs of departure. It shall be repaid by the person expelled, or by the research organization if the person affected was admitted for the purposes of carrying out a research project, and if the expulsion was ordered due to a non-fulfilment of the criteria of residence. The liability of the research organization remains in effect for six months following termination of the receiving contract.

115. Council Directive 2005/71/EC of 12 Oct. 2005 on a specific procedure for admitting third-country nationals for the purposes of scientific research.

164. The third-country nationals out of the hosting contract system can only avail themselves of the possibilities, as follows:

(a) As laid down in the PermitD. It means a *labour market test* (normal procedure) but the work permit shall be issued *without the assessment of the labour market* (benefited procedure) if the remunerating activity of an invited internationally respected academic (or artist) is not exceeding ten working days during a calendar year in a tertiary education, research institute or a public cultural institution; the third-country national researcher adds a teaching activity to the work on the grounds of the hosting contract.
(b) As laid down in the PermitD providing *exemptions* and free employment on the basis of international treaty or research activity that is within the ambit of a bilateral agreement concluded between Hungary and another state if it is certified by the Hungarian Academy of Sciences, or the research of the third-country national is based on a post-doc grant, or the scientific work is not exceeding ten days during a calendar year.

165. As a main rule, researchers of EEA nationality and their family members are granted free access to the Hungarian labour market. Hence, research activities are subject to a diploma and regulated professions are exempt from authorization. Pursuant to the general administrative rules, employers are obliged to report to the competent labour centre in the event of the employment of EEA nationals and their family members.

Chapter 4. Labour and Economic Migration

§1. Labour Employment

166. Due to the defensive, public order-oriented and less economic cost and benefit-based labour migration policy in Hungary (Tóth, 2008a), the MIPEX assessed Hungary as being a '*slightly unfavourable*' country in labour market access in comparison to other EU-Member States in 2007 and 2010.[116] Some bilateral agreements and ethnic preferences in domestic law could open some gates in the labour market. Moreover, the insecurity of residence of third-country nationals and the inadequacy in the integration measures also contribute to this perception. The following principles govern the regulation of labour migration:

(a) The entry to the *public sector for non-nationals is restrictive* in general. Although it is common in many states, the inconsistent Hungarian regulation and the great extent of exclusions can be criticized in the light of European integration (Forgács, 2006). Numerous ministerial decrees were issued that maintained the requirement of Hungarian citizenship as a '*hidden part of citizenship position*'. These 'privileges' are neither consensual, nor known to the public (Tóth, 2006b).
(b) Distinction between workers in access to employment in favour of EEA nationals and their family members is observed. Since 2004, the transposition of acquis communautaire has ensured '*Community preferences*', although transitional measures (2004–2011) are applicable against Hungarian labourers in some Member States and reciprocal restrictions are applicable towards workers of these old Member States here. The gradual liberalization in the EU is reducing the relevance of transitional instruments towards new Member States and as a parallel in Hungary, labour migration remains rather marginal or at the most remains regionally important in labour force supply (Tóth, 2008b).
(c) *Equal rights in labour conditions* have developed for socialist internationalism here previously, whereas they have been in the EC law for long decades as a component of freedoms (Lukács, 2009). With the accession to the EU, these equal rights did not have to be regulated but further controlling mechanisms had to be added.

However, the coherent principles of regulation on labour migration (e.g., selection of the best workers, attracting the qualified labourers to Hungary or facilitation of the family unification of the professionals) have not been seen (Lukács, 2007).

167. Labour migrants are excluded from all positions that require Hungarian nationality. The publicly financed and regulated positions shall be divided into the following groups by law:

116. Niessen, Jan – Huddleston, Thomas – Citron, Laura in cooperation with Geddes, Andrew and Jacobs, Dirk 'Migrant Integration Policy Index' Bruxelles 2007; Huddleston, Thomas and Niessen, Jan 'Migrant Integration Policy Index III' MPG – British Council, Brussels, 2011 <www.mipex.hu>.

(a) Certain elected positions defined by public law.
(b) Officers in defence.
(c) Officers at law enforcement (officers of police, prison, fire brigades, catastrophe dissolution, customs and secret services).
(d) Government officials.
(e) Public officials.
(f) Administrators of justice (court, public prosecutor office) having their own regulation on employment.
(g) Public servants.

The *Hungarian nationality* is strictly required in groups (a), (b) and (c). It can be said that dual nationality implies a hindering status that would be exempted by the competent minister. The decision-making workers in (d), (e) and (f) predominantly shall be nationals but *mechanic file-keepers or non-leading positions can be fulfilled by union citizens and family members* (persons entitled to right to move). Finally, employees in (g) can be either nationals or EEA nationals or third-country nationals as long-term migrants *equally*, but as exceptions in certain branches or positions they shall be nationals or speakers of the Hungarian language. Taking into account the frequent amendments in public sector provisions, opposite trends are evident. On one hand, the list of elected positions excluding non-nationals has become longer. On the other hand, accession to the public sector has become partly easier for EEA nationals. However, the reasons of exclusion are not explained in Bills or proposals. For instance, the local escort in environment protection was required to be a national but this requirement was modified to include the residing EEA nationals and third-country nationals as long-term migrants for the sake of this employment.[117] At the same time, the auctioneer as leader of mart[118] or as executive director in publicly financed media[119] is required to be a Hungarian citizen.

168. Elected positions defined in public law: Certain positions shall be fulfilled exclusively by Hungarian nationals, for instance, member of the Constitutional Court[120] and member of the Parliament.[121] Each of them is regulated in separate acts requiring citizenship directly (e.g., the member of the Monetary Council or Inspectoral Board of the National Bank) or indirectly (for instance, in case of the member of the National Auditor Office, the Parliament is entitled to elect the proper, qualified person regardless of his nationality[122]).

169. Officers in defence: Act CCV of 2012 on the legal standing of professional and mercenary (fixed-time) members of the National Defence requires nationality

117. Ministerial Decree on guards of natural protection No. 33 of 1997, 20 November (KTM) modified in 2010 (KvVM).
118. Ministerial Decree No.16 of 2001, 26 October (IM).
119. Act CLXXXV of 2010 on market and publicly financed media services, Art. 103 (1).
120. Act CLI of 2011 on the Constitutional Court, Art. 6(1).
121. Fundamental Law, Art XXIII(1).
122. Act CXXXIX of 2013 on Hungarian National Bank, Art. 9(5), 14(7), Act LXVI of 2011, Art. 7.

as a precondition in all jobs, in addition to a clean criminal record, determined qualification, proper health conditions and permanent residence in Hungary. For this reason, the legal relation is terminated in case of cessation of nationality or acquisition of another nationality. The Constitutional Court annulled the provision of the Act that bans recruitment of persons with dual nationality to the army, as being incompatible with the Constitution.[123] In accordance with this, the security screening and check that is statutorily required for the appointment of decisive positions can determine if there is any risk in the candidate's personal conditions. As a result, the automatic exclusion of applicants with multiple nationality implies an unconstitutional limitation upon the right to work or other fundamental rights, because the citizen's allegiance to the state and defence is a moral but not a legal phenomenon. The provision terminating the intentionally acquired second citizenship of an officer stays undisturbed in the said Act, going against this idea. In future, the annulment of the exclusive rule concerning the dual nationals in defence positions would lead to easier access to law enforcement for persons with dual nationality.

170. Officers at law enforcement (police, prison, fire brigades and catastrophe dissolution, customers, secret services) are regulated in Act XLIII of 1996 that was amended often. This Act covers members of police, national security services, border-guards, catastrophe-management, emergency-management, customs, fire brigades and officers in penology institutes. This is a wide and gradually growing group entitled to use coercive measures. In general, an applicant for employment in an officer's position has to be of the age of majority but below 35 years of age, and he/she shall have a standard residence in Hungary, a clean criminal record, qualification(s) as defined for the given position by law, Hungarian citizenship and confirmation by the security check. Further requirements for applicants of employment in police or civil security services are neglected now. For a person in possession of multiple nationality as a possible security risk, employment at any police, law enforcement unit or security service may be allowed only by the minister of the interior or the minister supervising the civil security services.

171. The '*government official*' as a new status was introduced by the new government (Act LVIII of 2010 amended by the Act LII of 2011) providing wide manoeuvring room for the employers (Prime Minister's Office, ministries, central and regional offices, agencies or law enforcement units) to remove and dismiss their skilled workers (previously public officials that were re-labelled by the Act as government officials to a great extent) and to provide more prerogatives for leaders. The government officials holding university degrees are entitled to act on behalf of public authority, while labourers with secondary education can be employed as additional, physical, administrative or technical worker.

172. The *public officials* were decimated in 2010 with the introduction of the legal standing of government officials. Thus, only the labourers in municipal authorities and non-governmental agencies (State President Office, Audit Office,

123. Constitutional Court Resolution No. 52 of 2009, 30 April.

Parliament, Constitutional Court, Ombudsman Office, National Media and Communication of Information Authority, National Competition Office, Financial Inspector Office, Secretariat of the Hungarian Academy of Sciences, National Public Procurement Office, etc.) belong to this regime. Their dismissal, removal were also unburdened by Act CLXXIV of 2010. Hence, the Constitutional Court annulled the rules on dismissal of officials without reasoning as incompatible to the Constitution and in violation of human dignity.[124] Preventing the further annulment, the Parliament passed new rules in 2011 determining, at least, formal criteria and reasoning of employment termination by the employer. Public officials are empowered to implement public power by adopting measures in legislation, disputes or conflicts. According to the PuboA, the public official shall be a national with a clean criminal record, and at least a medium level education (clerk) or a diploma (in all decision-making positions). Moreover, for stronger transparency and anti-corruption efforts, in certain confidential and leading positions a declaration on assets and a security check on the entire family of the applicant is necessary as ministerial decrees define in details. While the nationality is a general requirement, persons in ambit of the FreeA and 'nationals of party states of the European Social Charter'[125] can be employed as clerks (e.g., file managers) out of leading or confidential position, if the applicant has – beyond the above-mentioned, usual requirements – knowledge of the Hungarian language which is necessary to work in the given position.

173. Administrators of justice (court, public prosecutor office) have their own regulations on employment: For accession to employment in the administration of justice (as judge, administrator, expert in judicial/forensic sciences, protocol writer, typist, physical worker), the basic requirement is to be a national in possession of the voting right, clean criminal record and defined qualification(s). Certain exceptions are regulated in the Act in favour of EEA nationals and their family members. Thus, EEA nationals and their family members within the personal scope of the FreeA are employable as typists or physical workers at the Public Prosecutor's Office, if he/she has basic qualification(s), knows the Hungarian language which is necessary to work in the given position and has a clean criminal record. This exception cannot be implemented for a leading and confidential position.[126] Moreover, only a Hungarian national may be appointed to judge at court.[127] Also, EEA nationals and their family members within the personal scope of the FreeA are employable as typists, physical workers, experts of justice and candidates for expert – with the exception of protocol writer and editor at company court – at court administration, if he/she knows the Hungarian language as is necessary for the given position.[128] In brief, the key positions in justice (such as judge, member of tribunal, public prosecutor) shall belong to nationals.

124. Constitutional Court Resolution No. 29 of 2011, 7 April.
125. The revised Charter (1996) is published by the Act VI of 2009.
126. Act CLXIV of 2011 on public prosecutors' legal status and carrier, Arts 11, 109 and 122.
127. Act CLXII of 2011 on legal standing and remuneration of judges, Art. 4.
128. Act LXVIII of 1997 on legal standing of workers in administration of justice, Art 11(3) amended by the FreeA.

174. Public servants: It is a collective term providing workers for all kinds of publicly financed institutions (e.g., at public schools, hospitals, universities) on the basis of the Act on public servants and executive decrees on branches. The Hungarian nationals and the residing EEA nationals and their family members (persons under the ambit of the FreeA) and third-country nationals as long-term migrants are eligible for public servant employment. However, the Act delegates the regulation in two directions: either to require nationality and Hungarian/foreign language knowledge, or to liberalize the general conditions regarding jobs. The government is entitled to exempt the requirement of citizenship or right to free movement or long-term migrant status (liberalization) while in national defence, justice, law enforcement and security services the responsible minister can determine *working positions* in which the applicant is to be a Hungarian national with a clean criminal record, of the age of majority, or with knowledge of the Hungarian language.[129] Without the definition of the specific task or protected public interest, this delegated legislative power is not compatible with constitutional rule-of-law. Moreover, all public servants determined by law are required to regularly make a declaration on their assets, since 2007. The appointment despite the non-fulfilment of pre-conditions implies invalidity of the contract of employment. According to the recent modification, the public tenders of job would make the public service sector more competitive and transparent.

The executive decree requires, in certain positions, Hungarian nationality and/or knowledge of the Hungarian language:[130] For instance,

(a) A public servant in the position of security or asset-guard of *archives and public collections* (museum) must be a Hungarian national. Furthermore, Hungarian citizenship and security check is required from all public servants employed in public collections of defence, while leading positions in public cultural collections shall be fulfilled by public servants speaking properly in Hungarian[131] This acceptance is totally discretionary without determination of language ability or its testing method.
(b) The contract of public servant employment in all public institutions and organs under the *supervision of the minister of the interior (law enforcement)* requires proving the knowledge of the Hungarian language also without clear definition of language competences. Moreover, almost all positions in law enforcement shall be fulfilled by Hungarian nationals, such as mechanics or gatekeeper. The OIN may employ non-nationals only as physical workers so the 'integration of immigrants through work' is not applicable here.[132]

175. Within some years after the accession to the EU, the EEA nationals and their family members were given preferential treatment in Hungary, but amid a

129. Act XXXIII of 1992 on legal standing of public servants, Arts 20 and 85.
130. See in particular Ministerial Decree (HM) No. 27 of 2008, 31 December, Ministerial Decree without portfolio (TNM) No. 4 of 2008, 31 December, Ministerial Decree (IRM) No. 10 of 2009, 17 April and Ministerial Decree (BM) No. 37 of 2011, 28 October.
131. Government Decree No. 150 of 1992, 20 November, s. 2.
132. Ministerial Decree of the Interior No. 37 of 2011, 28 October, s.2.

diversity of applicable rules in a hardly clean system (e.g., on the grounds of the reciprocity principle, green card holders, registration-based free labour, Tóth, 2006b). Since 2009, *liberalized employment* has been ensured,[133] so there is no need for labour authorization for the employment of persons who are *entitled to the right to free movement and residence in the EU*, such as the citizens of the EU-Member States – including Croatia in recent enlargement – Iceland, Liechtenstein, Norway, Switzerland, and their – including Hungarian nationals' – family members, regardless of their nationality. However, this free accession to employment includes simplified employment and excludes many jobs in the public sector. Other nationals and distant family members (spouse, dependent child up to the age of twenty-one) are subject to *labour authorization*, obtaining visa/residence permit and labour permit (See paragraph 411-420.) as preconditions to lawful employment, with exceptions as made by international agreements or laws.

176. Third-country nationals residing lawfully in Hungary can be employed even for contractual work that is subordinated by other persons *without labour permission* as the UnemplA in part and the government regulates in an executive decree of the UnemplA (PermitD).[134] The following list is evolving while persons protected by international public law form its stable components:

(a) leaders in the branch/representative office of a business company with its seat in a foreign country[135] (exclusive to his/her directing activities, for example, participation in trading or selling work requires permit);
(b) staff of the consular office and the embassy of foreign states, including the employ of their family members, but only on the ground of reciprocity upon the declaration of the Ministry of Foreign Affairs;
(c) staff of an international organization operating in Hungary on the ground of seat agreement, including the employ of their family members;
(d) staff of interstate cooperation or its unit, including the employ of their family members, but only on the ground of reciprocity upon the declaration of the Ministry of Foreign Affairs;
(e) repair, servicing within warranty or commissioning of equipment not exceeding fifteen working days within a month if based on civil contract with a company seated in a foreign country;
(f) posting workers as service providers across the border if it is based on civil contract with a company seated in another EEA state;
(g) (foreign) workers employed if it is based on a manpower-lending contract with a company seated in another EEA state;
(h) the key responsible officer with high qualification(s) or membership activity in the board of supervisors in a partly foreign-owned company;

133. Government Decree No. 322 of 2008, 29 December on amendment of Decree No. 355 of 2007, 23 December on transitory measures in employment.
134. Government Decree No. 445 of 2013, 28 November on employment of third-country nationals in Hungary, s.15.
135. Act CXXXII of 1997 on branch offices and commercial representatives of companies with foreign seats.

(i) employ in postdoctoral (scientific, researching) application or by the Bólyai scholarship;
(j) employ of researcher based on an interstate agreement and proved by a document issued by the Hungarian Academy of Sciences;
(k) third-country national researcher's activities based on a reception agreement with an accredited research organization;
(l) teaching, scientific or artistic activities not exceeding ten working days per annum;
(m) third-country national student's activities within an international student exchange programme for professional trainee;
(n) student's work during the period of regular attendance (from enrolment to graduation) in a secondary, art or tertiary educational institution in Hungary;
(o) foreign language teaching in elementary, secondary or tertiary education if it is based on bilateral agreements on educational cooperation (proved by the document issued from the Ministry of Public Education);
(p) professional (pastoral) employ in a registered church or its institution;
(q) employ of third-country nationals as participants in the Comenius, Erasmus, Grundtvig and Leonardo da Vinci exchange (trainee) programme;
(r) professional athletes and employ of sport experts (trainer);
(s) employ of officers and civil staff members of units within the ambit of NATO-SOFA, including the employ of their family members;
(t) spouse of a Hungarian national living together or his/her widow/er if they were living together at least for a year prior to his/her death;
(u) employ of the third-country national family member of a sponsor who has a valid residence permit that is issued on the ground of family unification having resided for at least a year in Hungary, if the sponsor can be employed without labour permission;
(v) recognized refugees and persons under international protection (temporary or subsidiary protection) including a family member or guardian in possession of valid residence permit that is issued on the ground of family unification;
(w) employment of inmates (protection seekers) at refugee and reception centres;
(x) migrants in possession of a long-term residence permit (long-term migrants with EC/temporary[136] /national[137] settlement permit); and
(y) other persons exempted by international agreements.

Employer must notify the main statistical data of the worker and the beginning and the termination of the remunerated work to the regional labour office – with exception of posted workers in point (f) and (g) upper – within a day.[138] The legality of employment without labour permission shall be proved by the employer and its documentation shall be preserved for checking for three years after termination

136. In accordance with Directive 2003/109/EC providing mobility of third-country nationals inside the Union.
137. On the ground of ThirdA and UnemplA.
138. The national database of employment may provide yearly statistics and a basis for mirror-statistics of employed EEA and third-country nationals. See, http://nfsz.munka.hu/engine.aspx?page=stat_kulf_munkavall_mo-on/.

of the remunerated work, and a fine may be imposed for the failed notification or its documentation.

177. The term *'frontier worker'* construed in terms of the free movement of persons appears only in the social law[139] which expressly lays down that the precondition relating to residence is waived for frontier workers. If an EU citizen works in Hungary – irrespective of the duration of the work – in a legal employment relationship, he/she will fall within the ambit of social coordination rules (Regulation 1408/71/EEC) and if he/she resides in another Member State, he/she will be exempt from evidencing his/her Hungarian residence. The person will be entitled to claim family benefits as an EC worker for himself/herself and for his/her family. In this regard, the Hungarian law is not as sophisticated as would be allowed by the ECJ case law,[140] because it grants benefits to the workers, even if they have no real and sufficiently close links to Hungary. In practice, frontier workers are not problematic,[141] however, the concept of entitlements for frontier workers is not acknowledged in every Member State, leading to inequalities and unjust situations (Lukács & Gyulavári, 2009).

178. Accession to the labour market and position of labourers and economic migrants are strongly determined by the following:

(a) labour permission for non-preferential groups of workers;
(b) guarantees of equal treatment that are provided by the Labour Code, UnemplA and forum shopping of anti-discrimination authorities;
(c) recognition of qualification, diploma and certificates including the prior work experiences;
(d) requirements of language (Hungarian) knowledge to the given position and their testing method;
(e) registration of employee, family member preference of employed migrants, social insurance, family care and personal income regime.

These provisions – without repeating the visa and residence requirements – are described in Part VII.

§2. Seasonal Workers and Temporary Workers

179. Another kind of visa is the seasonal employment visa, for single or multiple entry, for residence and employment of a third-country national for a period longer than three months and a maximum of six months. The visa is applicable for

139. Act LXXXIV of 1998 on the support of families.
140. Hartmann and Geven cases (C-212/05 and C-213/05).
141. The volume of frontier workers claiming family benefits is rather marginal. There are around 35,000 family benefit cases related to EEA nationals among which a thousand affect frontier workers (almost exclusively Romanian and Slovak nationals). Compared to the annual 1.2 million family benefit beneficiaries, this means approximately 0.1%.

a maximum period of one year, according to the ThirdA. The visa application shall be refused, or the issued visa shall be withdrawn if the applicant fails to comply with the general requirements of entry and residence or he/she has disclosed false information or untrue facts to the competent authority (consular office to the place of domicile of the third-country national) in the interest of obtaining the right of residence. The decisions in seasonal visa applications shall be adopted within fifteen days. There is no appeal in the event of refusal or withdrawal of the visa. The seasonal labourer residing in Hungary is eligible neither for an interim permanent residence permit, nor an EC permanent residence permit. The other conditions of employment can be read in Part VII.

180. Hungarian law contains specific rules aimed at simplifying the administrative requirements of *atypical employment.*[142] Between 1997 and 2010, there has been the instrument of the Temporary Working Book that provided for a rather flexible way of employment for both the employer and the employee. Simplified administrative procedures, reduced labour law consequences and special social security arrangements were attached to this form, however, the many abuses and the difficult ways of state control made it debatable. A new Act on the new rules of atypical employment, called '*simplified employment*' enables an employee-employer relationship to be established in a simplified manner for seasonal work in agriculture, tourism or casual work. Simplification here means that only the most important labour law rules (e.g., minimum wage) need to be applied and other guarantees in the Labour Code (Article 201–203) are excluded (e.g., the maximum work hours per day). The administration for registering the start and end of employment is also simpler. The daily wages for persons in simplified employment are the same as for regular workers. However, the public revenues are less than in regular employment and the social insurance benefits are also limited (e.g., pension scheme, health care in the event of accident and unemployment benefit is provided)[143] There are numerical limits upon the number of workers and days in simplified employment. For example, if an employer employs five workers, the maximum number of workers in simplified employment is two. The same employee can only be employed with the same employer for a maximum of 120 days per annum.

The rules are equally applicable to Hungarian and EU citizens, their family members and long-term migrants who are third-country nationals. Other third-country nationals may be employed for agricultural seasonal work on the grounds of simplified employment (Article 5).

142. Act LXXV of 2010 on Simplified Employment in effect from 1 Aug. 2010 repealing Act CLII of 2009 on Act on Simplified Employment.

143. For instance, EUR 2 for agricultural seasonal work or tourism seasonal work and EUR 4 for casual work per day. However, these public revenues and insurance benefits cover on persons that are insured in Hungary and not in another state due to the social security coordination or bilateral agreement.

§3. Independent Economic Activities

181. During the decades of dominance of state property, remunerative work could hardly be differentiated from employment and unified regime of labour. Since 1989, individual and (family-sized) micro-entrepreneurship (e.g., agricultural farmers, office of attorney-at-law, public notary, patent agent, veterinary service) has gradually developed its own legal environment. Their common trait is that they undertake work on the basis of a civil law contract (order) and they operate with their own instruments (e.g., work accessories, raw material) at their own economic risk and liability. Unlike employment, the independent economic activity is not subordinated by an employer or leader, and the individual as a freelance professional or entrepreneur is responsible for directly paying the public revenues (taxation, social insurance and unemployment contributions). Hence, mental and/or financial capital, minimal administrative capacity and registration by a competent authority or professionals' chamber are required.

182. The independent economic activity may be pursued on the ground of a civil law contract, as professionals within the ambit of EchoA, as a special group of taxpayers with simplified entrepreneurial taxation rules (SeTax), rules on individual entrepreneurs or in the form of an individual company (CompA, PrivA). Due to incoherent rules on common public charges, registry, authority permission, control and legal entity, the government decided a campaign on to set up a stable sectorial scheme on self-employment.[144] The accession to the EU inspired this effort through the examples of applicable regulation on self-employment in various Member States. Even after years, the result is weak: there is a deficit in transparent principles and rules that would prevent further inflation of normative system or breach of market rules. There are more and more provisions on flat rate, tax deduction, exempted groups of entrepreneurs (e.g., farmers) and growing administrative burdens for independent entrepreneurs and corporate bodies. The other details can be found in Parts VII and VIII.

§4. Investment Activities

183. The migration law determines no specific benefit or legal status for foreign investors because Hungary welcomes investment in the absence of investors, and Act XXIV of 1988 on the investment of foreigners in Hungary is still in force after some amendments. The free investment with proper protection has been only gradually regulated. However, the equal treatment for non-nationals in real estate (e.g., in acquisition of arable land) or in certain economic activity (monopoly) is not provided. However, a small benefit for investors appeared in 2013: buying treasury

144. Government Resolution No. 1213, of 2002, 23 December, No. 2032 of 2004, 12 February and recently No. 1121 of 2013, 11 March on the strategy on development of small and medium entrepreneurship and self-employment sector in Hungary to 2014–2020 taking into account the EU policy (see COM(2008) 394 final).

bonds for at least in sum of EUR 250,000 a residence permit is issued to the foreign investor to five years. The ThirdA and ThirdD determine its application conditions.

184. Furthermore, if the investor who is a third-country national intends to work in his/her own company or entrepreneurship that is beyond the control of property or business, he/she needs labour permission (e.g., if he/she assists to sell in his/her own shoe-shop in labour peaks) unless he/she belongs to exempted migrant groups. The investor is eligible to enter and stay in the country if he/she can prove his/her self-subsistence and the subsistence of the family members. The purpose of establishing a company and business negotiations are taken into account in admission procedure (e.g., in approval of letter of invitation). The rules on investing and establishing companies are described in Part VIII.

Chapter 5. Humanitarian Reasons

§1. Humanitarian Grounds

185. The 'humanitarian reason' means a *lawful exception* from the general requirements set out in the ThirdA for authority in the admission of third-country nationals. According to the entitlement, exceptional entry and residence may be authorized not only on the grounds of urgent humanitarian needs but also on grounds of national interest or international obligations (Articles 13(2), 18(2) of ThirdA). The legislation is silent on what the humanitarian grounds are, and its interpretation belongs to law practitioners distinguishing between national interests (ethnic preference) and international obligations. However, the humanitarian law is part of international obligations (Varga, 2006) and human rights commitments are also considered a field of international obligations. In brief, the humanitarian grounds mean an amalgam of binding rules and margin of appreciations on the basis of international soft law, human misery of migrants and ethical principles if any. Their autonomous substance has not been determined yet.

186. Whereas, Article 29(1) of ThirdA determines the meaning of humanitarian reasons in the context of issuance of a specific residence permit. In the event of non-fulfilment of the general requirements of residence permission, the following persons shall be granted *a residence permit on humanitarian grounds*:[145]

(a) persons recognized by Hungary as a stateless person;
(b) persons who have been granted tolerated status in Hungary;
(c) any third-country national who applied to the refugee authority for asylum, or who applied to the refugee authority for any subsidiary form of protection or temporary protection;
(d) any third-country national who was born in Hungary and has been removed from the custody of his guardian who previously had custody according to Hungarian law, and also unaccompanied minors;
(e) for substantial national security or penal investigation reasons – by initiative of the national security, law enforcement agency, public prosecutor, customs authority or the court – any third-country national, or other affiliated third-country nationals on his/her account, who has cooperated with the authorities in a crime investigation and has provided significant assistance to gather evidence;
(f) any third-country national who has cooperated with the law enforcement agency in execution of removal, s/he is not in under penal procedure but his/her expulsion or exclusion measure is withdrawn because it is not applicable; or
(g) victims of severe exploitation including minors as third-country nationals who have been employed without valid residence and labour permit.

145. The humanitarian residence permit document means a document made out in the form and with the contents specified in Council Regulation (EC) No. 1030/2002 of 13 Jun. 2002 laying down a uniform format for residence permits for third-country nationals in an ID-2 format.

The immigration authority may *brush aside the expulsion* of unaccompanied minors, protection seekers and their family members or victims of human trafficking issuing them a residence permit on humanitarian grounds (Article 45(9) in ThirdA).

187. Furthermore, a *certificate of temporary residence* (Article 30(1) of ThirdA) shall be issued to any third-country national also on humanitarian grounds, as follows:

(a) who remained in Hungary beyond the duration of lawful residence due to humanitarian reasons or reasons in connection with his/her gainful employment, or for personal or some other unavoidable reasons beyond his/her control;
(b) who is a victim of human trafficking, if initiated by the victim support authority, for the reflection period;
(c) whose entry is authorized – in exceptional cases – on humanitarian grounds, on grounds of national interest or because of international obligations arising out of their failure to fulfil one or more of the conditions laid down by law, if s/he does not have any form of authorization to reside in Hungary;
(d) who has applied for stateless status, for the duration of such proceedings, if s/he does not have any form of authorization to reside in Hungary;

The certificate of temporary residence means a pending position of a residing migrant without specific rights or benefits – with the exception of victims of human trafficking – while residence permit holders enjoy a status that is eligible for certain legal and/or social supports or rights (tolerated migrant, protection seekers, stateless persons, unaccompanied minors, victims of human trafficking). Hence the above-mentioned question arises, as to what the reasons of exceptional admission are. There is only one common trait in these exceptions: they are regulated in ThirdA and ThirdD and not in AsylA or Asyld because these migrants are viewed from the perspective of law enforcement, public and security orders.

188. Concerning the *general position of residence permit holders if their permit is issued on the humanitarian grounds* ex officio, the following shall be emphasized:

(a) validity of residence permit issued on humanitarian grounds is shorter (six to twelve months) than that of regular residence permit, and its prolongation is also restrictive. For instance, if it was issued by the initiative of another law enforcement organization, the prolongation shall be provided with its consent;
(b) a third-country national shall submit to having his/her fingerprints and a photograph of his/her face taken;
(c) a residence permit may be issued for the purpose of gainful employment to third-country nationals who wish to engage in a gainful employment in possession of a residence permit granted on humanitarian grounds (unified procedure in Article 20/A of ThirdA);

(d) the immigration authority shall have powers to order the confinement of the holder of this permit in a designated place. The costs of confinement in a community hostel or refugee centre shall be borne by the third-country national, unless he is issued a residence permit on humanitarian grounds;

(e) if two months have lapsed from the date when compulsory confinement in a community hostel or refugee centre was ordered, but the circumstance serving grounds therefore still exists for reasons beyond the control of the third-country national in question, he/she shall be transferred to another place. However, the immigration authority may endorse – exceptionally, *on humanitarian considerations* – the third-country national's request to designate him other place of residence after two months, and he may obtain an approval from the OIN to be employed (Article 63–64 of ThirdA).

The status of a third-country national with a certificate of temporary residence is weaker than that of the residence permit holder whose permit is issued on humanitarian grounds, because the period of validity of the certificate is three to six months, its prolongation is excluded in many cases. Moreover, the certificate holder has no right to leave or return to Hungary, his/her document is applicable only in the event of his/her surrender to another state.

189. According to the ThirdA, the *tolerated migrant* shall mean any person who is authorized to stay and shall not be returned to the country of his/her nationality, or in the case of a stateless person, to the country of regular place of residence, for fear of facing the threat of death penalty, torture or any other form of inhumane or degrading treatment or punishment, and there is no safe third country admitting him/her, and who is not eligible for the recognition as a refugee or a stateless person, nor for any subsidiary form of protection or temporary protection. In the event of non-refoulement, the non-national has to be allowed to stay in the country.

190. The *prohibition of refoulement* shall be evaluated at the refusal of entry, in ordering expulsion or in the execution of expulsion order. In the event that there is any doubt as to whether or not the principle of non-refoulement applies as regards the refused entry and ordering of return, the Police shall request the opinion of the refugee authority (a unit inside the OIN). The refugee authority shall comply with the above request without delay. During the expulsion measure, the decisions shall evaluate the prohibition of removal as to whether the principle of non-refoulement applies as regards the proceedings for ordering the expulsion or for carrying out an expulsion measure. Where a lawfully expelled third-country national lodges a request directly to the sentencing judge, the judge shall contact the refugee authority to request a prompt opinion as to whether the principle of non-refoulement applies. Furthermore, the migration authority, when carrying out an expulsion measure, shall inform the person affected of his/her right to seek legal advice and representation, or the assistance of a registered legal aid organization. If there is no safe third country admitting him/her, and the return or the expulsion is not lawful, the competent Regional Directorate of the OIN shall adopt a decision to grant a *tolerant migrant status* to the third-country national in question, and shall issue a residence permit on the grounds of humanitarian reasons. It is valid for a year and may be extended for one year per occasion.

191. The status of *tolerated migrant* has a fragmented legal standing on the margin of alien policing and human rights.

(a) This fragile position is not only visible for an annually prolonged residence permit, but also for an easy withdrawal ex officio. The residence permit issued on humanitarian grounds may not be extended, or it shall be withdrawn when the grounds for tolerant status cease to apply. The immigration authority shall also withdraw the status if the third-country national was granted the right of residence on other grounds, or failed to appear before the competent authority in the course of the review of his/her status upon receipt of notice from the immigration authority, within three months from the date of the notice.
(b) Whereas, the tolerated migrant shall reside in a designated place, in a reception centre where asylum seekers and recognized refugees are accommodated, although their status and size of supports are different.
(c) S/he is in a legal limbo, and has no real chance to obtain a Blue Card or EC residence permit (the ThirdA excludes it *expressis verbis*) and living in a poorly equipped reception centre motivates him/her to re-migrate even illegally.
(d) Tolerated migrant must actively facilitate clarification of his/her own identity but for absence of proved identity refusal of his/her permit on humanitarian grounds is not lawful.
(e) ThirdD regulates on what kind of supports is provided for tolerant migrants.

192. The OIN shall provide *aid and support for the subsistence of tolerated migrants* who are third-country nationals and are in need together with their family members (by the definition of the SocialA): they have no assets available in Hungary constituting sufficient means of subsistence, or their income including that of family members living in the same household is not more than the mandatory minimum monthly old age pension[146] per capita. Requests submitted by the tolerated migrants for aid and support shall be evaluated by the regional directorate of the OIN and they are eligible for supports as the residence permit on humanitarian grounds is issued. The eligibility is certified by a card issued also by the Regional Directorate of the OIN. These supports are as follows by the ThirdD:

(a) personal care, such as room and board in a community hostel if migrant in need without proper income;
(b) basic and urgent medical services;
(c) financial provisions for up to twelve months, such as one-off moving allowance (in order to move out from the hostel or refugee centre and renting a solid flat on the grounds of a rental contract and registered address; the maximum amount being EUR 75 per month;
(d) attendance at public schools as nationals;

146. Its amount has been approximately EUR 90 since 2007.

(e) social and consultative mental health services, translation, information on rights and obligations if the OIN has concluded a contract with Red Cross, NGOs[147] or churches providing these services (inside the community hostel or in alternative accommodation places).

If the inmate's monthly income exceeds the aforementioned threshold, he/she shall pay the costs of the services received from the community hostel in the amount specified by the director of the community hostel. Otherwise, inmates may leave the community hostel if moving out is allowed by the competent Regional Directorate of the OIN and upon providing a statement before moving out (statement of relocation). A tolerated migrant who has moved to a private accommodation, may be allowed to return to the community hostel with the permission of the competent regional directorate, and if eligible for community hostel services by virtue of his/her financial standing and income.

§2. Unaccompanied Minor Children

193. The UN Convention on Child's Rights (1989) requires the party states to implement in all regulations the spirit of '*the best interest of the child*' and the child's need for protection by the state, society and family. The migration law has to respect not only these principles in the contact with migrant minors, but in the way that the protection of foreign minors must be integrated into the family- and child-protection system. The first is rather the task of the legislators, while the latter belongs to the municipals, the Police, the NGOs and the OIN institutional cooperation that would be developed further. While all important codes (e.g., the AdminA, the CrimPA, the SocialA, the Penal Code, the Labour Code, the FreeA or the ThirdA) contain some specific provisions on minors regardless of their nationality, the special homes for migrants, experts in child care who speak in foreign languages are available to a limited extent.

194. The term of '*unaccompanied minors*' has appeared in the Hungarian law during the accession preparatory period,[148] although it is obscure. Because a minor has a limited ability to act or is incapable, he/she is under the parental/guardian custody as the Civil Code determines. Due to this mirror-translation of the EC law and international documents, there is a (virtual) duality in the Hungarian law: minors who are incapable or with a limited act to perform, so their acts are valid with a parental/guardian approval/representation, and the foreign unaccompanied minors for whom an immediate *ad litem* legal representative or guardian shall be appointed as required according to all domestic laws without direct provisions in the FreeA and the ThirdA. In fact, the protection of a minor would be ensured through the

147. For instance, see Menedék – Hungarian Association for Migrants <www.menedek.hu>.
148. With reference on Council Directive 2003/86/EC and Council Conclusion adopted on 26 Jun. 1997. This fact is connected to the continuously high number of protected foreign unaccompanied minors. For instance, in 2012 there number was 875 and in 2013 it was 465 in OIN statistics.

most proper instruments.[149] But it is not required that an appointed *ad litem* representative or a guardian shall be able to communicate on the mother tongue with the minor in question or he/she shall participate in a special training in migration law, too. In brief, the protection for non-national minors is based on a secondary standard.

195. Taking into account that there is *no age limit* in claiming for an international protection including the refugee status, the assistance as a victim of smuggling/trafficking in human beings and for a stateless status, the specific and rather preventive provisions are as follows:

(a) The term of 'family member' within the ambit of the FreeA covers the third-country national who is entitled to a parental right on a minor with a Hungarian citizenship (Article 2). This provision can prevent the minor from becoming unaccompanied but only for a Hungarian minor.
(b) The right of residence for a period of longer than three months may be granted to a person who exercises the parental custody of a minor child who is a Hungarian citizen, in the non-fulfilment of the general requirements.
(c) The right of residence of a spouse who is a third-country national shall be retained in the previous status in the event of divorce or annulment of marriage where by court he/she has parental custody of the child of an EEA national who resides in Hungary, or by an agreement between the spouses has the parental custody to a minor child.
(d) In the event of the EEA national's death or the departure from Hungary, the right of residence of his/her child shall be retained – irrespective of age – for the period of the pursuit of studies, if already and continuously engaged in such studies. The right of residence of the other parent who has the parental custody of the child shall be retained for the period of studies of the minor.
(e) The exclusion may not be ordered if the expulsion measure was taken against a minor. Moreover, an expulsion measure may not be ordered against an EEA national or his/her family member who is a minor, except if the expulsion is necessary in the best interests of the child. In this case, the Regional Directorate of the OIN shall contact the competent guardian authority to provide support and care for the unaccompanied minor.
(f) In order to secure the enforcement of deportation, the competent authority shall order a detention, but the minor shall not be placed under detention prior to the deportation.

196. The ThirdA contains the definition of '*unaccompanied minor*' that means a third-country national below the age of eighteen, who arrives in the territory of Hungary unaccompanied by an adult responsible by law or custom, and for as long as they are not effectively taken into the care of such a person, or a minor who is left

149. The ombudsman regularly monitors the legal fate of unaccompanied foreign minors, his recent report (No. 2731/2012 AJAB) summaries shortages in their protection, including the fact that their majority disappears from the child care and guardian authority system and their expulsion or deportation to Serbia is pursued without protective measures.

unaccompanied after they entered the territory of Hungary (Article 2 e.). Furthermore, the migration authority shall conduct the immigration proceedings relating to a minor child who is a third-country national to investigate whether the protecting provisions concerning unaccompanied minors apply to the child in question. The inquiry shall, in particular, aim to determine whether he/she is in fact a minor, and if there is an adult who can be held responsible for him/her whether by law or custom. For the protection of the rights of unaccompanied minors, the migration authority shall take the adequate measures at the beginning of the proceeding to have a representative *ad litem* appointed. With a view to provide the support and care for him/her, the migration authority shall contact the competent guardian authority and the consular post of the country of origin of the minor in question in Hungary (ThirdD). Unaccompanied minor shall be treated as a person belonging to the vulnerable group that requires special attention and care (Article 2 t.) The other protective provisions are as follows:

(a) The visa applications shall be evaluated immediately but within a maximum of seven days of receipt if it comes from a minor and his/her accompanying legal guardian, or from a person with custody of an unaccompanied minor who is arriving to escort the minor home.
(b) The migration authority shall evaluate immediately but within a maximum of seven days of receipt the applications of minors and their accompanying legal guardians for a residence permit, if the substantiated purpose of the travel is a medical treatment for the minor; applications for a residence permit of persons with custody of an unaccompanied minor who are arriving to escort the minor home.
(c) The parent of the unaccompanied minor with a refugee status, or his/her legally appointed guardian may be granted a long-term visa or a residence permit on the grounds of the family reunification.
(d) Long-term visas or residence permits may be issued for the purpose of medical treatment to third-country nationals accompanying their minor children or family members in need of support for receiving medical treatment in Hungary.
(e) In the event of non-fulfilment of the general requirements for a residence permit, any third-country national who was born in Hungary and has been removed from the parental custody according to the Hungarian law, and unaccompanied minors shall also be granted a residence permit on humanitarian grounds. This permit shall be valid (renewed) until the assisted return to the home country and the family unification is ensured.
(f) The migration authority shall withdraw the settlement, the national settlement or immigration permit from the minor if his/her parental custody is ensured only by his/her parent living abroad.
(g) An unaccompanied minor may be expelled only if adequate protection is ensured in his country of origin or in a third country by means of reuniting him with other members of his family or by state or other institutional care. Until this is ensured, the migration authority shall notify the competent guardian authority immediately to proceed and to provide accommodation to the minor.
(h) The detention of a third-country national who is a minor according to the migration laws or prior to expulsion shall not be ordered. However, a compulsory

place of his/her residence shall be designated to him/her instead of the detention and/or to a parent whose minor would be left unattended if he/she was to be detained. For this place of residence, a reception centre shall be designated to minor and his/her guardian (parent), in the absence of which, a children's institution or a commercial or private accommodation maintained under contract shall be designated. Unaccompanied minors may be placed in a private accommodation with relatives other than immediate family members, if the relative undertakes a commitment in writing to provide a room and board and support for the minor, and if it is evident that such a placement is in the minor's best interest, by virtue of the relationship between the minor and the said relative.

(i) In the procedure for a stateless status, the appointment and the involvement of a representative *ad litem* is required. For instance, he/she has to be present on the hearing and to sign the protocol made on the hearing by the migration authority. As regards the recognition of the stateless status of an unaccompanied minor, a copy of the relevant resolution shall be sent to the competent guardian authority to the place where the permanent or temporary residence, or the accommodation of the minor is located with a view to the protection of the rights of the stateless minor, and for providing and monitoring care for them.

197. The AsylA also accentuates the *protection of unaccompanied minors* during the whole procedure[150] in separate provisions; however, the Hungarian legal system covers on all minors in need of protection. This duplication is visible in the AsylA, because there is a definition on unaccompanied minors and on other persons eligible for a preferential treatment including unaccompanied minors. The unaccompanied minor means a non-national below the age of eighteen, who arrives in the territory of Hungary unaccompanied by an adult responsible by law or custom, and for as long as he/she is not effectively taken into the care of such a person, or a minor who is left unattended after he/she entered Hungary until he/she is again under parental or guardian custody (Article 2(f)). It can be read in the ThirdA as well. Whereas, a person eligible for preferential treatment means a vulnerable person such as a minor, unaccompanied minor, disabled person, elderly, pregnant woman, single parent with minor children and person who has been subjected to torture, rape or other serious forms of psychological, physical or sexual violence, who has special needs on account of his/her specific situation (Article 2(k)). There is no a simple solution regarding the conflicting provisions on minors without parental custody and on membership in a vulnerable group, or in the event of cumulative disadvantages (e.g., a raped minor left alone as victim of trafficking) and whether benefits or preferences can be accumulated or not (for instance, applicant with minor may be kept in detention only for thirty days while unaccompanied minor not at all so it is better to be left alone by Article 31/A-B in AsylA). The answer, in fact, depends on the assessment of the OIN or the Regional Directorate and on which laws are implemented.

150. Transposing into the national law the Council Resolution of 26 Jun. 1997 on unaccompanied minors who are nationals of third-countries, and in part the Council Directive 2003/86/EC on family unification and in part the Qualification Directive.

198. The main protective and supportive *rules in favour of unaccompanied minors* in AsylA and AsylD are as follows:

(a) If the person seeking recognition of refugee status is an unaccompanied minor, the refugee authority shall forthwith provide for the appointment of a representative *ad litem*.
(b) If there is any doubt regarding the age of an unaccompanied minor, a medical examination may be performed. This examination may be conducted solely upon the consent of the person seeking recognition of refugee status, or if he/she is not in ability to act due to his/her condition, the consent of his/her legal representative or representative *ad litem* is required. Where the consent is absent, the application for recognition may not be refused solely on the grounds of such refusal to undergo the medical examination, however preferential rules pertaining to minors shall not apply to him/her, apart from the regulations relating to involvement of his/her parent, legal representative or the appointment of a representative *ad litem*.
(c) Asylum procedures for unaccompanied minors shall be conducted under priority without delay.
(d) As regards the unaccompanied minor, the obligation of non-refoulement applies where family reunification, or the state or other institutional support is not ensured either in the country of origin, nor in any other country liable to accept him/her. If the obligation of non-refoulement is applied, the immigration authority shall recognize, upon the recommendation of the refugee authority, the non-national in question as tolerated migrant. However, the implementation of non-refoulement is excluded if the minor's country of origin is neither proved nor probable (Article 45).
(e) The register and records of the refugee authority shall contain the following details of persons falling within the scope of AsylA – inter alia – the natural identification data; facial photograph; fingerprints, if over the age of fourteen, an indication if the person seeking asylum is an unaccompanied minor, the fact and date of recognition of refugee status, subsidiary protection or temporary protection status even for five years after the ceased status. It means that all information is available not only for complete refugee statistics but also for planning, managing and monitoring the supports for unaccompanied minors.
(f) The AsylD requires that the authority in proceedings for any kind of protection shall take into account the vulnerability of the applicant while implementing the relevant rules on this event. In dubious cases, an expert opinion may be sought from a psychologist or a physician on implementation of specific provisions but this examination shall be based on the consent of the applicant providing detailed information of its purpose in his/her mother tongue or spoken language. In the event of refused examination by the applicant, the preferential provisions are not applicable.
(g) The refugee authority must take measures to find the parent or that family member who may be responsible for the unattended minor (e.g., in administrative cooperation with another Member State, UNHCR, International Committee of Red Cross or the Hungarian Red Cross according to the general rules of the AdminA) unless it is endangers the best interests of the minor (e.g., there is

conflict of interest between the person responsible for the minor and the minor). If a proper family member is available, he/she has to sign a written understanding on guardianship, care and attendance of the minor in question. In the absence of proper family member, the refugee authority shall take action to trace the person responsible for the minor involving the guardianship authority to appoint a legal representative *ad litem* (e.g., a local attorney-at-law).

(h) The unaccompanied minor shall be accommodated in a child care institution (specific institute established for minors without families). For the inmates over the age of five, a preschool preparatory course in the Hungarian language shall be managed and their attendance at a public school shall be ensured during the obligatory school age (five to sixteen years old).

(i) While deciding on the location and accommodation of the unaccompanied minor, the available family members, in particular his/her brothers and sisters shall be taken into account. Minors may be accommodated at available relative if s/he undertakes his/her care and alimentation. This shall be notified to the local municipal guardianship authority.

(j) Persons belonging to the vulnerable groups may obtain health-care services, rehabilitation measures and psychological supports free of charge (and reimbursement to the service provider is burdened on the OIN). Moreover, the students who do not speak the Hungarian language, attending elementary and secondary school (all minors in possession of humanitarian permission, unaccompanied minors and recognized persons under protection, victims of human trafficking) are eligible for an additional preparatory course.

§3. Victims of Human Trafficking

199. The *victims of human trafficking* shall be provided with a certificate of temporary residence by the competent Regional Directorate of the OIN if it is initiated by the victim support authority (Justice Office) for the reflection period.[151] Its maximum length is one month that shall not be extended, and it becomes void if the migrant departs (e.g., he/she disappears within the reflection period after changing his/her mind). Whereas, he/she may be expelled during the reflection period, if his/her residence in Hungary constitutes any threat to national security, public security or public policy.[152] In the possession of a certificate of temporary residence, the legal position of victims is fragile (see paragraphs 85, 92, 187 and 189).

200. If he/she is able and ready to contribute to the success of the investigation against the smuggling or trafficking network, a residence permit on the grounds of *humanitarian* commitments will be issued according to the ThirdA even in case of

151. Transposing the Council Directive 2004/81/EC of 29 Apr. 2004 on the residence permit issued to the third-country nationals who are victims of human trafficking or who have been the subject of an action to facilitate illegal immigration, who cooperate with the competent authorities.

152. The Directive prohibits the victim's expulsion but allows termination of the reflection period at any time, taking into account the non-cooperative behaviour of migrant. The Hungarian legislator re-interprets it: due to the expulsion, the grounds of residence and the right of residence are automatically invalidated, thus the termination of reflection period is done by the authority's action.

any non-fulfilment of the requirements for a residence permit. The migration authority issues the residence permit upon the request of the Police, customs office or the NSO for substantial national security or law enforcement reasons to any third-country national, or other affiliated third-country nationals on his/her account, who has cooperated with the authorities in a crime investigation and has provided significant assistance in gathering evidence. The validity period of a residence permit granted on humanitarian grounds is six months, which may be extended by a maximum of six months at a time. Whereas, the residence permit may not be extended, or shall be withdrawn, and the consent of the initiating authority to the extension or the refusal of the permit is required. The competent Regional Directorate may order the victims to remain in the following compulsory places of confinement: in a reception centre or in other places of accommodation maintained under contract.

201. The victims of human trafficking shall be provided aid and support – the same as provided for the tolerated migrants – specified in the ThirdD, while he/she can never meet the requirements of regular residence permission. In this way, his/her perspective of integration and rehabilitation is greatly limited (see more details in paragraph 193).

§4. Others

202. Respecting the principles of humanitarian admission, Hungary has made an agreement with the US government in order to receive some persons from the Guantanamo Bay Detention Facility.[153] The US party commits to arrange and provide transportation of the former detainee from Guantanamo to an agreed upon location in Hungary, and to provide the former detainee with appropriate identity documents. It is the objective of this arrangement that the former detainee quickly becomes self-sufficient and integrated into Hungarian society. To this end, the Hungarian Government does the following:

(a) grants a residence permit on humanitarian grounds and with it, the entitlement to all the rights and responsibilities thereto appertaining as regulated in ThirdA;
(b) grants residence without extradition, removal or transfer of the former detainee to other countries or to the control of any third government, either directly or indirectly, except in accordance with its obligations under international law;
(c) provides integration support to include housing, job-seeking assistance, access to public health care and language instruction.

The US Government will provide assistance in support of this integration effort. These special provisions regarding the received ex-detainee shall be implemented by the immigration authority governed by the ministers responsible for defence, security services, interior and finance in Hungary. The only one received Palestine ex-detainee submitted a complaint to the ombudsman that urged the clarification of

153. Note Verbale published in Government Decree No. 260 of 2009, 25 November.

bilateral agreement, in particular of the supports to his integration, family unification and financial cover to these expenses.[154]

203. The AsylA and ThirdA equally draw special attention to vulnerable groups of protection seekers or migrants. *Person in need of special* treatment cannot be determined exhaustively, but the Acts provide examples, such as unaccompanied minors, other minors, elderly or disabled persons, pregnant women, single parent raising a minor child and persons who have suffered torture, rape or any other grave form of psychological, physical or sexual violence, and are found, after proper individual evaluation, to have special needs because of his/her individual situation. Hence, the rules shall be applied to these persons with due consideration arising from their situation.

These Acts regulate the following:

(a) the refugee authority shall examine whether in respect of the person seeking recognition as refugee or beneficiary of subsidiary or temporary protection (person seeking protection), furthermore in respect of refugees and beneficiaries of subsidiary and temporary protection, the rules applicable to persons requiring special treatment apply;
(b) to determine whether the person is in need of special treatment, the refugee and immigration authority may use the assistance of a medical or psychological expert; such examination shall be conducted with the consent of the person concerned; if the person seeking protection denies consenting to the examination by a specialist, the provisions applicable to persons requiring special treatment may not be applied to them;
(c) the refugee authority is obliged to inform the person seeking protection – in their mother tongue or in another language understood by them – in simple and understandable terms, regarding the examination procedure to be used and the consequences of the examination, as well as of their right to deny consent to the implementation of the examination as specified above;
(d) the deadline of leaving the country – voluntarily or by force in deportation, refusal or transport – shall be determined by the authority to the migrant in concern with due consideration arising from his/her personal, family and health conditions.

154. Szabó Máté's statement is cited in Origo (2011, 16 June).

Chapter 6. Asylum

§1. Conditions

204. The Amsterdam Treaty attached a Protocol to the EC Treaty setting up a presumption that EU citizens are excluded from the asylum, due to the criteria of accession, security, country of origin of such applicants, and the EU Treaty as a realm of common principles for all Member States (Article 6). The Geneva Convention (1954) is hardly compatible with a non-rebuttable presumption on the exclusion from the protection, so the Protocol considers the recognition of EU citizens as an exception defining its preconditions. The LisbonA modified this Protocol requiring a decision of the Council (Article 7(1) or (2) of the EU Treaty) concerning the Member State whose nationals are the applicants. Appendix 2 of the LisbonA incorporated the Charter of Fundamental Rights approved by the EU heads of state and the Government in December 2000 into the national legal system. Its Article 18 declares the following: '*The right to asylum*' shall be guaranteed with due respect for the rules of the Geneva Convention of 28 July 1951, and the Protocol of 31 January 1967 relating to the status of refugees, and in accordance with the Treaty establishing the European Community.' The secondary EC law uses the definition of 'applicant' and the term of 'recognition'[155] that relates to only a '*third-country national or a stateless person*'. The exception means that the presumption that not each Member State is safe shall be rebutted, but the burden of proof is shifted in this context to the applicants, because there is no provision on how to modify the previous refusal of applicants deriving from only that Member State on which the Council has issued a decision due to the violation of human rights. This external emphasis is transposed to the Hungarian law.

205. The Fundamental Law (Article XIV (3)) provides asylum and protection for any non-national who has well-founded fears of persecution on the grounds as the Geneva Convention (1951) determines and 'who may enjoy the protection neither in country of his/her origin, nor in another state'. The conditions of recognition shall be regulated in an act including the definition of safe country and provisions on what is to be done institutionally if a Member State is constituted by the Council as a non-safe entity. This burden is explicitly shifted to the applicant, as follows:

> the authority shall investigate in the procedure not the general conditions of human rights in the applicant's country of origin, but the individual conditions and reasons in the context of the applicant's persecution according to his/her

155. Article 2(c) and (f) in Council Directive 2005/85/EC on minimum standards on procedures in Member States for granting and withdrawing refugee status (hereinafter: Procedural Directive) – it will be replaced by the European Parliament and Council Directive 2013/32/EU up to July 2015; Art. 2(c), (d) and (e) in the Council Directive 2004/83/EC on minimum standards for the qualification and status of third-country nationals or stateless persons as refugees or as persons who otherwise need international protection and the content of the protection granted that was replaced by the European Parliament and Council Directive 2011/95/EU on 21 Dec. 2013 (hereinafter: Qualification Directive) Art. (e), (g) and (i).

claim, and on the basis of individual assessment as to whether the protection is available or not for the applicant in that country.[156]

Taking into account the legal text of the AsylA, there is no reference to the Council's decision on a Member State, while the protection seeker shall give evidence on non-safety of his/her country of origin if it is on the EU's list or the national list of safe countries (Articles 9 and 16(1)).

In sum, it is contrary to the object and purpose of the Geneva Convention (1951) and human rights instruments that a national of a Member State should only be admissible as a protection seeker if the country of origin has formally derogated from its human rights obligations or has been determined under a political process to be a serious and persistent violator of human rights (Nicholson, 2006), or the applicant can attest his/her persecution in a pre-screening phase of the procedure.

206. According to the reasons of protection and the substance of the legal standing enjoyed by the protected migrants, the following *categories* may be differentiated:

(a) The AsylA and the AsylD determine the definition of *refugee* and its recognition with reference to the Geneva Convention (1951) and the New York Protocol (1967).
(b) Persons under the *subsidiary protection* are under the ambit of the AsylA and the AsylD, while the main idea is stated in the Qualification Directive (Article 2(f)). Since 1993, a 'second class protection' has been existing in Hungarian law or in the administrative measures, but this subsidiary protection provides a clear position due to the AsylA.
(c) *Temporary protection* is constituted in the AsylA (Article 19) on the grounds of previous administrative practice in late 1990 designating the group of persons in need of protection (such as Balkan war victims) by the Government. This governmental entitlement is inserted to the AsylA while the transposition of the EC secondary law[157] means the reasons for temporary reception of mass influx that is based on the Council's decision. It is rather a theoretical class, as the war in the Balkans ended.

The legislators emphasize how the AsylA develops the rights and duties of the applicants under each category, depending on the purpose of protection and procedural guarantees. In this sense, it covers applicants for refugee status, subsidiary and temporary protection. They are common in launching a procedure, because all of them have to submit their own claim at the migration authority.

Tolerated migrants are authorized to stay in the territory of Hungary according to the ThirdA. It took a longer time to regulate certain benefits and rights for them also in the ThirdD, but the reluctant legislation has remained the most characteristic attitude towards them since early 1990s. (See paragraphs 5, 186–193, 198 and 201.)

156. Explanatory Report to the Bill (AsylA).
157. Council Directive 2001/55/EC, 20 Jul. 2011 on minimum standards giving temporary protection in the event of a mass influx of displaced persons, Art. 2.

207. However, these migrants in need of protection have to meet the following consecutive criteria:

(a) they shall be non-nationals, including stateless persons;
(b) they arrive from a non-safe transit country or a non-safe country of origin, and
(c) Hungary is responsible for examining their application in the merit on the basis of the results of a pre-screening or eligibility assessment.

I. Refugee Status

208. As regards the *positive conditions of recognition* on the grounds of the Geneva Convention (1951) and the Qualification Directive, the following cases by the AsylA can be outlined:

(a) Hungary shall grant refugee status to a non-national who is persecuted or, owing to a well-founded fear of being persecuted for reasons of race, religion, nationality, political opinion or membership of a particular social group, is outside the country of nationality and is unable or, owing to such fear, is unwilling to avail himself or herself of the protection of that country. A well-founded fear of being persecuted may be based on events which have taken place since the applicant left the country of origin, or on activities which have been engaged in by the applicant since he/she left the country of origin. This rule is relevant for refugees *sur place* without any procedural or substantial deadline for submission. In the absence of the exclusion reasons, the refugee authority shall grant a refugee status to the non-national applicant who verifies or establishes the probability that the mentioned requirements in concert with Article 1 of the Geneva Convention (1951) apply to him/her.
(b) The Minister in charge of immigration may, in the absence of the conditions for granting a refugee status, nonetheless grant a refugee status under special and equitable circumstances to a non-national, where this is substantiated on humanitarian grounds, insofar as there are no grounds for exclusion of the refugee protection. Due to the exception it is granted ex officio, and there is no legal remedy for the Minister's decision.
(c) The Minister may grant a refugee status to an alien who was granted recognition as a refugee by the Office of the United Nations High Commissioner for Refugees, and to whom the applicability of the Geneva Convention (1951) is declared by the refugee authority. The number of quota-refugees (based on the cooperation with other states and the UNHCR) shall be limited to a hundred persons annually.[158]

209. Refugee *recognition is excluded* if it is unnecessary, or the applicant is not worthy of the protection according to the Geneva Convention (1951). The AsylA

158. For instance, in 2013 ten quota refugees may be received by the Government Decree No. 210/2013, 19 June.

extends it, with reference on the Qualification Directive (at least in the Explanatory Report to the Bill).

(a) The first exclusionary term is the arrival from the safe country of origin or the safe transit country. The *safe country of origin* means a country that the Council of the European Union has included in the minimum common list of safe countries of origin, or in the list of countries of origin contained in the relevant Government Decree on the designation of third countries as safe countries of origin, or part of a country that is included in those lists. Being included in either of those lists of the safe countries of origin constitutes a rebuttable presumption of the safety of that country or part of that country with respect to the application of the asylum seeker, where it can be shown that there is generally and consistently no persecution, no torture or inhuman or degrading treatment or punishment, and the country in question provides for a system of effective remedies against the violations of these rights and freedoms. The safe third-country shall mean, with respect to the applicant, a country where, prior to entering the territory of Hungary, the applicant had stayed or travelled through, and had the opportunity to apply for a refugee status or a subsidiary protection, provided that the refugee authority is satisfied that the applicant's life and liberty are not threatened on account of race, religion, nationality, membership of a particular social group or political opinion, and the applicant is not exposed to any real risk of serious harm; the principle of non-refoulement in accordance with the Geneva Convention (1951) is respected; the prohibition of removal to a country where there is a substantial reason to believe that the person in question is likely to be subjected to torture or any other form of cruel, inhuman or degrading treatment or capital punishment, as laid down in the international law, is respected and applied; and the possibility to receive protection in accordance with the Geneva Convention (1951) exists. In both cases, the applicant has to face the documentation system of the countries regarding potential safety and he/she has to dispute these systematic items and documents in order to rebut the presumption or more, to attest the personal dangers. If the country of origin of the person seeking asylum is included in the common list of the EU or in the national list of safe countries, the burden of proof lies with the asylum seeker to verify that his/her country of origin cannot be considered to be a safe country of origin in his/her particular circumstances. Similarly, if the person seeking asylum had stayed or travelled through a safe third-country prior to entering Hungary, the burden of proof lies with the applicant to verify that he/she did not have the opportunity to apply for effective protection in that country. In brief, the non-rebutted presumption means the exclusion from the refugee recognition (and perhaps from the non-refoulement, too).[159]

(b) An applicant who files a *subsequent application* shall not be granted a refugee status if the risk of persecution is based on circumstances which the applicant has created by his/her own decision since leaving the country of origin, and if

159. In absence of a published, fixed national list of safe countries the Supreme Court Guidelines (No. 2 of 2012, 10 December (KMK vélemény) on safe third country are decisive. For instance, Serbia is not safe for protection seekers according to this document.

such a refusal is compatible with the Geneva Convention (1951). The applicant is excluded, because the danger is due to his/her 'malicious, spiteful and intentional behaviour after leaving the country of origin'.[160]

(c) Any non-national to whom either of the *exclusion clauses* contained in Article 1 D, E or F of the Geneva Convention apply shall not be granted a refugee status. In evaluating these events, the documents of the UNHCR, and of the UN General Assembly shall be taken into account; for instance, on the UN Charter, the definition of terrorism, the operation of the UN Relief and Works Agency for Palestine Refugees (UNRWA)[161] or war crimes. However, the AsylA gives only one interpretative provision to the exclusionary terms. Namely, within the meaning of Article 1F(b) of the Geneva Convention (1951), 'serious non-political crime' shall mean any act where – taking into account all applicable circumstances, such as the objective of the felony, the motivation, the mode of commission, the methods used or contemplated – the criminal elements of the offence outweigh the political aspects, and that is punishable under the Hungarian law by five years of imprisonment or more.

210. The *cessation of the refugee status* may be based on the termination or the withdrawal of the decision of recognition reflecting partly the absence of the necessity, or behaviour undeserving of the protection, partly the correction of the authority's assessment of conditions by the AsylA, as follows:

(a) the refugee status is terminated if the refugee has acquired Hungarian citizenship;
(b) the refugee has voluntarily re-availed himself/herself of the protection of the country of nationality;
(c) having lost his/ her nationality, the refugee has voluntarily re-acquired it;
(d) the refugee has acquired a new nationality, and enjoys the protection of the country of his/her new nationality;
(e) the refugee has voluntarily re-established himself/herself in the country which he/she left or outside which he/she remained owing to fear of persecution;
(f) the circumstances in connection with which he/she has been recognized as a refugee have ceased to exist. However, it shall not apply to a refugee who continues to refuse to avail himself/herself of the protection of the country of nationality claiming a well-founded fear of persecution;
(g) has renounced his/her recognition as a refugee;
(h) it was granted in spite of the existence of the exclusion clauses, or if falling under the said exclusion clauses;
(i) the conditions for the resolution on which the recognition was based did not exist at the time it was adopted;

160. Explanatory Report to the Bill (AsylA) with reference to the Art. 5(3) in the Qualification Directive.
161. The Capital Court (Budapest) claimed the interpretation of the Art. 12(1)a of the Qualification Directive in a preliminary ruling at the EUCJ. According to its judgment (C-364/11) the proceeding authority has to scrutiny how and in what conditions the protection of UNRWA has been provided or ceased avoiding automatism in exclusion. It is important for Palestine applicants in Hungary.

(j) the refugee has misled the authorities during the asylum procedure by presenting false information or documents or by withholding relevant information or documents, provided that it had a decisive impact on the decision for the granting of refugee status; or
(k) the refugee has been convicted by the court of law either in Hungary, or in another state for committing a crime punishable by imprisonment of five years or more.

II. Subsidiary Protection Status

211. In accordance with the Qualification Directive, the AsylA defines the 'second class status' for that non-national who does not qualify as a refugee, but in respect of whom substantial grounds have been shown for believing that the person concerned, if returned to his/her country of origin would face a real risk of suffering serious harm, and is unable, or, owing to such risk, unwilling to avail himself or herself of the protection of that country. A well-founded fear of being persecuted or a real risk of suffering a serious harm may be based on events which have taken place since the applicant left the country of origin, or based on activities which have been engaged in by him/her since he/she left the country of origin. The applicant has to rebut the presumption of the safe country of origin or the safe transit country, so the authority shall grant a *subsidiary protection* status to an alien who verifies the real risk of return or establishes its probability. In this context, all terms of the safe country, its presumption and the *sur place* protection seeker shall be implemented *mutatis mutandis*.

212. Despite its terminology, the subsidiary protection is not below the threshold of refugee recognition, so the safe country principle as well as the worthiness will also exclude the applicants. If the country of origin of the person seeking subsidiary protection is included in the common list of safe countries of origin of the EU or in the national list of the safe countries, the burden of proof lies with the applicant to verify that his/her country of origin cannot be considered to be a safe country of origin in his/her particular circumstances. Staying in or travelling through a safe third-country prior to entering the territory of Hungary, the burden of proof lies with the person seeking subsidiary protection to verify that he/she did not have the opportunity to apply for effective protection. It is difficult to prove the absence of the effective protection. The non-national is *excluded* from the subsidiary protection, where there are serious reasons for considering that he/she has committed a crime against peace, a war crime, or a crime against humanity, as defined in the international instruments drawn up to make a provision in respect of such crimes; he/she has committed a crime that is punishable under the Hungarian law by five years of imprisonment or more; he/she has been guilty of acts contrary to the purposes and principles of the United Nations; or he/she is considered a danger to the national security of Hungary. The last reason is particularly fluid because the person is not an offender or sentenced as referred before, and there is no legal practice or available reasoning as to the meaning of endangered national security.

213. The instability of the subsidiary protection may be illustrated by the rule that the refugee authority examines the compliance with the conditions for granting subsidiary protection status at a minimum of five-year intervals. Regardless of this regular revision, the status is ceased by *termination or withdrawal*, as follows:

(a) the subsidiary protection is terminated if the migrant has acquired a Hungarian citizenship;
(b) the subsidiary protection is withdrawn if the migrant has voluntarily re-availed himself/herself of the protection of the country of nationality; or
(c) having lost his/her nationality, the protected migrant has voluntarily re-acquired it;
(d) the holder has acquired a new nationality, and enjoys the protection of the country of his/her new nationality;
(e) the holder has voluntarily re-established himself/herself in the country which he/she left or outside which he/she remained owing to fear of persecution;
(f) the circumstances in connection with which he/she has been granted subsidiary protection have ceased to exist, but it shall not apply to the migrant who continues to refuse to avail himself/herself of the protection of the country of nationality stating a well-founded fear of persecution;
(g) the migrant has renounced his/her eligibility for subsidiary protection;
(h) the protection was granted in spite of the existence of the exclusion clauses, or if falling under the said exclusion clauses;
(i) the conditions for the recognition did not exist at the time it was adopted; or
(j) the migrant has misled the authorities during the procedure by presenting false information or documents or by withholding relevant information or documents, provided that it had a decisive impact on the decision for the granting of a subsidiary protection status.

III. Temporary Protection Status

214. The temporary protection status does not only require the event of a *mass influx* for the defined reasons in an abstract way, but also a designation of the received group by the EU Council or by the Government as a political body and an authority procedure implementing the abstract and concrete rules. The temporary protection is provided to members of the mass influx whom the Council of the European Union recognized as persons eligible for temporary protection[162] or whom the Government recognized as persons eligible for temporary protection, for they were forced to flee their country due to an armed conflict, civil war or other internal armed conflicts, or due to general, systematic and frequent violation of human rights – such as torture, cruel, inhuman and degrading treatment. The form of designation is a resolution passed by the Government, but there is no practice of this protection

162. Council Directive 2001/55/EC of 20 Jul. 2001 on the minimum standards for giving temporary protection in the event of a mass influx of displaced persons and on measures promoting a balance of efforts between Member States in receiving such persons and bearing the consequences thereof.

at all. The applicant has to verify or has to establish his/her membership in the designated group probability during the procedure for recognition.

215. In the event of a mass flight, the individual *exclusionary provisions* are hardly applicable but they are required. The non-national is excluded from being a beneficiary of temporary protection, wherein there are serious reasons for considering that the applicant has committed a crime against peace, a war crime, or a crime against humanity, as defined in the international instruments drawn up to make provisions in respect of such crimes; he/she has committed a serious non-political crime outside the territory of Hungary prior to his/her submission of the application. In this context, the serious non-political crime shall mean any act wherein – taking into account all applicable circumstances, such as the objective of the felony, the motivation, the mode of commission, the methods used or contemplated – the criminal element of the offence outweighs the political aspects, and the offence is punishable under Hungarian law by five years of imprisonment or more. Furthermore, the applicant is excluded if he/she has been guilty of acts contrary to the purposes and principles of the United Nations; if he/she is considered a danger to the national security of Hungary; or if, according to a final court judgment, he/she has committed a crime that is punishable under Hungarian law by five years of imprisonment or more. As can be seen, the prima facie recognition on the basis of the membership in the designated group is theoretically excluded whereas the threat to national security does not have any interpretative or illustrative provisions.

216. The duration of the temporary protection is one year, or as the Council of the EU or the Government in the designation defines or *prolongs* or *withdraws* it. As a result, the cessation of the protected status would be based on the deadline or event as determined in the designation decision or on individual procedure. In accordance with this, the status is terminated if the person enjoying temporary protection has acquired permanent resident status in Hungary; or the refugee authority has granted refugee status or subsidiary protection status to him/her because the opportunity for claiming another protected status shall not be excluded for him/her. The recognition is withdrawn by the migration authority if the temporary protection is granted to him/her – upon his/her consent – by another country;[163] it was granted in spite of the existence of the exclusion clauses, or if falling under the said exclusion clauses; the applicant has renounced his/her status in writing; or the conditions for the resolution on which the recognition was based did not exist at the time when it was adopted.

§2. Procedures

217. The asylum procedure as a collective term includes numerous restrictive and complicated provisions. Looking back at the history of legislation since 1989,

163. Under the Council Directive 2001/55/EC, for instance, as a burden-sharing certain parts of the group are received by other Member States.

it can be said that the fourth generation of regulation is the most complex, transposing all criticized components (Tóth, 1994) from the favourite destination countries' rules. This trend in the legislation has been independent from the number of asylum seekers. Without repetition of specific provisions on unaccompanied minors (see above), the *common rules on the procedure in protection seeking* can be defined.

218. From the perspective of the *applicant, he/she has some procedural rights, as follows*:

(a) The asylum procedure conducted by the refugee authority or the court shall be exempt from charges, when the application is submitted for the first time.
(b) The asylum procedure shall be launched upon the migrant's request submitted to the refugee authority. The applicant shall act in the procedure in person, including the persons with limited ability to act. It means that he/she shall present the claim for protection and at hearings at the proceedings, and in case of an applicant with limited ability to act, his/her legal representative (parent, guardian, legal representative *ad litem*) shall be involved. As regards the joint application of family members for recognition, it shall be submitted by the family member with legal capacity on behalf of all family members concerned, subject to their (or their legal representative's) prior written consent.
(c) In the asylum procedures, the applicant may use his/her native language or a language that he/she understands. The refugee authority may use an ad hoc interpreter subject to a contract between the authority and the interpreter, and the costs of interpreting services shall be borne by the authority. The decision shall be delivered orally and in writing to the applicant in his/her native language or in another language that he/she understands within eight days of the time it was adopted. If the applicant's whereabouts are not known, a decision shall be delivered by way of a posted announcement that shall be considered served on the eighth day following the day of posting. It shall not contain the subject matter of the case, and from the personal data of the applicant it may indicate his/her family name and surname only.
(d) The applicant has the opportunity to use the legal aid of his choice and expense, or to access it in accordance with the FreeLA free of charge, or to accept the free legal counselling offered by any registered non-governmental organization providing legal protection on a regular basis. The legal representative may attend the interview of the applicant, may have the access to the documents and files of the procedure and may make copies thereof; and may contact the inmates for counselling in a reception centre, in confinement or in detention.
(e) The applicant has the right to legal remedy in all substantial decisions of the OIN, requesting a judicial review at the competent (administrative) court located next to his/her place of registered residence or in the absence of his/her present residence, to the last registered place of registered residence. There are four administrative county courts (Szeged, Pécs, Debrecen, Győr) and the Capital Court, which adjudicate on all protection seekers' cases taking into account the place of applicants' residence (refugee centre).

219. The *proceeding authority has to pursue numerous obligations*:

(a) The refugee authority shall inform the applicant in writing, concerning his/her rights and duties in the proceedings, as well as the legal consequences of any breach of such duties in his/her native language or in another language he/she understands. This event shall be recorded in the file.
(b) The representative of the UNHCR may participate in procedures, including – subject to the consent of the applicant – attending his/her interview at the refugee authority, having the access to the documents and files of the procedure, and making copies thereof; receiving information concerning the procedure and on the decisions adopted, presenting his/her own views regarding the case during any stage of the procedure; entering the place of the confinement, the reception centre or the place of detention.
(c) The applicant shall be subjected to security checks (search of his/her belongings, clothing and/or vehicle), and have his/her facial photograph taken, and – if over the age of fourteen – fingerprints will also be taken.
(d) In the appeal of the asylum procedures, reopening the case and proceedings under the reasons of equity, or the suspension of the procedure and submission of application by way of electronic means is not permitted – derogating the AdminA.
(f) The authorities or the Court shall not contact the applicant's country of origin or any country if there are grounds to believe that it collaborates with the country of origin; any person or organization who or that are or could be considered as potential actors of persecution, or who collaborate with actors of persecution. It intends to preserve the physical integrity, liberty and security of his/her family members as yet living in the country of origin. However, it shall not apply if the same applicant submits an application after having two previous applications refused or dismissed by a final decision, and the refugee authority did not apply the obligation of non-refoulement.
(g) The refugee authority may neglect the personal hearing or interview with the applicant if he/she is not in a condition to be interviewed. The applicant under the age of fourteen arriving together with an adult family member may be interviewed only if it is essential to ascertain the relevant facts of a case. An application may not be refused solely based on the fact that the refugee authority did not interview the applicant.

220. During the asylum procedure, the *probability of the applicant's story* is challenged by the authority searching evidences, as follows in the AsylA and AsylD:

(a) In the asylum procedures, in order to verify or establish with a reasonable degree of certainty whether the person seeking the recognition of a refugee status is eligible for a refugee status, a subsidiary protection status or a temporary protection status, the following means of proof may be accepted – without the derogation of the free toolkit of evidences in the AdminA: facts and circumstances presented by the applicant in documents, a travel document or other document that is adequate to establish his/her identity and/or nationality; all relevant and timely information relating to the country of origin, including the laws and other statutory provisions of the country, and the way they are applied (*country information system*).

(b) The refugee authority and, if necessary, the Court shall obtain a report from the unit responsible to supply *country-specific information* under the supervision of the minister.[164] Furthermore, the refugee authority may accept the documents submitted by the applicant as authentic, that were made abroad, and any document certified by a foreign Court, administrative body, notary public or any other person vested with authenticity as affirmative proof without the diplomatic certification (apostille) by the Hungarian foreign mission in the country where it was issued, even without an official Hungarian translation. The assessment of an application for recognition shall be based on the individual position and personal circumstances of the applicant. For instance, the principle of *in dubio pro reo* shall be implemented.

(c) The obligation of non-refoulement shall be respected, wherein the applicant is exposed to the danger of being persecuted for reasons of race, religion, nationality, political opinion or membership of a particular social group, or is likely to be subjected to torture or any other form of cruel, inhuman or degrading treatment or capital punishment in his/her country of origin, and there is no safe third country offering refuge to the said person. The refugee authority, in its decision for the refusal or for the withdrawal of recognition shall establish whether or not the obligation of non-refoulement applies. In the event of non-refoulement, the migration authority shall recognize, upon the recommendation of the refugee authority, the non-national as tolerated migrant. In the event of refoulement, the refugee authority shall order the person in question to leave the territory of Hungary within thirty days, and the withdrawal of all issued cards. The obligation to leave the country shall not be imposed upon a non-national who is entitled to reside in Hungary on any other grounds; is in a condition, at the time when the decision is adopted, that prevents him/her from leaving the country for fear of suffering a serious, permanent and irreversible sickness or causing irreparable damage to his/her health, and if able to produce a medical diagnosis by a forensic expert to that extent. In the latter case, he/she shall be ordered to leave Hungary, when his/her health condition has improved. These provisions are based on the commitments of Article 33 of the Geneva Convention (1951) and Article 3 of the ECHR and its case law.

221. The procedure in recognition of refugee status or subsidiary protection consists of two phases: the first is the *preliminary examination*[165] and the second is the *investigation in merit*. If the refugee authority finds an application admissible, it shall follow the procedure at the second phase. In the event that the applicant shall

164. The Supreme Court's expert group in asylum and immigration cases (2012–2014) defines the criteria of credible information on the country of origin/transit in judicial procedure. The existing Information Group operates inside the OIN. Thus the Supreme Court has to set up own team or to initiate an independent centre of information in this domain with reference on the Art. 8(2) of the 2005/85/EC Directive.

165. Its conditions are determined in the Council Regulation 343/2003/EC establishing the criteria and mechanism for determining the Member State responsible for examining and asylum application lodged in one of the Member States by a third-country national and Commission Regulation 1560/

not be kept in detention ordered by the migration/refugee authority, he/she is accommodated in a reception centre or his/her private lodgings. Since 2013 the refugee authority may order detention of the applicant if s/he has no other entitlement of residence than the asylum claim, and other coercive measures (bail in EUR 500–EUR 5000, regular report to the authority, residence in a designated place) determined for the applicant are not enough, and:

(a) his identity (citizenship, personal conditions) and country of origin shall be clarified to the non-refoulement and requirement of international protection;
(b) s/he restrains or inhibits the recognition procedure (e.g., disappearing, hiding) or it is probable;
(c) his/her deprivation of liberty is necessary for security and public order;
(d) his/her claim is submitted at the airport; or
(e) his/her not presence at authority would obstruct the success of the Dublin procedure.

The maximal duration of the asylum detention is six months and for applicant (family) with minor shall not be than thirty days. The Regional Directorate of the OIN can order detention to seventy-two hours and its prolongation shall be decided by the local court if its necessity and legality is proved by the Regional Directorate. If detention is required over this maximal period, a confinement with full board shall be defined for the applicant. Furthermore, legal representative *ad litem* shall be ordered for applicant in detention if s/he cannot speak Hungarian. The conditions for the inmates in detention are determined in the ministerial decree.[166]

222. The main components of the *preliminary examination* are as follows:

(a) The preliminary examination procedure shall be completed within thirty days[167] without possibility for prolongation. The applicant that is placed in a reception centre until the decision is adopted on the conclusion of the preliminary examination procedure or the ruling is made regarding the transfer of the applicant to another responsible Member State can leave the centre with the permission of the refugee authority.
(b) Hungary concluded *cooperation agreements in administration* with relevant Member States to designate the competent partners (from Hungary, the Refugee Directorate of the OIN, its Co-ordination Division), deadlines to respond to the request, transfer and readmission.[168] Furthermore, this collaboration implies the implementation of the data in European fingerprints identification centre

2003/EC which sets out the detailed rules for the application of the Regulation. The third generation of the Dublin Regulations entered into force in 2014 replacing these rules: the European Parliament and the Council Regulation 604/2013/EU and Commission Regulation 118/2014/EU.

166. Ministerial Decree No. 29 of 2013, 28 April (BM).
167. It covers the Hungarian authority's act and not the deadline for response of the requested state that would take two months.
168. In the delegated power of the AdminA, the Government concluded these agreements (Government Decree No. 291 of 2008, 10 December publishing the agreement implementing the Reg. 343/2003/EC with the Bulgarian Government; No. 247 of 2008, 14 October with the Slovakian Government;

(EURODAC)[169] to screen out the dual applicants or other responsibility-oriented issues.[170] The purpose of taking and storing fingerprints is to establish the identity of persons seeking asylum and the repeated submissions of applications. The competent authority shall without delay transmit the recorded fingerprint data of the applicant along with his/her personal data as verified, or as supplied if unverified, his/her nationality, and an indication of his/her designated place of accommodation to the data processing agency designated by the minister. The designated data processor (Institute for Forensic Sciences) shall be responsible for the transmission of data to and the reception from the Central Unit of the EURODAC, as well as for their comparison.

(c) If the Member State contacted under the Dublin process is required to take charge of the applicant and to examine the application of the person concerned, the refugee authority shall transfer the applicant by way of a decision. The refugee authority may restrict the applicant from leaving the reception centre, until the transfer is completed, or for up to seventy-two hours in order to secure the implementation of the transfer.

(d) The decision on the *transfer of the applicant* may be subject to a judicial review. Its claim shall be submitted to the refugee authority within three days following the date of delivery of the decision. The refugee authority shall forthwith forward the claim for judicial review to the administrative court together with the documents in the file and its opinion. The Court shall decide on the claim without a suspensive effect within eight days in a non-litigation procedure, relying on the available documents without hearing the applicant. The Court's decision is final. The preliminary examination procedure shall be terminated at the time of the transfer of the applicant, but if the Member State finally refuses to take charge of the applicant and of the examination of his/her application, the preliminary examination procedure shall be carried on.

(e) Where the Dublin Regulations cannot be applied, the decision to determine as to whether an application is considered inadmissible lies with the refugee authority. An application shall be considered *inadmissible* if the applicant is a national of any Member State of the EU; the applicant was granted a refugee status in another Member State or in a third country, where this protection also applies at the time of examination of the application, and the country in question is liable to readmit the applicant; there is a safe third country for the applicant; or the applicant has lodged a repetitive application without new facts after a final decision for refusal. The reference on the safe third country is also applicable if it claims the extradition of the applicant.

No. 144 of 2008, 22 May with the Romanian Government; No. 302 of 2007, 13 November with the Slovenian Government; No. 128 of 2005, 1 July with the Austrian Federal Government).

169. Council Regulation (EC) No. 2725/2000 of 11 Dec. 2000 concerning the establishment of 'Eurodac' for the comparison of fingerprints for the effective application of the Dublin Convention was replaced by the European Parliament and the Council Regulation 603/2013/EU of 26 Jun. 2013.

170. For instance, Art. 4(2) of the Bulgarian Government's agreement says: 'If a request for taking back is based on data from the Eurodac system, the responsible authorities shall respond immediately but at the latest within 10 (ten) calendar days following the receipt of the request.'

(f) The application is manifestly unfounded if it contains only marginal or irrelevant information to the recognition; the applicant's country of origin is doubt due to his/her malicious behaviour; or the claim for recognition is submitted in delay without its acceptable reasons.
(g) The refugee authority shall refuse an application without any substantive investigation, if the inadmissibility is evidenced at once (manifestly unfounded) or during the preliminary procedure.
(h) The refugee authority shall terminate the preliminary examination procedure if the applicant withdraws his/her application in writing; fails to respond to requests to provide information hindering the examination; fails to appear at the personal interview in spite of a written notice, and fails to give a justification for his/her absence; his/her whereabouts are not known; or he/she refuses to give a facial photo and fingers printing. In the decisions, the refugee authority withdraws the residence permit on humanitarian grounds.
(i) The outright refusal of an application or termination of the procedure may be subject to judicial review with suspensive effect – if it is not a repetitive application on the same grounds – submitted within three days together with the documents of the case and any cross-complaint attached. Upon the receipt of the claim for a judicial review, the Court shall decide within eight days in a non-litigation procedure. In the proceedings, the personal interviews may be conducted if deemed necessary. The Court may alter the decision of the refugee authority. The Court's decision is final.

223. In order *to prevent the abusive application*, the AsylA (for instance in Article 54–55) introduces severe restrictions if the same applicant has submitted an application after having two previous applications refused or dismissed by final decision, and the refugee authority had not applied the principle of non-refoulement. As such, the application has no suspensive effect on the order to leave the country or on the expulsion order or the extradition. In recent years, the many applications were repetitive (while the reasoning part of the decisions was neither individualized nor conclusive in unfounded claims). Moreover, such repetitive applications mentioning the same person with different identification documents or personal data[171] have no right to access support, accommodation and contact with the UNHCR.

224. Although the protection seekers arrive primarily at land-borders, the AsylA determines some *specific rules for airport application* in accordance with the Procedural Directive. Where a non-national lodges an application before admission into the territory of Hungary, at the international airport frontier checkpoint, the provisions in the previous paragraphs shall be applied with certain exceptions, as follows:

(a) the applicant is not considered as a person who has the right to reside in the country issuing a residence permit on a humanitarian ground, he/she is not accommodated in a reception centre, and his/her internal employment is impossible;

171. It is added only in the Explanatory Report to the Bill (AsylA).

(b) the applicant is placed in the shelter (detention) inside the transport transit area (it is guarded, and nutrition, accommodation and basic medical care are provided);
(c) in the airport procedures, the preliminary examination procedure shall be completed within eight days. The refugee authority shall promptly communicate the decision adopted upon the preliminary examination procedure;
(d) the applicant shall be formally admitted into the territory of Hungary if the preliminary examination procedure is concluded with a ruling for submission for substantive proceedings; or eight days have elapsed since the submission of the application (without decision on the eligibility to the substantial procedure);
(d) (e) mentioned airport procedure shall not be implemented if applicant is eligible for the preferential treatment.

225. The Hungarian Helsinki Committee monitoring project on the access to the protection at airports in six European capitals, including Budapest, proves the common shortcomings in practice,[172] in particular not conducting an interview with all persons in the procedure to refuse entry into the country, the providing of formal information on the rights of asylum seekers and assistance, the poor communication skills of the border guards/checking staff in foreign languages. This comparative report strongly offers certain changes beyond the regular monitoring on the airports, based on a cooperation agreement between the NGO and the responsible migration agency. First, in order for remedies against the decision to refuse entry and the return order to be effective and meaningful, the request for judicial review must have an automatic suspensive effect. Once a foreigner is returned from the country, it is practically impossible to pursue legal remedies, which results in risking the life and security of the potential asylum seekers. Second, the state should ensure that facilities for foreigners confined at the airport or in an airport transit zone for more than twenty-four hours provide adequate living standards with as few restrictions as possible. The authorities must keep in mind that these foreigners have only committed a minor offence by entering the country without valid travel documents – in case of refugees for a legitimate reason – therefore keeping them under prison-like conditions exceeds the purpose of the measure and is not proportionate to the offence that they have committed. Due also to these critics the ThirdA prohibits refusal and expulsion of if migrant is 'under asylum procedure' and is eligible for residence by law (AsylA) since 2013. The recent border monitoring report of HHC released that the interpretation on how to get under the asylum procedure at borders is enigmatic. In 2013 about 85% of the apprehended (illegal) migrants could become protection seekers in average while at the airport only 45%.[173]

226. The *substantive proceedings* of the refugee recognition or the subsidiary protection shall be concluded within sixty days of the date of the ruling for the

172. The Researchers 2008/2: 25–26 (Refugee Documentation Centre, Ireland).
173. A menedékkérők hozzáférése az ország területéhez és a menedékjogi eljáráshoz Magyarországon [Access to the protection and asylum procedure at the Hungarian borders in 2013], Budapest, 2013. Magyar Helsinki Bizottság – ORFK – UNHCR www.helsinki.hu.

submission for substantive proceedings. Its major forces during this period are as follows:

(a) The NSO is involved in the procedure of giving an expert opinion as the authority within thirty days without any prolongation. It means that the duration of the proceedings of the special authorities shall be included within the administrative time limit of the substantive proceedings.
(b) The refugee authority shall examine the conditions for the recognition of the applicant's refugee status; and second – in their absence – the conditions for a subsidiary protection status. If the applicant fails to supply the facts and circumstances forming the reason for fleeing his/her country of origin, or the applicant has made inconsistent and contradictory representations which make his/her claim clearly unconvincing in relation to his/her having been the object of persecution or serious harm, it cannot be considered as an unfounded application, wherein an expert of forensic medicine explains that the inconsistent and contradictory representations made by the applicant are attributable to his/her health or mental condition. The refusal is probable, if the applicant deliberately provides false information or withholds information concerning his/her personal data and nationality; uses a forged or counterfeit document to identify himself/herself for entering the country and insists on the validity of the false contents thereof; conceals from the refugee authority his/her travel document or any other document based on which to establish his/her identity, destroys such documents, or intentionally obstructs the procedures aimed to establish his/her identity; or is making an application merely in order to delay the enforcement of his/her expulsion order.
(c) Under the influence of the Qualification Directive (Articles 6–10, Article 15), the AsylA defines persecution, serious harm, internal flight, actors of persecution, reasons for persecution, effective protection and causation of persecution and protection seeking but without additional examples or explanations than those found in the Qualification Directive. It means that the reading and teaching of EC law is replaced by the domestic regulation that would be disadvantaged (e.g., unintentional differences between the two legislations, alienation of the ECJ case law from the Hungarian law practitioners). Whereas, these definitions do not mean to establish more favourable standards (Article 3) as is inspired for Member States by the Qualification Directive. In brief, the legislators of the AsylA, as good pupils in a dualistic legal system, made applicable the EC law via transcription of the rules without their own standards or initiatives.

227. The substantive proceedings may be *completed with the following decisions*:

(a) The refugee authority terminates the substantive proceedings if the applicant withdraws his/her application in writing; fails to respond to requests to provide information hindering the examination; fails to appear at the personal interview in spite of a written notice, and fails to give justification for his/her absence; his/her whereabouts are unknown, or the application should have been rejected outright, however, the refugee authority received information concerning the reason for refusal subsequent to the initiation of the substantive proceedings. In the decisions wherein the refugee authority orders the applicant to leave the country within thirty days, and it is communicated without delay, no appeal is available – with an exception – but a claim for continuation may be requested within strictly three days. In the event of a continuation, the repetition of any reason for termination provides a basis for refusal. A judicial review may be submitted to the Court for the termination owing to the last mentioned reason of termination within thirty days. The Court in a non-litigation procedure after hearing the applicant shall decide within eight days.

(b) The refugee authority, if it accedes to the application for the recognition of a refugee status or a subsidiary protection status, shall simultaneously notify the alien in question in writing of his/her rights and obligations. If the applicant is dissatisfied with the granting of a subsidiary protection status instead of a legal remedy, a repetitive application may be submitted for a refugee status.

(c) If the refugee authority finds an application unfounded, it shall reject that application. The decision rejecting the application in merit may be subject to a judicial review. The claim for a judicial review with a suspensive effect shall be submitted to the refugee authority within eight days following the date of delivery of the decision. It shall be forwarded to the Court together with the documents of the file and any cross-complaint attached. The Court shall decide the claim within sixty days in the judicial proceedings in which the hearing of the applicant is required. The Court shall not conduct a personal interview if the applicant cannot be reached at the place of accommodation of record; his/her whereabouts are not known, or the new application is based on the same grounds. The Court may alter the decision of the refugee authority. The Court's decision is final. The refugee authority's notification obligation is applicable also if the Court has overruled the resolution of the refugee authority granting a refugee status or a subsidiary protection status to the applicant.

228. In the procedure of the regular *revision of the conditions* of the subsidiary protection and a review of compliance with the conditions prescribed for the recognition of a refugee status, the refugee authority shall advise the holder of the status to produce evidence to verify or establish the existence of the required conditions, or that there are no grounds for the exclusion of the recognition within the prescribed time limit. The refugee authority shall interview the holder, with the following exceptions: if he/she cannot be reached at the place of accommodation on record; his/her whereabouts are unknown, or he/she fails to appear at the interview in person in spite of the repeated written notices and is unable to justify his/her absence. The decision on the withdrawal of the status may be subject to a judicial review, except if the withdrawal is affected by the holder's renouncement of recognition. The claim for judicial review with suspensive effect shall be submitted to the refugee authority within fifteen days following the date of delivery of the decision. It is promptly forwarded to the Court, together with the documents in the file. The Court shall decide on the claim within sixty days in judicial proceedings. The applicant must be heard unless he/she cannot be reached at the place of accommodation on record; or his/her whereabouts are not known. The Court's decision is final, and it may not be appealed.

229. In proceedings for the *recognition of temporary protection status*, the refugee authority or the Court makes an assessment in two steps: first, it has to be determined whether the applicant belongs to the designated group inside the time frame of the resolution by the Council or by the Government. At this stage, it is not required to obtain the report on the country of origin but the applicant has to produce evidence to verify or establish that he/she is eligible for temporary protection. The second step is to clarify whether the recognition of temporary protection status is excluded or not. The procedure for the recognition of the temporary protection status shall be completed within forty-five days, and this time limit may not be extended. The expert opinion from the NSO shall comply with the refugee authority's request within thirty days. There is no appeal against refused or withdrawn recognition but a claim for judicial review may be submitted to the Court within eight days against refusal and within fifteen days against withdrawal with two exceptions: if the withdrawal is based on the resettlement and the reception by another Member State, or on the migrant's renunciation of the status. The Court shall decide the claim within sixty days.

230. Despite the complex set of provisions regarding protection against unlawful removal and judicial review on asylum cases – the *legal practice and judicial control in merit* has only gradually developed. First, the reasoning of decisions and judgments is weak or too short including the judicial review on applicant's detention.[174] Second, the non-litigation proceedings and unpublished judgments pertaining to the civil and professional control on refugee and Court assessment have not existed to a proper extent. For instance, a convicted Chinese citizen was imprisoned for illegal entry, kidnapping and forgery of official documents in 1995. After his release, in 1999 a request was made from China (Interpol Office in Peking) for his extradition for wilful injury and bodily harm of a person, committed with special cruelty. Thus, his detention prior to extradition was ordered by the Capital Court. The ECHR accepted the complaint from the person because he would have faced not only a deprivation of liberty but also capital punishment and unfair criminal procedure at home. 'On 18 January 2001 the Government submitted to the ECtHR] that they had decided to refrain from extraditing the applicant to China … .] Moreover, on 31 January 2001 they informed the Court that the applicant had left Hungary for Sierra Leone.' [175] The ECtHR decided to strike the case out of the list of complaints. The case contains no assessment or arguments of the Court or the Minister of Justice (Government) including the non-refoulement or relevance to Article 3. In the case of a Serbian family which fled from Kosovo to Hungary in 1999, the Capital Court at first obliged the OIN to repeat the administrative procedure due to inadequate fact-finding, as follows:

174. The Hungarian Helsinki Committee report on the practice of asylum detention in three centres and its formal judicial review is very critical, see www.helsinki.hu 28 Mar. 2014.

175. Case of Yang Chun Jin alias Yang Xiaolin versus Hungary, No. 58073/00, Strasbourg, 8 Mar. 2001.

> In the reasoning of the decision of the OIN it was questionable whether the story of the applicant's escape was genuine. It was established as a fact that the applicant's passport had not been withdrawn. It was also established that the war condemned by both the Hungarian society and the international community had come to an end not long after the applicant's escape. OIN gave no further reasons of the rejection. It recognized, however, due to the threat of imprisonment for the rejection of the military service, the applicant as a person authorized to stay.

Despite the repetition of the administrative procedure, the further OIN decision was also simplified. 'The Court fully concur[s with] the applicant's view that the refugee authorities shall properly have to substantiate their doubts.' Finally, the Capital Court changed the decision of the OIN (August 2000) and recognized the applicant as a refugee.[176] In another, very similar case involving a Serbian family's asylum, the Capital Court annulled the OIN decision (November 1999) and obliged the OIN to conduct a new procedure, as follows:

> since the OIN did not fully clarify the relevant facts of the case necessary to a well-founded decision, the circumstances were not assessed satisfactory. Therefore, the decision was not well-reasoned. ...] The OIN should have had a much more detailed interview with the applicant.[177]

The third request for preliminary ruling concerning the Qualification Directive was submitted by the Capital Court to the ECJ.[178] It relates to the meaning of Article 12(1)(a)[179] referring back to Article 1D of the Geneva Convention (1951). Perhaps these three questions and the UNHCR participation in the dialogue[180] represent the advanced sensitivity of the Court to the refugee law evolving therein.

§3. Legal Position of Protected Persons

231. The protection seekers' *accommodation* relates strongly to their opportunity to implement their rights to a fair procedure. However, the applicants in

176. Capital Court, non-litigations procedure, Budapest, 4 Oct. 2000. However, the OIN submitted an appeal to the Supreme Court that upheld the decision of the Capital Court as lawful and correct. Supreme Court, Budapest, Apr. 2001.
177. Capital Court, non-litigations procedure, Budapest, 28 Feb. 2000.
178. C-31/09 Bolbol Nawras versus Bevándorlási és Állampolgársági Hivatal (OJ C 82/15. 04 Apr. 2009).
179. 'A third-country national or a stateless person is excluded from being a refugee, if (a) he or she falls within the scope of Article 1 D of the Geneva Convention, relating to protection or assistance from organs or agencies of the United Nations other than the UNHCR. When such a protection or assistance has ceased for any reason, without the position of such persons being definitely settled in accordance with the relevant resolutions adopted by the General Assembly of the UN, these persons shall ipso facto be entitled to the benefits of this Directive'; see the EUCJ case No. C-364/11.
180. UNHCR Statement on the Art. 1D of the 1951 Convention. Issued in the context of the preliminary ruling reference to the Court of Justice of the European Communities from the Budapest Municipal Court regarding the interpretation of Art. 12(1)(a) of the Qualification Directive (May 2009).

detention (e.g., the detention prior to the expulsion) have no right to move to the opened reception centre, while his/her interview by the refugee authority shall be provided in the place of confinement. In this way, the legal position of the members in a vulnerable group and the applicants who entered lawfully is better than the legal position of illegally arrived, apprehended or other migrants under the migration authority's procedure as well as than that of the applicants with repetitive claims. However, the basic material conditions shall be provided to persons seeking asylum who are in asylum detention. Moreover, the general rules in the AsylA and the AsylD are decisive. Accordingly, *a person seeking protection*[181] is entitled to the following:

(a) to reside – with certain exceptions – in the territory of Hungary, or to receive an authorization to reside in the country by the ThirdA; the applicant shall be furnished with the residence permit on humanitarian grounds during the procedure;
(b) to be supported and to have accommodation and full board; the refugee authority in its ruling for the submission of an application for substantive proceedings shall specify the applicant's designated place of detention, accommodation, in a private lodging – upon request – or in a reception centre or some other place of accommodation maintained under contract. The applicant shall stay and live in the place of accommodation designated by the refugee authority during the period of the substantive proceedings;
(c) to have a standard of living adequate for the health of persons seeking asylum. The persons eligible for a preferential treatment shall be entitled – if in need – to the necessary medical assistance specified in other legislation, free of charge. In fact, this closure is fulfilled by very restrictive decrees on health care (e.g., the psychiatric treatment for the applicants in the post-traumatic stress syndrome (PTSS) is not financed by the Health Fund and some NGOs have managed it for decades). All applicants have to get vaccination and medical screening, too;
(d) to undertake employment inside the reception centre within a period of nine months from the date of submission of the application for asylum no more than eighty hours per month, and under the general rules applicable to third-country nationals thereafter;
(e) to contact the representatives of the UNHCR[182] or other relevant international non-governmental organizations for the duration of the asylum procedure;
(f) to obtain benefited public transport tickets for travelling to the refugee authority, to health care and to participation in a programme organized by NGOs on contractual basis with the OIN;
(g) to be buried at the cost of the OIN, in the absence of proper financial resources of the family members;

181. Transposing the Council Directive 2003/9/EC laying down minimum standards for the reception of applicants for asylum in Member States.
182. In accordance with Government Decree No. 23 of 1990, 7 February publishing the co-operation agreement concluded between the Hungarian Government and the UNHCR.

(h) to be supported in attending a public school when under the age of schooling but no more than to twenty-one (e.g., covering the costs of nutrition at elementary and nursery school, of dormitory, contribution to the pupils' kit annually up to the minimum lawful monthly pension per child and student's season ticket on public transport);
(i) to be supported with monthly pocket money depending on the age of inmates (minor or adult up to EUR 10-30 per capita)
(j) aid to his/her voluntary return home, having his/her ticket financed at least in part.

232. The *applicant must cooperate* with the refugee authority, such as, in particular, to elaborate the circumstances of his flight, to provide his personal data and help to establish his/her identity, to deliver his documents; to give an account of his/her wealth and income; to stay and live in the place of accommodation designated by the refugee authority observing the rules of conduct for inmates. This cooperation includes medical screening, examination and medical treatment, so he/she must receive any vaccinations prescribed by the competent public health authority in the event that there is a danger of contracting a disease. If the applicants and inmates violate these obligations (e.g., the infringement upon the obligation of cooperation, absence of over twenty-four hours from the designated place of accommodation without the refugee authority's consent, leaving the designated place of accommodation for a period of fifteen days or more, his/her whereabouts being unknown, he/she has disclosed false information or untrue facts concerning his/her assets or income, or a commission of a crime) including that 's/he re-submits his/her application for recognition unaltered', these supports and rights may be withdrawn or refused. This is not applicable to persons eligible for preferential treatment and to emergency medical treatment.

233. The refugee authority shall communicate its *decision for the withdrawal or reduction of the reception assistance* including its regular review upon request or ex officio. No legal remedy is available for the decision on the withdrawal or the refusal of the reception assistance, but it may be contested within three days and the local court shall decide it within six working days. It would be a sanction for aggressive or abusive manner of the applicant neglecting the domestic by-laws in reception centre. Two main forms of sanction are applicable: limitation of pocket money (with 25%–70%) for a defined/undefined period and to designate another reception centre or public shelter for the contentious applicant/family. The court decision is final.

234. The *recognized persons are entitled to obtain various forms of assistance* determined in the AsylD wherein they are in need, in the absence of their proper incomes and assets (by the definition of the SocialA): they have no assets available in Hungary constituting sufficient means of subsistence, or their income including that of family members living in the same household is no more than the mandatory minimum monthly old age pension[183] per capita, or living alone, no more than 150% of the mandatory monthly old age pension.

The main differences in comparison with the applicants' supports are as follows:

(a) after recognition refugee and subsidiary protected person is eligible for reception assistance in further sixty days while the temporary protected persons in need for undefined period;
(b) the person in refugee or temporary protected status is eligible to self-subsistence support up to six months if s/he is moving from the reception centre;
(c) the person in refugee or temporary protected status may initiate an integration contract with the OIN within sixty days of recognition. This contract is valid up to two years including a tutor, financial supports and restrictive rules on co-operation with the local (municipal) family care service in his/her integration. There are some further supports in kind and in finance aiming at their integration that are not available for applicants, such as Hungarian language training (within 24 months and 520 hours for adults and additional student courses at a public school attendance), support to establish one's own household and to rent an apartment for the family, contribution to translation fees of the required documents in study, work or in practice of a profession, regular support to self-subsistence of the family (for two years), and support to purchase a flat using a loan with a beneficial commission or with a non-payable contribution. However, the non-participation in the said language course – with the exception of old age or mental or physical obstacles – results in withdrawal of financial supports;
(b) the holder of a temporary protected status is not eligible for support to move out from the reception centre and establish his/her own household and to rent an apartment for the family, nor for support to purchase his/her own flat.

235. The aforementioned aid and support may also be withdrawn or refused in a formal decision of the refugee authority, if the recognized person violates the duties. The decision may be subject to a judicial review, and its claim with a suspensive effect shall be submitted to the refugee authority within three days following the date of delivery of the decision. The refugee authority shall forthwith forward the claim to the Court together with the documents of the file and any cross-complaint attached. The Court shall decide it within eight days following receipt of the claim in non-litigation proceedings, including a personal hearing of the claimant if deemed necessary. The Court may alter the decision of the refugee authority, and its decision will be final.

236. The *legal status of recognized refugees* is misunderstood for at least two reasons. First, the Fundamental Law applies the term 'asylum' with reference to the Geneva Convention (1951) while the AsylA regulates other protected status on different grounds labelling all of these persons as being under 'asylum'. According to

183. Its amount has been approximately EUR 100 since 2007.

the AsylA, 'asylum' shall mean authorization to reside in the territory of Hungary combined with protection against refoulement, expulsion and extradition (Article 2), whereas Article 3(2) says that '[p]ersons with a refugee status, beneficiaries of subsidiary protection and persons enjoying temporary protection in Hungary shall also have an access to asylum.' Furthermore, the AsylD states (in Article 2) that persons enjoying asylum shall be readmitted to Hungary. These may illustrate that 'asylum' is a collective term and a close reference only to the refugee status together with the grounds of the Geneva Convention (1951). In other words, the authority of the Constitution or today the Fundamental Law for legislative power has been overextended in the AsylA (Tóth, 2001c). Second, the recognized refugee 'unless otherwise expressly provided by an act of Parliament or Government decree, and with the exceptions set out in the AsylA – shall have *the same rights and obligations as Hungarian citizens*' (Article 10(1) of the AsylA). It means that a statutory law or a Government decree can derogate the AsylA. There are neither any limits, nor any specific reasons for derogation. In brief, the actual legal position of recognized refugees is partly based on the Geneva Convention (1951) and other international commitments, and partly on the directly applicable EC law, and partly on the changing incoherent national rules (Tóth, 2004a).

237. The *main rights of the recognized refugees* are as follows:

(a) he/she has the right to vote in the election of the local representatives and of the mayor, and in a local referendum and popular initiatives, whereas the other voting rights are not ensured to him/her;
(b) he/she may not hold a job or office or position which is required by law to be filled by a Hungarian citizen (e.g., in the public sector), but a free entry to the labour market without permission is ensured;
(c) he/she is obliged to request for and possess a personal identification document, but this identity card indicates his/her refugee status;
(d) he/she is entitled to a bilingual travel document, as defined in the Geneva Convention (1951); the PassD entitles the Regional Directorate of the OIN to issue the bilingual travelling document that is valid for one year; in possession of this document the holder may travel without a visa across the party states of the European Convention (1959);[184]
(e) he/she is entitled to the above-mentioned supports and accommodation when in need;
(f) he/she may acquire a Hungarian citizenship in a preferential manner (applicant can be naturalized if he/she has a residence for three years in Hungary after recognition instead of the generally required eighth years of residence as a settled migrant), while the other requirements shall be met by the applicant including taking an exam in Hungarian on the constitutional basics);[185]
(g) he/she is entitled to claim for a family unification;

184. Government Resolution No. 1076 of 2009, 27 May on becoming a party state in the European Convention on visa waiving for refugees (Strasbourg, 20 Apr. 1959).
185. Article 4(2) in the Act LV of the 1993 on Hungarian nationality.

(h) he/she is required to cooperate with the refugee authority; to undergo medical screening, examination and medical treatment, and to receive any vaccinations prescribed by the competent public health authority wherein there is any danger of contracting a disease; and to observe and abide by the laws of Hungary.

Since 1989,[186] the rationale of the refugee status has been based on maximum similarity to the status of the nationals, but Hungary's actions have been greatly limited in the international dialogue emphasizing protection (Tóth, 2002b) or the development of a coherent integration policy for refugees.

238. The *legal status of persons under the subsidiary protection* is also ambiguous, because 'the beneficiaries of the subsidiary protection – unless expressly provided by an act of Parliament or Government decree otherwise, and with the exceptions set out in the AsylA – shall have the same rights and obligations as refugees' (Article 17). It is clear that in any law and Government decree, a derogation from the refugee and national status may be defined, and

(a) he/she shall be entitled to a travel document issued by the Regional Directorate of the OIN, so it is not standardized in the Geneva Convention (1951): according to the PassD it contains thirty-two pages indicating the holder's personal data, photograph, legal status and the date of expiry. It is valid for one year;
(b) he/she shall not have voting rights and claim to preferential naturalisation.

239. The *temporary protected status* – without implementing the AsylA provisions – means also an amalgam of the right and obligations, as follows:

(a) he/she is entitled to a personal identification document. A residence permit issued in accordance with Council Regulation No. 1030/2002/EC in the format of identity card is valid for up to one year that may be extended by one more year per occasion until the end of the protection ex officio. It contains the personal data, validity and the address of the holder's place of residence, so if it is changed the refugee authority shall issue a new residence permit;
(b) he/she may obtain a travel document in the absence of a valid travel document of his/her country of origin. According to the ThirdA, the migration authority may issue a travelling document for returning to the home (domicile) country to that third-country national whose passport is lost or destroyed and he/she cannot obtain another. The PassD entitles the Regional Directorate of the OIN to issue (renew) a bilingual travelling document to a temporarily protected migrant upon his/her request. This document is valid for six months, and is applicable for leaving and returning to Hungary once. It contains the holder's personal data, photograph, legal status and the date of expiry, too;
(c) he/she can access the support and accommodation as defined in the AsylD; a card issued by the refugee authority shall be presented, when the supports or aids are applied;

186. See the Law-Decree No. 19 of 1989 on refugee status, Act CXXXIX of 1997 on asylum.

(d) he/she can be employed under the general rules of the third-country nationals (PermitD);
(e) he/she is required to register his/her place of accommodation and to notify the refugee authority of any changes therein; to cooperate with the refugee authority; to undergo medical screening, examination and medical treatment, and to receive any vaccinations prescribed by the competent public health authority in the event that there is any danger of contracting a disease; and to observe and abide by the laws of Hungary; and
(f) he/she may agree to transfer him/her and family member to/from another host state from/to Hungary, taking into account the solidarity and burden sharing in the event of mass influx.

§4. Position of Family Members

240. The applicants for any kind of protection *may arrive and claim together with the family members*, so their legal position is relevant during the entire procedure and the substantial decision as well. According to the AsylA, the term 'family member' shall mean the foreigner's minor child (including adopted and foster child), parent, if the person seeking recognition or enjoying international protection is a minor and spouse, if the family relation was already existent before their arrival in Hungary (Article 2(j)). Taking into account the best interests of the child, the unity of the family and the persons eligible for preferential treatment, and the rights of applicants to benefits, the following provisions shall be implemented:

(a) In order to preserve the family unity, subject to the exclusion reasons (Article 1 D, E or F of the Geneva Convention, 1951), the family member of a recognized refugee shall also be granted a refugee status upon request. The AsylA mentions no time frame, so the latter family member may also request the status on the grounds of close ties to the recognized person on the individual assessment of exclusive reasons. Furthermore, if a non-national who has been granted a refugee status has a child born in Hungary, the child shall also be granted a refugee status upon request.
(b) The family member of a non-national who has been granted a subsidiary protection status, with the exception of any exclusion reason having been proved with respect to him/her, shall also be granted the same status upon request, if he/she files a joint application for subsidiary protection, or the family member has submitted an application for subsidiary protection upon the consent of the beneficiary of the subsidiary protection, before the resolution for granting a subsidiary protection status is adopted. It implies the all applicants shall meet the requirements of recognition. Wherein a non-national with subsidiary protection status has a child born in Hungary, the child shall also be granted a subsidiary protection status upon request.
(c) In order to preserve the family unity, in the absence of a reason for exclusion, the family members of a non-national who has been granted temporary protection shall also be granted a temporary protection status upon request if such

family members were granted temporary protection in another Member State of the EU, subject to the consent of the person enjoying temporary protection.

241. The *family reunification of protected persons is more frequent* when they are integrating and establishing a new stage of life in Hungary. For recognized refugees and newborn babies, the legal standing is not hindered, but in all other cases the ThirdA[187] shall be applied together with the international provisions, such as the UN Convention on Child's Rights (1989) or between the Member States, the Convention on Jurisdiction, Applicable Law, Recognition, Enforcement and Cooperation in Respect of Parental Responsibility and Measures for the Protection of Children[188] (1996). The contradictions can be summarized as follows:

(a) different definitions of the term 'family members' in ThirdA and AsylA;
(b) documentation of family ties and self-subsistence; and
(c) recognition of travelling document of the family member(s) for visa and admission.

242. Without repetition of the description of the family unification for third-country nationals (in Part II), it has to be emphasized that all family members outside the protection criteria or stipulated time limits may request visas and residence permits only on the grounds of the ThirdA wherein the *definition of 'family members'* is different from the persons under the ambit of the AsylA. The term 'family member' shall mean, as per the ThirdA (Article 2(d)), the spouse of a third-country national; the minor child (including any adopted child) of a third-country national and his/her spouse; the minor child, including adopted and foster children, of a third-country national wherein this third-country national has parental custody and the children are dependent on him/her; and the minor child, including adopted and foster children, of the spouse of a third-country national, wherein the spouse has parental custody, and the children are dependent on him/her. For instance, in this respect, a family unification of an adult (e.g., to become a guardian, a responsible brother, or a grandfather) to a minor who is recognized as refugee was almost excluded. Whereas, the more frequently amended ThirdA now has specific rules on sponsor and family members in unification. The following persons may be granted

187. Transposing the Council Directive 2003/86/EC of 22 Sep. 2003 on the right to family reunification.
188. Act CXL of 2005 publishing the Convention. Its Arts 6–7 are relevant. In accordance with this, for refugee children and children who, due to disturbances occurring in their country, are internationally displaced, the authorities of the Contracting State on the territory of which these children are present as a result of their displacement have the jurisdiction required. It is also applicable to children whose habitual residence cannot be established. In the event of the wrongful removal or the retention of the child, the authorities of the Contracting State in which the child was habitually resident immediately before the removal or retention maintain their jurisdiction until the child has acquired a habitual residence in another State, and *(a)* each person, institution or other body having rights of custody has acquiesced in the removal or detention; or *(b)* the child has resided in that other State for a period of at least one year after the person, institution or other body having rights of custody has or should have had knowledge of the whereabouts of the child, no request for return lodged within that period is still pending, and the child is settled in his or her new environment. The text contains a definition of the wrongful removal or the retention of a child, when an urgent intervention is necessary for the protection of the person or property of the child.

a residence permit on the grounds of family reunification (discretion power of OIN): family members of persons with refugee status, and the parents of unaccompanied minors with refugee status, or their legally appointed guardian(s). Moreover, relatives of sponsors, the spouses of sponsors or persons with refugee status may be granted a residence permit on the grounds of family reunification: their parents who are dependants; their brothers and sisters, if they are unable to provide for themselves due to health reasons.

243. The ThirdA intends to support family unification saying that a decision rejecting an application for family reunification with a person holding refugee status may not be based solely on the fact that documentary evidence of the family relationship is lacking (Article 19(3)). At the same time, the ThirdA regulates that the spouse of a person holding refugee status may be issued a residence permit for the purpose of family reunification if their marriage was contracted before the entry of the person with refugee status into the territory of Hungary (Article 19(5)). Whereas, the ThirdD determines that relationship (e.g., parental line) in granting a long-term visa or a residence permit with reference to family unification of a recognized refugee or subsidiary protected person. Family relationship for the purpose of reunification with a person with refugee status or a beneficiary of a subsidiary protection may be verified by any reliable means, specifically by Deoxyribonucleic acid (DNA) analysis. A sample for DNA analysis shall be taken in the presence of an officer of the regional directorate, or the competent consulate officer. If the third-country national verifies the family relationship by means of a DNA analysis performed abroad, the regional directorate shall contact the *Hungarian Institute for Forensic Sciences* requesting an expert assessment with a view to verifying the admissibility of such proof. All costs related to such DNA analysis shall be borne by the applicant.

244. Furthermore, the ThirdA intends to combat not only the *marriage of convenience* but also the non-monogamous partnership because '[t]he spouse of a sponsor may not be issued a long-term visa or a residence permit if the other spouse of the sponsor has residence permit that was issued on the grounds of family reunification.' The requirement of self-subsistence is applied for refugees and family members because in the visa and residence permit authorization, a notarized statement shall be made by a family member having the right of residence in Hungary holding refugee status, promising support to the applicant along with a document in proof of the family member's ability to provide such support. This provision stems from a principle of principle and indirectly excludes genuine supports in the integration through the family unification of refugee. In accordance with this, a refugee can live with family members if he/she has become self-subsistent in Hungary. Moreover, only residing family members are eligible for supports and arrival of family members is not preferable in refugee supports. Due to differences in the regulation, in the absence of the social supports that would prepare for future reception of the family members and emphasis on public order emphasis in the legal practice as well (Tóth, 2006b), family unification has not been encouraged much in Hungary. In particular, the relationship to Article 8 of the ECHR can hardly be seen (Groenendijk et al., 2007; Gyeney, 2014).

245. The *age assessment of undocumented migrant children shall be done* in order to provide the necessary protection during the migration procedure, rights for unaccompanied minors, recognized persons under protection and family unification. For instance, as the AsylD determines when providing reception, the best interests of the minors seeking recognition shall be the primary consideration during the accommodation at the reception centre, and provision of food, clothing, mental hygiene, health care, attendance, education as well as housing separate from persons of age of majority shall be provided so as to advance the child's physical, mental, emotional and moral development, and as is adequate for the child's age, health and other needs. In order to determine whether the person seeking recognition, the refugee or the beneficiary of subsidiary or temporary protection, requires special treatment, the refugee authority may use the assistance of a medical or psychological expert. Such examination can only be conducted with the consent of the person concerned (See paragraph 198 b and f.). The method of medical and psychological determination is regulated. However, the Ombudsman has released some cases of maladministration in this context.[189] From this point of view, the proposal of the Commissioner for Human Rights regarding how the migrant child's age[190] is to be determined would be incorporated into the provisions.

246. The family unification is hindered by the *non-recognition of travelling document* of the family member applying for a visa. Four Somali male refugees submitted a request for constitutional review of whether Government Decree 328 of 2007, 12 December that determines the acceptable foreign travel documents required for the (Schengen) visa was compatible with the non-discrimination principle in the Constitution. Their family unification requests were denied by the OIN saying that their family members' documents were not acceptable by Hungary on account of not being on the list of proper documents. The applicants' travelling documents were issued during the civil war without proper guarantees, so the OIN decision was lawful. Furthermore, the right to family unification shall be provided equally without discrimination on the grounds of nationality, but the right to family life is preceded by the security rationale as part of public interest and hence the limitation of the fundamental right was proportional and necessary, staying within the constitution in the said Government Decree.[191]

247. A residence permit may be issued on the grounds of family reunification to a third-country national who is a relative of another third-country national who is in possession of a residence permit, immigration permit, permanent residence permit, interim permanent residence permit, a national or EC permanent residence permit, or – under the FreeA – in possession of a residence card or permanent residence card

189. See in the Report and Proposals AJB 7120/2009.

190. In Hungary as well, the X-ray test is implemented but the Proposal underlines its shortcomings. Furthermore it is not acceptable to expose children to ionizing radiation for examination done purely for administrative purposes. Quasi-automatic or routine medical screening of migrant children should therefore not be used. The incorrect age assessment may result in dramatic consequences including the wrongful detention of a separated or unaccompanied child. <http://commissioner.cws.coe.int/tiki-view_blog_post.php?postId=166> (downloaded 8 Aug. 2011).

191. Constitutional Resolution 766/B/2009.

(sponsor). Family members – unless they have obtained the right of residence on any other grounds – shall be authorized to extend his/her right of residence after five years from the date of issue of his/her first residence permit, or upon the death of the spouse or the persons with refugee status, and if other requirements for further residence are fulfilled. The children of third-country nationals holding a national visa or a residence permit and born in the territory of Hungary shall be issued a residence permit on the grounds of family reunification. The validity period for a residence permit granted for the purpose of family reunification shall be up to three years, and it may be extended by a maximum of three additional years at a time. However, the validity period of a family member's residence permit may not exceed the validity period of the sponsor's residence permit.

Chapter 7. Other Grounds

§1. Ethnic Preferences

248. Ethnic preferences: since the constitutional reforms have appeared in migration law in various legal sources frequently in a comprehensive manner. This nation-building policy (Tóth, 2000a) has gradually formed an amalgam of legal institutions in domestic law and international agreements in favour of ethnic Hungarians living across the border (Tóth, 2000b), supporting the entry and residence of kin-minority. The turning point of this kin-state policy was the adoption of the act on ethnic Hungarians living in adjacent states in 2001 (Tóth, 2002a) while its amendment in 2003 reducing the benefits of kin-minority members available partly in Hungary, and partly in the home state.[192] After the failure of the referendum in 2004 on the *ex lege* acquisition (dual) citizenship for ethnic Hungarians living in neighbouring states (Tóth, 2007b), a revision of *Diaspora law* has happened, taking into account the EC law but preserving the main principles in nationality law (Tóth, 2005) and political discourses (Kovács-Tóth, 2007). However, the Fundamental Law and the Act on Ethnic Hungarians living across the borders has institutionalized a separate budgetary supports to their culture, education, visiting programmes, research, religious life, travelling fares and small investors in favour of kin-minority.

249. Today, the following components of *Diaspora law* shall be considered relevant in migration law:

(a) The national visa and national residence permit is available for activities conducted to preserve and maintain the Hungarian language, cultural and ethnic identity, family ties, learning and enlightenment in an establishment of secondary or higher education recognized by the state for third-country nationals (ThirdA). The other efforts of Hungary to obtain facilitated visa or reduction of the Schengen visa fee in the EU legislation also belong to this policy in favour of neighbours (in particular the West-Balkan and Ukraine).
(b) The national settlement (migration) permission may be issued despite meeting lesser requirements than the EC long-term migrant permission for third-country nationals.
(c) The local border traffic agreement and permission is based on the EC Regulation. Not only its adoption but also its content was actively supported by Hungary only for neighbours living in the border zone, making it easier for them to cross the border.

192. Despite stormy political debates, in 2001 the Parliament adopted an Act that introduces a specific certificate for ethnic Hungarians living in Slovakia, Romania, Ukraine, Slovenia, Serbia-Montenegro and Croatia. Because of constitutional and international inconsistency, the law was modified in 2003 ceasing some individual benefits (employment, social insurance and public health) in Hungary that were available in the possession of the Ethnic Hungarian Certificate. (Act LXII of 2001 on Ethnic Hungarians living in neighbouring states was amended by Act LVII of 2003. Its executive rules on financial, technical and procedural issues can be found in approximately ten Government and Ministerial decrees.)

(d) The preferential naturalization required shorter time of residence prior to submission than for other applicants (1993–2004), then it was exempted from any time of residence prior to submission of the application (2005–2010) and it has been exempted from any residence in Hungary since recent amendments of nationality law entered into force in 2011. In 1993–2010, the preferential acquisition of Hungarian citizenship was in line with the principle of kin-minority cultural proximity without any genuine integration policy being offered for migrants.

(e) The list of bilateral agreements on labour, trainee, sport, youth exchange, minority protection, scholarships and municipals' cross-border cooperation concluded with neighbouring states may also intend to support migration and people-to-people contact enjoyed by kin-minorities as well.

§2. Stateless Persons

250. Hungary is a party state in all important international agreements that intend to prevent statelessness and provide protection for stateless persons, such as the UN Convention on the Reduction of Statelessness (1961), the European Convention on Nationality (1997), the UN Convention on the Legal Status of Stateless Persons (1954), and recently the European Convention on the Avoidance of Statelessness in relation to State Succession (2006).[193] In addition, Hungary joined the International Commission of Civil Status (CIEC) that developed certain practical rules concerning nationality, citizenship and stateless status. The Recommendation No. R (99) 18 of the Committee of Ministers of the Council of Europe on the avoidance and the reduction of statelessness (1999) also influences legislation.[194] However, this contracting position means no automatic implementation of all guarantees by the domestic regulation for at least two reasons. First, Hungary had made some reservations to the international commitments excluding certain guarantees,[195] and does not intend to revise those from time to time. Second, the new commitments would require systematic efforts in legislation and training of law practitioners. However, this procedure was upgraded by the European integration of Hungary and supported by the UNHCR.[196]

193. Published in the Act III of 2002, Act II of 2002, Act XCVIII of 2008, Act XV of 2009.

194. This recommendation recalls partly the principles already formulated in the European Convention on Nationality insofar as they have relevance for the avoidance and reduction of cases of statelessness, but some of these principles are further elaborated through specific and concrete guidelines. It is referred to in the Explanatory Report to the Bill (ThirdA).

195. European Convention on Nationality: reservations to Arts 11–12 exclude reasoning of decision and legal remedy in nationality law decisions; UN Convention on the Legal Status of Stateless Persons (1954): reservations to Art. 23: Public relief; Art. 24: Labour legislation and social security; Art. 28: Travel documents.

196. For instance, the UNHCR published in Hungarian and distributed among the decision-makers the booklet on this topic in 2007 (United Nations High Commissioner for Refugees / Inter-Parliamentary Union, Nationality and statelessness: A handbook for parliamentarians, Geneva: 2005).

251. It takes a longer time to recognize: statelessness is already, as such, in breach of the guarantee that everybody must be able to enjoy all human rights. The main concern is how rights and protection are to be provided for de facto stateless persons in Hungary. A de jure stateless person is every person 'who is not considered as a national by any State under the operation of its law' according to the UN Convention (1954). As a result, if a foreign state refuses to recognize a certain person as a national, other states are absolutely not entitled to conclude that the person in question is nevertheless a national of this foreign state. If no information can be acquired within a reasonable time on the nationality of a person, he/she should be deemed to be stateless. The EU should promote the development of an international legal instrument in which this principle is codified, preferably with a concrete indication of the length of time which is 'reasonable'. In addition, it is therefore preferable to define a de facto stateless person as 'a person without effective nationality and therefore not enjoying any protection of his/her national state' (de Groot, 2007).

252. In the absence of specific rules, *stateless persons are treated as other third-country nationals*. For instance, the FreeA determines that 'for the purposes of this Act third-country national shall mean – with the exception of Hungarian citizens – any person who is not a citizen of the EEA, including stateless persons'. On the grounds of this rationale, 'travel document shall mean a passport or another instrument or document that is recognized by Hungary as proper means of identification for its holder for crossing the border of Hungary and to certify his/her citizenship or stateless status' (Article 2). The ResD also considers all others who are non-nationals and are outside the scope of the FreeA as stateless persons. As is obvious, the *legal status of statelessness is not automatic* and the migrant has the options to choose a refugee status or other protected position by the AsylA, or to claim for a document providing lawful residence according to the ThirdA or to obtain a certification by the FreeA as a family member. In other words, there are severe *competitors* to the legal status of statelessness in Hungary, in particular in the context of social, labour and economic rights. Furthermore, the regulation recognizes, tacitly, the existing status of statelessness proving it by a travel document issued in another state not only for persons within the ambit of the FreeA but for visa holders or passengers within the ambit of the ThirdA, because 'travel document shall mean a passport or another instrument or document that is recognized by Hungary as proper means of identification for its holder for crossing the border of Hungary and to certify his/her citizenship or stateless status' (Article 2).

253. Hungary has been the first country in the region to adopt, through an amendment in 2007, *separate and detailed legislation on the determination of statelessness*, which not only elaborates upon the procedural criteria, but also creates – as a highly progressive measure – a separate legal identity and protection status for stateless persons (Gyulai, 2007). *The statelessness determination procedure* is regulated in the ThirdA and the ThirdD.[197] It is not so simple to conclude at the end of

197. The stateless migrant could request a residence permit on humanitarian grounds in 2001–2007 but without any specific determination procedure. The ThirdA incorporated the specific rules on determination in 2007.

the procedure that the applicant is a stateless person that 'shall mean a person who is not recognized as a citizen by any country under his/her national law' (Article 2 of the ThirdA). In 2007–2014 (until July), the total number of applicants was 203, and out of them only 121 migrants were recognized as de jure stateless persons in Hungary according to the UNHCR data. The others in need of protection had and has to choose other legal channels.

254. In accordance with this, the main components of the *procedure to recognize statelessness* are as follows:

(a) The recognition of statelessness status is based on *claim of the migrant* concerned, and there is no procedure launched ex officio. Whereas, when under the proceedings governed by the ThirdA there is any possibility that a third-country national should be considered stateless, the migration authority shall inform the person in question concerning his/her option to request for the stateless status. The provision of this information shall be recorded in writing.
(b) A certificate of temporary residence shall be issued to the applicant, for the duration of such proceedings, if he/she does not have any form of authorization to reside in Hungary.
(c) An application made in writing, or made verbally, may be submitted to the competent Regional Directorate of OIN near the place of residence only by a person who *lawfully resides* in Hungary (Article 76 of ThirdA) 'in order to diminish the chance for abusive application'.[198] It means that Hungary in practice excludes the entry of all de facto stateless persons who have no valid passport and/or the opportunity to obtain a visa. The other migrants, including the illegal migrants and victims of smuggling or trafficking, have to choose the asylum or the family membership channel to enter and reside lawfully if they are (de facto) stateless persons. However, the lawful residence of asylum seekers and victims has not been generally accepted by the migration authority staff refusing the legal entitlement of these applicants for residence on the grounds of international commitments, so they are mostly considered tolerated migrants during the procedure.
(d) Any request submitted verbally shall be recorded in writing by the immigration authority. Upon submitting the application, the applicant shall be informed of his/her rights and obligations in the proceedings (e.g., the FreeLA considers the applicant eligible for free legal aid irrespective of his/her monthly income or assets), the legal consequences of any breach of such obligations and of the designated place of accommodation. Its acceptance is recorded in the file.
(e) The applicant shall attend the proceedings in person and be interviewed. He/she may use his/her mother tongue or a language he/she understands for verbal and written communication. He/she shall be provided access to legal counselling. Apart from the applicant, his/her legal representative and/or another duly authorized person may also be involved in the case on the applicant's behalf, subject

198. The Explanatory Report to the Bill (ThirdA) said further: 'The Bill intends to exclude illegally entered or residing migrants who just after their apprehension submit spitefully the application for recognition of statelessness.'

to providing proof of their power of representation or written authorization. A person with limited ability to act also has the right to participate in such proceedings as a party. The representative of the UNHCR – subject to the applicant's consent – may attend the hearing of the applicant. The competent Regional Directorate shall inform the applicant's legal representative and the UNHCR at least three working days in advance concerning the scheduled date of the hearing.

(f) In the proceedings for the recognition of the stateless status, the applicant has to substantiate or establish the probability of his/her stateless status, with particular regard to the state which is his/her place of birth, or where his/her previous permanent or habitual residence is located; of the nationality of his/her family members and parents. During the procedure, the authority records data of identification of the applicant, his/her data regarding the travel documents, marital status, date of marriage; occupation and education; reasons for application, permanent or temporary residence in the country of customary residence; and permanent or temporary residence or place of accommodation in Hungary. The migration authority shall – upon request – provide administrative assistance in fact-finding[199] via the Hungarian foreign missions but the applicant must attach all available documents of identification to the application. The competent Regional Directorate may consider any foreign document enclosed by the applicant as a substantiating document in the absence of the requirements set out in the AdminA.

(g) The representative of the Office of the UNHCR may participate in any stage of the proceedings for the recognition of the stateless status. Such representative may be present when the applicant is interviewed; he/she may provide administrative assistance to the applicant; he/she may access the documents of the file and make copies thereof. The migration authority shall send the administrative decision and Court decision to the Office of the UNHCR. Whereas, the representative of the NSO and counter-terrorism unit of the Police may interview the applicant towards providing an expert opinion in the procedure.

255. The proceedings shall be *terminated* if the applicant dies; he/she withdraws the application in writing; he/she fails to appear in the interview in person in spite of repeated written notices and is unable to justify his/her absence; or the procedure cannot continue because the applicant's whereabouts are unknown. The application for the stateless status shall be *refused* by way of a formal decision if the applicant falls within the scope of Article 1(2) of the UN Convention relating to the Status of Stateless Persons (1954),[200] or he/she terminated his/her nationality

199. Pursuant to the Art. 25 of the UN Convention (1954) including the co-operation with the UNHCR. The Explanatory Report to the Bill emphasizes this contribution to establish the high probability or evidences of statelessness.

200. This Convention shall not apply to the following: (i) to persons who are at present receiving, from organs or agencies of the UN other than the UNHCR, protection or assistance so long as they are receiving such protection or assistance; (ii) to persons who are recognized by the competent authorities of the country in which they have taken residence as having the rights and obligations which are attached to the possession of the nationality of that country; (iii) to persons with respect to whom there are serious reasons for considering that: (a) they have committed a crime against

deliberately, with a view to obtaining the stateless status.[201] The competent Regional Directorate shall adopt a *decision in merit* within two months following the date of submission. A copy of the decision shall be sent to the NSO, the counter-terrorism unit of the Police and to the UNHCR.

256. A *decision adopted in proceedings for the recognition of stateless status* may not be appealed. A claim for the judicial review of such decision may be submitted to the migration authority within fifteen days from the date when it was communicated. The migration authority shall forward the claim without delay to the Capital Administrative Court together with the documents of the file. The Capital Court shall adopt a decision within ninety days of receipt of the claim in a non-litigation procedure that does not automatically have a suspensive effect. Upon the applicant's request, the suspensive effect (i.e., to reside in the country until the final decision) may be ensured by the Court. The applicant's hearing is required unless the applicant cannot be reached at the address on record or if he/she has moved to a place unknown. The Court may overturn the decision. The proceedings for the recognition of stateless status are exempt from charges.

257. The elements of *legal status of the recognized stateless persons* 'are deficient and are regulated in fragmented provisions of the Hungarian legal system'.[202] The existing parts of their legal standing can be summarized such that statelessness to a large extent means lawlessness (Tóth, 2004b). The main components of their status are as follows:

(a) In the absence of the requirements for a residence permit specified in the ThirdA, the migrant shall be granted a residence permit on humanitarian grounds if he/she is recognized by the Hungarian authority as a stateless person (ThirdA, Article 29). A residence permit is issued and prolonged by the competent Regional Directorate of the OIN ex officio. However, the migrant has to complete a format determined in the MinD and attach a photograph. The form of the 'Humanitarian residence permit' is determined in the ThirdD in accordance with the EC law.[203] The validity period of this residence permit shall be one year which may be extended by a maximum of one year at a time. This pending situation is the target of critics,[204] and it may explain why the stateless

peace, a war crime, or a crime against humanity, as defined in the international instruments drawn up to make provisions in respect of such crimes; (b) they have committed a serious non-political crime outside the country of their residence prior to their admission to that country; (c) they have been guilty of acts contrary to the purposes and principles of the UN.

201. This provision is compatible with the Recommendation of the Council of Ministers No. R (99)18 that avoids the abusive accession to the status of statelessness according to the Explanatory Report to the Bill (ThirdA).

202. Explanatory Report to the Bill (ThirdA).

203. It shall mean a document made out in the form and with the contents specified in Council Regulation (EC) No. 1030/2002 of 13 Jun. 2002 laying down a uniform format for residence permits for third-country nationals. The document format: ID-2 card with a remark (residence permit granted on humanitarian grounds).

204. Conference on the procedure of recognition of statelessness (9 Jul. 2007, Budapest) held by the UNHCR and the Hungarian Helsinki Committee.

status is not too attractive in comparison to the refugee status or the long-term migrant status. A residence permit granted on humanitarian grounds may not be extended, or it shall be withdrawn if any requirement for issue is no longer satisfied; the third-country national in question has disclosed false information or untrue facts to the competent authority in the interest of obtaining the right of residence; or withdrawal is requested by the authority or body on whose initiative it was issued.

(b) The stateless person who has a domicile in Hungary has a personal right that is part of the Hungarian law (e.g., he/she belongs to the personal scope of the family law and civil law as a national) but his/her existing marital status at the time of recognition by the Hungarian authority shall be respected.[205]

(c) The central immigration register contains the natural identification data of the persons recognized as holding the stateless status as well (surname and forename, place and date of birth; sex; mother's surname and forename at birth). However, it does not mean that statistics on applicants, recognition, refusal or loss of this status is also available.

(d) The stateless status is not eligible for free employment or even for a facilitated permission (without labour market test). These persons can be employed only in possession of a labour permit if there is an employer who intends to use a labourer with a short-term residence permit (up to one year including the months of authorization procedure). It is not in the same spirit as offered by the UN Convention (1954) to party states.[206] Moreover, the European Social Charter's provisions that may protect the migrant workers are not applicable.[207]

(e) The public relief and the social benefits are available for resident stateless persons on an equal basis as for nationals. However, in possession of the humanitarian residence permit, holders are not eligible to these non-contributory benefits.[208]

---

205. Articles 11(3) and 15(1) of Law-Decree No. 13 of 1979 on the international private law deal with stateless persons without any reference to recognition because Hungary was not a party state in the international treaties concerning stateless persons or reduction of statelessness. For many decades, stateless persons have obtained genuine rights when they had settlement permits (long-term migrant status) so the term of domicile or registered place of residence/address reflects this rationale.

206. Article 17: 1. The Contracting States shall accord to stateless persons lawfully staying in their territory treatment as favourable as possible and, in any event, not less favourable than that accorded to aliens generally in the same circumstances, as regards the right to engage in wage-earning employment. 2. The Contracting States shall give sympathetic consideration to assimilating the rights of all stateless persons with regard to wage-earning employment to those of nationals, and in particular of those stateless persons who have entered their territory pursuant to programmes of labour recruitment or under immigration schemes.

207. The Revised European Social Charter is published by the Act VI of 2009, its Arts 18–19 were not opted by Hungary although the Charter shall be implemented on stateless persons as well under the jurisdiction of a party state.

208. Hungary revoked the declaration made to the Article 23 and 24 of the UN Convention on stateless persons (1954) in 2012 (see the Act LIII of 2012). Thus lawfully residing stateless persons have right to enjoy the same labour, social insurance and public relief conditions as nationals. For instance, the family care benefit (Act LXXXIV of 1998) was extended to recognized stateless persons.

(f) Stateless persons only as minors may acquire Hungarian citizenship in a preferential way if they are permanent residents. Acquisition of citizenship with presumption is provided *ex lege* by birth for the child of stateless parents in possession of a permanent residence permit in Hungary. However, there is no time limit for rebuttal, so this *ius soli* acquisition is conditional. The other way of acquisition is based on declaration (claim for citizenship to the President of the State). The applicant was born in Hungary and has not acquired any other nationality of his/her parents by birth provided that at the time of his birth he resided in Hungary, he/she has lived continuously in Hungary for a period of at least five years by the time of submission of the declaration and he/she is no older than nineteen years. The amended preferential naturalization may be granted to stateless person if his/her domicile has been in Hungary at least for three years. Whereas, these preferences are independent from the statelessness status. However, the OIN shall take into account the applicant's conditions (de facto and de jure statelessness).

258. The *free travel for stateless persons* would be ensured as much as possible. First, the visa-free short-term travel is required in accordance with the EC law if stateless persons are furnished with the proper travelling documents.[209] Second, the competent Regional Directorate of the OIN may issue a travel document – upon request – to a stateless person residing in Hungary for the purpose of departure and re-entry to Hungary, within the period of validity.[210] The ThirdA does not require status but only a Hungarian residence of (de facto and de jure) stateless persons to obtain the travelling document (Article 28 of the Convention, 1954). 'For instance, a person who is recognized as stateless in another state but s/he resides lawfully in Hungary may claim for this special travelling document.'[211] There is a difference between the passport and the travel document that is defined by international agreements or the Government Decree because the latter is issued not by the regular passport office, and its validity and applicability are limited (PassA, PassD).[212] Stateless persons residing in Hungary shall have issued a bilingual document entitled '*Utazási igazolvány hontalan személy részére*/Travel document for Stateless Person' made out in Hungarian and English, containing the indication specified in Article 1(1) of the Appendix of the UN Convention (1954). This travel document is valid for one year from the date of issue, and its validity period may be extended once, by six months, according to the ThirdA. The applicant shall present the claim in person in a completed standard form, and he/she must pay the fee (EUR 11–18 per capita depending on whether the application is for issuing the travel document,

209. Taking into consideration the contents of Council Regulation 539/2001/EC, the right of entry for the purpose of residence not exceeding three months without a visa and the visas with a validity period not exceeding three months shall be granted to third-country nationals who are treated as stateless persons and holding a travel document listed under Annex II of Council Regulation 539/2001/EC. And see the Government Decree No. 328 of 2007, 11 December on accepted travelling documents for entry into Hungary issued for third-country nationals.

210. According to the OIN data, within three years (2007–2010), 261 travelling documents were issued for stateless persons.

211. Explanatory Report to the Bill (ThirdA).

212. Those transpose – inter alia – the 2004/83/EC Council Directive.

its renewal or replacement) as determined by the FeeD. If the travel document issued by the migration authority to a stateless person residing in Hungary is confiscated by the Court, the public prosecutor or the investigation authority in the course of criminal proceedings, or if they contacted the migration authority to withhold such travel document, the migration authority shall withdraw the travel document in question. Furthermore, the competent Regional Directorate of OIN shall confiscate the previous travel document issued to the stateless person by the competent authority of another state, and shall return it to the issuing authority via the diplomatic mission or consular post of the country in question. If he/she is granted citizenship, his/her travel document must be surrendered within fifteen days at the competent Regional Directorate to the place where his/her permanent or temporary residence or accommodation is located.

259. Although the stateless status exists, the surrounding legislation is criticized. The following *proposals* based on the regional survey made by the Hungarian Helsinki Committee (Gyulai, 2010) would be acceptable for further legislation:

(a) It would be necessary to include de facto stateless persons within the definition of stateless persons, and treat them similar to the de jure stateless persons in the legislation regarding statelessness and alien policing.
(b) Hungary should consider establishing a specialized unit of dedicated, professional and trained decision-makers with an exclusive right to decide claims regarding the stateless status. Furthermore, it is encouraged to adopt provisions that enable a stateless status determination procedure to be initiated ex officio, in particular for unaccompanied minors.
(c) It is urged to include provisions in its own statelessness legislation that provide for the sharing of the burden of proof between the applicant for stateless status and the processing authority.
(d) Hungary is urged to provide for legal residence for stateless persons not limited in time, or at least to apply the same standard in this respect as in the case of refugees.
(e) A better facilitation of stateless persons – in particular their vulnerable members, such as elderly or sick persons – would mean the acquisition of the Hungarian citizenship if they are residing permanently in the country. Moreover, Hungary should consider amending the Act on Hungarian Nationality to facilitate access to citizenship of newborn babies regardless of the status of their parents and to those stateless persons residing on their territory on a long-term basis, notably by exempting stateless applicants from the obligation of passing the examination (of constitutional studies in Hungarian). An amendment of the said Act would be required to allow for an effective administrative and judicial review system in case of rejected applications for citizenship, at least in case of stateless applicants, as a minimum standard.
(f) Granting full access to the labour market for stateless persons is necessary.
(g) Hungary is encouraged to facilitate the access of stateless persons to primary, secondary and higher education under the scheme applied to nationals.
(h) Hungary is also encouraged to make efforts to collect and publish comparable and transparent statistics on stateless persons who appear in the

framework of asylum, alien policing and statelessness determination procedures. It may support the enhanced and necessary cooperation with the UNHCR and non-governmental organizations to effectively train the personnel of administrative and judicial bodies dealing with statelessness determination on the legal and procedural issues related thereto.

Part IV. Loss of the Right of Residence

Chapter 1. Conditions under Which the Right of Residence Might Be Lost

260. No subjective right to residence in the territory of Hungary is ensured, with the exception of Hungarian citizens including multiple nationals. The Fundamental Law has two relevant provisions that prove the restriction of the right to entry and residence for all non-nationals:

(a) The Hungarian citizen may at any time return to Hungary from abroad (Article XIV(1)). It means that he/she must meet the only requirement, which is to present a document on Hungarian citizenship (passport, identity card or citizenship certificate issued by the OIN that is valid for a year[213]). If the passport or identity card is void, it is not an automatic reason for refusal because the consulate or the Police checking the borders are entitled to control its data in different registries. However, if a passenger presents a travel document issued by a non-Hungarian authority, he/she shall be treated as a non-national until Hungarian citizenship is not proved (ThirdD). Whereas, non-nationals can enter and reside in Hungary as determined by laws.

(b) All persons who lawfully reside in the territory of Hungary – with the exceptions determined in statutory law – have the right to free movement inside the country and free exit from the country. The lawfully residing foreigner may be expelled exclusively on the grounds of a lawfully decided expulsion order (Article XIV(1)). In accordance with this, the unlimited right of residence belongs only to nationals, while others residing lawfully (as per EC law, international law or domestic rules) are entitled to remain until a substantial and formal lawful, final expulsion order is not issued by the competent authority. It requires an individual assessment of endangering behaviour of a non-national and respect for fundamental and human rights as well (right to private life, family life, to legal remedy). Furthermore, the substance of the right to entry, residence and exit, including its limitation shall be regulated in statutory law.

For this reason, the loss of right to residence – if exists this right anyhow – implies the various ways of limiting this right through the authorization.

213. Act LV of 1993 on Hungarian citizenship.

261. The *forms of the ceased legal basis* of residence are as follows:

(a) The renouncement of residence means a voluntary departure, as done by millions of passengers. For instance, the EEA nationals and their family members shall notify the competent Regional Directorate of the OIN when they no longer wish to exercise their right to residence.
(b) The validity of the lawful residence arising from the authorization (visa, residence permit), the EC law or the international law has expired.
(c) The validity of the issued permission becomes void *ex lege.*
(d) The prolongation of lawful residence (visa, residence permission) is refused.
(e) The valid document for lawful residence is withdrawn by the competent authority.
(f) The migrant's legal status is changing (for instance he/she is moving out of the scope of the FreeA, his/her marital status has changed, he/she has acquired Hungarian citizenship, or his/her claim for asylum has been refused).
(g) The exclusion and/or expulsion measure is ordered, enforcing the migrant's departure and prohibiting his/her return to Hungary (exclusion).

The FreeA and ThirdA contain these preconditions under the collective term of 'loss of right of residence'.

262. Regardless of the method(s) in which the criteria of lawful residence are regulated, in a positive or a negative way, the following *reasons can be considered as abolishment of this right:*

(a) the absence of the material cover of the migrant's residence in Hungary including his/her (full) health care insurance;
(b) the absence or the waiving of family ties to the breadwinner if the family member cannot obtain an autonomous right to residence. However, the material cover and the family ties imply a derivative right arising from the breadwinner meeting all requirements of lawful residence;
(c) reasons concerning risky health conditions and threat to public health; or
(d) public order/security risks constituted by expulsion measures, exclusion order or deportation.

263. The *loss of the right to residence has some consequences* – with the exception of voluntary renouncement of right of residence – as follows:

(a) forced departure from the territory of Hungary within a date as determined in the authority's decision;
(b) no return to Hungary for a definite (or indefinite) period of time;
(c) other sanctions (e.g., refused application for entry exceptionally);
(d) modification in legal relationships (e.g., interruption in continuously lawful residence, employment, studies and professional practice) and the invalidation of the issued documents.

264. The legal basis and procedure of the right to residence for persons within the ambit of the FreeA and the ThirdA are different. Due to the wide margin of appreciations of the immigration authority, the loss of right to residence of persons within the ambit of ThirdA can be spoken of indirectly. It is better to mention their limited right to residence including easy termination, withdrawal or invalidation of their admission. First, the rules on EEA and their third-country family members are discussed (see below in paragraphs 266–273) and second, the provisions on non-preferential foreigners are summarized.

265. The right of residence of EEA nationals shall *terminate* in the following circumstances:

(a) in the event of the EEA national's death;
(b) the EEA national no longer being able to comply with the conditions for the exercise of such right;
(c) he/she has disclosed false information or untrue facts in the interest of obtaining the document evidencing the right to residence, on account of which he/she has been found guilty by a final court verdict; or
(d) he/she has been excluded/expelled from the territory of Hungary.

The competent authority shall adopt a resolution to declare the termination of the right of residence, and the EEA national concerned shall leave the country before the last day of the third month following the operative date of the resolution. These rules shall be properly applied to third-country family members. Moreover, the right to residence of a family member who is a third-country national shall terminate when their relationship is terminated within twelve months from the time when the right to residence was obtained, provided that it was established solely for the purpose of obtaining the right to residence. Finally, the right to residence of a person who is a third-country national and has parental custody of a child shall terminate when the right to exercise parental care is terminated, and if such a person is not entitled to further residence on any other ground.

266. The *discretionary family members* (see paragraph 133) will lose their right to residence on the following grounds:

(a) in the event of the Hungarian citizen's death or if his citizenship is terminated;
(b) in the event of the EEA national's death or if his right to residence is withdrawn, or if the EEA national no longer exercises the right to residence.

267. An EEA national who is *no longer engaged in any gainful employment* shall not retain his/her right of residence if he/she is temporarily unable to work, not as the result of an illness or accident requiring medical treatment; he/she has not been registered as a job-seeker as prescribed in any specific separate legislation following termination of his/her gainful employment, his/her registration as job-seeker is longer than the period of eligibility for job-seeking assistance (six months); or he/she does not embark on a vocational training with a view to improve his/her professional aptitude, provided that he/she had obtained the experience prescribed for vocational training during the previous employment.

268. The competent Regional Directorate of the OIN shall adopt a decision to declare that the EEA national or his/her family member has *abandoned the right to residence* in the territory of Hungary if such an EEA national or his/her family member has left the country and has not returned for over six months before obtaining the right to permanent residence. This provision shall not apply if the reason for the absence is in compliance with a compulsory military service; or if it is in connection with one absence of a maximum of twelve consecutive months for an important reason such as pregnancy and childbirth, serious illness, study or a vocational training, or a posting. The residence card shall be cancelled in the event that the holder has abandoned the right of residence in the territory of Hungary, or if his right of residence is terminated.

269. A *visa issued for a family member of an EEA national shall be considered void* if the data and information it contains are no longer correct (in this case, a new visa shall be issued with the correct data); it contains false or untrue information or has been forged; the holder was issued a document evidencing the right to free movement and residence; the holder is granted Hungarian citizenship or citizenship of a country whose nationals are not required to obtain a visa for entry to the territory of Hungary by virtue of any directly applicable EC legislation or an international agreement; or the holder has died. Wherein the visa authority learns of any reason during its proceedings under which the visa has to be invalidated, it shall withdraw the visa in question. Wherein a visa issued by another Schengen state is withdrawn, the issuing Schengen state shall be notified without delay.

270. An existing *local border traffic permit shall be withdrawn* if the applicant or the holder of the local border traffic permit fails to comply with the requirements for the issue of a local border traffic permit; has supplied false or untrue information in his/her application for a local border traffic permit; or has made an attempt to mislead the competent authority as far as the purpose of entry and residence is concerned. A local border traffic permit shall be considered invalid if it was withdrawn by a final decision; the data and information it contains are no longer legally applicable; it contains false or untrue information or has been forged; or the holder has died.

271. The right of permanent residence of the EEA national and his/her family member shall be lost under the following circumstances:

(a) the absence of the EEA national for a period exceeding two consecutive years; or
(b) if his/her exclusion/expulsion from Hungary is ordered;
(c) if the family relationship was established solely for the purpose of obtaining the right to residence; or

(d) false information or untrue facts are disclosed in the interest of obtaining the document evidencing right to permanent residence, on account of which the EEA national or family member has been found guilty by a final court judgment.

The Regional Directorate of the OIN shall communicate the loss of the right to permanent residence by way of a resolution. The permanent residence card shall be invalid in the event that the right to permanent residence has terminated.

272. Without repetition of the loss or terminated right to residence for persons within the ambit of the FreeA, the *legal consequences* of the lost right to residence are discussed here:

(a) The EEA national whose right to residence had been terminated shall leave the territory of Hungary. The family member who is a third-country national shall leave the country, except if granted the permission to reside on autonomous grounds. The compliance with the obligation to leave the country shall be carried out within three months from the date of the final decision.
(b) Wherein an EEA national or his/her family member has abandoned his/her right to residence in Hungary and returned to the territory of Hungary for a period of over three months, the duration required for the right to permanent residence shall begin from this time.
(c) The registration certificate shall be cancelled when the right to residence is terminated.
(d) The residence card shall be cancelled in the event of the holder's departure from Hungary, or if his right to residence is terminated.
(e) The cancellation of the registration certificate and the residence card shall be notified to the central authority of the population registry and address.
(f) With a view to enforce the compliance with exclusion orders, the authority ordering expulsion under migration laws or carrying out the expulsion ordered by the Court shall take the fingerprints and photograph of the person expelled by a Court order, or by the competent authority in conjunction with the exclusion.
(g) The data may be processed in the sub-registers maintained on documents evidencing the right to residence for five years following the termination of the right to residence, or the date of registered departure of the data subject. The central body operating the register of the personal data and addresses of citizens shall notify the central data administration authority concerning the death of an EEA national or his/her family member in Hungary, or their change of name; the termination of registered residence of an EEA national or his/her family member; and the termination of processing of the data of an EEA national or his/her family member.
(h) The competent authority shall inform the central body operating the register of the personal data and addresses of the citizens concerning the termination of the right of residence, or the date of registered departure of a data subject; the death of an EEA national or his/her family member abroad, or their change of name.

273. The visa with a validity period not exceeding three months shall be withdrawn from the third-country national under the following circumstances:

(a) he/she fails to comply with either of the requirements set out in the Schengen Borders Code (absence of valid travelling documents, the purpose of travel and residence is not proved, the required financial cover on residence and return to the home country is not ensured; he/she is under the exclusion order by a SIS alert system, he/she is endangering the public order, health, security and international relations of any Member State); in this case, the visa issued by another Schengen country shall also be invalidated;
(b) he/she has disclosed false information or untrue facts to the competent authority in the interest of obtaining the right of residence; or
(c) he/she attempted to mislead the competent authority as to the purpose of entry and stay.

274. Whereas, a visa with a validity period not exceeding three months shall be considered *void* by the ThirA if the visa has expired; the visa with a validity period not exceeding three months was withdrawn; the third-country national was issued a new visa in the proceedings for the exchange or replacement of the visa or for the extension of his/her visa's validity period; the data and information that it contains are no longer legible; it contains false or untrue information or has been forged; the holder is granted a visa for a validity period of longer than three months, interim permanent residence permit or a document evidencing the right to free movement and residence; or the holder has died.

275. A visa for a validity period of *longer than three months* shall be considered cancelled if it is no longer valid for entry into the territory of Hungary and residence in the country (expired); the visa with a validity period of longer than three months was finally withdrawn; the third-country national was issued a new visa in the proceedings for the exchange or replacement of the visa; the data and information that it contains are no longer legible; it contains false or untrue information or has been forged; the holder is granted a residence permit, a document evidencing a permanent resident status or the right to free movement and residence; or the holder has died.

276. The visa for obtaining *residence permission shall be considered invalid* if the residence permit, as the grounds for the visa was withdrawn or visa would have been withdrawn. In addition, a visa for seasonal labour and a national staying visa shall be withdrawn from third-country nationals who fail to comply with either of the requirements of entry and residence (the absence of valid travelling document, the purpose of the travel and residence not being proved, the required financial cover on residence, health care/insurance and the return to the home country not being ensured; he/she is under the exclusion or expulsion order); or the applicant has disclosed false information or untrue facts to the competent authority in the interest of obtaining the right of residence.

277. The application for a residence permit or the extension of the *residence permit* shall be refused, or if already issued, it shall be withdrawn from third-country nationals under the following circumstances:

(a) he/she fails to comply with either of the requirements of entry and residence (absence of the valid travelling document, the purpose of the travel and residence not being proved, the required financial cover on residence, health care/insurance and return to the home country not being ensured; he/she is under the exclusion or expulsion order).;
(b) he/she has disclosed false information or untrue facts to the competent authority in the interest of obtaining the right to residence;
(c) he/she suffers from any disease that is considered to constitute a threat to public health, and he/she refuses to submit to the appropriate compulsory medical treatment, or he/she fails to abide by the Hungarian health regulations while staying in Hungary; or
(d) he/she established the family relationship solely for the purpose of obtaining a residence permit on the grounds of family reunification.
(e) The Blue Card shall be withdrawn if he/she do not meet the requirement of permission, his/her high qualification is missing, his/her subsistence in Hungary is not ensured, he/she has disclosed false information or untrue facts to the competent authority in the interest of obtaining the Blue Card, his/her purpose for residence is differing form the Blue Card system, he/she has been unemployed at least for continuously three months, his/her employment was terminated at least two times since issuance of the Card, or he/she was employed for two years in a job that was different from that was determined in the labour permission.

As an exception, the residence permission may be granted for a third-country national being under the order of exclusion in the SIS alert system, taking into account the international or humanitarian commitments or the national interests. In this event, the withdrawal may be neglected.

278. A *residence permit shall be considered void* if the authorized duration of residence has expired; the residence permit was withdrawn by a final decision; the third-country national was issued a new residence permit in the proceedings for the exchange or the replacement of the residence permit, or for the extension of the residence permit; the data and information that it contains are no longer legible; it contains false or untrue information, or has been forged; the holder is granted a document evidencing a permanent resident status or the right to free movement and residence; or the holder has died.

279. A *local border traffic permit* may be withdrawn if the third-country national leaves the border area defined in the relevant international agreement without authorization. For instance, the Ukraine permit holders may enter, stay 'for a definite reason and in a definite area, and exit' without a precise definition which refers back to the 'border area' according to the party state rules (Article 1(5) and Article 2 of the Agreement between the Government of the Republic of Hungary and the Cabinet of Ministers of Ukraine on the Rules of Local Border Traffic). However, the general closure on lawful entry and residence is also ambiguous: the passengers may enter and reside 'if border residents are not considered to be a threat to public policy, internal security, public health, or the international relations of the states of the Contracting Parties, and in particular are not subject to any expulsion or ban on entry or stay on the same grounds' (Article 1(4)). Furthermore, the permit must be refused, or an existing local border traffic permit shall be withdrawn if the applicant or the holder fails to comply with the requirements for the issue of a local border traffic permit; has supplied false or untrue information in his/her application for a local border traffic permit; or has made an attempt to mislead the competent authority as far as the purpose of entry and residence is concerned.

280. A local border traffic permit shall be considered void if it was withdrawn by a final decision; the data and information that it contains are no longer legible; it contains false or untrue information or has been forged; or the holder has died. The decision for the withdrawal of the local border traffic permit lies with the authority that has issued the local border traffic permit, or if held by a third-country national who resides in Hungary, with the competent Regional Directorate to the place where the residence of the third-country national is located.

281. An *interim permanent residence permit may be withdrawn* if the third-country national no longer satisfies the requirements of self-subsistence, accommodation and holding a health insurance or ability to cover a health care payment. It shall be withdrawn from a third-country national who has been expelled or excluded. The interim permanent residence permit issued to a family member of a third-country national living with the said third-country national shall be withdrawn if the breadwinner's permanent residence permit has been withdrawn; or the family relationship no longer exists, unless the family member in question independently satisfies the conditions of residence (self-subsistence, accommodation being ensured and holding a health insurance or ability to cover a health care payment) following the breadwinner's death. The migration authority shall notify the authority of another Member State of the EU concerning the issuance of an interim permanent residence permit, and also if withdrawn with the reasons indicated, wherein the EC long-term residence permit was issued for the third-country national.

282. An *interim permanent residence permit shall be considered void* if the authorized period of residence has expired; the interim permanent residence permit was withdrawn by a final decision; the third-country national was issued a new document in the proceedings for the exchange or replacement of the interim permanent residence permit or for the extension of his/her interim permanent residence permit's validity period; the data and information it contains are no longer legible; it contains false or untrue information or has been forged; the holder is granted a Hungarian citizenship, a national permanent residence permit, EC permanent residence permit, or a document evidencing the right to free movement and residence; or the holder has died.

283. The migration authority *may withdraw the permit of settlement, the national permanent residence permit or the immigration permit* in the following cases:

(a) the circumstances based on which they were issued have changed to an extent that the criteria for the permission are no longer satisfied, and if a period of five years has not elapsed from the date of issuance of the permit;
(b) it was issued on the grounds of family reunification, and the marriage was dissolved within three years from receipt of the permit for reasons other than the spouse's death, or if the third-country national no longer has parental custody, unless the third-country national in question has resided in Hungary for at least four years as a permanent resident or in possession of the immigrant status;
(c) the third-country national has departed from the territory of Hungary and remained absent for a period of over six months.

284. The migration authority shall withdraw the *permit of settlement, immigration or the national permanent residence permit* under the following circumstances:

(a) the permit holder has disclosed false information or untrue facts to the competent authority in the interest of obtaining the permit;
(b) the permit holder is a minor and the right to residence from the parent exercising parental custody who is also a third-country national is withdrawn, while the requirements of the minor's residence in Hungary by the other parent exercising parental custody are not ensured in the country;
(c) it was granted to a third-country national on the grounds of family reunification, and his/her spouse with a Hungarian citizenship has departed from Hungary with a view to establish residence elsewhere, or the lawful residence of the third-country national's spouse in the territory of Hungary has been terminated; or
(d) the third-country national to whom it was issued is expelled or excluded.

285. An immigration permit, permanent residence permit and national permanent residence permit shall be considered *invalid* if its validity period has expired; the permit was withdrawn by a final decision; the third-country national was issued a new document in the proceedings for the exchange or replacement of the document, or for the extension of the document's validity period; the data and information that it contains are no longer legible; it contains false or untrue information or has been forged; the holder is granted Hungarian citizenship, an EC permanent residence permit or document evidencing the right to free movement and residence; or the holder has died.

286. The migration authority shall withdraw the *EC permanent residence permit* if the holder was absent from the territory of the EC for a period of over twelve months – the Blue Card holder and his/her family member for an uninterrupted period of twenty-four months – ; was granted a long-term resident status in another Member State of the EU; was absent from Hungary for a period of over six years; has disclosed false information or untrue facts to the migration authority in the interest of obtaining the permit; or his/her expulsion or exclusion is ordered. However, an EC permanent residence permit shall be considered void if its validity period has expired; it was withdrawn by a final decision; the holder was issued a new document in the proceedings for the exchange or replacement of the document or for the extension of the document's validity period; the data and information that it contains are no longer legible; it contains false or untrue information or has been forged; the holder is granted a document evidencing the right to free movement and residence, or Hungarian citizenship; or the holder has died. Any third-country national whose EC permanent residence permit has been withdrawn by the migration authority for departure, shall be granted a new EC permanent residence permit when re-applying, without checking the conditions of permission.

287. The *legal consequences of the lost right to residence* for the persons within the ambit of the ThirdA are as follows:

(a) The migration authority, if it finds that a third-country national who has lawfully resided in Hungary no longer has the right of residence, shall adopt a decision to withdraw the document evidencing his/her lawful residence, and shall order him/her to leave the country within thirty days, or exceptionally within sixty days. It shall not apply if the right of residence was terminated due to the expulsion or exclusion of the third-country national due to a SIS alert or he/she has expressly refused to leave the country.
(b) With a view to avoiding any overlap in the proceedings and for establishing the identity of the third-country national, the authority ordering the obligation to leave the country, the expulsion by migration laws, compulsory confinement, exclusion, detention by migration laws or carrying out the expulsion ordered by the Court shall take his/her fingerprints and photograph.
(c) The competent Regional Directorate of the OIN shall send an official copy of the final and executable resolution for the withdrawal of an immigration permit, permanent residence permit, interim permanent residence permit, national permanent residence permit, or an EC permanent residence permit to the central body operating the register of the personal data and addresses of habitants within five working days, and shall confiscate the personal identification document, the personal identification number and official address card of the third-country national affected. These documents shall be sent to the central body operating the register of the personal data and addresses of the habitants.
(d) The migration authority shall process the defined personal data of the third-country national in connection with applications for a immigration permit, permanent residence permit, interim permanent residence permit, national permanent residence permit or an EC permanent residence permit as well as the issued permit (e.g., natural identification data; photograph of the face; particulars of travel document; the date of first entry and final exit; home address) that shall be kept in stock for twenty years in connection with the refusal of an application for these permits from the date of refusal, or from the date of termination of the legal status in question, according to the ThirdA.

Chapter 2. Legal and Administrative Procedures

288. The family member of the EEA national *shall notify any changes* in his/her title of residence, and shall provide proof for the right to further residence. Moreover, he/she has to notify the termination of his/her relationship underlying his/her right of residence. In this context, the meaning of 'household' is relevant. It covers the community of persons living with an EEA national or a Hungarian citizen under the same roof, and using this address as the registered permanent or customary residence. The right to residence of the third-country national whose residence was granted on the grounds of family reunification as a dependant or a member of the household of a Hungarian citizen or an EEA national shall terminate when their *relationship* is terminated (living under the same roof, death of the person who was the legal reference on residence, abandonment of the right to residence, invalidation of marriage or divorce) unless the family member obtains an autonomous right to residence alone. As is obvious, if the breadwinner no longer exercises the right to residence or if there is any other change in his/her status, it influences the right to residence of the family member. In this context, the absence of sufficient resources for himself/herself to become an unreasonable burden on the social assistance system is a key factor in the loss of right to residence.

289. Where the residence of an EEA national or his/her family member represents a threat and is potentially *dangerous to the national security* of Hungary, the NSO or the counter-terrorism unit of the Police shall contact the competent Regional Directorate of the OIN to adopt the decision on termination of right to residence due to the non-fulfilment of its requirements. The migration laws define no conditions of threat or danger for national security and how it can be endangered by migrants, so the security services shall implement the abstract definition in the SecA without specifications or examples on the migratory movements or the migrants' behaviour. In accordance with this, the security services must determine whether the entry and residence of the migrant endangers the national security interests (the integrity of the state, constitutional order and sovereignty that would be threatened by covert and aggressive efforts in contact with the economy, governance, defence, political freedom and human rights including terror actions, illicit drug traffic and technology transfer, as per Article 74 a.).

290. At the time of the registration of residence, the EEA nationals and family members who are third-country nationals shall – enclosed with their application for residence card – supply a statement as to whether they *suffer from any infectious disease* or contagious parasitic disease as specified in the HealthD and considered to constitute a threat to public health, or if they receive a compulsory and regular treatment with regard to the said diseases. If, according to the EEA national's or his/her family member's statement, the *health risk* exists, the Regional Directorate of the OIN shall notify the competent institute of the health care authority. The institute may compel the EEA national or his/her family member to undergo the necessary medical examinations. Violating the rules of conduct and official decisions concerning medical treatment or therapy, the institute (health care authority) shall take the necessary disease control measures; or shall initiate the expulsion or propose the duration of the exclusion of the persons in concern.

291. The *unreasonable social burden* means a lawful reason for the loss of the right to residence (For more details, see paragraphs 288 and 137.). An EEA national or his/her family member shall be considered to have become an unreasonable burden on the social assistance system of Hungary if he/she draws social benefit for the elderly under the SocialA, regular social aid under the SocialA including any periods of suspension and reinstatement of its payment, or benefit to home care of a sick family member under the SocialA for any period of more than three months. If any of the aforementioned benefits is not provided on a regular basis, the period shall be calculated within one year prior to the first day of payment included. Furthermore, for the purposes of determining whether an EEA national and his/her family member have become an unreasonable burden, the competent Regional Directorate of the OIN shall take into account the personal circumstances of the person in question, such as the duration of residence in Hungary, the duration of payment of benefits and whether the difficulties are to be considered permanent or temporary.

292. A document evidencing the right to residence shall be invalidated if the EEA national or his/her family member has *abandoned the right to residence* in the territory of Hungary, or the right to residence or permanent right to residence is terminated. In addition, a document evidencing the right to residence shall be void if there are any changes in the particulars contained in the document, exclusive of the address; if the document has expired; if the document is damaged and the data it contains is no longer correct and legible; if the document contains false or untrue information or has been forged; if the holder has died; or if the holder was granted Hungarian citizenship. A registration certificate and residence card shall be *invalidated* if the holder is issued a document evidencing the right to permanent residence. The issuing authority shall withdraw these invalid documents in a decision declaring that the document is void. The competent Regional Directorate of the OIN that ordered the withdrawal of a document shall provide for the invalidation of the document, and to record in the appropriate sub-register or to issue a new document.

293. The competent Regional Directorate of the OIN follows some *common procedural provisions* in the assessment of the loss of the right to residence, as follows:

(a) In the proceedings launched upon the request in accordance with the FreeA or ThirdA, the client shall submit his/her request in person, and shall appear in person in front of the competent migration authority to collect his/her registration certificate. It may not require an applicant to appear in person if he/she is unable to do so due to health reasons.
(b) If the application or the request that is submitted by the client is incomplete, the competent authority shall promptly make out a notice for requesting the missing information or documents.
(c) Those proceedings in which the applicant is required to appear in person cannot be administered by way of electronic means.

(d) The competent migration authority is entitled to check the compliance with the conditions for residence and with the requirements of notifications as set out in the FreeA or ThirdA, if there is any reason to believe that these conditions are not satisfied or that the person affected failed to comply with any requirement of the notification.

294. The decision for the *withdrawal of a visa* for a validity period not exceeding three months before entry belongs to the competence of the visa authority that obtains the official information regarding the relevant conditions of the migrant. If the third-country national resides in Hungary, the visa is invalidated by the local Regional Directorate of the OIN near his/her address in the country. Wherein a transit visa or a short-stay visa issued by another Schengen state is withdrawn, the issuing Schengen state shall be notified without delay, within seventy-two hours at the most. The decision of the Regional Directorate rejecting the application for the extension of a visa for a validity period not exceeding three months shall contain a command ordering the affected third-country national to exit the territory of the Schengen area upon the expiry of his/her visa.

295. The *significant changes in the circumstances* imply in the context of the third-country national with a permanent/resident status that he/she is no longer able to support himself/herself and his/her dependent family members, nor is he/she able to provide a place of abode; he/she is receiving social welfare benefits and support in spite of having full capacity to work; or he/she is no longer provided support or a place of abode by the family member who had previously agreed to provide the same. In order to implement the criteria of right to residence, any third-country national who received his/her permanent residence permit or national permanent residence permit on the grounds of family relations is obliged to report to the competent Regional Directorate of the OIN next to the place of his/her residence if his/her marriage is dissolved or in the event of the death of his/her spouse within sixty days following the spouse's death or the final Court ruling for the dissolution of the marriage with the relevant documents attached. The third-country national with an immigrant or permanent resident status must notify the competent Regional Directorate if he/she leaves Hungary for resettlement in another country. Furthermore, the third-country nationals with an immigration permit, permanent residence permit or a national permanent residence permit shall be required to notify, in writing, the competent Regional Directorate located near his/her place of residence concerning his/her intention to exit the territory of Hungary for a period longer than six months, with the reasons and the planned duration of foreign residence indicated. If he/she leaves Hungary for a period not exceeding two years for reasons other than resettlement, the competent Regional Directorate may not withdraw his/her immigration permit, permanent residence permit, or national permanent residence permit, provided that the third-country national in question resided in Hungary for at least one hundred and eighty days within a period of one year before the notice was filed.

Part V. Sanctions

Chapter 1. Sanctions

296. Describing the system of sanctions, a differentiation may be done on the grounds of *who are subjected to sanctions*, as follows:

(a) the migrant (and his/her family as directly affected), but 'collective punishment' is incompatible with the Fundamental Law and collective expulsion in the Additional Protocol to the European Convention of Human Rights;
(b) the smuggler and human trafficker as offender who exploits other persons;
(c) the employer of the migrant;
(d) the carrier company;
(e) the legal personality (corporate entity); or
(f) other facilitator for illicit entry, residence or movement.

297. The other differentiating method is based on the *nature of the legal consequences*, such as the following:

(a) derogation or limitation of rights (prohibition of free movement, entry and residence in the territory of Hungary, right to family and private life, right to property, right to participate on public procurement);
(b) withdrawal or refusal of a certificate, entitlement or permission issued by an authority that are frequently required for the practice of rights;
(c) deprivation of liberty;
(d) imposition of a fine;
(e) the sanction is applicable once, for a fixed period or for an indefinite period; however, its maintenance may be reviewed.

These negative outcomes may depend on the culpability or not, and together with the procedural guarantees they would form the institutions belonging to various legal branches (administrative, penal, labour or civil law).

298. The legal rules on the entry and residence in Hungary and the removal of non-nationals contain numerous restrictions and entitlements for the discretionary power of the authority in the proceedings. In this context, the expulsion, deportation and exclusion (prohibited entry and residence) can be considered to be the main sanctions against migrants, while fines and imprisonment would be the most painful consequences for others who intended to gain from the exploitation of other people. However, the other coercive measures and administrative requirements overlap with and secure the genuine sanctions. Furthermore, the Constitutional Court confirms that the rules on accession and the residence in Hungary have *some specificity forming those to a separate field of legislation (alien policing rules)*:[214]

(a) The alien policing procedures occupy a special position within the procedural codes, because the protection of national and state interests shall be observed together with the EC law and the constitutional requirements.
(b) Exceptional measures or decisions may be issued without the right to remedy (e.g., the minister, as an exception, relaxes some requirements of the non-eligible application), or a single instance in remedy is compatible with constitutional system. The dual level in legal remedies (appeal and judicial review) is not a general requirement, or the decisions would not be contested on the ground of equity.
(c) The hardly coherent normative text is not an automatic violation of the Constitution, for instance, the right to legal remedy and the rules on movement including amendments equally require a qualified majority of votes in legislation, so their hierarchical positions are the same.
(d) The distinction among subjects of law means no discrimination or violation of the equality of rights. For instance, more rights for family members of EEA nationals than for other non-nationals or different sanctions in connection with movement remain within the constitutional framework. However, the limitation in entry and residence right of the family member of a Hungarian citizen was urgently modified in the legislation as an unconstitutional provision.
(e) The data of the presented documents of the passenger and the vehicle shall be controlled on the ground of alien policing databases (registries) in order to screen out excluded travellers, persons under arrest warrants, false or forged documents or abusive persons. This control mechanism is a necessary and lawful data management based on the national and the EC (Schengen Border Code[215]) regulations. If the personal and other data shall be preserved, the duration of this data storage shall be determined by law in connection with the third-country nationals' control on legality. In this context, it is necessary and reasonable, and it implies a proportional limitation of the right to self-determination of personal data.
(f) The repetition of abstract criteria of the constitutional values in the legislation cannot meet the requirements of constitutional law-making. This simplification is acceptable neither in statutory laws on deprivation of liberty, nor on any other limitation of the fundamental rights. As a result, the legislator has to determine the precise conditions of confinement and accomplishment of the public interest.

214. Constitutional Court's decisions (775/B/2006. AB határozat, 220/B/2005. AB végzés, 718/B/2000. AB határozat, 35/1991. (VI. 20.) AB határozat).

215. Regulation 562/2006/EC on the rules governing the movement of persons across the borders.

However, these decisions of the Constitutional Court can be considered to form marginal parts of its jurisdiction as well as the entire migration law within the legislation.

299. There are two sensitive points in the sanctioning and implementation of alien policing measures, as follows:

(a) the *respect for non-refoulement* together with the *prohibition of torture* and capital punishment; and
(b) the *respect for family and private life* (Articles 3 and 8 of ECHR).

The first requires substantial and procedural guarantees against arbitrary refusal or removal of migrants in each authorization procedure. For instance, the Optional Protocol of the CAT was ratified by Hungary setting up a proper scheme for prevention of torture, inhuman and degrading treatment. The national controlling mechanism belongs to the competence of the Ombudsman that starts to operate in late 2014.[216] That would be vital in alien policing which implements re-admission, Dublin and Prüm Treaty procedures or expulsion and detention of non-nationals.[217] The case law of the ECHR and the ECJ has been developed, but incorporating its conclusion into the legislation requires less energy and time than into the legal (authority) praxis. Nevertheless, this process has taken at least fifteen years in part and has not finished yet. Moreover, the AsylA, the ThirdA, the FreeA and the implementing decrees provide details on the evaluation of prohibition, removal and prevention of torture, capital punishment or persecution, but the substance of the family and private life (and the best interests of a child) has been fragmented in the regulation in Hungary (Gyeney, 2014). Beyond the general conclusions from the case law, the message of the ECHR is not simple enough to be adapted in particular towards promoting public and personal security. The cases pertaining to Article 8 are notable for their lack of clarity and precision (Harvey, 2001). In an area where economic reasoning and instrumental thinking can dominate, it is for the Court, and on its basis the national Courts, to uphold the value of human dignity and the importance of rights which attach to personhood and not to the status. After the accession to the EU, these two points of reference have been extended by the EC law as regards the limitation on the power of exclusion and expulsion of EU citizens because exclusion or expulsion form an exception to the right to free movement, or the right to continued economic activity. Therefore, it is always for the authority to justify *on strict grounds* its use against persons residing on the state territory, whose right of residence derives from the EC law (Guild, 2001).

---

216. Act CXLIII of 2011 on promulgation of the OPCAT.
217. It was urged recently in twenty-nine proposals made by the Human Rights Council within the universal periodic reporting (UPR) procedure in UN to the national report on human rights in Hungary. (July 2011), <www.kormany.hu>.

300. The secondary EC law[218] on the basis of the Treaty (Article 39) clearly requires the narrow interpretation of grounds for expulsion from the Member States, in the transposition and implementation:[219]

(a) The distinction shall be made between the public policy and the public security. The latter is generally interpreted to cover the internal and the external security along the lines of preserving the integrity of the territory of a Member State and its institutions. The public policy is below this threshold, and it is generally interpreted along the lines of preventing the disturbance of social order. For instance, the non-registration of a migrant does not threaten the public policy and public order.
(b) Restrictive measures may be taken only on the individual evaluation of the behaviour that represents a genuine and sufficiently serious, real threat affecting one of the fundamental interests of the society. Preventive or automatic expulsion (e.g., following a criminal conviction) is not allowed.
(c) The authority must conduct a proportionality assessment to decide whether the person concerned can be denied entry or removed on the grounds of public policy or public order if the protected interests are identified. It has to carefully take into account the personal and family situation of the migrant concerned and assess whether the measure is strictly necessary.
(d) There is a need for increased protection against expulsion (in the case of permanent residents after having resided for five years in the country, residence more than ten years and minors).
(e) Adopting an expulsion measure on imperative or serious grounds does not necessarily imply urgency. The assessment of urgency must be clearly and separately substantiated (e.g., why a one-month deadline is imposed in an expulsion).
(f) The procedural safeguards shall be provided (fully recorded factual and legal grounds, right to defence, judicial review, effective remedy and notification of the decision).

The EU law at present does not provide for any specific sanctions for abuse or fraud (e.g., marriage of convenience in order to obtain the right to family unification and residence) beyond ceasing the right to residence. Therefore it belongs to the competence of the Member States under the civil, administrative or criminal law – but all of them shall be effective, non-discriminatory and proportionate in their sanctions. The Hungarian legislation has hardly fulfilled this set of requirements, because the expulsion and protection against removal have been basically dependent on the legal status of the migrant (settlement permit holders, residence permit holders, union citizens and stateless persons) instead of clearly determined conditions of threatened public security and public order that cannot be measured mechanically with the number of years of imprisonment (Tóth, 2001a). The

218. Directive 2004/38/EC on the right of citizens of the EU and their family members to move and reside freely within the territory of the Member States.
219. Communication from the Commission to the European Parliament and the Council on guidance for better transposition and application of Directive 2004/38/EC – COM (2009) 313/4.

individualization of the threat and the assessment of the migrant's personal conditions have remained the most visible shortcoming yet.

301. From a logical point of view, the illegal entry may cover a short part of illicit movement, because the migrant has to be apprehended only at the crossing point or along the border zone. Otherwise, the starting point of unlawful behaviour cannot be determined, so for practical reasons the entire sanction system is based on illegal residence that automatically shall include an illegal entry, with the exception of the overstayed (registered) or abusive (irregular) migrants. For this reason, the *illegal residence and its facilitators* are at the centre of sanctioning.

§1. Administrative Sanctions

302. The refusal of entry and sending back from the state border are not sanctions, but they would be the consequence of an expulsion or exclusion order (prohibited entry and residence for some years or for an indefinite period) including the issuance of an SIS alert or a European Arrest Warrant. The authority carrying out border checks may *refuse the entry* of an EEA national or his/her family member(s) who have been excluded from the territory of Hungary due to the ordered prohibition of entry and residence. According to the FreeA, a refused person shall be returned to the country of origin; to the country that is liable to readmit him/her; to the country where his/her customary residence is located; or to a third country receiving him/her. This return shall be ordered by a decision explaining the precise reasons, and it shall take effect immediately with some exceptions. Any person whose entry was refused must remain on the means of transport that is scheduled to depart, or to transfer onto another means of transport of the carrier that is liable to provide return transport for the person in question. Until departure, the person ordered to return shall remain in a designated place located in the frontier zone (transit zone) of the state for a maximum period of seventy-two hours, as instructed by the Police carrying out border checks. If the return procedure cannot be carried out within seventy-two hours or the waiting period for the missing documents or evidence for entry expires without success, such that the withdrawal of the return order is not possible, he/she may then be expelled (See other details in paragraph 60).

303. The *refusal of entry* of the person within the ambit of the ThirdA shall be based on the Schengen Border Code, and the passenger must return to the country of origin, to the country that is liable to accept him/her, to the country where his/her customary residence is located or to any third country receiving him/her. In the event of non-compliance with the requirements of entry and residence, the third-country national shall be authorized only on humanitarian grounds, on the grounds of national interest or because of international obligations. If the entry is refused, because the third-country national is under prohibition of entry and residence, the *issued visa shall be void.* A third-country national whose entry was refused and is turned back shall remain for a maximum period of eight hours on the means *of transport that is scheduled* to depart to the point of origin or another destination of transit; he/she will remain in a *designated place* located in the frontier zone for a maximum period of seventy-two hours, or if having arrived by means of air transport, in a designated place of the airport for a maximum period of eight days; or s/he will transfer onto another means of transport of the carrier that is liable to provide return transport. If the return procedure cannot be carried out within seventy-two hours or eight days, the third-country national shall *be expelled following his/her admission*. In this case, the expulsion must not be accompanied by a *ban of entry and residence* (exclusion) with the exception that his/her exclusion is based on international obligation(s), or whose exclusion is determined by the EU Council or whose entry and stay interfere with national security or public order.

304. The apprehended, unlawfully entered migrants – either regarding the refused entry, or regarding the expulsion – are sent back on the grounds of *readmission agreements*.[220] These agreements have been concluded with approximately forty states, providing a less formal procedure on return and admission by the host country.[221] Concurrently liability for the minor offence of illegal entry would be established but it takes a longer time at police and court without chance to pay the imposed (instant or regular) fine (For more details see paragraphs 305 and 309.). According to these agreements, the return of citizens of the other party state, the readmission of its own nationals and the transit of all other migrants who have trespassed the rules on entry and residence are undertaken without specific formalities (e.g., the citizenship of the requested state shall be probable or proved in connection with the apprehended migrant) within a defined short period. If a counter-proof is available on a non-citizen, his/her admission may be refused, and the requesting state shall receive him/her back. In the event of proved citizenship of the returned migrant or a migrant who was provided with a valid visa, the residence or settlement permit issued by a requested party state, his/her readmission is promptly provided in the country of origin or transit within thirty-ninety days since his/her apprehension. Although these agreements contain some references to the non-refoulement, protection seekers, personal data protection and persons in need of assistance in travel, the most important guarantees on accessing the fair procedure (on asylum, victims' protection, family unification, interpretation, medical and child care) are missing. Formally, the readmission agreement is not a sanction, but its effect would hinder the access of genuine protection and destination. This type of

220. The Schengen Handbook (Appendix No. 39) determines the main components of readmission of illegal migrants, and the Council has concluded agreements or negotiated it with about twenty states. The Frontex, the European Return Fund and IOM also assist the transfer of illegal migrant. Finally the European Parliament and the Council Directive 2008/115/EC (16 Dec. 2008) on common standards and procedure in Member States for returning illegally staying third-country nationals (Return Directive) sets up the frame of co-operation. However about 80% of removal of illegal migrant within five–seven days are executed on the grounds of bilateral agreements, yearly 1500–3500 persons.

221. For instance, Act XXIV of 2000 on the publication of the agreement concluded between the governments of the Hungarian Republic and the Moldovan Republic on return and reception of illegally residing persons in Moldova or in Hungary; Act XXII of 2003 on publication of the agreement concluded between the governments of the Hungarian Republic and the Serbia-Montenegro on return and reception of illegally residing persons in Serbia-Montenegro or in Hungary.

agreement has been an organic part of visa facilitation or waiving programmes and the cooperation in justice, security and home affairs alongside the EU (Tóth, 2001b).

305. The Act *on Minor Offences* (MinofA) contains certain administrative legal sanctions against migrants who trespassed the rules on border crossing and registration. According to the MinofA, 'minor offence' means an unlawful action or omission that accomplishes a misdemeanour constituted and punished by the law and a decree (adopted by the government or local municipals concerning details or the amount of fine). 'Misdemeanour' implies threatening public order to a lower extent than would constitute an offence – so the behaviour shall be constituted either a crime or a misdemeanour. The culpability of a natural person over the age of fourteen years is required; however, certain minor offences are not punished if the perpetrator was only negligent. The legal treatment of the abettor and the instigator is the same as of the perpetrator in minor offences. The procedure for a minor offence may be launched within six months from the commission. The ongoing trial, investigation and measures of the public prosecutor or the Court interrupt this prescription period of the minor offence (e.g., in the last phase of a procedure, it is proved that the behaviour in question is not an offence but a misdemeanour), but for over two years after the action the perpetrator is not held responsible for a misdemeanour. Due to the diversity of minor offences, the sanctions (fine, detention, instant fine) are imposed in the most cases by the Police and the district governmental office. The complaint of the perpetrator or a legality-based protest of the public prosecutor shall be decided by the local Court (single judge) passing the final decision within thirty days. Moreover, the Policemen may haul up the perpetrator of the minor offence in connection with alien policing, travel document, prohibited border crossing, and it may limit his/her liberty for a maximum of twelve hours by the PolA. Its reason shall be indicated to the apprehended person giving him/her a certificate on the length of limited liberty. Many apprehended migrants are not able to pay the fine (EUR 17 up to EUR 1,500) while proceeding authority may seize their assets for guarantee. The MinofA determines some minor offences relating to migrants as follows:

(a) a fine may be imposed by the Police upon a person (whether national or non-national) who *attempts to cross the state border without permission or in a non-permissible way, or the same has been done by him/her.* The illegal border crossing includes trespassing the legal rules on travel documents (e.g., using valid passport of another person) (Article 204). These terms are ambiguous, because the subject (perpetrator) and the commission of this minor offence are misunderstood: the internal and external borders are legally different, and the persons within the ambit of the FreeA or the ThirdA are merged.
(b) a fine may be imposed by the Police on a person who *trespasses the provisions in connection with order, protection and control on state borders, including a violated restriction* on how to use any real estate in the border zone (e.g., reconstruction of a building without permission of the Police). Theoretically, he/she can move across the border during this action irregularly (Article 205).

(c) a fine may be imposed by the Police on a person who *trespasses the rules on registration and residence of non-nationals* (Article 208). This term is too wide without special reference on diversity in reasons and threat on public order.
(d) a detention up to sixty days may be imposed on a person who relocates, takes away or removes the *signal of the state border* (e.g., an illegal migrant is crossing the green border at night and he kicks it) (Article 177(2a)).
(e) a fine may be imposed on a person who cannot *present a document on his/her identity* (e.g., showing up the passport or residence permit), or he/she refuses to present it, or he/she states untrue personal data in police street check (Article 207). This trespassing may cumulate with other minor offence if foreigner is a beggar (together with a minor) or a suit-case trader without permission in a public place. Naturally, apprehended foreigner dislikes being identified and putting his/her name to the register of minor offences.

306. The immigration authority, if it finds that a third-country national who has lawfully resided in Hungary no longer has the right to residence, shall adopt a resolution *to refuse his/her application for a residence permit or to withdraw the document* evidencing right to residence of the third-country national in question, and shall order him/her to leave the territory of the EU. The third-country nationals may seek remedy against the expulsion order in the appeal submitted to challenge the resolution adopted to refuse the application for residence permit or to withdraw the document evidencing right to residence. If the court's decision is in favour of expulsion or the immigration authority declares the stay of the third-country national to be illegal, the immigration authority shall adopt a *decision ordering his/her exit from the territory of the EU.*

307. The authority shall prescribe the time limit for *voluntary departure* in its resolution ordering expulsion, or in its ruling adopted for carrying out the expulsion ordered by the court so that it falls between the seventh and the thirtieth day following the time of delivery of the resolution for expulsion, if the third-country national agrees to leave the country on his/her own accord. Upon request with reference to personal circumstances (such as the length of stay in Hungary, on account of which more time is required for making preparations for departure, or the existence of other family and social links), the authority may extend the period for voluntary departure up to sixty days. If the child who is in the parental custody of an expelled third-country national pursues studies in an public education institution, the immigration authority may – upon request or on its motion – extend the period for voluntary departure by a period up to the end of the current semester. Extension of the time limit for voluntary departure shall be ordered by way of a ruling. Enforcement of the ruling on the extension of the time limit for voluntary departure may be contested.

308. No time limit for voluntary departure shall be specified, or the immigration authority may set the deadline for leaving the territory of the EU before the seventh day following the time of delivery of the resolution for expulsion (immediately) in the following cases:

(a) the third-country national's right of residence was terminated due to his/her expulsion or exclusion, or an alert has been issued in the SIS regarding him/her for the purpose of refusing entry and the right to residence;
(b) the third-country national's application for residence permit was refused by the authority because he/she has disclosed false information or untrue facts to the competent authority in the interest of obtaining the right to residence, or misled the competent authority in respect of the purpose of residence, or he/she established the family relationship for the purpose of obtaining a residence permit on the grounds of family reunification;
(c) the third-country national has expressly refused to leave the country voluntarily, or, based on other substantiated reasons, is not expected to abide by the decision in favour of his/her expulsion; or
(d) the third-country national's residence in Hungary represents a serious threat to public security, public policy or national security.

If, according to the immigration authority's resolution, expulsion is to be carried out by way of deportation, a time limit shall not be specified for voluntary departure.

309. The immigration authority shall *independently order the exclusion* of a third-country national whose whereabouts are unknown or who resides outside the territory of Hungary, and: who must not be allowed to enter the territory of Hungary under international commitment; or who is to be excluded as per the decision of the Council of the European Union; whose entry and residence represent a threat to national security, public security or public policy; who has failed to repay any refundable financial aid received from the State of Hungary; who has failed to pay any instant fine or a fine imposed in conclusion of a misdemeanour proceeding within the prescribed deadline, and it cannot be recovered or collected.

310. The immigration authority shall order the *expulsion* of a third-country national under immigration laws who meets the following conditions:

(a) has crossed the frontier of Hungary illegally, or has attempted to do so;
(b) fails to comply with the requirements set out in ThirdA for the right to residence;
(c) was engaged in any gainful employment in the absence of the prescribed work permit or any permit prescribed in ThirdA;
(d) whose entry and residence represent a threat to national security, public security or public policy; or
(e) whose entry and residence represent a threat and is potentially dangerous to public health.

An independent exclusion order and an expulsion order under immigration laws may be issued upon the initiative of law enforcement agencies within the framework of discharging their duties relating to the protection of public policies as defined by law. The duration of exclusion that was ordered independently shall be adapted to the period of the underlying obligation or exclusion, or for a period of up to three years, and it may be extended by a maximum of three additional years at a time. An exclusion order shall be cancelled forthwith when the relevant grounds no longer exist. An exclusion ordered independently may not be appealed while independently ordered exclusion for reasons in (point of (a) and (b) shall not be contested at all.

311. The immigration authority shall not order the *expulsion* of any third-country national who meets the following conditions:

(a) has been expelled by the competent authority of another Member State of the EU, for the reason that the person in question represents a genuine, present and sufficiently serious threat affecting national security or public security; in connection with a conviction under the laws of the country where the resolution was adopted for an offence punishable by a penalty involving imprisonment of at least one year; based on suspicion of serious criminal offences; or based on failure to comply with regulations on the entry or residence of foreign nationals. In this case the existing expulsion order of other state shall be executed;
(b) is residing unlawfully in Hungary but another Member State of the EU shall readmit him/her on the grounds of a readmission or other agreement concluded before 13 January 2009. The readmission is ordered in a resolution that may be contested within twenty-four hours without delay. In the execution of the readmission order, the rules of deportation shall be implemented.

312. According to the ThirdA, *exclusion shall be ordered in conjunction with expulsion* ordered under immigration laws, if the immigration authority has ordered the deportation of the third-country national concerned. The third-country national affected shall have the right to appeal the resolution adopted separately on exclusion. There shall be no further appeal against the resolution. The appeal shall be submitted within twenty-four hours from the time of delivery of the resolution, and it shall be decided within eight days. Where expulsion is ordered on the grounds of ThirdA above, the immigration authority may also order exclusion taking into account the nature and severity of the infringement, the personal circumstances of the third-country national concerned, and considering whether his/her continued residence represents a serious threat to public security, public policy or national security. The duration of an exclusion measure shall be determined in years, and it may not exceed five years with the exception of the case when the residence of the third-country national in Hungary represents a serious threat to public security, public policy or national security. In this latter event, the maximum period of exclusion may be ten years. The exclusion ordered in conjunction with expulsion shall apply from the date of departure, or if this is not known, from the deadline prescribed therein. Third-country nationals whose exclusion was ordered may enter the territory of Hungary only upon the special consent of the ordering authority. The immigration authority may withdraw – upon request or on its own motion – the exclusion order if continued enforcement is no longer justified due to major changes in the underlying circumstances.

313. The immigration authority shall have regard for *numerous personal conditions in expulsion decisions as a kind of protection for third-country nationals.*

(a) The following factors are taken into account before adopting an expulsion order under immigration laws concerning a third-country national who is holding a residence permit issued on the grounds of family reunification: the duration of stay; the age and family status of the third-country national affected, possible consequences of his/her expulsion on his/her family members; links of the third-country national to Hungary, or the absence of links with the country of origin.
(b) Any third-country national who resides in Hungary under immigrant or permanent resident status or he/she is bound to a third-country national residing also in the country under immigrant or permanent resident status by marriage or registered partnership, and has a residence permit, may be expelled only if his/her continued residence represents a serious threat to national security, public security or public policy.
(c) Immediate family members of a third-country national who has applied to the refugee authority for refugee status for the duration of the application pending, and those with refugee status or to whom any subsidiary form of protection or temporary protection was granted, may be expelled only if his/her continued residence represents a serious threat to national security, public security or public policy.
(d) Third-country nationals who are victims of human trafficking may be expelled during the reflection period they are afforded, only if their residence in Hungary constitutes any threat to national security, public security or public policy.
(e) An unaccompanied minor may be expelled only if adequate protection is ensured in his country of origin or in a third country by means of reuniting him/her with other members of his family or by state or other institutional care.
(f) The immigration authority may abstain from ordering the expulsion of a third-country national who resides in Hungary illegally, if he/she is the subject of a pending procedure for renewing his/her residence permit or other authorization offering a right to stay in the country.
(g) Expulsion may not be ordered under immigration laws, and exclusion may not be ordered independently against a third-country national who was convicted for a crime in the Court, yet the sentence did not include expulsion in any form, neither as a principal punishment nor as an ancillary punishment.
(h) A third-country national holding an authorization issued by another Member State of the EU offering a right to stay or international protection status in the territory of that Member State, may be expelled only if he/she refused to leave the territory of Hungary upon receipt of notice from the immigration authority in writing, or his/her residence here represents a serious threat to national security, public security or public policy. If EC residence permit or protected status holders and their family members expelled from other Member State of the EU, their return to Hungary shall be allowed.
(i) A third-country national in possession of a valid residence permit or (expired) Blue Card issued by another Member State of the EU may be expelled by the immigration authority to that state. If the Blue Card holder is expelled by another Member State of the EU, his/her return to Hungary shall be allowed.

If the immigration authority decided to abstain from ordering expulsion, and the third-country national is unable to satisfy the statutory requirements of residence, the immigration authority shall issue a humanitarian residence permit on his/her behalf.

314. If during immigration proceedings for the expulsion of a third-country national there is any indication that the Dublin Regulations should be applied, and he/she did not submit an application for recognition in accordance with the AsylA, the immigration authority shall move to request the refugee unit of the OIN to carry out the Dublin process, and shall suspend the immigration proceedings until the conclusion of the Dublin process. The suspension of expulsion order is also required until the final decision on recognition if third-country national's expulsion was ordered before his/her asylum claim. The ruling for the suspension of the procedure may not be appealed. Where, in accordance with the Dublin Regulations, any state that applies the Dublin Regulations is required to take the applicant back, the refugee authority shall adopt a ruling on returning the third-country national affected. The ruling on the return order may be subject to judicial review, and its request shall be submitted within three days following the date of delivery of the ruling. The refugee authority shall forthwith forward the request for judicial review to the competent Court together with the documents of the case and any cross-complaint attached. The judicial review without any delay shall be completed within eight days in non-litigation proceedings, relying on the available documents. In the proceedings, personal interviews may not be conducted. The court's decision is final, and it may not be appealed. If the Dublin process culminates in the third-country national's return, the immigration proceedings shall be terminated at the time of return. The ruling adopted for terminating the immigration procedure may not be appealed.

315. Third-country nationals may not be turned back or expelled to the territory of a country that fails to satisfy the criteria of safe country of origin or safe third country regarding the person in question, in particular where the third-country national is likely to be subjected to persecution on the grounds of his/her race, religion, nationality, belonging to a special social group or political conviction, nor to the territory or the frontier of a country where there is substantial reason to believe that the expelled third-country national is likely to be subjected to the death penalty, torture or any other form of cruel, inhuman or degrading treatment or punishment (*non-refoulement,* Article XIV(2) of the Fundamental Law). According to the ThirdA, any third-country national whose application for protection is pending may be turned back or expelled only if his application is refused by a final and executable decision of the refugee authority. Furthermore, the immigration authority shall take into account the principle of non-refoulement in the proceedings relating to the refusal of the entry and to expulsion. Also, in expulsion cases, the Court shall take into account the non-refoulement ex officio or upon request of the third-country national concerned without delay. The enforcement of expulsion shall be suspended for the duration of the proceedings of the sentencing judge. If there is no safe third country offering protection to the third-country national affected but the prohibition of removal exists, the immigration authority shall grant him/her tolerant migrant status, and shall issue a humanitarian residence permit. When the grounds for tolerant migrant status cease to apply, the immigration authority shall withdraw the status unless there is another legal basis for granting permission to reside.

316. Further administrative sanctions may be imposed against the local border traffic permit holders on the grounds of the bilateral agreements. For instance, during their stay in the territory of Hungary or Ukraine[222] the local border traffic regime shall be respected, and border residents shall abide by the laws and regulations of this state. 'The states of the contracting parties impose penalties determined by their national regulations in case of any kind of misuse of the permit.' There is no definition or example defined in the text – so its interpretation is based on the national regulation and the aims of the agreement. Penalties that may be imposed by the states are determined in the agreement, as follows:

(a) In Hungary: the obligation to leave the territory of Hungary, alien policing expulsion and ban on entry and stay;
(b) In the Ukraine: the obligation to leave the territory of Ukraine, the expulsion and ban on entry and stay.

317. The immigration authority may *prohibit the exit* of a third-country national whose travel document is to be confiscated by the immigration authority as requested by the court, the public prosecutor or the investigation authority. This means a confiscation of his/her travel document after issuing a resolution that may not be appealed. The immigration authority, upon receipt of a notice from the court, the public prosecutor or the investigation authority for lifting the prohibition of leaving the country, shall cancel the prohibition without delay and shall release the third-country national's travel document as well.

318. Exclusion orders shall be imposed in connection with any person within the ambit of the FreeA who must not be allowed to enter the territory of Hungary under international commitment; or is to be excluded as per the decision of the Council of the EU. The competent authority shall – by way of a resolution – order the exclusion of any person whose whereabouts are unknown or who resides outside the country. The duration of an exclusion order shall be determined by the imposing authority; it may not be longer than three years on the first instance, and may be extended by three additional years per occasion if the underlying circumstances still exist at the time of expiry of the exclusion order. A copy of the exclusion order (decision) is sent to the data management unit for registry, because the person whose exclusion was ordered independently may enter Hungary only upon the consent of the ordering authority, granted at the request of the Court. There is no legal remedy against the exclusion order. The exclusion order shall be lifted if the underlying circumstances no longer exist. Where exclusion is ordered in conjunction with

222. Act CLIII of 2007. It defines the list of settlements in both party states of that local habitants may submit application for small border traffic permit. On the Hungarian side, it covers 244 settlements and in the neighbouring area it covers 382 settlements.

expulsion, it shall be contained in the resolution ordering the expulsion. If expulsion is ordered by the court, the authority carrying out the expulsion shall provide for the registration of the related exclusion order.

319. The expulsion order together with exclusion against the person under the scope of the FreeA may be issued by the migration authority as follows:

(a) at the request of the public health authority for public health reasons if he/she suffers from any infectious disease or contagious parasitic disease as specified in the HealthD and considered to constitute a threat to public health, and if he/she refuses to submit to the appropriate compulsory medical treatment, except if the infectious disease or contagious parasitic disease is contracted after three months following the date of entry;
(b) if he/she refuses to comply with an order to leave the territory of Hungary within the prescribed time limit;
(c) if he/she does not have the right to residence, and he/she has provided false or misleading information to the competent authority to verify his/her right to residence; or
(d) if he/she represents a genuine, present and sufficiently serious threat to the internal security of Hungary, if granted the right to entry or residence. It is applicable if the NSO or the Police initiate this order or the Court passed a final judgment adopted in criminal proceedings which may not, in itself, constitute grounds for expulsion. However, the EEA nationals and their family members with right to permanent residence may not be expelled from the territory of Hungary with the exception of this serious threat to security.

The expulsion together with the exclusion is ordered for a period of not less than one year and not more than five years. Where the expulsion is ordered on the grounds of public health, the public health authority shall propose the duration of exclusion. The reasons shall be reviewed after two years from the date when the expulsion is carried out upon request.

320. Exclusion may not be ordered against a person within the ambit of the FreeA if the following conditions are met:

(a) the expulsion was ordered because the assisted return could not have been carried out, for reasons beyond the control of the person in question;
(b) the expulsion measure was taken against a minor;
(c) the EEA national or his/her family member has resided in the territory of Hungary for more than ten years; or is a minor, except if the expulsion is necessary in the best interests of the child.

An expulsion measure may not be imposed in connection with a criminal offence wherein the court sentence did not include expulsion. The data administration agency referred to FreeA shall be notified of any expulsion measure imposed.

321. The migration authority shall evaluate the following criteria in the *expulsion order* process relating to the person within the ambit of the FreeA:

(a) the nature and gravity of the crime committed;
(b) the age and health conditions of the person affected;
(c) the family situation of the person in question, the duration of the family relationship;
(d) the number of children of the person in question and the ages of the children, relations with the children including visitation rights;
(e) if there is another state where there are no legal obstacles in exercising the right to family reunification, no such difficulties which the family members are likely to face if they had no other choice but to take up residence in this country;
(f) the financial situation of the person affected;
(g) the duration of residence in Hungary of the person in question; and
(h) the social and cultural integration of the person in question, and the extent of his/her links with the country of origin.

322. The natural and legal person as well as an unincorporated company providing passenger *transport services (carrier)* that transports a family member of the EEA national who is a third-country national or other third-country national by means of air, water or scheduled road transport – not including the railway companies – shall be required to check the travel document and visa of the passenger before boarding for travelling to Hungary or to another country via Hungary to ensure that they have travel documents required for entry or for transit. This check cannot screen out false, manipulated documents or determine whether the passenger has been excluded from Hungary. Hence the carrier's obligation on transfer and bearing the cost prior to departure is a sanction imposed without culpability of the carrier. It means a delegation of the public power of checking passengers' entry to private companies (Tóth, 1997). The carrier transporting any family member who is a third-country national or other third-country national by means of air, water, road or railway transport shall provide for the return of such family member to the country of departure or to the country which is liable to accept him/her, if he/she is refused admission to Hungary for lacking any of the requirements specified by law, or he/she is refused admission to another country and is turned back to Hungary; or the carrier to which the passenger was scheduled to be transferred refused to admit him/her on his means of transport. If the return cannot be promptly executed, the carrier in question shall bear all costs incurred in connection with the stay of the family member or the other third-country national until his/her return. When the carrier disputes its obligation to transfer the person in question or to finance his/her stay, the migration authority shall adopt a formal decision to order the carrier to comply. It shall be implemented immediately. If a carrier fails to fulfil his/her liability to return a non-admitted passenger within the deadline (seventy-two hours or eight days), the Police shall advance the cost of the return of such a person and shall execute it by way of another carrier. If the carrier responsible refuses to repay the costs advanced by the Police, the Police shall seek recourse to recover such expenses under the civil law.

323. For any failure to comply with the obligation to transfer and bear the cost until the departure of the family member of the EEA national or other third-country national, a *fine for the protection of public order* shall be imposed upon the carrier in question by the Police. A penalty for the protection of public order shall be imposed upon the carrier in question, between EUR 3,000 and EUR 5,000 per person. Its exact amount may be determined with regard to all prevailing circumstances, such as any recidivism, where applicable. A carrier shall be exempted from the payment of penalty under the following circumstances:

(a) if it can be verified that the carrier proceeded with due care and diligence to ensure compliance with the obligation to check the travel document and visa of the passenger;
(b) if the family member who is a third-country national, or another third-country national applies for asylum, or for any subsidiary form of protection or temporary protection, the obligation to return a non-admitted passenger may not be enforced.

324. The Police carrying out border checks shall impose a *penalty for the protection of public order* upon any air carrier who meets the following conditions:

(a) fails to supply information – in violation of the provisions set out in a specific separate legislation[223] – regarding passengers it transports from outside of any Member State of the EU or from outside of the territory of any Schengen State into the territory of Hungary;
(b) provides incomplete information; or
(c) supplies untrue information stemming from its failure to exercise due care and diligence.

According to the FreeD and ThirdD, the fine for the protection of public order shall be specified in the amount of EUR 3,000 – EUR 5,000. For any repeat infringement, the penalty may be imposed cumulatively for each journey for which the passenger's information was not communicated or was communicated incorrectly. However, its concrete amount may be determined with regard to all prevailing circumstances, such as any recidivism, where applicable. The carrier may not request the suspension of any proceeding aimed to determine their liability.

325. The EEA nationals and their family members whose *exclusion* was ordered independently may enter the territory of Hungary only upon the consent of the ordering authority, granted at the request of the Court. The competent authority may authorize the entry for persons who are the subject of an exclusion measure ordered in conjunction with expulsion for the purpose of appearing before the Court in the process of review of the expulsion order, if the Court has summoned or consented for the person(s) affected to appear. Expulsion and exclusion orders may not be appealed but judicial review may be requested. The Court shall adopt a decision

223. Its details can be found in Directive 2004/82/EC.

within eight days, and the applicant shall be provided the opportunity to present his/her own views in person in the hearing unless he/she cannot be reached at the address on record, or his/her place of residence is unknown.

326. Moreover, EEA nationals and their family members who are subject to exclusion ordered in conjunction with expulsion may apply after one year from the date the expulsion order was directed to be lifted on grounds of changes in his/her state of health or family status in connection with which he/she is required to enter the territory of Hungary. This request shall be decided by the immigration authority within three months. If the competent authority cancels the exclusion measure, it shall ensure that the exclusion is erased from the records. Expulsion measures ordered against third-country nationals under the prior Alien Act, ThirdA and the alerts issued on the basis of such expulsion orders in the SIS alert in accordance with Article 96 of the Schengen Implementation Agreement between 2001 and 2010[224] shall be reviewed before the expulsion of family members of third-country nationals is carried out or during the proceedings for the issue of a document evidencing right to residence. If keeping the expulsion order or the SIS alert in force is likely to bring unreasonable harm, the competent authority shall withdraw the resolution containing the order of expulsion. The competent authority shall carry out the procedure within twenty days and shall adopt a decision by way of a resolution.

327. EEA nationals and their family members shall not be authorized to exit the territory of Hungary if placed under pre-trial detention, if subject to house arrest or confined to quarters, if detained, placed under custody awaiting extradition, arrested for extradition, arrested for transfer, placed under provisional detention for transfer or if placed under involuntary temporary treatment in a mental institution. Moreover, in order to secure the enforcement of an expulsion measure the competent authority shall be authorized to *confiscate (withhold) the travel document* of the EEA national or family member affected; this resolution cannot be contested. The travel document shall be confiscated for the duration of the restraining measure to which the EEA national or his/her family member is subjected in the aforementioned proceedings.

328. The employers shall control the validity of residence and labour permit to third-country national entering employment, keep a copy of these documents during the entire period of employment and be required to report within five days to the competent authority if the employment of an EEA national or a family member has materialized, or if his/her employment is terminated. Any employer who fails to satisfy any of these obligations may be charged a *fine for the protection of the public order* by the migration authority. It shall not be imposed if employer proves that report was made or despite of due diligence in legal entitlement control the falsified/invalid documents cannot be recognized. According to the FreeD, its amount is a maximum of EUR 1,700 per employee. Its exact amount may be determined with regard to all prevailing circumstances, such as any recidivism, where applicable.

224. Enlargement of the Schengen system and the EU explains this temporary measure.

The Regional Directorate of the OIN shall not be authorized to impose the aforementioned penalty after one year following knowledge of the event. Employers may not request suspension of any proceeding aimed to determine their liability.

329. The failed registration of the persons within the ambit of the FreeA is not directly sanctioned, but it shall be presented in street or public place checks. In its absence, the most important consequence is that the conditions of residence rights shall be proved by the non-national, and all deadlines (to permanent residence) begin from the finding of this evidence. Furthermore, a fine may be imposed on the basis of the MinofA as against all undocumented inhabitants during street checks (see section 315 (e)).

§2. Penal Sanctions

330. Illicit entry into the territory of the country is not an offence in itself because this action constitutes a misdemeanour. However, if a person who *assists a third-country national to unlawful residence in the territory of a Member State of the EU or EEA* (including Hungary) for a material gain, he/she commits a delinquency that shall be punished up to two years imprisonment (Penal Code, Article 354).

331. The Penal Code contains another delinquency related to family ties: any adult person who *establishes family tie in an abusive manner* (marriage, paternity declaration) in order to access residence right and its documentation for a material gain is guilty of a delinquency punishable by imprisonment for up to two years (Article 355). Furthermore, *illegal employment* of third-country national regularly or for a longer period or in a group exceeding at least five persons without necessary permission to the remunerated work means a delinquency that shall be punished up to two years imprisonment. The punishment shall be at least three years if employment is exploitative as determined in the ThirdA or the employee is a victim of human trafficking (Article 356).

332. In practice, many foreigners are charged with *forgery or/and abuse of public or private documents* also in the immigration authorization, police checks or as protection seekers in admission.[225] The Penal Code (in Articles 342, 344, 345, 346) determines punishment partly for foreigners and partly for their assisting persons:

(a) Any person who prepares a forged public document, or falsifies the contents of a public document, uses a bogus or forged public document or a public

225. For instance, the Supreme Court annulled the judgement of the first and second instances of penal justice because the formal felony of a Somalian refugee did not violate the public security. He used forged identity and travel documents in police check arriving from Greece as a non-safe transit country. He was recognized as refugees but was punished for abuse with official documents. The Supreme Court explained how the Geneva Convention (Art. 31) and safe third country and public security in criminal justice shall be in harmony through a fair fact-finding process (Legfelsőbb Bíróság Bfv. I. 652/2011).

document issued under the name of another person, or collaborates in the inclusion of false data, facts or declarations in a public document regarding the existence, changing or termination of a right or obligation, is guilty of a felony punishable by imprisonment for up to three years.

(b) Any person who falsifies or unlawfully uses valid security document to entry is guilty of delinquency punishable by imprisonment for up to two years.

(c) Any person who uses falsified, forged or substantially untrue private document in order to prove facts or rights shall be punishable for a delinquency with imprisonment up to one year.

(d) Any person who unlawfully acquires a public document or a document which is not his own or not exclusively his own, from another person without the latter's consent, or destroys, damages or conceals the same, is guilty of a delinquency punishable by imprisonment for up to two years. Any person who perpetrates the act defined above in respect of a private document in order to gain unlawful advantage or to cause unlawful disadvantage is guilty of delinquency punishable by imprisonment for up to one year.

333. The Penal Code prescribes *expulsion as an additional punishment for foreigners*. It means that expulsion may form either an administrative or a penal sanction under the same name, while it is regulated under different codes (the Penal Code, the ThirdA and the FreeA). According to the Penal Code (Article 59), the non-national perpetrator whose presence in the country is endangering seriously the public order, shall be expelled from the territory of Hungary. Persons expelled shall leave the territory of the country and may not return for the duration of the term of expulsion. Its term would be definite or permanent, as follows:

(a) Permanent expulsion may be imposed against any person who has been sentenced to imprisonment for ten years or more and whose presence in the country would significantly jeopardize public safety. Upon request, the Court may release a person subject to permanent expulsion from the effect of such expulsion if such person is deemed worthy and if ten years have passed since the expulsion.

(b) The duration of expulsion for a specific term shall be a minimum of one year and a maximum of ten years.

Expulsion shall take effect upon the judgment becoming definitive. The duration of imprisonment served by the prisoner shall not be included in the term of expulsion.

334. Beyond the general rules, the above *specific guarantees can be found in the Penal Code:*

(a) Permanent expulsion may not be imposed upon persons within the ambit of the FreeA.

(b) Expulsion may be imposed upon a person within the ambit of the FreeA or a third-country national with long-term migrant status only in connection with the commission of a crime that is punishable by imprisonment for at least five years.

(c) Expulsion may be imposed only upon a person who has been living in Hungary legitimately for not less than ten years; who is minor; or whose right to family life would be injured; and his/her presence in the country would significantly jeopardize public safety, if he/she has committed a crime that is sentenced by the Court with imprisonment for at least ten years.

(d) Persons who have been granted refugee status (pursuant to the AsylA) may not be expelled. As is evident, the expulsion as well as the protection against expulsion decided by the penal Court are based a lot more on the legal status (category) of the perpetrators than on the individual assessment of his/her genuine threat to public security.

The phrase 'presence in the country is endangering the public safety' is enigmatic, because the duration of imprisonment or possible imprisonment is not per se evidence of threat or endangered security by the perpetrator. The new Penal Code is strict in length of punishment so these guarantees are weak.

335. One of the measures *attached to the criminal procedure* is the limitation of leaving. EEA nationals and their family members shall *not be authorized to exit* the territory of Hungary if placed under pre-trial detention, if subject to house arrest or confined to quarters, if detained, placed under custody awaiting extradition, arrested for extradition, arrested for transfer, placed under provisional detention for transfer, or if placed under involuntary temporary treatment in a mental institution. However the provisions on measures concerning ban of exit were deleted from the CrimPA in 2013 because the ThirdA (Article 66) and FreeA (Article 64) regulate it properly. The competent authority may withhold the travel documents by way of a non-appealable decision, if notified by the Court conducting the criminal proceedings, the public prosecutor or the investigating authority for having ordered any of the restraining measures aforementioned. The travel document shall be withheld for the duration of the restraining measure to which he/she is subjected. A similar measure is applicable against third-country nationals. The migration authority may prohibit, by a non-appealable decision, the exit of a third-country national whose travel document is to be withheld upon request by the Court, the public prosecutor or the investigation authority. The migration authority, upon receipt of a notice for lifting the prohibition of leaving the country, shall cancel the prohibition without delay and shall release the third-country national's travel document as well.

§3. Detention

336. Detention is a *collective term of limitation of internal and external movement* of non-nationals that is ordered to execute his/her removal (extradition, expulsion, surrender, deportation or refusal) on the grounds of the ThirdA, the FreeA or the AsylA. In the event of illegal entry, irregular residence or unknown identity of applicant, the detention pursuant to these acts is considered an administrative measure. However, detention in criminal procedure is applicable as defined in CrimPA, providing for the confinement of the perpetrator during the investigation and trial. In case of a delinquency, detention during the investigation and trial is not applicable against the perpetrator. Here the main rules of detention by the ThirdA, the AslyA and the FreeA will be discussed, and the procedural guarantees can be found in Part VI.

337. *I*n order to secure the deportation of a third-country national, or his/her transfer, the *immigration authority may order his/her detention*, if the any of the following conditions are met:

(a) he/she is hiding from the authorities or is obstructing the enforcement of the deportation or transfer in some other way;
(b) he/she has refused to leave the country, or, based on other substantiated reasons, is allegedly delaying or preventing the enforcement of expulsion (risk of absconding);
(c) he/she has seriously or repeatedly violated the code of conduct of the place of compulsory confinement;
(d) he/she has failed to report as ordered, by means of which to forestall the conclusion of the pending immigration procedure; or
(e) he/she is released from imprisonment as sentenced for a deliberate crime.

Detention under immigration laws shall be ordered by way of a formal resolution, and shall be carried out when communicated. Detention under immigration laws may be ordered for a maximum duration of seventy-two hours, and it may be extended by the local court of jurisdiction by reference to the place of detention until the third-country national's deportation or transfer, or for a maximum of sixty days at a time.

338. *Detention under immigration laws* may be extended by up to six additional months on the expiry of a period of six months, if the carrying out of the expulsion order takes more than six months, in spite of having taken all necessary measures, due to the following circumstances:

(a) the failure of the affected third-country national to cooperate with the competent authority, or
(b) delays in obtaining the documents required for deportation, attributable to the authorities of the third-country national's country of origin, or another state liable for readmission under a readmission agreement or which is otherwise liable to accept him/her.

339. Detention ordered under immigration laws shall be *terminated* immediately under the following circumstances:

(a) when the conditions for carrying out the expulsion or transfer of third-country national are secured;
(b) when it becomes evident that the expulsion or transfer cannot be executed; or

(c) after six months from the date when ordered, or twelve months under the conditions mentioned above. In the implementation of this rule, the duration of detention prior to expulsion shall be included in the total duration of detention;
(d) third-country national acquires right to residence as asylum seeker or his/her asylum detention is ordered.

The immigration authority ordering the termination of detention in point (b) and (c) shall designate a compulsory place of confinement for the third-country national affected.

340. The immigration authority may order the *detention of the third-country national prior to expulsion* in order to secure the conclusion of the immigration proceedings pending, if his/her identity or the legal grounds of his/her residence are not conclusively established, or his/her surrender to another Member State of the EU is pending on the grounds of a bilateral agreement. Detention prior to expulsion shall be ordered by way of a formal resolution, and shall be carried out when communicated. Detention prior to expulsion may be ordered for a maximum duration of seventy-two hours, and it may be extended by the local court of jurisdiction by reference to the place of detention until the third-country national's identity or the legal grounds of his/her residence are conclusively established, or for a maximum of thirty days.

341. The detention of a third-country national under immigration laws or *prior to expulsion* may not be ordered for the sole reason that the third-country national is an applicant for asylum. This principle has been advanced frequently by the UNHCR and the Universal Periodical Report to the UN Human Rights Council made by Hungary (May 2011) was strongly criticized for detention of protection seekers as a main rule in Hungary.[226] Not in this spirit but since July 2013 the refugee authority may order *detention of the applicant* if s/he has no other grounds of residence than the asylum claim, and other coercive measures (bail in EUR 500–EUR 5,000, regular report to the authority, residence in a designated place) determined for the applicant are not enough, and

(a) his identity (citizenship, personal conditions) and country of origin shall be clarified to the non-refoulement and requirement of international protection;
(b) s/he restrains or inhibits the recognition procedure (e.g., disappearing, hiding) or it is probable;
(c) his/her deprivation of liberty is necessary for security and public order;
(d) his/her claim is submitted at the airport; or
(e) his/her not presence at authority would obstruct the success of the Dublin procedure.

226. Mexico and the Czech Republic requested to change this practice of the Hungarian authorities that was refused by the Government saying that 'our practice and regulation is fully compatible to the substance of their proposal'. (August, 2011 <www.kormany.hu>)

The maximal duration of the asylum detention is six months and for applicant (family) with minor shall not be than thirty days. The Regional Directorate of the OIN can order detention to seventy-two hours and its prolongation shall be decided by the local court if its necessity and legality is proved by the Regional Directorate. If detention is terminated exceeding this maximal period, a confinement shall be defined for the applicant. Furthermore, legal representative *ad litem* shall be ordered for applicant in detention if s/he cannot speak Hungarian (Article 30/A-H of AsylA).

342. The detention of a third-country national who is *a minor* may not be ordered, with the following exception: 'families with minors shall only be detained as a measure of last resort and for not more than thirty days where the best interests of the child shall be a primary consideration, if the immigration authority is of the opinion that the objective of detention cannot be ensured by other measures'. This provision of the ThirdA formally protects child rights but detention or living in a designated place of residence (confinement with cameras, grids on windows and locked doors) can hardly be a proper place for a minor or a family with children.

343. According to the ThirdA and the FreeA together with its executive ministerial decree on detention of migrants (DetD), the following rules determine the *position of migrants in detention:*

(a) he/she shall be informed of his/her rights and obligations in his/her native language or another language which he/she understands;
(b) upon his/her request or on the grounds of a bilateral consular agreement, the authority ordering detention shall inform the consular or diplomatic mission of the third-country national concerning his/her detention without delay, the obligation of compulsory confinement, and the extension of the duration of detention; moreover, detainee may communicate freely with public prosecutor's office as controlling organ on legality of detention, with the ombudsman, watchdog NGOs and CPT using the translation service that shall be provided by the detention centre (sections 12–13 of DetD);
(c) as a provisional measure, the authority ordering the detention shall immediately provide for the placement of dependent family members who have remained without supervision, and/or for the safeguarding of his/her valuables which have been left unattended;
(d) he/she shall be kept in a specific place designated for this purpose. It implies that migrants are kept in separate institutions operated by the Police (while nationals may be placed in detention only in penal institutions);
(e) with the exception of married couples, men placed under detention shall be housed in quarters separate from women, furthermore, families with minors shall be provided with accommodation separate from all other detainees guaranteeing adequate privacy;
(f) he/she shall be accommodated (housing and nourishment shall be provided) and basic medical care shall be provided; he/she has the right to consult his/her legal representative or a member of the consular representation without any censorship, and to be visited by relatives under censorship; he/she can receive

visitors; he/she may submit complaints and requests to the local director; he/she may spend at least one hour outdoors each day;

(g) minors in detention shall have the opportunity to engage in leisure activities, including play and recreational activities appropriate to their age; minors in detention shall have, depending on the length of their stay, access to education. These provisions would diminish the relevance of child rights because the best interests of child are obviously preceded by the public order consideration.

Inmates must take part in cleaning the areas they use, without any compensation, and subject themselves to any examinations, permit the searching of their clothing, not obstruct the confiscation of any contrabands, repay the costs of their keep and support and cover the costs of any damage caused wilfully.

344. The *facilities of detention* are determined in the FreeD and the ThirdD in the same manner. The place of detention (guarded dormitory, community hostel) has to meet the following relevant requirements:

(a) the living quarters of detainees must have at least fifteen cubic metres of air space and five square metres of floor space per person;
(b) it must have a common area for dining, for recreational purposes and for receiving visitors;
(c) it must have separate washrooms, showers and toilets for men and women, with hot and cold running water, in a sufficient capacity consistent with the number of detainees;
(d) it must have an infirmary for providing the basic medical care; a medical examination room and an isolation room;
(e) it must have sufficient space for outdoor activities; it must have lighting sufficient to satisfy the standards laid down in the national requirements concerning the regional development and construction;
(f) it must have appropriate telephone facilities; and
(g) it must have natural ventilation in the living quarters and in the staff rooms, in the medical rooms, in the visitors' areas, in the kitchen, in the dining room and in the common areas.

345. Certain rights of third-country nationals in detention are conditional 'in situation where an exceptionally large number of third-country nationals to be returned places an unforeseen heavy burden on the capacity of hostels of restricted access, or on the immigration authority itself' – as the ThirdA outlines in the '*Lampedusa closure*'. In such situations:

(a) detention under immigration laws may be ordered for a maximum duration of seventy-two hours but it may be extended without the consent of the local court. As long as the exceptional situation persists, the immigration authority may decide to appeal to the local court within five days from the date when the detention was ordered to extend the period of detention beyond seven days;
(b) the immigration authority may carry out the detention at a place other than the place set up for migrants.

346. The immigration authority may *order the compulsory confinement* of a third-country national in a designated place, if he/she meets any of the following conditions:

(a) he/she cannot be returned or expelled due to commitments of Hungary as conferred in international agreements;
(b) he/she is a minor who should not be placed under detention;
(c) he/she should be placed under detention, in consequence of which his/her minor child residing in the territory of Hungary would be left unattended if he/she was to be detained;
(d) he/she is released from detention, however, there are still grounds for his/her detention;
(e) he/she has a residence permit granted on humanitarian grounds;
(f) he/she has been expelled, and is lacking adequate financial resources to support himself/herself and/or does not have adequate accommodation facilities;
(g) he/she should be placed under detention under immigration laws obstructing or refusing the enforcement of removal, but detention would result in a disproportionate measure taking into account his/her state of health and age.

347. The resolution shall specify the place of compulsory confinement, the code of conduct to be observed[227] and the obligation to appear at specific intervals before the authority if the place of confinement is not a community hostel or a refugee centre. However, in an overwhelming majority of cases, the third-country national is not able to support himself/herself, and has no adequate place of abode, financial resources, income, or host or relative who can be compelled to provide support. Hence the compulsory place of confinement is designated at a community hostel or a refugee centre while the costs of confinement in a community hostel or refugee centre shall be borne by the third-country national, unless he is issued a residence permit on humanitarian grounds.

348. If two months have lapsed from the date when compulsory confinement in a community hostel or refugee centre was ordered, but the circumstance serving as grounds therein still exist for reasons beyond the control of the third-country national in question, the immigration authority may *designate another place of residence* (e.g., a flat financed by an NGO), or prolong his/her residence in the community hostel of the refugee centre upon request, taking into account the personal circumstances. Any third-country national who has been ordered by the immigration authority to remain in a designated place shall be entitled to engage in gainful employment – subject to the immigration authority's consent – if holding a valid work permit.

227. For instance, the inmate has to keep his/her surroundings clean or notify the competent Regional Directorate in advance concerning his/her temporary absence in excess of twenty-four hours but not more than 120 hours, and shall disclose the destination and the duration of the absence.

349. The medical care for persons in detention and in compulsory confinement shall be provided. Any migrant who is detained or the inmate in an obligatory designated place of residence, if not covered by any social security system, shall be provided the urgent and basic health care services free of charge, including the obligatory vaccinations.[228] The panel doctor's care shall be provided to the inmates in the place of detention or confinement, while a special medical care shall be provided by the regular health care provider responsible for the region in question. The payment of expensive medicine and medicinal products depends on whether Hungary undertakes to compensate the same or not. In this latter case, the inevitable costs of health care shall be paid by the operator of the detention institute, the refugee centre, the community hostel or the Regional Directorate to the service provider by law.[229] However, health care services may be obtained if a certificate of eligibility for provisions is possessed.

350. In order to locate a third-country national whose whereabouts are unknown, the immigration authority may issue a *warrant* if he/she is subject to any restrictive immigration proceeding; has escaped from detention or is on unauthorized absence from the place of compulsory confinement in violation of the code of conduct; or failed to comply with the final decision of expulsion. When the grounds for such a warrant cease to prevail, it shall be withdrawn forthwith.

351. The rules on *detention of refugee or subsidiary protection seekers*[230] follow the pattern of DetD thus the following specificities are observed:

(a) the detention centres run by the OIN shall respect for family and private life of couples and families with minors;
(b) at the time of reception a medical protocol shall be made on injured, tortured or victimized persons;
(c) rehabilitation and psychological services shall be provided for vulnerable, victimized, tortured inmates; and
(d) employment of social workers is required to support for inmates and to ensure the co-operation with external health-care and child-care services.

352. In order to secure deportation the immigration authority may order the detention of an *adult in ambit of the FreeA* if his/her expulsion is permanent, or he/she is released from the imprisonment for a deliberate crime with the additional punishment of expulsion, or he/she has failed to leave the country within the deadline as the expulsion order determined. The maximum length of detention is seventy-two hours, and it may be extended by the local court of jurisdiction by reference to the place of detention until the deportation is carried out, or for a maximum of thirty days at a time up to three months. Detention shall be terminated immediately, under the following circumstances: when the relevant grounds no

228. Article 142 in Act CLIV of 1997 on Health-care.
229. Health-care services may be obtained a certificate of eligibility for provisions is possessed. Compensation shall be governed by the Government Decree No. 301 of 2007, 9 November.
230. Ministerial Decree No. 29 of 2013, 28 June (BM) on asylum applicants' detention and bail.

longer exist, when it becomes evident that the expulsion cannot be executed, or three months have elapsed since the date of the order.

§4. Expulsion Measures

353. Expulsion orders issued against third-country nationals shall specify the criteria in connection with the decisions adopted as required in the ThirdA, the duration of exclusion, the country to which the person in question is expelled (to another Member State of the EU, the Schengen system if third-country national shall be admitted, or out from the territory of the EU), the time limit for voluntary departure from the territory of the EU, a warning to the affected third-country national regarding deportation in the eventuality of his/her refusal to depart voluntarily, and the obligation to be photographed and fingerprinted. Expulsion orders may not be appealed; however, a petition for judicial review may be lodged within eight days of the date when the resolution was delivered. The court shall adopt a decision within fifteen days upon receipt of the petition. The final decision of expulsion and the duration of exclusion shall be recorded in the passport in the form of an entry, unless the foreign national affected leaves Hungary within the framework of a voluntary return program[231]or he/she has a valid residence permission issued by the authority in another Member State of the EU.

354. Where expulsion of the third-country national is ordered by the Court, it shall be carried out by the immigration authority by way of a ruling; this measure may be contested. The Court or the penal institution shall forthwith notify the immigration authority to carry out the expulsion when it becomes final. The immigration authority, upon receipt of the notice referred, shall order the expulsion to be enforced.

355. The costs associated with expulsion shall be borne by the person expelled or – if lacking the financial means necessary – by his/her host. In order to secure the costs of departure, the competent authority may seize the travel ticket if the third-country national in question has one, or – if sufficient financial means cannot be ensured otherwise – may confiscate his money in the amount as is required to purchase the ticket and to obtain a travel document. These actions may not be contested. Where the expulsion measure cannot be carried out because neither the person being expelled nor his/her host has the financial means necessary, the competent authority shall advance the costs of departure. These costs shall be repaid by the person expelled; by the host if the person affected was invited; by the employer, if the expulsion was ordered in the context of illegal labour, or by the research organization if the person affected was admitted for the purposes of carrying out a research project but requirements of residence were not met. The liability of the research organization shall remain in effect for six months following termination of the hosting agreement.

231. The Ministry of the Interior has co-operated with the IOM on voluntary return of irregular migrants, in 2012 it covered on 415 persons and in 2013 on 353 persons (OIN data).

356. With a view to avoiding any overlap in proceedings and for establishing the identity of third-country nationals, the authority ordering detention prior to expulsion or expulsion under immigration laws, compulsory confinement, detention under immigration laws or carrying out the expulsion ordered by the Court shall take the photograph of the face and fingerprints of the third-country national affected. They shall submit to having his/her fingerprints and a photograph of his/her face taken.

357. If the *return procedure* of the person within the ambit of the FreeA cannot be carried out within seventy-two hours, or the waiting period for the missing documents or the evidence for entry has expired without success, and hence the withdrawal of the return order is not possible, he/she may be expelled. Similarly, in case of refusal of entry of the person under the scope of the ThirdA whose return procedure cannot be carried out within seventy-two hours or eight days, he/she shall be expelled following his/her admission. In this case, the expulsion must not be accompanied by an exclusion order (ban of entry and residence), with the exception that his/her exclusion is based on international obligation, or whose exclusion is determined by the EU Council or whose entry and stay interfere the national security or the public order.

358. A return (refusal at border) or expulsion measure ordered by the Court or the immigration authority shall be enforced by way of transporting the third-country national affected under official escort (*deportation*) if he/she meets any of the following conditions:

(a) he/she is released from imprisonment as sentenced for a deliberate crime;
(b) he/she makes it necessary to supervise his/her exit for national security reasons, if so required by commitment under international treaty, or for the protection of public security or public policy; or
(c) he/she failed to leave the territory of the Member States of the EU by the day following the deadline prescribed in the resolution for expulsion.

Deportation shall be ordered in the resolution ordering expulsion under immigration laws or in the ruling for the enforcement of expulsion if ordered by the Court. In all other instances, it shall be ordered by a specific resolution or ruling. The competent public prosecutor shall oversee the deportation procedure in accordance with the relevant regulations, such as Act CLXIII of 2011 on public prosecutors[232] (Article 22), the ThirdA and the DeptD.

359. On the grounds of the mutual recognition of the authority's decision in another Schengen state, the Hungarian authority may implement its expulsion order if the third-country national's residence implies a genuine and severe threat to public security or it jeopardizes the public security or national security; the third-country national committed an intentional criminal act or offence that is punishable

232. The Chief Public Prosecutor determines how prosecutors must control the legality of deportation procedures by CPP Order No. 5 of 2012, 27 January (LÜ) s. 23.

with imprisonment for at least one year by the Court in another Member State; there is a well-founded suspicion of a committed act or criminal offence by the third-country national concerned; or his/her expulsion is ordered for severe violation of migration law concerning the rules on entry and residence. The immigration authority may cooperate in the enforcement of the expulsion ordered by a country whose territory is required for transit for the purposes of removal by air.[233] The deportation of a person shall be suspended if the entry of the person deported to the country of destination is no longer an option; the person deported requires urgent medical care; the country from whom the permission was requested for using its territory for transit by air in connection with the deportation as prescribed in the DeptD did not grant its consent, or revoked its previous consent; or the person deported entered the territory of the requested state without authorization during the transit.

360. The cooperation between the Member States shall mean the authorization of the transit through the territory of Hungary in cases of removal by air of the third-country nationals in the enforcement of expulsion ordered by a country that is required to apply the provisions of the Council Directive including any official escort and all other persons required to accompany the third-country national in question, such persons will be liable to provide medical care, interpretation and assistance with regard to such removals by air. The OIN, upon the receipt of a request submitted by the requesting state on a standard form (see in the DeptD), shall notify the competent authority of the requesting state concerning its approval immediately, within a maximum of two days. This time limit may be extended in justified cases by forty-eight hours, of which the competent authority of the requesting state shall be promptly notified. The OIN shall promptly notify the Police of its authorization for transit for the purposes of removal by air, because it implements the deportation order taking into account the transit. Whereas, the OIN shall refuse to authorize the transit through Hungary for the purposes of removal by air, or shall withdraw its authorization if the principle of non-refoulement applies. The OIN may refuse to authorize the transit through Hungary for the purposes of removal by air, or may withdraw its authorization if any of the following circumstances arise:

(a) the third-country national affected under the Hungarian laws is charged with criminal acts or offences or is wanted for the carrying out of a sentence;
(b) transit through other states or admission by the country of destination is not feasible;
(c) the removal measure requires a change of airports and between them a land transport;
(d) the personal and material conditions for the requested assistance are not available, or the transit for the purposes of removal by air is impossible at a particular moment for practical reasons;
(e) the transit of the third-country national will be a threat to public policy, public security, public health or to the international relations of Hungary.

233. Applying the provisions of Council Directive 2003/110/EC.

The OIN shall promptly inform the requesting statutory authority when authorization for transit for the purposes of removal by air is revoked, or of any other reason why the transit is not possible, including an explanation of the reasons. However, a deportation measure that was ordered by another Schengen state may be enforced if the OIN finds the requirements satisfied following a consultation with the Schengen state that has issued the order. If the deportation measure is carried out or if it cannot be executed, the competent authority of the Schengen state that has issued the order shall be notified.

361. The third-country national ordered to be deported shall be escorted to the frontier of the country. The deported person shall be escorted to the country of origin or to another state liable for readmission if his/her travel by air transport without safeguards is likely to jeopardize the aviation safety or an escort is prescribed under treaty (readmission agreement). He/she shall be informed – in a language that he/she understands – of the way deportation is to be carried out and of the opportunity to lodge a complaint. The information shall include the date of deportation, which is to be conveyed at least thirty-six hours in advance in the case of deportation by air transport; the destination; the means of transport planned to be used and whether or not the deportation will be carried out under escort. In certain cases a psychologist or doctor may be called in to assist in the procedure, if the person affected – due to his/her mental condition or health – is unable to endure the trauma of deportation or he/she requires special assistance during the proceedings. Before and after the deportation procedure, the third-country national deported shall be examined for any marks of injury, and, if any mark of injury is observed on him/her, a medical report shall be obtained. The person affected may lodge a complaint in writing within eight days after detention is carried out against the mode of enforcement, to be sent by mail. The compliant shall be investigated, in accordance with the provisions of the PolA.[234] In accordance with this, the complaint has no suspensive effect and it shall be decided by the County captain or the Headquarters of the Police.

362. According to the FreeA, the main rules on *enforcement of expulsion* orders imply as follows:

(a) wherein expulsion is ordered by the court, it shall be carried out by the Police by way of a ruling; this measure may be contested;
(b) if expulsion cannot be carried out due to non-refoulement rules, the same reasons shall apply where expulsion is ordered by the court. In this case, expulsion shall be declared non-enforceable by the sentencing judge of the competent court; and the person expelled may appeal directly to the sentencing judge to declare the expulsion non-enforceable. The enforcement of expulsion shall be suspended for the duration of the proceeding of the sentencing judge;

234. Act XXXIV of 1994 on Police (it shall be adopted along with its amendments by a qualified majority of votes in legislation).

(c) in order to secure the enforcement of an expulsion measure ordered by the court, the competent authority shall be authorized to confiscate the travel document of the EEA national or family member affected; this action cannot be contested;
(d) if an expulsion ordered by the court – with the exception of imprisonment – is enforced more than two years after it was issued, the competent authority shall re-submit the case to the court ordering the expulsion to have the sentence reviewed. The court shall check whether any material change has taken place in the circumstances of the person expelled since the expulsion order was adopted, or whether the person concerned continues to constitute a serious and genuine threat to public policy or public security, and shall adopt a decision whether to retain or lift the expulsion order.

363. Removal of persons within the ambit of the FreeA may be enforced by way of *deportation*, as follows:

(a) an expulsion ordered by the Court shall be enforced – if the non-refoulement rule is not applicable – by way of transporting the person affected under official escort (deportation), if the court has expelled him/her permanently because he/she does not have the right to free movement and residence;
(b) an expulsion ordered by the court or under immigration laws may be enforced by way of deportation, if the expelled person is released from imprisonment as sentenced for a deliberate crime; or was expelled under immigration laws but failed to leave the country within a month as the expulsion order is final;
(c) the deportation shall be ordered in the resolution ordering the expulsion measure under immigration laws or in a separate resolution. If expulsion is ordered by the court, deportation shall be ordered by way of a ruling on the execution of deportation by court order or in a separate ruling; these rulings may not be contested with the exception of the proposed means of deportation;
(d) suspension of the enforcement of a resolution or ruling ordering deportation may not be requested;
(e) the deportation of a person shall be abandoned if the entry of the person deported to the country of destination is no longer an option; or the person deported requires urgent medical attention;
(f) the competent authority also may cooperate in the enforcement of expulsion ordered by a country that is required to apply the above-mentioned provisions,[235] and
(g) the above-mentioned provisions on deportation by air of third-country nationals shall be applied strictly to the persons within the ambit of the FreeA.

363.1. The deportation of migrants is a pending situation, and its implementation according to the DeptD depends on interstate cooperation[236] and how soon the OIN can prepare all conditions for the escorted expulsion and the entry to the

235. See Council Directive 2003/110/EC of 25 Nov. 2003 on assistance in cases of transit for the purposes of removal by air.
236. Directive 2003/110/EC on assistance to authority in proceedings of deportation by air also intends to upgrade this practical co-operation and Council resolution 2004/573/EC (29 Apr. 2004).

destination country (e.g., obtaining visa, flight ticket, managing transport, transit and accession on the ground of the readmission agreement) '*respecting* [sic] *for the human dignity of deported person during its implementation*' (section 2) as follows:

(a) The personal belongings of the deported person that endanger life, security and public order or flight safety shall be confiscated.
(b) Nutrition for the deported person shall be ensured if the journey takes more than six hours or in case of a person below fourteen, takes more than two hours.
(c) Drinking water is provided every hour.
(d) At least one of the escorts (policeman, OIN officer, psychologist, interpreter, doctor) shall be a female if there is a female and/or a minor among deported persons.
(e) The deported persons on all lawfully applicable coercive measures by the escort shall be informed. '*The limitation of breath is prohibited and to mute the deported person by a tape or another instrument, to give him/her a sedative drug without consent, to addict medicine without a physician's order, to use toxic or paralyzing gas to the migrant is not allowed, as wearing a mask or cowl by the escorts are restricted*' (section 6). This codification rationale is strange: while it follows the law enforcement traditions in applying the general and abstract terms, such as respect for human dignity, the list of restraints suggest that a non-specified behaviour of escorts is lawful or at least tolerated. However, the Ombudsman had required, after the death of a deported person, to set up the minimum criteria of deportation in the legislation – and here the results are evident (Tóth, 2004b).

Chapter 2. Sanctions against Persons Helping Illegal Entry and Residence

§1. Human Smuggling

364. The Penal Code orders to punish *smuggling and trafficking of human beings that are strongly connected to* assistance in illicit stay, abuse with family ties and forgery of public documents (see sections 330–332.). The common feature of these is that they exploit migrants and vulnerable mobile people and it can hardly be divided into accession- and residence-based activities. They overlap one another but are considered as forms of organized crime. Due to this label, the victims of illegal activities are stigmatized and treated as perpetrators, at least in certain public discourses. The CrimPA provides a limited role of the witnessing or injured victims that cannot compensate this one-sided approach: the migrant's consent to the illegal actions is, in fact, supposed by the investigators despite international treaties.

365. *Aiding illegal crossing the state borders* is a delinquency (Article 354 in the Penal Code): if a person who *assists a third-country national to unlawful residence in the territory of a Member State of the EU or EEA* (including Hungary) for financial gain or advantage shall be punished up to two years imprisonment.

366. *Smuggling of human beings* means a delinquency or a felony (Article 353 of the Penal Code):

(a) Any person who provides aid to another person for crossing the state borders: without authorization; or in an unauthorized manner is guilty of a felony punishable by imprisonment for up to three years.
(b) The punishment shall be imprisonment for up to five years for smuggling illegal aliens if it involves several persons.
(c) The punishment shall be imprisonment for up to eight years for smuggling illegal aliens by tormenting the smuggled person, or in a pattern of business operation or in an organized gang.
(d) Any person who engages in preparations for smuggling of illegal aliens, as set forth in (a), (b) or (c) is guilty of a delinquency punishable by imprisonment for up to two years.

§2. Human Trafficking

367. According to the Penal Code, *human trafficking* (Article 192) is a felony. Any person who sells, purchases, conveys or receives another person or exchanges a person for another person, also the person who recruits, transports, houses, hides or appropriates people for such purposes for another party, is guilty of a felony punishable by imprisonment for up to three years.

(a) The punishment shall be imprisonment between one to five years if the criminal act is committed to the detriment of a person under eighteen years of age; to the detriment of a person kept in captivity; to subject the victim to forced labour; for the purpose of sexual perversion or intercourse; for the unlawful use of the human body; in criminal conspiracy; or in a pattern of business operation.
(b) The punishment shall be imprisonment between two to eight years, if the criminal act is committed to the detriment of a person who is in the care, custody, supervision or treatment of the perpetrator; or the motivation is to subject the victim to forced labour; for the purpose of sexual perversion or intercourse or for the unlawful use of the human body, and by force or by threat of force; by deception or by tormenting an injured person.
(c) The punishment shall be imprisonment between five to ten years if the criminal act is committed to the detriment of a person under eighteen years of age; to the detriment of a person kept in captivity or to the detriment of a person who is in the care, custody, supervision or treatment of the perpetrator; any of the motivations being to subject the victim to forced labour; for the purpose of sexual perversion or intercourse or for the unlawful use of the human body, or by force or by threat of force; by deception or by tormenting the injured person or for the purpose of making illegal pornographic materials.
(d) The punishment shall be imprisonment between five to fifteen years or life imprisonment if the criminal act is committed to the detriment of a person under fourteen years of age for any of the motivations to subject the victim to forced labour; for the purpose of sexual perversion or intercourse; for the unlawful use of the human body, or by force or by threat of force; by deception or by tormenting the injured person or for the purpose of making illegal pornographic materials.
(e) Any person who engages in the preparations for human trafficking is guilty of delinquency punishable by imprisonment for up to two years.

368. Trans-border criminality urged a more *effective cooperation* at an international stage among the law enforcement and the administration of justice including that of the Hungarian authorities. The UN Convention passed in Palermo (2000) against T*ransnational Organized Crime* strongly modified the legislation in Hungary in this context, so the ratification and the publication of the Convention[237] took six years, although the Hungarian Ministries were involved in the preparatory phase of the Convention. Its purpose is to criminalize the organized crime on a common basis and to maximize the effectiveness of law enforcement measures in respect of those offences and with due regard to the need to deter the commission of such offences. The legislators had to introduce to the national law the notions of organized criminal group (a structured group of three or more persons, existing for a period of time and acting in concert with the aim of committing one or more serious crimes or offences established in accordance with this Convention, in order to obtain, directly or indirectly, a financial or other material benefit), of structured group (a group that is not randomly formed for the immediate commission of an

237. Act CI of 2006 on publishing the United Nations Convention against Transnational Organized Crime (concluded on 14 Dec. 2000).

offence and that does not need to have formally defined roles for its members, continuity of its membership or a developed structure), while the serious crime shall mean a conduct constituting an offence punishable by a maximum deprivation of liberty for at least four years or a more serious penalty (Article 2). Furthermore, an offence is transnational in nature if it is committed in more than one state; or it is committed in one state, but a substantial part of its preparation, planning, direction or control takes place in another state; or it is committed in one state but involves an organized criminal group that engages in criminal activities in more than one state; or it is committed in one state but has substantial effects in another state (Article 3). In order to upgrade the international judicial cooperation, the Convention determines the modes of mutual legal assistance for the following purposes: taking evidence or statements from persons; effecting service of judicial documents; executing searches, seizures and freezing; examining objects and sites; providing information, evidentiary items and expert evaluations; providing originals or certified copies of relevant documents and records, including Government, bank, financial, corporate or business records; identifying or tracing proceeds of crime, property, instrumentalities or other things for evidentiary purposes; facilitating the voluntary appearance of persons in the requesting state party; or any other type of assistance that is not contrary to the domestic law of the requested state party (Article 18).

369. The Protocol against the smuggling of migrants by land, sea and air, supplementing the UN Convention against Transnational Organized Crime[238] determines the ways and emphasizes the role of international cooperation in smuggling of human beings. In accordance with this, the *smuggling of migrants* means the procurement, in order to obtain, directly or indirectly, a financial or other material benefit, from the illegal entry of a person into a state party of which the person is not a national or a permanent resident. It includes the illegal entry (crossing borders without complying with the necessary requirements for legal entry into the receiving state) and the implementation of a fraudulent travel or identity document that has been falsely made or altered in some material way by anyone other than a person or agency lawfully authorized to make or issue the travel or identity document on behalf of a state; or that has been improperly issued or obtained through misrepresentation, corruption or duress or in any other unlawful manner; or that is being used by a person other than the rightful holder. It implies that the main challenge for the Hungarian legislation and law practitioners means that the migrants shall not become liable to criminal prosecution under this Protocol for the fact of having been the object of conduct set forth in Article 6. It says that each state party shall adopt such legislative and other measures as may be necessary to establish certain kinds of conduct as criminal offences, when committed intentionally and in order to obtain, directly or indirectly, a financial or other material benefit from the smuggling of migrants; when committed for the purpose of enabling the smuggling of migrants: producing a fraudulent travel or identity document; procuring, providing or possessing such a document; enabling a person who is not a national or a permanent resident to remain in the state concerned without complying with the

238. Act CIII of 2006 publishing the Protocol. against the Smuggling of Migrants by Land, Air and Sea

necessary requirements for legally remaining in the state by the aforementioned means or by other illegal means. Criminalization includes attempting to commit this offence, organizing and directing other persons to commit this offence, and as aggravating circumstances pertaining to the offences (endangering lives or safety of the migrants concerned; or inhuman, degrading treatment and exploitation of migrants). The Protocol intends to facilitate the return of a person who has been the object of conduct set forth in Article 6 of this Protocol and is without proper documentation; the state party, of which that person is a national or in which he or she has the right of permanent residence, shall agree to issue, at the request of the receiving state party, such travel documents or other authorization as may be necessary to enable the person to travel to and re-enter its territory.

370. The other Protocol aims to prevent, suppress and punish human trafficking, especially the trafficking of women and children, supplementing the UN Convention.[239] The purposes of this Protocol are to prevent and combat human trafficking, paying particular attention to women and children; to protect and assist the victims of such trafficking, with full respect for their human rights; and to promote cooperation among states parties in this field. According to Article 3, *trafficking in persons* means the recruitment, transportation, transfer, harbouring or receipt of persons, by means of threat or use of force or other forms of coercion, of abduction, of fraud, of deception, of the abuse of power or of a position of vulnerability or of the giving or receiving of payments or benefits to achieve the consent of a person having control over another person, for the purpose of exploitation. The exploitation includes, at a minimum, the exploitation of the prostitution of others or other forms of sexual exploitation, forced labour or services, slavery or practices similar to slavery, servitude or the removal of organs. The consent of a victim of human trafficking to the intended exploitation shall be irrelevant. The recruitment, transportation, transfer, harbouring or receipt of a child for the purpose of exploitation shall be considered 'trafficking in persons', even if this does not involve any of the aforementioned means. Similar to the other protocol, its goal is to adopt such legislative and other measures as may be necessary to establish as criminal offences the conduct set forth in Article 3, when committed intentionally, including the attempt to commit this offence, organizing and directing other persons to commit this offence. Furthermore, the party states shall ensure for victims the information regarding relevant Court and administrative proceedings; assistance to enable their views and concerns to be presented and considered at appropriate stages of criminal proceedings against offenders, in a manner not prejudicial to the rights of the defence. The proper support for the victims covers the physical, psychological and social recovery of the victims of human trafficking, appropriate housing, counselling in a language that the victims of human trafficking can understand, medical and material assistance and employment, educational and training opportunities. The final aim is the repatriation of victims supporting their return (Article 8).

239. Act CII of 2006 publishing the Protocol to Prevent, Suppress and Punish Trafficking in Persons, Especially Women and Children.

371. The Council of Europe has also a convention supporting the victims of human trafficking and aiming at the criminalization of this felony.[240] That Convention shall apply to all forms of *trafficking in human beings*, whether national or transnational, whether or not connected with organized crime. The definition of 'trafficking in human beings' is the same as in the Protocol to prevent, suppress and punish trafficking in persons, especially women and children, supplementing the UN Convention. However, it contains provisions on the recovery, reflection period and the residence permit of the victims in cooperation with the investigation or judicial authority combating organized crime and trafficking networks. Moreover, it intends to set up the common substantial criminal legal basis towards the enhanced international cooperation in fighting against human trafficking (Chapter IV). Each party shall adopt such legislative and other measures as may be necessary to establish as criminal offences the conduct contained in the definition, when committed intentionally; the use of services which are the object of exploitation, with the knowledge that the person is a victim of human trafficking; forging a travel or identity document; procuring or providing such a document; retaining, removing, concealing, damaging or destroying a travel or identity document of another person. It defines a corporate liability for a criminal offence established in accordance with this Convention (e.g., the lack of supervision or control by a natural person). The group of experts on the action against human trafficking (GRETA) shall monitor the implementation of this Convention by the parties. Although human trafficking was incorporated to the Penal Code in 1998, it had to modify soon (Act CXXI of 2001) due to the Protocol. The amendment implies the extension of the list of forbidden behaviour.

372. Finally, the efforts on combating organized crime are to be noted, in hindering the channelization of earnings from the illicit criminal activities to legal transactions as well as further unlawful transactions or economy. For instance, Hungary is a party state of the UN Convention for the suppression of the financing of terrorism.[241]

373. In sum, there are three main differences between the trafficking and smuggling in human beings by the international public law that shall be expressed clearly in the domestic legislation and in the counter-strategy.[242] The consent of migrants is absent or is based on the abusive or misleading conduct of traffickers, while in smuggling the migrants have consented to be carried across the borders. The exploitation is a leading character of trafficking as a gainful activity in a longer or continuous abuse while the smugglers' activity is practically over after crossing the border. Finally, smuggling by definition requires a border crossing, while human

240. Council of Europe, CETS No. 197 Convention against Trafficking in Human Beings (Warsaw, 16 May 2005) was entered into force on 1 Feb. 2008. It is published in the Act XVIII of 2013 applicable in Hungary since August 2013 although it was signed in 2007.

241. Act LIX of 2002 on publishing the International Convention for the suppression of the financing of terrorism (9 Dec. 1999).

242. See the National program combating human trafficking (2013-206 as determined in the Government Resolution No. 1351 of 9 Jun. 2013).

trafficking may be conducted inside the country (e.g., through forced sexual services or forced labour).

374. Taking into account the aims of the harmonization of substantive criminal law, the *mutual assistance in criminal procedure and investigation or the extradition* is inevitable at the international level. It is ensured in the following legal sources, beyond the Criminal Code (recognition of the judgment of a foreign authority) and the CrimPA:

(a) According to the UN Convention cited above, all severe felonies committed in an organized form between the party states constitute extraditable offences. Moreover, these *extraditable offences* shall be included in any extradition treaty.
(b) Legal assistance in criminal matters is regulated in international (bilateral, regional) agreements and in a supplementary way in laws. For instance, the agreement of the South-Eastern European Initiative on Cooperation (SECI)[243] intends to upgrade the collaboration of party states in combating transnational offences. It covers the investigation authorities (Police, customs offices) within the region, engaged in fighting against organized crime. The Secretariat of the SECI through the national contact points assists the party states in the prevention, investigation, suppression and prosecution of trans-border offences without the derogation of the Schengen acquis and the implementation of the existing treaties or treaties that will be concluded in the future. Furthermore, the Secretariat is in contact with the ICPO-Interpol in Police issues and the World Customs Organisation (WCO) in customs issues exchanging data. The mutual legal assistance may be performed in the way of providing information and data (e.g., in control of persons, techniques of checking). Under the aegis of the Council of Europe, conventions on *extradition*[244] *and transfer of sentenced perpetrators* were developed. Hungary as party state has made some declarations to those. In accordance with this, the extradition of a Hungarian citizen may be allowed if he/she is a dual citizen and his/her domicile is out of Hungary while the claim for the extradition of a migrant with a permanent residence permit in Hungary may be refused. The claim for extradition shall be denied if the requested person is subject to the implementation or the sentence of capital punishment, unless the requesting state guarantees the non-implementation of such a judgment. Also, the claim for the transfer of a sentenced Hungarian citizen and migrant with a permanent residence permit in Hungary shall be refused. A notice on the transport of a sentenced person by air via Hungary is required in advance.
(c) In the absence of specific (international) provisions on the legal assistance in trans-border criminal cases, Act XXXVIII of 1996 shall be applied, including

243. Act CXV of 2000 on publishing the SECI agreement (26 May 1999, Bucharest).
244. Act XVIII of 1994 on publishing the European Convention on Extradition (1957, Paris) and its additional Protocol; Act XX of 1994 on publishing the Convention on Transfer of Sentenced Persons (1983, Strasbourg); Act LXVII of 2001 on publishing the Supplementary Protocol (1997) to the Convention on Transfer of Sentenced Persons (1983, Strasbourg).

the surrender of the criminal procedure.[245] The extradition shall not be provided, when the felony in question has lapsed either in Hungary, or in the requesting state; the claimed person or offence has obtained a pardon; the necessary submission or approval to the criminal procedure is missing; the requested claim relates to res judicata. The extradition of the Hungarian national may be decided if the dual national has the domicile abroad. The surrender of the Hungarian citizen is allowed to a third-country if he/she was extradited to Hungary and the criminal procedure was completed here. The extradition of the refugees to a non-safe country (the AsylA) is forbidden, while the protection seekers shall not be extradited to their country of origin at least until the completion of the asylum procedure; however, the detention prior to the extradition shall not be prolonged for up to twenty-four months. The temporary protected and persons in subsidiary protection shall not be extradited to their country of origin. The claim for the extradition shall be denied if the requested person is subject to the implementation or a sentence of capital punishment unless the requesting state guarantees the non-implementation of such a judgment to the minister of justice and law enforcement. Furthermore, the Minister may allow the extradition if there will be no further criminal procedure for the requested offence, and the requested person will not be surrendered to a third country, and he/she may leave the country after the completed (implemented) criminal procedure. The Capital Court upon the request of the public prosecutor's office is competent in the procedure pertaining to the extradition claim including the negotiation, personal hearing and involvement of the defender of the extraditing person and ordering detention prior to extradition.

(d) Act CLXXX of 2012 defines the procedure on the cooperation with the Member States of the EU in criminal matters.[246] It covers the implementation and the procedure pertaining to the European Arrest Warrant, and the surrender of the perpetrators. This Act is applicable to criminal acts and offences – including the covert and joint investigation and co-operation with Europol and Eurojust – that are enlisted in the Appendix in conformity with the EC law.[247] The EAW may be applied – inter alia – in the following offences referring to the Penal Code: human trafficking, smuggling in human beings for gain or on the grounds of business, aiding illegal residence, illegal usage of (part from a) human body as well as criminal offences of racism (violence against national, ethnical, racial or a religious community).

245. The consolidated Act transposes the framework decision of 2008/675/IB and s. 25 of European Parliament and the Council Directive 2011/93/EU, 13 December.

246. The scope of the Act LIV of 2002 on co-operation among the criminal investigation organizations covers the Police, customs officers and public prosecutor's control on investigation and these organizations' trans-border collaboration in international criminal offences. The judicial phase of criminal procedure is not within the ambit of this Act. Also, the data exchange within the Schengen Implementation Agreement belongs to another law (Act CV of 2007).

247. The secondary law appears in the framework of decisions such as 2006/980/IB, 2009/829/IB, 2008/909/IB.

375. The *National Strategy* on countering human trafficking was adopted by the Government[248]due to the critics of the GRETA and the transposing deadline of the Directive on prevention and fighting against trafficking of human beings in the European Union.[249] It covers the period 2013–2016 on the grounds of prior national strategy (2008–2012) laying down the responsibility of the Ministry of Justice and Public Administration that had to prepare an action plan including the raising of awareness, the co-ordination and research projects assessing the prior experiences (e.g., the manual made by the IOM and the ministries, joint committee and working group of the Ministry of Foreign Affairs and the American statutory authority (TIP Office)[250]). The national co-ordinator in the Ministry of the Interior maintains contacts with all Governmental, law enforcement and international actors (in particular with Austria, Belgium, Switzerland, Germany and Netherlands). The Headquarters of the Police[251] issued a resolution on the Police tasks combating prostitution and human trafficking in late 2007. Division of Counter-Trafficking in Human Beings (National Investigation Office – Headquarters of the Police)[252] operates only with eleven workers but in strong cooperation with the Interpol, the Europol, the SECI and the OIN. Moreover, the reform of the Penal Code in 2012, the amendment of the Act CXXXV of 2005 on compensation of victims in criminal offences including the victims of human trafficking and a new regulation on identification of these victims[253] may demonstrate the regulative efforts. The amended Act provides assistance for victims of human trafficking regardless their co-operation with investigation authority. The Act LXXXV of 2001 on the protection of the parties in the criminal procedure and the supporters to criminal justice introduced the assistance for victims of human trafficking. This protection programme relates to the Justice Office and the Police providing a new living environment and furnishing a new identity, personal documents and social assistance to persons (witnesses, collaborators in criminal investigation and trial) that are endangered. This regime fits to the penal law measures applicable against the corporate, legal entities (Act CIV of 2001) if their key personnel commit intentional criminal acts or offences supporting human trafficking (for instance, providing finances to this exploitative business). The victims of illegal migration and smuggling in human beings may obtain a temporary residence permit on humanitarian grounds (in the absence of the formal criteria of lawful residence) if they actively cooperate with the Police or other investigation authority in the disclosure of illicit migration networks and supporters (see the ThirdA and the ThirdD). The national strategy sets up five priorities: the efficiency of the prevention and investigation of crimes shall be improved; the level of protection of victims shall be upgraded; horizontal and vertical co-ordination in combat human trafficking at national and at international level shall be enhanced

248. Government Resolution No.1351 of 9 Jun. 2013.
249. European Parliament and the Council Directive 2011/36/EU, 5 Apr. 2011 shall be transposed up to Apr. 2013.
250. Its Report (12 Jun. 2007) considers Hungary as a progressive state fighting against human trafficking on the grounds of national priorities in prevention, assistance for victims, efforts to raise awareness and proper legislation. However, it criticized the weak co-ordination regime in combat.
251. HQP resolution No. 46 of 2007, 20 December.
252. Decree of the Minister of Justice and Law Enforcement No. 3 of 2008, 16 January.
253. Government Decree No.354 of 2012, 13 December.

including the regular exchange of statistical data; return of victims must be elaborated and assisted. A shelter for victims was opened in 2005, operated by an NGO and financed by the OIN. Since its opening, some dozens of victims of trafficking were accommodated in it. A further shelter is projected to 2015. It is regrettable that necessary human and financial resources of these priorities are only planned but not ensured properly to the period in concern.

376. The CrimPA contains the entitlement for the criminal Court and the investigation authority to deprive the liberty of the alleged perpetrator in *detention* and *pre-trial detention* if there is a well-founded suspicion of the commission of a criminal offence, and his/her confinement is necessary to prevent the disappearance or other disturbance of the investigation or the criminal procedure. The detention shall not be longer than seventy-two hours, while the pre-trial detention from one month to the end of the trial would take, and the close family members of the person concerned shall be informed within twenty-four hours. However, neither the detention nor the pre-trial detention are sanctions, they are only penal procedural measures securing the proceedings.

Part VI. Legal Remedies and Procedural Safeguards

Chapter 1. Legal Remedies in Case of Refusal of Right to Enter, Stay or Reside

377. Without repetition of substantial and certain procedural rules, including the special categories of migrants in Parts I-V, the following provisions on legal remedy shall be summarized in the context of entry and residence of persons within the ambit of the ThirdA and the FreeA:

Table 16 Remedy in Entry and Residence Authorization

Scope	*Legal Measure*	*Remedy*	*With Delaying Effect*	*Submission Deadline*	*Final Decision Made by*	*Decision Deadline*	*Impacts*
FreeA	Refusal at border by decision	No	Entry is allowed if proper documents are submitted within seventy-two hours				
ThirdA	Refusal at border	No	Until departure (by vehicle) foreigner shall stay on board or in designated place at border				
ThirdD	Short-term visa is refused at border	Appeal	No	Within three days to border police	OIN	Within five days	Issuance of visa
FreeD	Short-term visa is refused at border	Appeal	No	Within three days to regional directorate	OIN	Within five days	Issuance of visa or not
ThirdD FreeA	Short-term visa is refused	Appeal	No	Within eight days to consular official	Minister	Within fifteen days	Issuance of visa or not
FreeD	Short-term visa is annulled or withdrawn	Appeal	Yes	Within three days to the police, or to the regional directorate	HQ of the Police OIN	Within five days	Issuance of new visa or not

ThirdD	Short-term visa is annulled or withdrawn	Appeal	Yes	Within three days to consular official, or to police, or to the regional directorate	Minister HQ of Police OIN	Within five days	Issuance of new visa
ThirdD	Short-term visa extension is refused	Appeal	Yes	Within three days to regional directorate	OIN	Within three days	Extension of visa
ThirdD FreeD	Refusal of small border traffic certificate	Appeal	Yes	to consular official (within fifteen days)	Minister	(within twenty-one days)	Issuance of the certificate or not
ThirdA FreeA	Short-term visa is refused, annulled or withdrawn by public administration	Judicial review	No	Within three days to first instance admin. authority	Capital Administrative Court	Within eight days in a non-litigation procedure	New procedure is ordered or not

Scope	*Legal Measure*	*Remedy*	*With Delaying Effect*	*Submission Deadline*	*Final Decision Made by*	*Decision Deadline*	*Impacts*
ThirdA	Refusal of seasonal labour visa, national visa, withdrawal of national visa	No appeal					
ThirdD	Residence permit is refused	Appeal	Yes	Within eight days to consular official	OIN	Within twenty-one days	
ThirdD	Withdrawal of residence permit	Appeal	Yes	Within eight days to regional directorate	OIN	Within twenty-one days	Issuance of a new permit
ThirdD	National or EC settlement permit is refused	Appeal	Yes	(within fifteen days)	OIN	Within one month	Issuance of the permit or not

378. Procedural provision on entry and residence of migrants: Rules on entry and residence authorization of migrants are within the ambit of the ThirdA, the FreeA and its executive decrees while AdminA is secondary in comparison to these special legal sources. This fact is indicated in the tables wherein the deadline is stated within parentheses. For instance, if there is no administrative remedy, the County/Capital Court is entitled to review the decision unless it is directly prohibited. If judicial review is available, the Court is entitled to modify the administrative organ's decision on prohibited entry and residence. From the above list, it is clear that guarantees are not the same for persons within the ambit of the FreeA and those within the ambit of the ThirdA. However, the differences are more obvious in coercive measures as can be seen below (Table 17).

Table 17 Remedy for Coercive Measures

Scope	*Legal Measure*	*Remedy*	*With Delaying Effect*	*Submission Deadline*	*Final Decision Made by*	*Decision Deadline*	*Impacts*
FreeA	Expulsion order	Only judicial review	No	Personal hearing if possible	County/ Capital Court	Within eight days	Annulled order or repetition of administrative procedure or refusal
FreeA	Exclusion order						
ThirdA	Expulsion order	Judicial review	No	Within eight days	County/ Capital Court	Within fifteen days	Annulled order or repetition of administrative procedure or refusal
FreeA	Revision of exclusion order	Request	No	After one year of final decision on exclusion order	OIN	Within three months	Refusal or deleted prohibition of entry
FreeA	Enforcement of expulsion ordered by the Court in a penal case	Complaint	No	(within fifteen days)	OIN	(within twenty-one days)	Refusal or acceptance
FreeA		Request for non-refoulement	Yes	Opinion of OIN is attached	County/ Capital Court		Annulled order or refusal

FreeA FreeD	Deportation order	Complaint for method of enforcement	No	Within eight days after enforcement in writing by post	OIN	Within fifteen days	Apology or refusal
FreeD	Deletion of deportation order (in absence of enforcement criteria)	No	If necessary conditions to the enforcement are provided, deletion is annulled				
ThirdA	Expulsion (together with withdrawal of residence permit, visa, or its refusal)	Joint remedy	Judicial review				
ThirdA	Independently ordered exclusion	Appeal only	Yes	Within twenty-four hours	OIN	Within eight days	Annulled order or refusal
ThirdA	Surrender on the grounds of readmission agreement	Complaint	No	Within twenty-four hours	OIN	(within twenty-one days)	Annulled order or refusal
ThirdA	Refusal of prolongation the deadline for voluntary leaving the country	Complaint	No	Immediately	OIN	(within twenty-one days)	Refusal or prolongation of the deadline

Scope	*Legal Measure*	*Remedy*	*With Delaying Effect*	*Submission Deadline*	*Final Decision Made by*	*Decision Deadline*	*Impacts*
ThirdA	Suspension of enforcement of expulsion order (e.g., in absence of its preconditions)	No					
ThirdA	Surrender to another Member State of the EU on the grounds of Dublin regime	Judicial review	No	Within three days	County/ Capital Court in non-litigation process (no hearing of migrant)	Within eight days	Annulled order or repetition of administrative procedure or refusal No further remedy
ThirdA	Enforcement of expulsion ordered by the Court in a penal case	Complaint	No	(within fifteen days)	OIN	(within twenty-one days)	Annulled order or refusal
ThirdA		Request for non-refoulement	Yes	Before release from the penal institution	Judge of penal institution		Annulled order or refusal
ThirdA	Enforcement of deportation order (in a determined way)	Complaint	No	Within twenty-four hours	OIN or HQ of the Police	Within eight days	Annulled order or refusal

ThirdA	Enforcement of deportation order	(complaint)	No		County/ Capital Public prosecutor Office		Unlawful order is annulled and instruction is given on the grounds of legality

379. Without repeating the other procedural guarantees, the common safeguards are summarized below, as shall be available for all persons under the personal scope of the ThirdA and the FreeA:

(a) The right to free movement and residence (the FreeA) may be restricted incompliance with the principle of proportionality and based exclusively on the personal conduct of the individual concerned, where such personal conduct represents a genuine, present and sufficiently serious threat affecting public policy, public security or public health.[254] Naturally, these criteria (Article 33 of FreeA) require a longer practice at the migration authority and other practitioners taking into account the relevant and evolving case law of the European Court of Justice (Tóth, 2007a; Carlier, 2008). While the continental legal system of Hungary dislikes implementing the case law, the legal education and the notion of rule-of-law alienates law practitioners from the case law either in a domestic or in an international context. For this reason, the requirements of proportionality, individualization in the sanctioning and the real threat had to be defined in the legislation.
(b) The non-refoulement requirement shall be respected in all phases of the proceedings, including the expulsion by the Court. This implies that the migrant shall not be turned back or expelled to the territory of a country that fails to satisfy the criteria of safe country of origin or safe third-country regarding the person in question, in particular where the foreign national is likely to be subjected to persecution on the grounds of his race, religion, nationality, social affiliation or political conviction, nor to the territory or the frontier of a country where there is substantial reason to believe that the expelled foreign national is likely to be subjected to torture or any other form of cruel, inhuman or degrading treatment or capital punishment. Furthermore, any foreign national whose application for refugee status is pending may be turned back or expelled only if his application is refused by the final and executable decision of the refugee authority.
(c) In addition, the competent authority, before the implementation of measures for the return, carrying out an expulsion order, and before the enforcement of the Court-ordered expulsion shall investigate whether this restriction applies towards a non-EEA state. In this process, the competent authority shall request the opinion of the refugee unit of the OIN that shall comply with the above request without delay. The competent authority shall suspend any pending immigration-related proceedings or the enforcement of such a resolution, and shall request the competent Regional Directorate to issue a humanitarian residence permit to the person in question if it determines that this restriction applies. The Regional Directorate shall monitor whether the restriction of return applies on a regular basis, or shall check once a year by contacting the central immigration records office. Where the restriction of return no longer applies to an EEA national or his/her family member whose immigration-related procedure has been suspended, the competent authority shall resume the proceeding.

254. Rutili case (C-36/75), Bonsignore case (C-67/74).

(d) The competent authority shall inform the parties affected – in the language that the person in question understands – about their rights and obligations conferred in the FreeA or the ThirdA, in particular their right to legal recourse, claim for compensation, and the means for enforcing their rights. The following shall also be conveyed verbally to the client in his/her native language or in another language that he/she understands: decisions, the Court's decision adopted in the judicial review, including a decision ordering detention prior to the deportation and in connection with the extension of such a detention.
(e) In the proceedings launched upon the request in accordance with the FreeA or the ThirdA, the client shall submit his/her request in person, and shall appear in person in front of the competent authority to collect his/her registration certificate. The competent authority may not require an applicant to appear in person if he/she is unable to do so due to health reasons. Those proceedings in which the applicant is required to appear in person cannot be administered by way of electronic means.
(f) If the exclusion (prohibited entry and residence) is ordered, the operative part of the resolution shall be displayed on a website specified in the specific separate legislation.
(g) Where no appeal is permitted under the FreeA or the ThirdA, the reopening of the case and the proceedings under reasons of equity may not be requested.
(h) In proceedings for the issuance of visas, the costs of translation and interpretation services and the fees of a sign language interpreter (costs of language services) shall be borne by the applicant. In addition, in the proceedings launched upon request, the costs of the delivery of the decision and the costs of language services, as well as these costs in proceedings launched ex officio, shall be covered by the authority.
(i) The immigration authority, when carrying out an expulsion measure against the third-country national, shall inform the person affected of his/her right to seek legal advice and representation, or the assistance of a registered legal aid organization.

380. According to the PolA, a person subjected to measures taken by the policeman may submit a complaint to the commander (supervisor) of the policeman within thirty days. The complaint shall be decided within thirty days stating whether the measure was lawful or illegitimate. Appeal against the commander's decision may be submitted also within thirty days to the higher police unit (e.g., a police check conducted by a policeman of the city, his vertical superior unit being the county police station). If the measure was taken by a central unit of the Police, the complaint is excluded (e.g., when deportation by air is enforced by the Headquarters of the Police and the OIN), but a judicial review is available (Article 93/B).

381. With reference to the information in paragraphs 25 and 26, the AdminA is secondary in relation to entry, residence and coercive measures taken for persons within the ambit of the FreeA and the ThirdA, if these acts are silent regarding certain procedural issues. It means that these acts would destroy the guarantees provided in AdminA without special explicit reasons. The implicit reason for specific legislation implies a security risk relating to non-nationals' presence in the country.

Article 13 of AdminA ensures the right to derogation in the event of the implementation and direct enforcement of EU legal acts and international commitments published in the act. As a result, the appeal may be excluded in the ThirdA and the FreeA, and the judicial review of the contested decision will be available without delay. However, the derogation implies also the exclusion of all kinds of legal remedy against certain measures. If the appeal is ensured in decisions on the grounds of the ThirdA and the FreeA, the applicant may submit new evidences and refer to new facts, and the superior authority may modify the substantial decision or annul the unlawful decision at first instance, issuing a final, lawful and fair decision. The general cost of administrative appeal is 16 EUR. AdminA (Article 100) generally excludes appeal (remedy inside the administrative procedure) if the first instance decision was made by a central authority (e.g., the OIN or the minister). In this case, the first instance administrative decision becomes final. The judicial remedy against the final administrative decision (if the appeal has been decided or is excluded) may be submitted within thirty days from the delivery of the decision with reference only to the unlawful action of the administrative organization. Differing from the appeal, the judicial review does not involve any delay unless the Court, upon request of the applicant, orders the suspension of the decision. The Administrative Court (at county or capital level) proceeds in a non-litigation (without meeting the applicant) process as a main rule without a determined deadline (Article 109).

382. The MinofA prohibits violation of the rules on border crossing and residence (See paragraph 305). The first instance procedure in these minor offences belongs to the joint directorate of Police stations, and the submitted complaint against the Police's decision including the Public Prosecutor's protest is reviewed by the local (District) Court (single judge or justice secretary) within thirteen days from the submission without negotiation. The Court decision may confirm the Police decision refusing the protest of the Public Prosecutor or the complaint, modify the decision or order a new fair procedure by the Police accepting the protest. With the approval of the Public Prosecutor, the perpetrator of the minor offence may be forced by the Police to appear at the Police directorate or at the Court if despite the official order he/she had failed to appear without providing a justification in advance.

383. The Penal Code orders the punishment of smuggling, human trafficking, and any assistance in illicit staying (See the paragraphs 332, 364-367, 373). Beyond the right to a fair procedure, the provisions in connection with remedy are summarized in accordance with the CrimPA, as follows:

(a) The legal remedy is ensured against decisions, measures or the default of the Court, Public Prosecutor and the investigation authority with certain exceptions by law (e.g., the Supreme Court's decision cannot be reviewed in a regular remedy procedure).
(b) The appeal against the first instance judgment with a suspensive effect refers either to facts or the legal interpretation, including the appeal, only on the reasoning of the judgment. However, the suspension of the implementation covers the parts of the judgment that are reviewed by the second instance Court.

Moreover, the second instance Court verifies all the documents of investigation and the trial including facts, evidences, legal conclusions of judges and the implied punishment regardless of who submitted the appeal and why. If the appeal relates to a procedural decision of the Court, it shall be decided without litigation if a fact-finding is not necessary. Considering the unfounded judgment of the Court of first instance, the Court of second instance has to modify the facts of the case (through an additional fact-finding) and/or its legal interpretation, conclusions and decision on the basis of documents confirming or refusing the first instance judgment and acquit the charged person or abolish the trial.

(c) The decision in the second instance may be reviewed if the Court violated the substantial penal law, for example, the guilt of the perpetrator was stated in an action that was not part of the facts in the first instance, or it acquits the perpetrator who was sentenced in the first instance judgment. New facts and evidences cannot be announced in the appeal against the second instance decision of the Court.

(d) The prohibition of aggravated punishment, including the withdrawal of acquittal, limits the power of the second instance Court in decision if the appeal is submitted without the claim for a greater punishment of the charged perpetrator.

(e) Anybody may capture the perpetrator *in situ* of commission, notifying the Police or delivering him/her to the investigation authority. The apprehension of the perpetrator takes a maximum of seventy-two hours that has to be confirmed by the public prosecutor, the pre-trial detention ordered by the investigation authority may take a maximum of one month, otherwise upon the proposal of the Public Prosecutor it can be ordered by the judge or the Court. Instead of the pre-trial detention, a prohibition for leaving the place of residence or custody at home may be determined. The apprehension and the pre-trial detention are accompanied by the withholding of the perpetrator's passport for the duration of the detention. Furthermore, the ordered prohibition for leaving the place of residence or custody at home shall be announced to the passport authority or to the OIN to declare the names of persons whose exit is forbidden.

(f) The CrimPA – as other codes – prevents the disadvantages that could be faced by non-Hungarian speakers during the procedure. To this aim, the usage of the native language in oral and written communication shall be ensured for the participants in the proceedings in accordance with international agreements, including the convention on regional and minority languages. It covers the free usage of alternative language upon the request of the participants. Each document that shall be communicated to the participants shall be translated to the aforementioned language by the issuing authority (Court, Public Prosecutor or investigating authority) unless the participant concerned manifestly dispenses with translation.

Chapter 2. Legal Remedies in Case of Detention

384. Limitation of liberty includes detention prior to expulsion or deportation and the designated compulsory confinement in special shelters run by the Police as well as the compulsion to stay in a designated area in the border zone before departure (surrender, removal or refusal at borders). Without repeating the main reasons and conditions regarding how persons within the purview of migration laws can be deprived of their liberty, it is important to compare the requirement stated in Article 5 of the ECHR to the domestic rules. Article 5 states that 'No one shall be deprived of his liberty save in the following cases and in accordance with a procedure prescribed by law – inter alia – as the lawful arrest or detention of a person for non-compliance with the lawful order of a court or in order to secure the fulfilment of any obligation prescribed by law (point b); or the lawful arrest or detention of a person to prevent his effecting an unauthorized entry into the country or of a person against whom action is being taken with a view to deportation or extradition (point f).' It is notable that migrants are not offenders, and their expulsion – and the corresponding exclusion from the country – is based on convictions only in exceptional cases. In the majority of cases, they cannot meet the requirements of lawful entry and/or residence for various reasons and their deprivation of liberty under different terminologies (detention, designated place of residence in community hostel, confinement) are ordered for a wider set of reasons than in Article 5. Moreover, it would be important to ensure for them a speedy revision of court and release if the detention is not lawful (subsection 5) and an enforceable right to compensation (subsection 6). The Table 18 may demonstrate as follows:

(a) there is a difference between the position of persons within the ambit of the FreeA and the ThirdA: EEA nationals and family members may be detained for up to three months and the other migrants may be detained for up to twelve months whereas the legal reasoning is substantially the same. It implies a discrimination within a homogeneous group;
(b) compulsory confinement is formally neither arrest nor detention but these institutes are run by the Police furnished with cameras, security checks and a strict regime of entry and residence. The questions arise as to why migrants have to reside for long periods in closed institutions and whether they severely endanger the public order. Their criminality is not significant;
(c) there is no deadline for the passing of the judicial decision. It is rather a tradition that the Court is entitled to proceed at its own pace and there is a deadline for its decision only in exceptional cases. Hence the evaluation of 'reasonable time' in a fair procedure in habeas corpus is hardly possible;[255]

255. See the similar cases in the ECHR, *Maglódi v. Hungary* – C-30103/02, 9 Nov. 2004; *Imre v. Hungary* C-53129/99, 2 Dec. 2003, violation of Art. 5 for very long detention without individual threat-evaluation in its prolongation.

(d) judicial review is made by the local (District) court as a single judge, whereas at the local level there is no judge responsible for the revision of administrative decisions. The local court has only two kinds of cases: penal and civil law. Hence, in many cases the penal judge proceeds to implement (directly or indirectly) the principles and provisions of CrimPA in cases of non-convicted persons.
(e) there is no suspensive effect of judicial review, unless the Court orders the non-enforcement of the administrative decision for public policy or the acceptable private interest of the applicant;
(f) there is no personal hearing in judicial review (of administrative decision or non-litigation process). If personal hearing is required, it appears directly in the provisions;
(g) there is no *ex lege* compensation for unlawful administrative limitation and deprivation of liberty. It is available only in CrimPA.

Table 18 Legal Remedies in Case of Detention

Scope	*Legal Measure*	*Remedy*	*With Delaying Effect*	*Submission Deadline*	*Final Decision Made by*	*Decision Deadline*	*Impacts*
FreeA	Detention prior to deportation	Judicial review	No	Within seventy-two hours in writing or orally	Local (District) Court	Immediately but within eight days	Termination of detention or refusal No further remedy
FreeA FreeD	Prolongation of detention prior to deportation with thirty days at a time (up to three months)			Within twenty-four hours in writing or orally			
FreeD	Designation of the place for detention prior to deportation	No					

ThirdA	Detention order by immigration laws	Judicial review	No	Within seventy-two hours	Local (District) Court		Termination of detention or refusal No further remedy
ThirdA ThirdD	Prolongation of detention order by the immigration laws up with thirty days at a time (up to twelve months)	Judicial review	No	Within twenty-four hours in writing or orally	Local (District) Court		
ThirdA	Detention order prior to expulsion	Judicial review	No	Within seventy-two hours	Local (District) Court	Within eight days	
ThirdA	Prolongation of detention prior to expulsion with thirty days	Judicial review	No	Within twenty-four hours	Local (District) Court		
ThirdA	Detention order (how it is enforced)	Complaint	No		Local (District) Court	Within eight days	

Scope	*Legal Measure*	*Remedy*	*With Delaying Effect*	*Submission Deadline*	*Final Decision Made by*	*Decision Deadline*	*Impacts*
ThirdA	Exceptional conditions for mass-detention prior to expulsion (its length)	Judicial review for its prolongation after the seventh day	No	Within five days	Local (District) Court		Termination of detention or refusal
ThirdA	Order and prolongation of designated place in compulsory confinement	Complaint	No	At any time	Local (District) Court	Within eight days	Termination of designation or refusal if all necessary documents are supplemented
DetD	Conditions in detention and legality of order if inmate's complaint is refused	Complaint	No	Within eight days	County/ Capital Police Commander	Immediately but within fifteen days	Modification of decision or immediate refusal if it is a repeated claim within three months and not relating to health conditions

DetD	Conditions in detention, confinement	Complaint	No	At any time	County/ Capital Public Prosecutor or Ombudsman	Personal hearing	Request to annul the unlawful decision
DetD	Decision on repay the cost of caused damages in detention by inmate	Judicial review	No	Within thirty days	County/ Capital Court		Modification or annulment of the decision

385. Some guarantees can be found in the *detention procedure* for the EEA national and the family members in the FreeA and FreeD as follows:

(a) If an expulsion ordered by the Court – with the exception of imprisonment – is enforced more than two years after it was issued, the competent authority shall re-submit the case to the court ordering the expulsion to have the sentence reviewed. The court shall check whether any material change has taken place in the circumstances of the person expelled since the expulsion order was adopted, or whether the person concerned continues to constitute a serious and genuine threat to public policy or public security, and shall adopt a decision whether to retain or lift the expulsion order.
(b) The court shall proceed with a single judge presiding in proceedings concerning complaints and for the extension of detention prior to deportation and shall conclude the case by way of a ruling. If the judge has dismissed a complaint or a motion for extension, another request or motion may not be lodged on the same grounds.
(c) In any case concerning the extension of detention prior to deportation beyond the seventy-two-hour time limit by the court, and in proceedings relating to complaints and further extension of detention, the detainee shall be granted a personal hearing upon request.
(d) The hearing may be conducted at the place of detention and in the absence of the legal representative. The court may disregard the holding of a hearing if the person under detention prior to deportation is unable to attend because he/she is being treated in an in-patient medical institution, or if the complaint or the motion does not originate with a party entitled to do so. The EEA national or his/her family member, and the immigration authority shall present their evidence in writing or verbally during the hearing. Parties shall be given the opportunity to study the evidence presented. If the EEA national or his/her family member is not present, or the proponent authority is not represented, but they have submitted their comments in advance in writing, they will be introduced by the judge.
(e) The court's decision shall be delivered to the EEA national or his/her family member who has been affected, and to the immigration authority. If the EEA national or his/her family member has a legal representative or a representative *ad litem*, they shall be informed as well. The court decision shall be announced verbally and shall also be delivered in writing without delay.
(f) The court proceedings are exempt from charges.

386. The ThirdA contains partly similar, partly different *procedural safeguards in detention*:

(a) A ban for the enforcement of expulsion measures ordered by the Court may be imposed by the sentencing judge. If it is applied, the person expelled may appeal directly to the sentencing judge on one occasion – in connection with the execution of the same judgment – to declare the expulsion non-enforceable. If the person expelled submits his request which was addressed to the sentencing judge to the immigration authority, the immigration authority shall forward it without undue delay to the competent sentencing judge with its opinion attached.

(b) The enforcement of expulsion shall be suspended for the duration of the proceeding of the sentencing judge.

(c) The Court shall proceed with a single judge presiding in proceedings concerning complaints and for the extension of detention and shall conclude the case by way of a ruling. If the court has dismissed a complaint or a motion for extension, another request or motion may not be lodged on the same grounds.

(d) In the Court proceedings, representation for the third-country national may only be provided by a legal representative. The Court shall appoint a representative *ad litem* for any third-country national or his/her family member who does not understand the Hungarian language and is unable to contract the services of a legal representative on his/her own.

(e) In any case concerning the extension of detention beyond the seventy-two-hour time limit by the Court, and in proceedings relating to complaints and further extension of detention, the detainee shall be granted a personal hearing upon request. The hearing may be conducted at the place of detention and in the absence of the third-country national's legal representative. The court may disregard the holding of a hearing if the third-country national is unable to attend because he/she is being treated in an in-patient medical institution, or if the complaint or the motion does not originate with a party entitled to do so.

(f) The third-country national and the immigration authority shall present their evidence in writing or verbally during the hearing. Parties shall be given the opportunity to study the evidence presented. If the third-country national is not present, or the proponent authority is not represented, but they have submitted their comments in advance in writing, they will be introduced by the court.

(g) The Court's decision shall be delivered to the third-country national affected, and to the immigration authority. If he/she has a legal representative or a representative *ad litem*, they shall be informed as well. The court decision shall be announced verbally and shall also be delivered in writing without delay.

(h) The Court's decision is final and proceedings are exempt from charges.

387. The ruling on the return order (expulsion on the grounds of a readmission agreement or the Dublin process) may be subject to judicial review. The petition for judicial review shall be submitted to the refugee authority within three days following the date of delivery of the ruling. The refugee authority shall forthwith forward the petition for judicial review to the competent court together with the documents of the case and any cross-complaint attached. The petition for judicial review shall be adjudged by the court – within eight days following receipt of the petition for judicial review – in non-judicial proceedings, relying on the available documents. In the proceedings, personal interviews may not be conducted. The court's decision is final, and it may not be appealed. Pending judicial review, implementation of the ruling on the return order shall not be suspended upon receipt of a request therein.

388. Third-country nationals may not apply for the suspension of proceedings for ordering their detention. The resolution ordering detention may not be appealed. He/she while placed under detention may lodge a complaint in the event of the immigration authority's failure to comply with its obligations to provide proper information regarding his/her rights or if a proper place is not designated for him/her. The complaint shall be adjudged by the local (District) court of jurisdiction by reference to the place of detention. In accordance with the court's decision, any measure that has been omitted must be carried out, and/or any infringement must be remedied. The Court shall adopt a decision for such complaints within eight days.

389. A return for a rejected entry or the expulsion order of the migrant under the scope of the ThirdA shall be enforced by way of transporting him/her with an official escort if the third-country national is released from imprisonment as sentenced for a deliberate crime; is under detention; makes it necessary to supervise his/her departure for national security reasons, if so required by the commitment under an international treaty, or for the protection of public security or public policy. The third-country national residing in Hungary may be deported in the implementation of the decision of another Schengen Member State authority if his/her deportation was ordered for violation or severe threat to national security or public order; for at least one year of imprisonment as sentenced for a deliberate crime, for the suspicion of the commission of a serious crime, or for severely trespassing rules on accession and residence in the migration law. The third-country national affected may lodge a complaint against the deportation order. The immigration authority may cooperate in the enforcement of the deportation (removal) by air with another Member State that ordered the expulsion of the third-country national or in transit.[256] The deportation of a person shall be interrupted if the entry of the person deported to the country of destination fails; he/she requires urgent medical attention; the country from whom permission was requested for using its territory for transit by air in connection with deportation did not grant consent, or revoked its previous consent; the person deported entered the territory of the transit state without authorization.

390. Persons within the ambit of the ThirdA may be deported on jointly operated flights to the country of access if there is no direct flight. The DeptD requires the consent and the assistance in transit from the relevant authority of Member States in the EU. Upon the sending Member State's request submitted on a format to a transit country's authority two days prior to the planned transit, it may be accepted and supported. The silence of the requested competent authority (no answer within a minimum of two and a maximum of four days) means the acceptance and notice on the migrant's deportation by air shall be forwarded to the tacitly consenting state. The transit shall be completed within seventy-two hours unless its suspension is necessary. The escort in the deportation process, despite his/her policeman status, wears civilian clothes without arms, but his/her entitlement to implement coercive measures beyond the aforementioned restrictions has not been regulated. If the OIN is requested by another Member State to assist in a transit, it implies that a tight escort from the arrival until the departure of a deported person,

256. Council Directive 2003/110/EC of 25 Nov. 2003 on assistance in cases of transit for the purposes of removal by air.

and the urgent medical care, nutrition and accommodation of persons in need may be ensured.

391. The CrimPA (Article 146) determines that the travelling document(s) of a person shall be confiscated and retained and also detained until the completion of the coercive measure(s) ordered by Court, public prosecutor or investigation authority within the criminal procedure. In order to ensure the success of the criminal proceedings, the ban on the non-national's exit from the country may be also ordered. This act shall be notified to the OIN also wherein the coercive measure is withdrawn by the ordering authority.

392. The public prosecutors must control the legality of public administrative organs, Police or the OIN – ordering coercive measures. Act CLXIII of 2011 regulates what measures may be taken by the public prosecutors (in particular by their County/Capital Office) in order to enforce lawful actions inside the public administration procedure within the ambit of the AdminA, the MinofA and law enforcement. This task ('protection of public interest') signifies the legal basis of legal remedy for migrants in detention, in compulsory confinement or in other places depriving inmates of liberty, who may submit complaints to the competent office of public prosecutor. All organizations that are complained against shall correct any prior unlawful action, measure or decision upon the instruction of the public prosecutor (Article 120 of AdminA, Chapter 4 of Act CLXIII of 2011).

Chapter 3. Other Legal Remedies

393. The authorization of entry, residence and coercive measures (detention, expulsion and deportation) are supplemented with other administrative decisions in which remedy is not necessarily available. As proved by Table 19, administrative sanctions, such as fines, can be contested by appeal and the final administrative decision may be reviewed by the County/Capital Court. Its claim shall be submitted within thirty days (Article 330 of CivPA). Whereas, the withholding of passport and the usage of money to enforce removal of migrants cannot be contested. This asymmetry in remedies would be explained by the strong public administration law and weak law enforcement (alien policing) rules from the clients' perspective.

Table 19 Legal Remedies in Connecting Actions

Scope	*Legal Measure*	*Remedy*	*With Delaying Effect*	*Submission Deadline*	*Final Decision Made by*	*Decision Deadline*	*Impacts*
FreeA ThirdA	Refused approval of invitation letter	Appeal	Yes	(within fifteen days)	OIN	(within twenty-one days)	Approval or refusal
FreeD ThirdD	Fine for public order imposed on carrier	Appeal	Yes	(within fifteen days)	HQ of the Police	(within twenty-one days)	Annulment or modification or refusal
FreeD ThirdD	Fine for public order imposed on employer	Appeal	Yes	(within fifteen days)	OIN	(within twenty-one days)	Annulment or modification or refusal
FreeA ThirdA	Confiscation of travelling document in order to ensure expulsion order	No					
FreeA ThirdA	Retention of travelling document until the end of ongoing process (e.g., trial)	No					

Scope	Legal Measure	Remedy	With Delaying Effect	Submission Deadline	Final Decision Made by	Decision Deadline	Impacts
ThirdA	Seizure of money for purchase travel ticket, other documents in order to enforce expulsion order	No					
ThirdA ThirdD	Apprehension and police custody of alien not verifying identity and legality of residence in Hungary (12+12 hours)	Complaint	No	Within twelve hours	Police commander at superior station	Within thirty days	Release or refusal

394. In order to apprehend the EEA national or his/her family member whose whereabouts are unknown, the competent authority may *issue a public security warrant*, for such person who has escaped from the detention prior to the deportation; or has left the place designated in the border zone by the authority to an unknown location. This warrant may be issued also on a third-country national, who is subject to any immigration proceeding and has disappeared before a final decision, or has escaped from the detention or is on unauthorized absence from the place of the compulsory confinement in violation of the code of conduct; has failed to comply with the final decision of expulsion. The warrant shall be issued by way of a decision, and a copy of it shall be sent to the nearest Police headquarters and to the consular official.[257] When the grounds for such a warrant cease to prevail, it shall be withdrawn forthwith by the ordering (law enforcement) authority.

395. Upon request of a person within the ambit of the ThirdA, or if so prescribed by a bilateral consular agreement, the authority ordering detention shall promptly *inform* the consular or diplomatic mission of the third-country national concerning his/her detention, the obligation of the compulsory confinement, and the extension of the duration of the detention via the minister in charge of foreign affairs. As a provisional measure, the immigration authority shall immediately provide for the placement of the dependent family members of the third-country national apprehended, who have remained without supervision, and/or for the safeguarding of his/her valuables which have been left unattended.

396. The decision on imposing a public order fine belongs to the competence of the Police station nearest to the (illegal) border crossings of the passenger or to the nearest Regional Directorate of the OIN to the (unlawful) employment. Its decision may be appealed to the Headquarters of the Police or to the OIN. The claim to a judicial review of a final administrative decision is also available according the general provisions in the AdminA.

397. Separate chapters in the FreeA and the ThirdA regulate personal data proceeding, data storage, exchange and the right to protection. It meets the constitutional requirements, the general act on personal data protection[258] and the control system of the SIRENE, and the Data Protection and Freedom of Information Authority (NAIH). For instance, in order to monitor the right to residence of foreign nationals, the immigration authority shall keep the following sub-registers – within the central immigration register – on the personal data of the EEA nationals and their family members: the register of EEA nationals holding registration certificates, holders of residence cards; holders of permanent residence cards; EEA nationals and family members subject to expulsion or exclusion; whose travel document or personal identification document was reported lost. The FreeA and the ThirdA determine what data of the data subjects, relating to their documents evidencing their right of residence, are processed. These data may be processed in the

257. Act LXXXVIII of 2013 on register of missing persons and objects and their search.
258. Act CXII of 2011 on personal data protection and publicity of publicly relevant information.

sub-registers maintained for five years following the termination of the right to residence or the date of the registered departure of the data subject.

398. Some examples may demonstrate the relevance of immigration registers and data processing[259] as new electronic borders in the borderless Europe, as follows:

(a) If the applicant is a third-country national for whom an alert has been issued in the SIS for the purposes of refusing entry and residence, a residence permit (or its prolongation) may be issued upon consultation with the competent authority of the Schengen state that has issued the alert via the (national) SIRENE Office. A residence permit granted on humanitarian grounds shall not be extended, or it shall be withdrawn if any requirement for its issue is no longer satisfied; he/she has disclosed false information or untrue facts to the competent authority in the interest of obtaining the right to residence; or a withdrawal is requested by the authority or body on whose initiative it was issued. An appeal against a decision for the refusal of residence permission or on withdrawal of a residence permit shall be lodged within five working days following the communication of the decision.

(b) The Government has appointed the OIN for maintaining the records referred to in Article 34 of the Visa Information System Regulation,[260] and for functioning as the national authority providing access as the data administration agency. According to the VIS Regulation, the following authorities shall have access to the system for the exchange of visa data established under Council Decision 2004/512/EC: visa authority, the Police and Regional Directorates of OIN. Moreover, the Government designates the OIN for discharging the official duties relating to national document-signatory functions and nationwide signatory attestation functions, and the official functions of national document certification and attestation bodies in biometric data processing. The Office, in its capacity as the signatory attestation authority, shall – inter alia – compile and maintain – with a view to controlling local border traffic permits, residence permits, as well as immigration permits with storage mediums containing biometric identifiers – the certificates of the national document-signatory authorities of all Member States of the International Civil Aviation Organization (ICAO) and their certificate revocation lists, and the distribution points of certificate revocation lists.

(c) In connection with applications for local border traffic permits and different kinds of residence permits, the biometric identifiers shall be recorded by the competent consulate officer, or the officer at the Regional Directorate of the OIN. Upon receipt of an application for interim permanent residence permit, national permanent residence permit, or EC permanent residence permit, or for

259. The Act CLXXXI of 2012 determines the data exchange within the SIS II as it entered into force in April 2013. The national SIRENE office (in Centre for International Criminal Co-operation – HQP) tasks and final remedy for unlawful data process by NAIH are also regulated in the executive rules (Government Decree No. 15 of 2013, 28 January).

260. Regulation of the European Parliament and the Council No. 767/2008/EC, 9 Jul. 2008.

the exchange or replacement of a permanent residence permit or immigration permit, the biometric identifiers (Article 99 of the ThirdA) shall be recorded by the Regional Directorate.

399. The cooperation among the law-enforcement agencies is institutionally regulated in admission and migrant's authorization. The common points of cooperation arise from the AdminA. In accordance with this, a joint-competence, or a right to approve or veto, or a compulsory expert opinion shall be required in certain issues in public administration. Without this approval or opinion issued by another agency, the proceeding authority's decision is void. In some cases, the opinion is optional.

(a) As the FreeD determines, the minister of foreign affairs and the competent consulate officer may request the opinion of the NSOs (Agency for Constitutional Protections as new name since 2011 and the Counter-Terrorism Centre as a unit of the Police) concerning any visa application by a third-country family member of an EEA national. They shall provide the aforesaid opinion within six or ten days.
(b) In connection with applications of third-country nationals for various kinds of residence permits, to determine whether the residence of a third-country national is considered to constitute a threat to the national security of Hungary, these agencies are appointed to function as the competent authority in the first instance, and the minister of the interior supervising the national security services in the second instance. According to the ThirdD, the competent Regional Directorate of the OIN shall forward the personal data of third-country nationals applying for residence permission from the central immigration register to these agencies. At the request of the competent Regional Directorate, it shall allow access to the documents enclosed with such applications, or shall make copies of them. Their opinion shall be provided within twenty and forty-five days in a different authorization to the proceeding authority. In the event of any information arising which is attributable to the special authority after the official assessment is delivered concerning the third-country national to whom it pertains, based on which the official assessment is to be revoked, the aforesaid special authority shall forthwith send a new assessment to the Regional Directorate. An appeal filed against the official assessment shall be heard by the minister of the interior in the second instance. The minister shall make available the official assessment to the OIN. The minister shall issue the opinion on permission within fifteen or twenty days.
(c) In connection with applications of third-country nationals for interim permanent residence permits, national permanent residence permits and EC permanent residence permits, in order to determine whether the residence of a third-country national is considered to constitute a threat to the public security of Hungary, the Government appointed the relevant county police headquarters to function as the competent authority in the first instance, and the National Police Headquarters in the second instance. Their rights in accession to data registers and duty to prepare an official assessment to the competent Regional Directorate are the same as the aforementioned agencies.

The AsylA regulates these agencies how they provide expert opinion on each protection seeker's application, and ThirdA extends their screening activities to the procedure on recognition of stateless status.

400. Before the accession to the EU, Hungary had to establish a system of *free legal aid* which was present in the procedural codes in a fragmented way, without common principles and an institutional basis. A new act in 2003 established the institution, while the fragmentation in the codes and the prior incoherence of provisions remained. For instance, the anti-discrimination lawyers' network led by the Ministry of Justice (and Law Enforcement) or the free legal aid at the Courts' client service has been untouched although the Justice Office was born with the implementation of the FreeLA. Legal counselling was freely available in the communist past, provided by trade unions for workers. It was liquidated in the early 1990s, and in the social-economic transition this public service was not available only for persons in need. Finally, the transposition of the *acquis communautaire* compelled the setting up of a free legal counselling on equal footing for the EU citizens who hardly wanted to use the service of the '*attorney-at-law of paupers*' or the '*people's solicitor*'. This subsidized legal support system was developed over years, gradually beginning in non-litigation, civil and criminal law cases. Law firms, NGOs and academics keeping up legal counselling services may join the legal supporters' registry of the Justice Office that concludes a service contract with registered members for a fixed tariff and conditional payment in counselling. The list of supporters is available on the homepage of the Justice Office so that poor clients may choose from the list after a hard screening of the eligibility at the Office. This may illustrate the controversial harmonization of law and the apathy towards the growing inequality in society. Moreover, conflict-oriented justice is deeply rooted in the Eastern European region instead of the consensus-finding model, even more than in other parts of the world (Fleck, 2008).

(a) In non-litigation procedures, the client (Hungarian national, person under the scope of the FreeA, the ThirdA or international agreements) is eligible for free legal support including a free of charge application if his/her monthly personal income does not exceed the lowest pension and he/she has no property (as defined by the SocialA). If the client's income crosses this threshold but is below the average income of employees, a reimbursement of service price may be allowed for him/her within one year and therein he/she has paid all reimbursement in a prior supporting period. Regardless of the income level, the applicant for international protection and status of statelessness as well as the third-country national under the expulsion order[261] or in possession of residence permit issued on the grounds of humanitarian reason, applicant for visa, residence or settlement permission or naturalization if his/her ancestor is/was a Hungarian citizen is eligible for this free legal aid (counselling and letter writing). Victims of criminal offences shall be freely informed of their own rights.

261. Implementing the European Parliament and the Council Directive 2008/115/EC on return of illegal migrants.

Free legal aid includes free service of interpreters or translation to the applicants for international protection[262] and third-country nationals in expulsion procedure as well as to third-country nationals with humanitarian residence permit.

(b) A state-financed legal representative may be provided for the client who is not able to protect his/her own interests in the civil law suit or the legal representative of a party to an action at law (at a higher Court procedure) is required, but he/she is below the above-mentioned income threshold. The legal representative has to represent the client during the entire procedure until the judgment enters into force. The applicant would be automatically eligible for a free legal representative if he/she needs a judicial review of a refused asylum request, or his/her claim is in connection with damages from a criminal offence. However, the CrimPA determines who is eligible for a free (state-financed) legal representative in a trial through the requirement to be defended by a professional legal representative in severe felonies. If the perpetrator does not employ a lawyer, the investigation authority is obliged to nominate without delay a lawyer from the list of the Bar paid by the state as per a fixed tariff.[263]

(c) Justice Office (incorporated into the county governmental offices in 2011[264]) makes decisions regarding the eligibility of a client without delay, but within a maximum of one to fifteen days. This screening process is free of charge but it requires a lot of personal data and documents (from tax office and pension scheme). A refused claim may be reviewed at Administrative Court in a non-litigation procedure submitting a statement of claim within thirty days of rejection to the Court. A rejected claim to be registered as legal supporter may be also reviewed at the Administrative Court submitting a statement of claim within thirty days of rejection to the Court. The register of legal supporters in Justice Office is public.

401. The permanent residents (newly naturalized persons, settlement permit holders, recognized refugees and third-country national with subsidiary protected status) as well as the nationals in Hungary shall be furnished with an *identity card.*[265] Before its expiration, a request for a new identity card shall be requested at the local (District) governmental office. In the enlarged Europe, the holders are eligible for travelling inside the EU with this machine-readable document with the biometrically identified photograph, signature and the personal data of the holder.[266] This small plastic card has gained more importance than it had in the communist past, when it served only for the verification of a person. The identity card is state property, so its destruction, loss, falsification, use as deposit or preservation after the holder's death by family members is restricted, and it shall be carried by the holder

262. The low budget cannot cover the honorarium of attorney-at-law and translators in many cases with the exception of certain projects, such as the Project on effective legal aid for asylum seekers and translation service financed by the European Refugee Fund (2012).
263. The honorarium of attorney-at-law in state financed legal aid is symbolic: EUR 13 per hour (2014).
264. See the Government Decree No. 177 of 2012, 26 July on the Administrative and Justice Office.
265. Government Decree No. 168 of 1999, 24 November on issuing and registration of identity card.
266. The issued permanent residence permit contains the holder's forename in a Hungarian version, if it was determined in the authorization procedure.

in public places. Thus in the event of its non-presentation upon the authority's request, a minor offence fine up to EUR 500 may be imposed by the Police (Article 207 of MinofA). The lost, disappeared or destroyed identity cards shall be notified within three working days to the local (District) governmental office. Police station or the consular office residing abroad. If the card is lost, a temporary identity card would be issued (and the lost document shall be put on the list of searched objects by the Police) and there is no appeal to this decision. The AdminA shall be implemented regarding the procedure of issuance of certificate and the authority registry (Chapter 5) with the exceptions provided by law. On these grounds, the most relevant provisions are as follows:

(a) The certificate shall be issued within twenty days if it cannot be provided immediately.
(b) If its issuance is refused or withdrawn (e.g., it was misused, falsified or the legal status of the holder is changing) the governmental office passes a formal decision on it. The rejection of a certificate shall be based on a lawful exclusion (e.g., there is no evidence or data on the fact that would be certified). An appeal may be submitted within ten working days from the communication of the refusal.
(c) The appeal is decided by the Central Office of Electronic Registry (under the aegis of the Ministry of Justice and Public Administration).
(d) If the validity or the authenticity of the certificate is questionable in a procedure, the authority in proceedings shall announce it, providing the facts and evidence to the issuing organ if the immediate withholding is not necessary. On certain grounds, the correction, supplement or withdrawal of the certificate would be required.

It is a very common reason for the refusal that the migrant has no original and/or officially translated document regarding his birth and marital status, and in the absence of those, neither a Hungarian birth nor marriage registration,[267] nor is the issuance of an identity card allowed. The ICCS[268] as a regional European organization has developed the basis for a common documentary substance and a list of codes applicable in the register office of the party states. Although Hungary is a party state, the translation and ratification of its agreements or the implementation of its proposals have not been accomplished.

402. The *procedural expenditures* are relevant also to migrants. The AdminA determines the main components of the procedural costs: fee, administration service price, payments relating to appearance of applicant at the authority proceeding, costs of (non-Hungarian) language usage in the proceedings, inspection of

267. Act I of 2010 on birth, death and marriage register and procedural rules entered totally into force in July 2014. It provides a unified, electronic registry system in Hungary.
268. International Commission on Civil Status (Strasbourg) has sixteen party states. It provides studies on marriage of convenience (Bogus marriages, September 2010) or on undocumented migrants (Persons deprived of civil status and identity documents, October 2010) with reference on missing identification documents.

documents in the file, payments of representation, honoraria of expert, translator, costs of communication, expenditures of the execution of the authority decision and measures, costs of a local survey and witness. If the proceeding authority allows a free of charge application for the client having taken into account his/her poor economic conditions, although the procedure is important to protect his/her own rights and interests, these financial components are fully avoided, unless the conditions of the applicant have changed strongly. The decision on the procedural expenditures shall be notified to the applicant and other authorities involved in the process concerned. Certain organizations (e.g., the Red Cross) would be exempted from the payment of the fees by law.[269] However, these provisions are secondarily anticipated by the migration rules. For instance, on the grounds of the FreeD, the consular office, the OIN or the Police may allow the exemption from the procedural expenditures for the visa applicant within the ambit of the FreeA and the ThirdA as well as international agreements including cultural exchange, humanitarian relief, sport, artistic and scientific or study programmes (e.g., obtaining a state-financed scholarship). The family member of an EEA national or a third-country national visiting a close family member who is suffering from a disease or an accident in Hungary, the family member of a foreigner with a supplementary protected status, a minor below six years of age, a pupil as the member of a group of visitors, a third-country national as a researcher on the grounds of receiving contact are exempted by law. Persons under the scope of the FreeA may be arrested securing the deportation order, and the complaint to the Court is free of charge.

403. All inhabitants (nationals and migrants) shall produce and surrender their identification document upon request for checks in public places by Policemen and/or customs officers. The migrant will have to surrender the document on the legal basis of his/her residence in Hungary. Any third-country national who is unable to verify his/her lawful residence in Hungary or is unable to produce a credible evidence of his/her identity (with a valid, non-expired, non-manipulated document), or who violates the provisions of the ThirdA shall be apprehended and taken into custody by the immigration authority. If the grounds for his/her residence or identity cannot be established while in custody, the third-country national may be kept in custody for an additional period of a maximum of twelve hours. This measure may be appealed. No remedy is available for this measure. In the event that any travel document is found in the possession of a third-country national that is issued to another person, and is held illegally by the third-country national, it shall be confiscated and – if no criminal charges are filed – sent to the Hungarian mission of the issuing state, or failing this, it shall be returned to the issuing agency via the minister in charge of foreign affairs.

---

269. For instance, Act XL of 1993 on the Hungarian Red Cross (Art. 4).

Part VII. Access to the Labour Market

Chapter 1. Overview of the Applicable Legislation

404. The most important legal sources in relation to the labour market for migrants are as follows:

(a) The Fundamental Law ensures the right to a freely chosen profession and job, or to engage in entrepreneurship (Article XII).[270] Within this provision is in part the right to work. The right to safe and non-discriminative labour conditions and to paid holidays and breaks is also promised (in Article XVII).[271] Unlike classical liberties, these rights are conditional, requiring contribution of individual's to enrichment of the whole society and activity of the state and proper institutional environment. Furthermore, the right to work overlaps with the right to free entrepreneurship, undertaking, social rights and non-discrimination (Takács, 2003). While the right to free undertakings is a protected subjective right, the right to work can be guaranteed by proper employment and economic policy, social and political pledges. These are ensured partly in the legislation restricting employment contracts through public law components.[272]
(b) The Labour Code, the UnemplA and the LabInA determine the labour conditions and benefits in the period of unemployment.
(c) PermitD represents distinctive rules on third-country nationals and other labourers who are outside the Community preferences.
(d) The rules on public sector restrict non-nationals' access to this labour market and the circle of exemptions is narrow (See paragraphs 167-174).
(e) The Act of Accession contains short-term measures towards labourers from new Member States and entitlement to introduce equal reciprocity measures in ExD against old Member States' workers after enlargement. These rules are now

270. (1) Everyone shall have the right to freely chosen his or her job or profession, or to engage in entrepreneurial activities. Everyone shall have a duty to contribute to the enrichment of the community through his or her, performed according to his or her abilities and possibilities. (2) Hungary shall strive to create conditions ensuring that everyone who is able and willing to work has the opportunity to do so.
271. Its relevant parts: (3) Every employee shall have the right to working conditions that respect his or her health, safety and dignity. (4) Every employee shall have the right to daily and weekly rest period, and to an annual period of paid leave.
272. See the interpretation of the Constitutional Court decisions (e.g., 327/B/1992.AB határozat, 54/1993.(X.13.) AB határozat, 41/1995. (VI.27.) AB határozat).

outdated, and persons in ambit of FreeA are freely employed but their employment shall be noticed according to the ExD.

405. The International Labour Organization (ILO) conventions and the UN Covenant on Economic, Social and Cultural Rights (1966) contain the general labour requirements without specifications regarding labour migrants. Hungary is *not a party state of the UN and the Council of Europe conventions protecting labour and social rights of migrant workers and their family members* including self-employed persons. This policy is based on a *defensive migration policy* also against labour migrants, although thousands of Hungarian emigrants have been excluded from reciprocal protective measures in target countries in this manner. Due to this reluctant migration policy, Hungary ratified neither the European Convention on Establishment (Paris, 1955) nor the Articles 18–19[273] of the European Social Charter.[274] Despite the accession to the EU and the implementation of the *acquis communautaire* at the time of ratification of the Revised European Social Charter,[275] the policy of *minimalism in migration pledges* has continued. In brief, only the most relevant articles that would be extended to self-employed persons and their family members were not chosen from the optional rules[276] in the Charter. Furthermore, guarantees of the social security of migrants on bilateral agreements are also excluded from undertakings,[277] while Hungary has concluded numerous treaties in this field (e.g., with Ukraine, Serbia, Montenegro). Whereas, the ratification covers the following:

(a) maintaining a proper labour inspection system (Article A 4/4.) requiring at least the visibility of controllers in asymmetrical contracts of a powerful company with self-employed persons. Today, the capacity of labour inspection is much below this fulfilment, in particular respecting micro-entrepreneurs and their employees, their health and safety protection (Article 22[278]);

273. Article 18: The right to engage in a gainful occupation in the territory of other Contracting Parties. Art. 19: The right of migrant workers and their families to protection and assistance.
274. Act C of 1999 on publishing the European Social Charter (Turin, 1961).
275. Act VI of 2009 on publishing of Revised European Social Charter (Strasbourg, 1996).
276. Article 18: The right to engage in a gainful occupation in the territory of other Parties. Art. 19: The right of migrant workers and their families to protection and assistance. It contains the statement that 'With a view to ensuring the effective exercise of the right of migrant workers and their families to protection and assistance in the territory of any other Party, the Parties undertake: 10. to extend the protection and assistance provided for in this article to self-employed migrants insofar as such measures apply.'
277. Article 12: The right to social security. In accordance with this, 'With a view to ensuring the effective exercise of the right to social security, the Parties undertake: 4. to take steps, by the conclusion of appropriate bilateral and multilateral agreements or by other means, and subject to the conditions laid down in such agreements, in order to ensure: a equal treatment with their own nationals of the nationals of other Parties in respect of social security rights, including the retention of benefits arising out of social security legislation, whatever movements the persons protected may undertake between the territories of the Parties; b the granting, maintenance and resumption of social security rights by such means as the accumulation of insurance or employment periods completed under the legislation of each of the Parties.'
278. Article 22: The right to take part in the determination and improvement of the working conditions and working environment. In accordance with this, 'With a view to ensuring the effective exercise

(b) non-discrimination in enjoyment of rights set forth in the Charter including equal treatment on the grounds of language, race and colour (Article V/E).
(c) principle of more favourable treatment would be accorded to persons protected (Article V/H).

406. Regardless of the accession to the EU, the constitutional rule-of-law requires respect for equality of citizens in all types of legal conditions, such as in the labour issues. Three provisions shall be underlined as relevant guarantees to non-discrimination in employment (Article XV of the Fundamental Law):

(a) Hungary shall respect *the fundamental rights* of all persons in the country without discrimination on the basis of race, colour, gender, language, religion, political or other opinion, national or social origins, financial situation, birth or on any other grounds whatsoever;
(b) The state shall ensure the equality of *men and women;*
(c) Hungary shall support social inclusion and equal treatment for everyone through *measures that create fair opportunities.*

In this spirit, the Labour Code, Act LXXV of 1996 on Labour Inspection (hereinafter LabInA) or Penal Code as well as other provisions, action plans together are intending to provide equal access to remunerative work.

407. The principle of equal treatment is enshrined *expressis verbis* in the Labour Code in general and in special areas, as follows:

(a) First, the principle of equal treatment shall be respected in employment relations an in particular in remuneration. However, legal remedy shall not result in any violation of or harm to the rights of another employee (Article 12).
(b) The Labour Code expressly deals with the equal treatment principle in terms of trade union, right to the collective bargaining, free membership in and operation of trade unions. For instance, it is prohibited to discriminate worker in accession to benefits on the grounds of his membership or activity in trade union (Article 231 and 271).
(c) The equal treatment and non-discrimination shall be ensured for posted (foreign) workers and lended (migrant) workers, for instance in favour of young workers, females and mothers with small children. However, remuneration shall be equal with local workers only from the 184th day of lending employment contract (Article 219 and 295).

---

of the right of workers to take part in the determination and improvement of the working conditions and working environment in the undertaking, the Parties undertake to adopt or encourage measures enabling workers or their representatives, in accordance with national legislation and practice, to contribute: a to the determination and the improvement of the working conditions, work organization and working environment; b to the protection of health and safety within the undertaking; c to the organization of social and socio-cultural services and facilities within the undertaking; d to the supervision of the observance of regulations on these matters.'

408. The personal and institutional scope of the EqualA and its Chapter III (Articles 21–32) *covers also the private and public labour relations,* thus all definitions of prohibited behaviours (direct/indirect discrimination, segregation, harassment, retorsion, instruction for discriminative action) and sanctions shall be applicable on this area. It is considered a particular violation of the principle of equal treatment if the employer inflicts direct or indirect negative discrimination upon an employee, especially when the following provisions are made or applied in any of the following:[279]

(a) access to employment, especially in public job advertisements, hiring, and in the conditions of employment;
(b) a provision made before the establishment of the employment relationship or other relationship related to employment, related to the procedure facilitating the establishment of such a relationship;
(c) establishing and terminating the employment relationship or other relationship related to employment;
(d) relation to any training before or during the work;
(e) determining and providing working conditions;
(f) establishing and providing benefits due to the basis of the employment relationship or other relationship related to work, especially in establishing and providing wages;
(g) relation to membership or participation in employees' organizations;
(h) the promotion system;
(i) the enforcement of liability for damages or disciplinary liability.

The EqualA prescribes non-discriminative advertisements and hiring procedures, training, working conditions, membership in certain organizations and increment opportunities.

409. The principle of equal treatment in labour is not violated under the following circumstances:

(a) the discrimination is proportional, justified by the characteristic or nature of the work and is based on all relevant and legitimate terms and conditions; or
(b) discrimination arises directly from a religious or other ideological conviction or national or ethnic origin fundamentally determining the nature of the organization, and it is proportional and justified by the nature of the employment activity or the conditions of its pursuit.

410. The legal consequences of discrimination in labour are not incorporated into Table 15 that mentions many responsible organizations. Hence, there is an

279. These provisions laid down in Art. 21 of the EqualA mirror the obligations of a Member State pursuant to Regulation 1612/68/EC. Moreover, this Act transposes a dozen of non-discrimination regulations and directives, e.g. the Council Directive 2000/78/EC, 2000/43/EC, 2004/113/EC and European Parliament and Council Directive 2011/98/EU.

'*embarrassment due to abundance*' of fora (Kádár, 2009), while the level of public awareness in discrimination issues and legal measures for possible clients and victims was 39% in 2007 but the number of cases, disputes and complaints have been really low in Hungary (Demeter, 2009). The Eurobarometer 2012 proves that 23% of Hungarian respondent has been discriminated personally (mainly in employment, social and health care) within twelve months prior to the survey while the average in the EU was only 17%. However, one third of the population can identify the name and functions of ETA in Hungary in 2011, and the total number of complaints is about 1,000 per annum in ETA.[280]

(a) The civil lawsuit can be launched for invasion of privacy and personality at the local Court on the grounds of the Civil Code. Paying compensation may be most difficult for the defendant but the procedure takes years, and fact-finding and providing evidence are difficult due to interpersonal relations in employment. It is the same at the disputes relating to the Labour Code at the labour Court.
(b) Since 2014 labour inspectors cannot impose a fine in minor offence procedure for discriminative behaviour/action of employer as they could in past. The LabInA entitles them to control employers – in particular corporate entities – and the maximal fine has been upgraded to EUR 66 500 but for other unlawful conducts (such as unlawful employment of third-country national, failed registry or remuneration below the lawful minimum). Minor offences in employment were deleted from the MinofA recently.
(c) The most specific procedure introduced in 2004 on the grounds of the EqualA is led by the ETA[281] as a semi-independent authority under the aegis of the Parliament that must not instruct it in individual cases. The ETA was given strong competencies and the power to impose sanctions. The provisions of the EqualA shall be implemented through a complaint procedure if a violation is supposed. However, the ETA can act on the basis of an application and ex officio as well. The ETA publishes its annual report regularly.[282] The most important decisions of the ETA are also available in English. Its fact-finding and burden-sharing procedural provisions were modified in 2006 resolving the collision between the Community law and national law on burden of proof. However, theoretically, anti-discrimination rules transposed into the Hungarian labour law would be implemented for protection of privacy of employee against the employer, and freedom in concluding contracts can be limited in favour of the worker only in public service contracts. It means that the practical impact of anti-discrimination provisions on employment, in particular on the private sector, is supplementary. The task foreseen for the coming years is the fine-tuning and simplification of the system as regards definitions, exemptions and some

280. See www.egyenlobanasmod.hu/tamop/kutatasok=tanulmanyok (2010–2013).
281. Chapter 5/A of EqualA defines the status of ETA, its procedural rules are inserted into the EqualA and AdminA.
282. <www.egyenlobanasmod.hu>. In English: Report on the activities of the Equal Treatment Authority in 2007. For instance, in 2008 the ETA announced the breach of equal treatment in thirty-seven cases, most of which concerned discrimination in employment, including rejection of a non-national applicant for a job as public servant.

procedural rules (Gyulavári, 2007). However, ETA is entitled since 2012 to register employers being inflicted fine for discrimination in prior two years. It means that employers in public registry are excluded from public benefits and public procurement competitions.[283]

283. Ministerial Decree No. 1 of 2012, 26 January (NGM) on fair employment relations.

Chapter 2. Conditions for Entitlement to Work in Hungary as an Employed Person

§1. General Conditions

411. The Labour Code prescribes the *common criteria of employment* and other gainful work. In accordance with this, individuals who have a limited ability to act and are at least sixteen years of age (the end of obligatory attendance of school) can lawfully be employed. Exceptions in employment or gainful work are available for fifteen-year-old students in summer holidays, youngsters below sixteen with the consent of the guardian authority can be employed in the fields of art, sport, advertisement or the fashion industry (Article 34). Further, the required health and qualification conditions – if there are any – shall be met. The Labour Code lays down that women and young persons (between sixteen and eighteen years of age) shall not be employed in work which may result in detrimental effects with a view to their physical condition or development. The particular jobs for which women or young persons may not be employed, or may only perform if the specific working conditions are provided or on the basis of a preliminary medical examination, shall be determined by the legal regulation. Moreover, it is provided that a woman, from the time her pregnancy is diagnosed until her child reaches one year of age, shall be temporarily reassigned to a position suitable for her condition from a medical standpoint, or the working conditions in her existing position shall be modified as appropriate, on the basis of a medical report pertaining to employment. The new position shall be designated upon the employee's approval.

412. Third-country nationals are subject to *labour authorization* taking into account international commitments, domestic exceptions (see paragraph 176) and the quota of foreign labourers per annum. The latter may be defined by the responsible minister considering the views of stakeholders (ministers, trade unions and social partners) on migratory processes, data of (un)employment and vacancies in labour registry. The Ministerial Communication is published in the Official Gazette up to the 1st of February of the given calendar year. For instance, in 2007 the maximum number of employable foreigners was 83,000, in 2009 it was 60,000 and in recent years this figure has been decreasing. The general requirement of labour authorization for non-EEA nationals (third-country nationals) shall be applicable on classical employment relations (under the Labour Code) and on other remunerated works done under the supervision of another person (employer, principal or master) including trainee's practice, labour in the public sector, in a cooperative as member, long-distance work or other occasional works. In contrast, small/agricultural producers, private entrepreneurs are working independently (self-employed persons), so they are outside the scope of this authorization. However, there are some economic activities in which neither the type of legal contract (civil or labour), nor the substance of labour (e.g., commissioning of equipment's *in situ*, repair within warranty) can clearly demarcate whether a work shall be under the ambit of PermitD. In many cases, the (projected) length of work determines it. Without a permit, the valid labour contract cannot be concluded with the migrant worker, and lawful exceptions from authorization by UnemplA or ExD (see paragraphs 176, 404 and

443) shall be attested by the employer within the entire period of work and for three years after the termination (e.g., in a labour inspection). As a result, it is necessary to check the alleged exempted cases by the employer at the labour office before employment taking into account that the issued permit is valid for the requested employer (to a registered office), for the requested work with the employer and within the determined period of time. However, this check or scrutiny of documents is required unless employers want to pay a fine (Article 71 of ThirdA).

413. Taking into account international commitments or specificity of employment, the labour permit shall be issued within the authorization *without labour market test*, almost automatically with limited discretion power, for the following third-country national applicants who are third-country nationals (section 9 of PermitD):

(a) Labourers within the framework and quota determined in a bilateral agreement.
(b) Key personnel doing outstanding, qualified work (directing, supervision on business activities in fact beyond the definition of the Civil Code).
(c) Labourers forming up to 5% of all employers (in average) in a foreign dominant share company.
(d) Family member of consular/embassy staff if the employment is out of consular office/embassy, and upon deceleration of the Ministry of Foreign Affairs the reciprocity is absent in the relationship between Hungary and the sending state.
(e) Internationally known visiting professors, outstanding artists and researchers in teaching, scientific or artistic work not exceeding ten working days per annum upon declaration of the inviting institutions.
(f) Family member living together at least for five years in Hungary with a breadwinner migrant worker – without a Blue Card – who has been employed here for at least eight years if applicant is not eligible to family unification (e.g., he is a farer relative).
(g) Spouse living together at least one year in Hungary with a breadwinner who is a recognized refugee, a temporary or subsidiary protected person or a long-term migrant.
(h) Widow/er of recognized refugee, temporary or subsidiary protected person or person with right to free movement (EEA national) with whom he/she was living together for at least a year in Hungary before the breadwinner died.
(i) Repair, servicing within warranty or commissioning of equipment exceeding fifteen working days within a month if is based on a civil contract with a foreign-seated company (out of the EEA).
(j) Migrant with residence permit issued on the grounds of humanitarian reason whose employment is supported upon deceleration of the OIN.
(k) Tolerant migrant as inmate of reception centre whose employment out of the centre is supported by the OIN.
(l) Non-delegated foreign person at consular office, embassy for local employment.
(m) Worker in a film which is a co-production registered by the National Movie Agency (inside the National Media and Infocommunications Authority).
(n) Professional trainee for not more than three months per year.
(o) Surplus teaching work of a researcher who arrived on the grounds of a hosting agreement to an accredited research organization.

(p) Family member of the Blue Card holder if they are living together.
(q) Prolongation of the seasonal agricultural employment – in the same job by the same employer if application is submitted before fifteen days of expiry in a required format.

The permission may be issued without labour market assessment if employee meets the necessary health and qualification requirements.

414. The access to employment is strongly determined not only by the entry, residence and labour permit system but also by the *recognition of qualifications* and diplomas. Its framework is outlined in the Act on recognition of various qualifications and diplomas (Act C of 2001, hereinafter QualA)[284] that entitles ministers and chambers to regulate and control the specific requirements in the professions and branches of occupations belonging to their own competence.[285] During the recognition process, the authority declares the legal force of the foreign degree equivalent to the legal force of a degree obtainable in Hungary. The resolution on the recognition of the level of qualification determines which Hungarian qualification is equivalent to the foreign degree, thus, whether the foreign degree is equivalent to a Hungarian university or a college degree, or to a degree obtainable at a postgraduate training following a college or university degree. The Educational Office (and its agency, the Hungarian Equivalence and Information Centre – HEIC – as a contact point for international communication and exchange of data[286]) is responsible for recognition in general.

(a) The recognition or equivalence in the legal force of a qualification is automatic on the grounds of an international (regional, bilateral) agreement, such as issued in a party state of the Lisbon Convention.[287] In other cases, an individualized procedure shall be managed before the issuance of a certificate of recognition or equivalence.
(b) The certificate on elementary school studies may be recognized if it contains at least eight years of curricula. Its relevance in the labour market is marginal, because unskilled work is often done by medium-skilled workers. It is more relevant for migrant pupils, but on the basis of the age of schooling (between five and sixteen years of age) all children regardless of their nationality or legal status, below the age of sixteen years have to attend public school independently of the documentation of prior curricula or qualification.
(c) The certificate on grammar school completed with a maturity examination may be given if its holder is entitled, in the country of issuance, for entry into the tertiary education, or if it is based on at least twelve years of curricula and it

284. It is in conformity with Directive 2005/36/EC.
285. For instance, Decree of the Minister of Health Affairs (EÜM) No. 4 of 2008, 16 January on the Unconditional Recognition of Diplomas, Qualifications in the Health Sector Issued in the EU (determining the year of reference for recognition) while the procedural rules of recognition is regulated in the Ministerial Decree (EÜM) No. 30 of 2008, 25 July.
286. For instance, HEIC is the national contact point in NARIC and ENIC network.
287. On the recognition of degrees in tertiary education in the European Region (11 Apr. 1997) that was published in Act XCIX of 2001.

certifies that its holder took final examinations on at least four subject matters. In the absence of this certificate, there is an obstacle to participate in any kind of vocational training.

(d) If the certificate on occupation is partly different from the Hungarian structure, a professional examination may be ordered taking into account the applicant's working/professional experience, practice and requiring the major components of the curricula in Hungary. It shall be implemented *mutatis mutandis* to a master examination.

(e) The certificate on the first grade of tertiary education may be recognized if it attests to the completion of at least three years of studies (Bachelor of Arts) or it entitles the holder to enter the master studies unless that given profession has two grades that are required to be completed, or to enter the doctoral degree course.

(f) The recognition of scientific degrees issued by a foreign higher education institution falls within the sphere of authority of those Hungarian universities which are entitled to provide PhD training and award scientific degrees in the field of study, or in its identifiable branch, testified by the foreign degree. During this process, the university examines whether the degree issued abroad is equivalent to a PhD or a Doctor of Liberal Arts (DLA) degree obtainable in Hungary. The recognition takes place in one procedure at the university chosen by the applicant but it is not a prerequisite to have the level of the qualification recognized.[288] As a result, the recognition of academic diplomas falls within the competence of the high-level educational establishments the governmental authorities are not competent.

415. The QualA regulates the recognition of degrees obtained at foreign higher education institutions in three main procedures: automatic recognition; recognition with conditions of EEA diplomas of EEA nationals; moreover, the recognition process for non-EEA nationals or non-EEA diplomas (Hudák et al., 2003). The main differences are connected to the free movement of workers in the EU (and in the EEA) as follows:

(a) Procedures and conditions within the ambit of the QualA shall be the same for EEA nationals, Hungarian nationals, their family members (persons within the personal scope of the FreeA), researchers as residence permit holders, long-term migrants, Blue Card or unified permit[289] holders who are third-country nationals residing in Hungary (national treatment).

288. Nevertheless, it is possible to request the recognition of the level testified by the foreign scientific degree from the responsible (general or sectoral) governmental authority. For instance, it is the Office of Health Authorization and Administrative Procedures in health sector while the Educational Office is in charge of recognition in general providing information for the public <www.oh.gov.hu/hungarian-equivalence/recognition-of-foreign> – its homepage contains the main provisions on recognition. The list of responsible authorities and chambers are determined in the Government Decree No. 33 of 2008, 21 February.

289. Residence and labour authorization is issued in a one-stop-shop procedure by the OIN in accordance with the European Parliament and Council Directive 2011/98/EU.

(b) Due to existing common minimal qualification requirements, diploma on physician, specialist doctor, nurse, midwife, dentist, specialist dentist, veterinary, pharmacist and architect issued in the EEA Member State without any conditions shall be considered equivalent to qualification obtained in Hungary, if the date of reference in each qualification in Member States is determined.[290]

(c) The applicant meeting the requirements of the regulated profession (in EC and transposed national law[291]) shall be entitled to the right to use the designation of the profession that is in conformity with the Hungarian term and also in the language in which he/she has obtained it. The recognition of the diploma of veterinaries, physicians, dentists or lawyers (attorney-at-law) covers an entitlement for the usage of the doctor as qualification in public documents (Dr med/jur/vet).

(d) The authority in the proceedings may communicate with the responsible authority relating to the applicant's qualification in the country of issuance in order to clarify the validity of the documents attached to the recognition.

(e) No longer than three years of adaptation period or aptitude test (e.g., theoretical and practical examination in Hungarian, assessing the ability and the required knowledge in the regulated profession of the applicant) may be determined for the applicant if his/her qualification period or curricula is different from that in the Hungarian regulation, or his/her integrated qualification is not applicable in Hungary. During the adaptation period, the applicant's profession is engaged under the supervision of a qualified professional according to the Hungarian regulation, or his/her participation in training may be required. At the end of the adaptation period, the authority shall evaluate it.

416. The Hungarian *language requirements* are relevant in the recognition of foreign diplomas, qualifications and in access to the labour market. The majority of rules relate to the public sector. Further, the authorization at the labour office does not cover how migrant workers can communicate and what communication demands are parts of the given job (with clients, colleagues or the employer).

(a) In the QualA, the rules deal with language requirements regarding the recognition of diplomas of persons within the ambit of national treatment. These persons are entitled to exercise a regulated profession in Hungary if they dispose of the language skills necessary for the pursuit of the concrete profession. An aptitude test is made by the competent authorities in the Hungarian language with the aim of assessing the practical and theoretical ability of the applicant to pursue a regulated profession in the country. The aptitude test takes into account the fact that the applicant is a qualified professional in the Member State of origin, and the test concerns only those abilities which are inevitable in the pursuit

---

290. These common requirements in each field require some years in university education, so accession to the EU member states have to define the date since that issued diploma is in conformity with common requirements ('date of reference'). For instance, Romania did not indicate this date of reference up to 2009, so thousands of physicians, dentists and nurses after enlargement could not enjoy this preferential treatment in Hungary.

291. For instance, Ministerial Decree No. 22 of 2012, 14 September (EMMI) on acquisition of qualification of dentist, specialist dentist, specialist pharmacist and clinical psychiatrist.

of the given profession in Hungary. Moreover, it is applicable in case of free provision of services, so the competent authority may require the applicant to provide evidence that he/she obtained the necessary information on Hungarian laws and ethical rules. Employers in Hungary are free to offer employment on terms laid down by them. In these cases, the degree of the necessary language abilities is set by the employer; however, they are required to comply with the case law of the ECJ.

(b) In the public sector – if the public servant or low level public official positions are open for non-nationals – language ability and its testing is regulated in a fragmented manner. The refrain is 'if the applicant has the *proper Hungarian language skills which are necessary to work in the given task/position*'. There are no internal or derivative regulations on how language skills of non-native applicants can be defined, measured or developed. Despite the on-going reform in public administration, the language ability test has not been developed.

417. The private sectors' practice on *language conditions* is unknown and partly regulated. It would be necessary to conduct a survey (e.g., in chambers, lobby-organizations of the economic branch) on the home-grown rules and practical conditions in the labour market. Employers in Hungary are free to offer employment on terms laid down by them. Some articles and news items prove how competition among professionals may upgrade the level of tests. For instance, the Ministerial Decree on the recognition of health care diplomas regulates the language requirements in the same spirit. It declares that the competent authority inform the applicant in Hungarian or in English regarding the professional and ethical rules, the applicable social security laws and the possibilities of learning the Hungarian language. The Ministerial Decree issued by the Ministry of Economy and Trade (GKM) No.17 of 2008, 30 April determined the language requirements for skilled workers in the air navigation service that is operated by a private company. Due to traffic security, the employment criteria, testing method, language ability in English and Hungarian, its evaluation system of trainee, junior and senior workers are clearly regulated (see its section 14 and Annex). According to qualification and requirements of obtaining a certificate for captains, nationality and knowledge of language would signify unequal treatment. For instance, an examination towards obtaining the certificate shall be taken in Hungarian, with some exceptions.[292]

418. Prior *labour and professional experiences* would be important in the qualification and in remuneration or labour law. While the first is regulated in the QualA taking into account work experiences in another EEA state together with sectorial specificities,[293] the previous jobs or training in other parts of the world are not

292. Applicant for certificate on Danube-lines shall take the exam in specific terminology in Russian or German language (see the International Treaty on Danube) and for certificate on sea-lines in English.

293. For instance, Ministerial Decree No. 36 of 2007, 13 November (OKM) on the enlisting of professional activities that fall within the scope of recognition of professional experience (in accordance with NICE and ISIC nomenclatures in the industry, agriculture, trade and other sectors), or Ministerial Decree No. 31 of 2009, 18 September (OKM) on the enlisting of organizations that regulate professional activities in the member states of the EU.

included in the regulation. In addition, the Labour Code and rules on public sector define prerogatives and benefits which are measured on the basis of the work years of the labourer – but those per se refer to the labour experience obtained in Hungary, or more strictly, within the same types of public organization.

419. There are some legal rules on self-employed or contract-driven occupations on the basis of which the evidence of professional experience is determined. For instance, Government Decree No.266 of 2013, 11 July contains the preconditions of how to operate as an expert the building and technical superintendent. Although the membership in the relevant chamber is optional for entrepreneur if it implies a cross-border service supply, the exam for entitlement by the national chamber is required in order to practice these professions lawfully and to be included in the list of entitled professionals. The appendix to the Decree regulates the required qualification, professional practice, exam procedure and minimum abilities of the applicant. The EEA national has to submit his application to the Capital Chamber of Engineers or Architects attaching the documents of fee paid, prior practice(s) in other Member State(s) also in Hungarian translation, professional Curriculum Vitae (CV) and references. According to the Ministerial Decree issued by the Ministry of the Interior No. 22 of 2006, 25 April, the lawful operation of private investigator, safeguard and bodyguard requires his/her individual license issued by the police authority, membership in the responsible chamber (consolidated Act CXXXIII of 2005) or as a company in possession of permit issued by the police authority. The applicant may also be a registered local office of a company established in another EEA state or an EEA national in possession of the individual entrepreneurship card. In case of non-national applicants, the documents shall be translated into Hungarian and clean criminal record issued by the place of (foreign or Hungarian) residence shall be also attached. In case of EEA national entrepreneur with license issued in another EEA Member State, only its validity and expiry data can be controlled in police authorization. It means that there is no specific criterion of prior professional practice of applicant if it implies a cross-border service supply.

420. The courts interpret the professional experience tightly in the public sector (e.g., working for years in a Police station was not considerable legal practice in the application to a position in local municipal).[294] The Ombudsman received some complaints from migrant workers regarding their working years abroad not having been taken into account in the calculation of jubilee payment and premium period in the public sector. The Ombudsman interpreted the applicable provisions and ascertained that exclusion from jubilee payment was lawful, but the exclusion from the premium period of the public servant is unlawful.[295]The new provisions on public officials require exceptionally prior professional experience of candidates, and transversal mobility among public administrative and law enforcement organs is accepted for workers but the practice out of Hungary has not been accepted

294. Bírósági Határozatok periodical for published cases of the Supreme Court] 1488/2006.
295. Állampolgári Jogok Országgylési Biztosa beszámolója, Budapest, 2007. Annual report to the Parliament of the Ombudsman, 2007, 80.

although persons in ambit of FreeA may be employed in certain positions of the public sector.[296]

§2. Conditions for Special Categories of Workers

421. The *skilled third-country national workers with Blue Card* enjoy certain exceptions in ThirdA admission (See paragraphs 85, 88, 90, 92, 102, 107-108, 157 and 191.) and labour authorization in the UnemplA as well as in the PermitD and QualA (See the paragraphs 277, 286, 313, 413 and 415.). The legal position of qualified workers is determined by the following rules:

(a) The Government may regulate the annual quota of employed third-country nationals including the Blue Card holders and the professions in which their employment is excluded on the grounds of data of labour force supply. In absence of employment strategy neither this exclusion nor the preferential professions in which there are deficit have been defined.
(b) The applicant for the Blue Card must prove a written commitment on employ issued by the potential employer that establishes the authorization. This commitment shall contain the name of position, the length of employment (no longer than four years), the minimum monthly salary of the worker and the required qualification. These conditions must not be changed because the labour contract becomes void if its substance is different from the written commitment. The minimal amount of salary shall not below than 120-150% of the gross monthly salary in national average in two years prior to the application.[297]
(c) According to LablnA, the labour inspector checks the legality of the third-country national's employment, including the existence of a valid Blue Card (or labour permit). In the absence of the Blue Card (or other labour permission), the employer must pay a contribution to the state budget: the minimum at first contribution being EUR 2,750 and in the event of repetition within three years, it costs a minimum of EUR 5,200. The decision on implied fine is communicated to the OIN.
(d) The Blue Card holder may enter and reside for a short term (up to ninety days) in another Member State of the EU; after eighteen months of residence may request new Card in another Member State to be employed, and after two years he or she may be employed freely out of the original job or sector in Hungary.
(e) The SocialA provides old age benefit for the Blue Card holder in need if he/she has a registered address in Hungary.

422. Having deep roots in agricultural production, it was an achievement in Hungary when the permission for *seasonal workers in agriculture* was deleted in

296. Act CXCIX of 2011 on public officials and Government Decree No. 29 of 2012, 7 March on their qualification.
297. Ministerial Decree No. 44 of 2011, 16 December (NGM) allows the lower (120%) amount in health sector. For instance, in 2015 it will be at least EUR 950 while in other sectors at least EUR 1200 monthly.

2005 if they would be employed in possession of a Temporary Work Book[298] (TWB) as a form of an atypical work. Between 2005 and 2010, upon the request of migrants, the competent capital/county labour office to the place of residence of migrants issued the TWB. The PermitD regulates how the labour permission is to be issued for seasonal agricultural workers:

(a) a third-country national migrant is eligible for employment up to 180 days – continuously or in more parts – within twelve months in plant-growing, forestry, animal breeding and fishing. If seasonal employment will take up to sixty days, a labour market test is not required in the authorization process. The validity of the permit cannot be extended;
(b) the labour office may issue the permit if the employer has notified the vacancy in advance, the labour market test is negative and applicant meets the requirements of qualification and health conditions – if there are any;
(c) seasonal workers can be employed through the manpower agency if it is registered at the labour office. In this case, the exclusionary reasons in the permission shall be assessed in connection with the manpower agent/agency (e.g., the salary would be below the national average or a fine was imposed against the agent for the violation of labour law within a year).
(d) The labour contract would be simplified as the Labour Code (Articles 201–203) offers providing a sample that contains the minimal guarantees for seasonal and occasional workers.

423. Due to the widespread principle of *ius sanguinis* in acquisition of nationality and benefited naturalization, the number of migrants with dual or multiple nationalities is growing (See paragraphs 3 and 15.). Employment of a person with *multiple nationalities* at any law enforcement and militant unit would be evaluated as a security risk so applicant's exclusion from a job is allowed on the grounds of the security check in individual cases but not automatically. Further, certain positions shall be filled by Hungarian nationals in public sector by the ministerial decrees on employment at police, security services and defence without open reference second/first nationality. Thus avoiding unconstitutional regulation.[299] Perhaps these rules also express mistrust on (first or second generation of) migrants without any reasoning in refusal (Tóth, 2004b).

424. In the sports sector, the *migration of athletes and sport experts* (trainers, managers) is sometimes confronted with the logic of competition among nations and not teams of sportsmen (Nemes & Tóth, 2002). This free movement can be hindered by three main obstacles, as follows:

(a) The *equivalent qualification* (certificate or diploma, qualified or master trainer, human-kinesiologist, physical education teacher) in the field of sport has been

298. Act LXXIV of 1997 on Employment with Temporary Work Book and the Simplified Payment of Public Contributions – not in force since 2011.
299. Constitutional Court judgement No. 52 of 2009, 30 April (AB határozat).

changed several times due to amendments in the tertiary education system.[300] Until January 2013 the minister in charge of the sport could exempt the qualification for employment that is determined in these professionals in the Appendix of the Decree on on the basis of applicant's age or prior practice in the sport sector. The qualification of sport experts is relevant for employment: all professional sportsmen or member of sport organizations have to meet this qualification Decree that shall be implemented 'in accordance with the internal rules of the sport federations'. Because the nationality requirement of the applicant is not defined, this universal requirement of qualification shall be equally applied by EU and non-EU nationals. Until 31 December 2007, each sport federation had to define in each sport field and branch the qualification which would be considered as a sport expert and the position which would be fulfilled by a qualified or master trainer. This requirement is relevant in the labour authorization for third-country nationals (PermitD).

(b) Since 1 July 2007, employment of professional athletes and trainers has been lawful without labour permits, regardless of nationality (PermitD). The legality of the exception shall be proved by the employee, for example, for a labour inspector's check. The second possible repercussion would be the rules of employment and the change of the employer, including provisions on transfer. The professional athlete shall be *remunerated* exclusively on the base of the Labour Code regardless of his nationality according to the SportA. In the possession of a racing permit, he/she has to conclude on a fixed-time (close-ended) written *employment contract* with a sport club or association as a labourer with certain specific exceptions as defined in the Act. This racing right is assigned from the athlete to the employer sport organization that shall be registered by the sport federation on the basis of the internal rules. This transfer of racing right means a financial compensation for the athlete. Due to termination of employment, this racing right returns free of charge to the athlete. The sport organization obtaining this racing right temporarily or permanently may transfer it to another sport club with the consent of the athlete who is entitled to receive *compensation* from the transferring sport organization that can obtain a *fee* from the hosting sport organization. The financial compensation and the fee are *consensual* but shall be announced to the sport federation; moreover 1% of it shall be paid to the sport federation and 4% to the fund supporting the training of supplies. If this transfer is not temporarily, a new labour contract shall be concluded. During the validity of the employment contract, it includes the fixed-time transfer of the right for racing to another sport club/association according to a contract. In this case, the athlete is considered as a posted worker. The SportA provides the athletes' free movement as employees. The transfer of racing right can be prepared and managed by commercial agents as a lucrative activity (commission) if he/she is registered at the international and national sport federation. Any other share in the transaction costs (beyond the athlete's compensation, commission, fee and sport federation) is invalid.

(c) The third objection would be the nationality quotas or other specific treatments of non-nationals in racing. According to the SportA, the *national sport league*

300. Government Decree No. 157 of 2004, 18 May.

(federation) in each branch of sport is entitled to regulate the Racing Conditions (e.g., of national championship), the Code on Transferring, to register the racing rights of athletes and clubs, to issue or reject the racing license, authorization 'for *Hungarian [national] athletes* participating in races held abroad and for *foreign [national] athletes* participating in races held in Hungary'. However, *there are no quotas of non-national athletes defined in the public legal rules.* For instance, the Hungarian Football League published the racing requirements and conditions in the season of 2013–2014. In accordance with this, 'the participation of players as EU citizens and citizens from the party states of Cotonou Treaty enjoying the equal treatment at a national championship is not limited. The maximal number of other foreign players is five who are playing in the same match on the ground. The list of the states whose nationals shall be equally treated with union nationals as well as the states in the ambit of the Cotonou Treaty the League shall publish regularly by the League' The definition of foreign player means that he has spent less than three years in the frame of the League (its clubs). [301] The Statute of the Hungarian Handball League defines that foreign player is a third-country national without three active years with racing right in the national championship. However, the Regulation for Transfer between Federations has no specific rule on nationality.[302] According to the Racing Statute of the Hungarian Athletic League, only Hungarian nationals are eligible to race in a national assorted team, and the maximum number of non-nationals per club in a race is one athlete. However '*there is differentiation between national and EEA citizens*' – said the president.[303] In recent years, the equal (national) treatment of EEA nationals has been more and more regulated in by-laws of sport federations, including the right to transfer and participate in a championship.

(d) Only Hungarian nationals are eligible for sport allowances (for Olympic winners, their trainers or sport leaders in SportA) finance from the budget. A preferential naturalization is assured for foreign athletes to become members in the national assorted and Olympic team, so allowances are available for outstanding ('Sport-Hungarian') nationals but not for non-national trainers.

425. The *key personnel* is an independent, functional term in the PermitD differing from the legal position of 'leading officer' in the Civil Code that may be employed without labour permission. The key personnel refers on third-country-nationals who are employed by a company in decisive part in foreign property that is seated in Hungary, and they are directing, supervising the whole company or its units but they are not owners; or they have high qualification that is vital to the business or servicing activities of the employer. Their labour authorization shall be decided within five days because the labour market test is not required. The

301. Championship requirements are applicable since 1 Jul. 2013, details see <www.doumentumtar.mlsz.hu/02_Szabalyzatok/02.>.
302. International Handball Federation (July 2011) and www.keziszovetseg.hu.
303. The Hungarian Athletic Alliance includes 113 sport clubs. All internal regulations (Statute, Racing Provisions, Disciplinary Rules, etc.) were adopted in 2005–2007 and reformed in 2014 providing equal treatment for EEA nationals with Hungarians. See further in <www.masz.hu>.

relocation of key personnel is a daily practice of multinational companies. The *posted workers* in ambit of the Directive 96/71/EC are neither authorized nor notified at labour centre/office in PermitD thus their number is not known is Hungary. Although certain groups of posted workers are regulated in PermitD as exempted from the permission (see the paragraph 32, 176, 407) only the Labour Code uses the term of secondment, transfer and loaning of workers. The provisions of the Code shall be implemented on work or employment that is performed regularly in Hungary (Article 3) unless lawful exception is ensured as in the Article 295–297. Accordingly, posted worker employed by foreign employer in Hungary (and inside the same group of companies) is subjected to the national law (Code)[304] and the collective agreements in the following aspects if these provisions are more favourable than his or her own national law: the maximum work periods and minimum rest periods; minimum paid annual holidays; the lawful, gross minimum rates of pay, including overtime rates; conditions of hiring out workers (Article 214-222), in particular the supply of workers by temporary employment undertakings;[305] health, safety and hygiene at work; protective measures in the terms and conditions of employment of pregnant women or those who have recently given birth, of children and of young people, and; equal treatment between men and women and other provisions on non-discrimination. These rules shall be implemented together with sectoral collective agreements in the construction industry. Protecting the labour market environment, its guarantee shall not be ignored. However, the social security of posted workers belongs to the own national regulation and social insurance system.

426. In the absence of more preferential provisions in law, the *family member* of a sponsor who is a third-country national may be employed with a labour and residence permit on the grounds of family unification in Hungary. The circle of family members is defined in the ThirdA, and their exceptions in labour market test and free employment in UenmplA and PermitD (See paragraphs 176 and 413.). The family member's work permit may be issued for the term of the residence permit on the grounds of family unification but not for more than two years. A family member's application for work permit shall be refused, if the validity period of the residence permit has expired or if the permit is withdrawn. Rules on collective or seasonal agricultural labour permission shall not be applied to family member's applications. The third-country national losing his or her job is eligible to the unemployment benefit and assistance if he or she had a unified (residence and

304. The assignment is also covered by the Code. 'Employers shall be entitled to temporarily reassign their employees to jobs and workplaces other than what is contained in the employment contracts, or to another employer.' (Art. 53) The new Labour Code uses only the expression 'temporarily reassigned' instead of secondment or transfer.

305. Loaning in Article 214: 'temporary agency work' shall mean when an employee is hired out by a temporary-work agency to a user enterprise for remunerated temporary work, provided there is an employment relationship between the worker and the temporary-work agency (placement). The duration of assignment may not exceed five years, including any period of extended assignment and reassignment within a period of six months from the time of termination of his/her previous employment, irrespective of whether the assignment was made by the same or by a different temporary-work agency.

labour) permit and he or she was employed at least for six months prior to the registry as jobseeker (Article 2(3) of the UnemplA).

427. Volunteers involving them to social, charity, health, cultural, human rights or youth activity are attracted from abroad and vice versa. The Act on community work by volunteers (hereinafter VolA) follows the rationale of labour law providing for non-gainful activity of migrants in the receiving organization (municipal, minority self-government, public institution, NGO, church or public service provider). In accordance with this, a volunteer over the age of ten (up to the age of eighteen with the consent of the parents) may conclude a contract on work if his/her age, health conditions and qualification are in conformity with the possible requirements to the given task. However, below the age of sixteen as volunteer shall not be sent abroad. The main duties of the receiving organization are the following:

(a) Proper information on the task and protective measures, labour instruments, instructions and control by a professional person shall be provided.
(b) The young volunteer's daily work is limited (e.g., between ages sixteen and eighteen, the maximum is four and half hours per day but not more than eighteen hours weekly).
(c) A symbolic compensation for his/her work (e.g., per diem to a migrant without domicile in Hungary) may be given that shall not exceed one-fifth of the lawful minimum salary per month.
(d) The foreign volunteer of an organization shall be received on the grounds of a contract between the sending and the receiving organizations involving the mediator organization (e.g., the relief action is organized by a youth organization managing the contact between the foreign sending organization and the Hungarian receiving organization).
(e) The liability insurance of the receiving organization shall be covered regarding labour and damage in connection with the volunteers' activity.
(f) Migrants within the ambit of the ThirdA (see the rules of admission in paragraph 90) – not including refugees, temporary protected persons, settled and long-term migrants – can lawfully work as volunteers if the receiving organization has concluded a liability insurance contract on damage caused by them, accommodation (nutrition, residence and internal travel) and return travel is ensured, and their health care eligibility (by law or on contractual basis) or cover on their health care costs is provided. Furthermore, their contracts shall be in writing.
(g) Before the reception of volunteers, a notice in format shall be completed and submitted to the Ministry of Human Resources electronically by the receiving organization that maintains a registry of volunteers' movement. Moreover, the data from the registered receiving organizations shall be forwarded to the labour inspection and the taxation office in order to use these data to prompt check in receiving organizations.

Volunteers are within the margin of labour migration as well as foreign students, researchers under the personal scope of ThirdA. Their employment is rather occasional (e.g., for a teaching activity) beyond the researcher employed on the grounds of the reception contract issued by the registered institute in Hungary.

Chapter 3. Sanctions against Illegal Participation in the Labour Market

428. The legality of the employment of foreign labourers is checked in an integrated manner involving *labour inspectors* together with Police and customs officers determining whether the residence of the employee is lawful, the labourer is registered and the payment of public revenues by the employer is in order. Numerous requirements have to be met in labour sanctions although they are implemented in parallel without the cost, benefit and implication assessment. The major direction of punishment targets the shadow economy, while the reduction of transaction costs in employment administration, the simplification of the labour and visa permission or introduction of the one-stop-shop has hardly been deliberated.

§1. Sanctions against Employers

429. Regional labour inspectors are entitled to control lawful employment including the legality of foreign (third-country national posted and lent)[306] labourers by the LabInA. It is partly based on the terms of non-permitted and irregular employment in the PermitD. In accordance with this, the employment is not lawful if the gainful activity of a third-country national does not suit the labour law or permission (e.g., the work is done out of the determined place or a different working activity is conducted). The administrative practice proves its rigid interpretation. For instance, the employment was considered as unlawful because the labourer was working in the territory of another county and not in the county defined in the permit; or the labourer was sent to the countryside for a concrete delegated task.[307] In addition, the labour inspector is entitled for a complex control, not only on the rules in connection with employment of third-country nationals, but all labour conditions and provisions of other laws.[308] The labour inspector is entitled to take the following *measures*:

(a) A fine is imposed for the proved *violation of labour documentation and notice shall be paid by* employers. The amount of the fine depends on how many individuals were illegally employed, the type of employer (e.g., a small entrepreneur or a multinational company) the frequency of sanctions against the same employer. Thus the minimal fine is EUR 100 and the maximum is EUR 67,000.
(b) A payment to the budget (Employment Fund) shall be ordered if illegal employment of third-country national is proved. Its amount is at first 400% of the paid remuneration to the illegally employed persons but at least 800% of the actual lawful monthly minimum salary per capita. The repetitive fine within three years is up to 800% of the paid remuneration or at least 400%–1500% of the

306. The used term is not coherent, the UnemplA and LabInA refers either to foreigners or third-country nationals because the full liberalization on employment of EEA nationals has not been incorporated to their text.
307. EBH 2008/1811. ügy, KGD 2004/171. ügy.
308. For instance, EBH 2002/799.ügy.

lawful monthly minimum salary per capita). If application for labour permit prolongation is failed, the payment is the paid remuneration to the employed worker but at least 200% of the actual lawful monthly minimum salary per capita.
(c) The inspector may initiate different administrative sanctions to the competent authority (e.g., closure of the shop or withdrawal of its licence).
(d) Putting the name of the employer to a public list of final decisions on labour infringement the employer is being excluded from public benefits or public procurement procedure.

430. A *work order fine* shall be paid also to the state budget in the following circumstances:[309]

(a) failing to announce data or providing false data in relation to the start and the termination of a third-country national's employment that may be employed without permission; or
(b) not maintaining in an archive the documents of employment for three years after its termination; or
(c) not being registered as a private labour exchange service provider at the labour office, or
(d) failing to announce or providing incomplete or false data in relation to lending manpower.

The UnemplA defines its amount: it is between EUR 17 and EUR 1,700, and the county labour authority (inside the governmental office) evaluates the frequency and repetition of irregularity.

431. The employers shall check before the employment of a third-country national that he/she has proper permits (visa and residence permit) for engaging in gainful employment. Furthermore, the employer shall report to the migration authority if the third-country national failed to start his/her labour as authorized, or if his/her employment is terminated before the expiration of the validity period of the work permit. A *public order fine* may be imposed by the Regional Directorate of the OIN under the following circumstances:

(a) the employer of persons under the ThirdA did not check the residence and labour documents of the potential employee to verify whether he/she was eligible for gainful activity in Hungary;
(b) the employer failed to announce to the Police/OIN or other responsible authority within five working days that a person under the ThirdA or the FreeA (family member) did not start the work despite the permission or the employment being terminated.

309. Decree of the Minister of Labour No. 3 of 1996, 5 April (MüM) on labour order fine.

The employer is exempted from paying the fine if his/her representative has checked the documents and despite careful scrutiny the falsification could not be revealed. The direct employer and main contractor – if work pursues a civil law contract – are jointly responsible for paying the imposed fine if the representative of the main contractor was or would have been aware of the illegal employment of the third-country national (in the absence of a valid residence permit or labour permission). This failure would cost up to EUR 1,700 per employed foreign person in the FreeD and the ThirdD if it is revealed by the authority within one year. Its appeal is decided by the Headquarters of the Police or OIN.

432. The disclosure of illicit employment of migrants under the personal scope of the ThirdA means that *all costs of return and expulsion* shall be covered by the employer (including e.g., the receiving research institute within six months after the expired reception period).

433. In accordance with the PermitD, the *labour permit may be denied* – inter alia – under the following circumstances:

(a) if a fine was imposed with a final decision against the prospective employer for any infringement of employment and occupational safety regulations within one year preceding the date of the application;
(b) if the prospective employer was ordered, in accordance with the LabInA, to make a mandatory contribution to the Employment Fund for illegal employment of a third-country national within three years preceding the date of the application, and the employer failed to comply with such payment obligation;
(c) in the event of authorization of seasonal agricultural work, the permit may be refused if a work order fine against the private labour exchange company was imposed with a final decision, or the labour exchange company was ordered in accordance with the LabInA to make a mandatory contribution to the Employment Fund for illegal employment of a third-country national, and the labour exchange company failed to comply with such payment obligation.

434. In accordance with the VolA, if the receiving organization has failed to notify the employment of volunteers to the responsible Ministry, the checking labour authority, labour inspector, the tax authority or the public prosecutor must indicate this fact to the responsible Ministry. The responsible Ministry shall order the recovery of the registration within thirty days. In the absence of this performance, the *receiving organization may exclude volunteers from lawful employment* for a maximum time period of one year.

435. The PermitD intends to give a small guarantee for illegally employed third-country national: employer shall *reimburse the remuneration to him or her* if the infringement of the labour law is disclosed. The labour authority supports (somehow) the migrant worker to get this money in Hungary or abroad. If its amount cannot be defined in the given case by the authority at least 300% of the lawful minimal monthly salary per capita shall be paid by the employer (section 23).[310]

§2. SANCTIONS AGAINST WORKERS

436. The most relevant sanction against an unlawfully employed foreigner is that he/she cannot reside in the country. Subject to the exception set out in ThirdA (e.g., non-refoulement, family conditions are taken into account), the immigration authority shall order the *expulsion* of such third-country national under immigration laws who fails to comply with the requirements set out in ThirdA for the right to residence (e.g., proper material means of subsistence from documented, lawful economic activities) or who was engaged in any gainful employment in the absence of the prescribed work permit or any permit prescribed under statutory provision. However, the immigration authority shall not expel the third-country national if he/she shall be readmitted on a bilateral agreement that was concluded between the EU and any third country before 13 January 2009. The order on his/her surrender may be contested within twenty-four hours without suspensive effect. In the event of expulsion, its judicial review may be initiated within eight days, and shall be decided within fifteen days by the court. If the third-country national has been expelled for security or public order reasons by another EU Member State, and while residing in Hungary he/she is engaged in any gainful employment without proper permission, the existing expulsion order shall be executed by the Hungarian authority.

437. Where expulsion is ordered, the immigration authority may also order *exclusion* taking into account the nature and severity of the infringement, the personal circumstances of the third-country national concerned, and as to whether his/her continued residence represents a serious threat to public security, public policy or national security. The period of non-entry may be ordered for a maximum of five years in case of serious threat to public security, public policy or national security up to ten years. Third-country nationals whose exclusion was ordered may enter the territory of Hungary only upon the special consent of the ordering authority.

438. Due to the free movement of persons within the ambit of the FreeA, their expulsion and exclusion may be ordered in exceptional cases. While the EC law requires prohibition on the grounds of individual behaviour in connection with severe threat to public order, security or public health without economic reasons,[311] the simple violation of administrative labour rules or statutory provisions on self-employment cannot justify ordering the *prohibition of entry and residence.*

310. It is considered the transposition of the European Parliament and the Council Directive 2009/52/EU, 18 June but its executive rules are fragmented.
311. Directive of 2004/38/EC and case law of ECJ.

Chapter 4. Legal Remedies and Procedural Safeguards

439. The *labour permission procedure* can be divided into two parts: the notification of vacancy by the employer to the non-preferential procedure that is based on labour market assessment and the preferential authorization without this test by the PermitD. These can be elaborated as follows:

(a) Vacancy and labour force demand of the potential employer is notified to the capital/county labour centre (inside the governmental office) defining precisely the kind of worker requested (his/her qualification, language knowledge, labour experience and other components of the job) before the formal application submission within fifteen to sixty days. During this period the labour office recruits such worker available for the position in question, who is registered as a job-seeker according to the UnemplA and who satisfies the conditions of employment prescribed by the employer's labour requirement; the UnemplA defines the meaning of labour-readiness and ability of individuals in an active age. In the absence of labour force supply (with preferences for EEA nationals and family members and others on the grounds of international agreements[312]) the permission for employment of a third-country national may be issued within thirty days. This procedure, including the labour market test, is applicable on the seasonal agricultural labourer's permission.
(b) If the third-country national is exempted the labour market test, the permit shall be issued within ten days and within five days for key personnel's permission. The documents on health conditions and qualifications of a labourer as required by law in the given position or job shall be attached to the application.

If the residence and labour authorization for a third-country national applicant – including for the application for the Blue Card – is decided in a unified procedure, the Regional Directorate shall request the expert opinion from the county labour centre that evaluates the local labour market assessment on the grounds of vacancy and claims. The expert opinion shall be issued within twenty-one days while the entire procedure shall be finished by the Directorate within ninety days. Despite of this recently introduce 'one-stop-shop' process, the bureaucratic spirit of substantial and procedural provisions have been continuous as well as their critics. The labour market test is not based on up-to-date and comprehensive data of job-seekers, and Community preferences and employer's economic interests are not clearly expressed in the rules (Tóth, 2011). If the labour conditions in employment are changing, a new permission or a modification procedure shall be initiated. This rigidity of permission has been criticized by NGOs[313] and authors (Berke et al., 2002; Kovách et al., 2007).

---

312. PermitD is silent regarding direct reference on Association Agreements and other connected rules, such as Council Decision 2008/157/EC of 18 Feb. 2008 on the principles, priorities and conditions contained in the Accession Partnership with the Republic of Turkey and repealing Decision 200635/EC or Resolution of Association Council No.1/80.

313. Oltalomkeresők – Migrációs Hírlevél (Menedék – Migránsokat Segítő Egyesület) <www.menedek.hu> Newsletter on migratory movements, social events and statistics – published by the Hungarian Association for Migrants in 2006–2008.

440. The application *shall be refused* by the labour authority if the following circumstances arise:

(a) the employment is scheduled to start after 120 days from the date of submission;
(b) the genuine employer differs from the applicant or the submitted documents (e.g., on qualification of the worker) are manipulated or falsified;
(c) there is a worker available for the position for which the third-country national is to be hired who satisfies the qualification requirements and the employment conditions prescribed by the relevant legislation or specified by the employer, and if the employment of such worker is hindered due to reasons attributable to the employer;
(d) instead of employment by the applicant, a labour exchange (lending the labour force to another) is intended;
(e) the employment is out of the annual quota for third-country nationals or the job is on the list of excluded positions for third-country nationals in the labour market as determined by the minister;
(f) Hungarian labourers are obviously hindered in employment in the state of the nationality of the potential worker who is a third-country national (reciprocity);
(g) or the conditions of entry, residence and public order as determined in the ThirdA are not met by the third-country-national in a unified procedure.

441. The *application may be refused* – beyond the above-mentioned grounds on sanctions that are applicable against the employer – if the following circumstances arise:

(a) the employer was imposed a labour or public order fine or reimbursement of remuneration for illegally employed workers was forced by the labour authority within one year of the date of application;
(b) a strike is on during the period of authorization at applicant employer;
(c) the employer carried out collective redundancy within one year of the date of application,
(d) the employer is apparently unable to provide the employment conditions required; or
(e) the indicated monthly salary for the employee is below the average in the given economic sector in the country according to the Central Statistical Office data (this rejection is based on the ground of statistics from the previous calendar year and not on a collective bargain, and the acceptable threshold is 80%).

442. All documents (e.g., on qualification of foreign labourer, medical check) shall be attached with the authentic translation into Hungarian. If the applicability of a labourer's qualification or an employer's legal status is questionable, the labour office may contact other competent authorities for clarification. The permit determines the concrete job, its time frame, locality and employer's data in advance. It is valid only to this work done by that nominated labourer without any modification by the employer or the employee. The maximum length of validity is two years in permit, but it can be prolonged before its expiration. The permit is renewable if it based exclusively on the prolongation of employment if other conditions are not changed. In this case, a format shall be submitted to the competent labour office without attachments before the expiration of the permit within thirty-sixty days.

443. The employer is obliged to announce the start, failure and cessation of the foreign worker's employment as well as the given job falling out of permission to the competent county labour authority or the immigration authority within five days. In these cases, the labour authority or the Regional Directorate of the OIN withdraws the permit by the UnemplA and the PermitD. The OIN, the tax office and the social insurance authority are entitled to obtain the personal data of employees (e.g., nationality, qualification, legal status, address, job and salary) from the National Employment Service (Central Labour Registry[314]). It has to be added that all employees *ex lege* are subject to the health care and social insurance/pension scheme, so the data of the employee shall be provided immediately to these organs by the employer during the existence of the employment status. In addition, a social and employment electronic database on the grounds of information on active aged persons given by the registrar at the municipal and labour office assists in controlling the eligibility and incompatibility of social and labour benefits, supports and conditions at the individual level. This new database set up in 2009 extended the data provision obligation for all employers regarding the employee, including persons under the personal scope of the FreeA and migrants out of the labour permission regime in ExD and PermitD. In accordance with this, the start of employment on the first day of employment and the cessation of employment within twenty-four hours shall be notified to the competent labour centre. This announcement includes the nationality, legal basis of work and family membership, too. The permit and its documentation shall be preserved for three years after the cessation of employment (for instance, during a labour inspection or tax authority check these documents shall be presented).

444. All labourers regardless of their nationality or legal status are entitled to use, free of charge, the *labour services* (labour exchange, counselling and legal aid) at the labour centres as the sort of services defined in the UnemplA. Important labour services and benefits are based on the registry of unemployment and cooperation with the labour authority in job seeking. While the foreigners whose employment is within the ambit of the labour permission cannot enter and remain in the country after ceased employment as job seekers, the persons entitled to the right to free movement and residence (the FreeA) are eligible to enter, reside and be registered as job seekers with a valid desire to find a job, for up to six months. They can use portable document (U1) issued by another Member State authority to prove job-seeking position and prior employment. Similarly, third-country national losing his or her job is eligible to the unemployment benefit and assistance if he or she had a unified (residence and labour) permit and he or she was employed at least for six months prior to the registry as jobseeker. Due to this distinction, the former group practically has no opportunity to enjoy labour services unless he/she has proper

314. All workers can control whether their processed data in the registry are correct or not due to the labour, social insurance and tax consequences <www.emma185.hu>.

financial resources to be considered a self-sufficient person. In addition, this '*lawless group*' has to pay the same unemployment contribution as other labourers do, but without accession to unemployment benefit, re/training, support to become a self-employed person, support to the employer towards recruitment of disadvantageous labourers (unskilled, middle-aged, in poor health conditions). In brief, the labour service and support system, in fact, has not been prepared for job-seeking migrants. Whereas, persons under the scope of the FreeA and others who can be employed without labour permission are treated as nationals in law, but in practice, the conditions in labour services have not been developed (e.g., foreign language communication with clients, supports to vocational training/exam for non-native workers and special integration courses regarding the labour market are missing). In an economic crisis, non-contributory services as well as contributory benefits (their eligibility being dependent on work and contribution-paying period of the worker) are limited, so migrants remain marginal in this context, at least in the near future. Decisions in connection with unemployment supports and job seeking benefits for migrant workers shall be issued sixty days by the competent labour centre. The labour office decision may be appealed and the final decision regarding only the infringement of law may be reviewed at the court and can be modified substantially. If the court annuls the administrative decision, a repeated procedure shall be pursued.

445. The rules on legal remedy and the *procedure in employment* and labour office authorization (permission of foreign labourer's employment, renewal of permission and unemployment benefits) are regulated in the UnemplA and the PermitD, and as a supplementary character in the AdminA and the CivPA. In the absence of special provisions in labour law, the AdminA shall be implemented as in all administrative procedures. For instance, the interpretation of the scope of labour permission was clarified in a judicial review. It was the Supreme Court that clarified whether a labour permission is required or not for a commissioning work. By law, its fifteen days is a threshold, but the Supreme Court states that these fifteen days shall not be consecutive, and the permission depends on the number of days on which work is accomplished in fact, while commissioning implies a skilled work that shall not necessarily be technically complicated work but will rather be based on an unusual method in Hungary.[315] Furthermore, provisions on specificities (in the UnemplA and the PermitD) say the following:

(a) the first instance decisions on labour permission and unemployment benefits belong to the capital/county labour office, and the appeal is decided by the national labour service;
(b) the first instance decision on labour permission takes twenty days in general, but in cases without labour market test (e.g., application for key personnel) it takes only five days;
(c) additional attachments to the applications shall be submitted within ten days;
(d) permitted unemployment benefits (labour seeking, support to re/training, etc.) are available within a year, and after this period their eligibility expires.

315. LB-H-MJ 2008/23.bírósági határozat, Complex Döntvénytár (LB 2008.január 23.).

446. Decisions regarding the fine imposed on the labour inspectors may be reviewed by the Court. It can be annulled and a repetition of procedure can be ordered because of violation of laws by the administrative organ in proceedings. Decisions on fines are often executed after the modification of the implemented legal rules or the dissolution of entrepreneurship.

447. In other cases, the AdminA shall be applied. The AdminA is a general codex in almost each administrative procedure that provides a legal remedy in all substantial decisions of the authority, such as refusal of application, withdrawal of permit, refused prolongation of permit or imposition a fine. In accordance with this, within fifteen days of the substantial decision's notice to the client, an appeal may be submitted to the higher administrative organ of the proceedings authority. The appeal has a delaying effect unless the execution of the issued decision has to be immediately ordered on the ground of public policy, protection of life, property or national security. Regardless of the reasons for legal remedy, the second instance of administrative procedure involves checking the legality, formality and functionality of the first instance decision, and it may finally modify, supplement, annul or confirm the first decision. The rules on entry and residence of non-nationals (alien policing proceedings) precede the rules in the AdminA, and in labour migrants' cases form an amalgam from the procedural provisions (the ThirdA, the FreeA, the Labour Code, the UnemplA and these executive norms together with the AdminA and the CivPA) not necessarily in favour of clients. In brief, the effective protection of public order and the formal legality of decisions would be the leading principles. The controlling mechanism on first instance decisions is ensured through the public prosecutor's review and the regular supervision by the second instance authority as well. The final administrative decision may be reviewed at the County/Capital Court exclusively on the ground of violation of law that shall be indicated by the client.

448. The review of decisions based on labour law is ensured. In accordance with this, the CivPA's special chapter is applicable on social insurance, decisions by labour inspectors including check on foreign labourers' employment, labour safety issues, benefits and supports in connection with the UnemplA. Beyond the general rules, it has been emphasized that the Administrative and Labour Court is competent in this judicial review that operates in each county and in the capital, while the appeal against its judgment belongs to the normal (universally competent) county/capital Court, and in exceptional cases the Supreme Court is also entitled to issue a final judgment. While the judicial review has no suspensive effect, the suspension of the execution may be ordered by the proceeding Court upon the request of the plaintiff as well as ex officio. The application for a judicial review may be submitted to the Labour Court within thirty days of notice of the administrative decision to the client. The judicial review intends to clarify whether the legality of the prior (administrative) procedure was provided or not. Its judgment means the abrogation of the decision, the abrogation and order of repetition of the entire administrative procedure or the amendment of the prior decision.

449. The authority in the *recognition of qualification* procedure shall apply the rules of the AdminA with some specificities determined in the QualA, as follows:

(a) The original document on qualification (certificate, diploma) shall be presented, but due to probable personal or reasonable conditions exemption may be allowed for refugees, other internationally protected persons or persons who request the recognition only for the continuation of studies.
(b) The recognition authorities (approximately thirty[316] in number) shall publish on their own homepage the languages in which the non-authentic translation of the attached documents is acceptable. Otherwise, an authentic translation in Hungarian made by the National Translation Authentication Office (under the aegis of the Ministry of Justice and Law Enforcement) or attested by the public notary and the consular office is required.
(c) The procedure takes three months.
(d) The applicant has to prove residence in Hungary by an address card or identity card, and migrants out of the personal scope of the FreeA – with the exception of persons who request recognition only for the continuation of their studies – have to present a residence permit issued for family unification or gainful work It means that lawful residence of migrant is the basis for recognition, employment and entrepreneurship. (This latter is not logical, because the recognition of qualification is a precondition to the establishment of a private entrepreneurship or to a self-employed person or a labourer.)
(e) A fee (up to 250% of lawful minimum monthly salary) that greatly exceeds the general fee has to be paid in advance. For instance, the recognition or the equivalence certificate of elementary or secondary school document by international agreement requires only 12.5% of the lawful minimum monthly salary, while taking a master examination costs two and half times that salary or fee for the aptitude test costs only the expenses of its management. Persons under the EC preference and the scope of the FreeA, including Hungarian nationals, may request exemption, and the applicant's financial conditions may be verified from the data provided by the OIN. It means a doubled check due to missing cooperation between authorities. (This national treatment principle based on trust is challenged by the doubled check concerning the statement of migrant: OIN data on are requested again in mirror declaration of migrant in other administrative procedure whether he/she tells a lie to the tax office or the social affairs office in municipal.)
(f) The Educational Office[317] (under the subordination of the ministry in charge of public education) is competent in the recognition of certificates issued on elementary school, grammar school education and professional branches in confirmation of the level of graduation obtained in tertiary and scientific studies. This office is the contact point in the European and the worldwide cooperation of administrators in tertiary education and qualification issues (and it operates as a national information centre on the recognition of the free movement of labourers inside the EU. Universities are entitled for recognition of diplomas issued abroad, while in regulated professions the HEIC or a specific office is

316. See the consolidated text of the Government Decree No. 33 of 2008, 21 February and its Appendix on foreign certificate recognition authorities at first and second instances implementing Act C of 2001 and on cross-border services that shall be notified.
317. Government Decree No. 121 of 2013, 26 April.

competent if it belongs to the subordination of the branch ministry concerned. For instance, the Office of Health Authorization and Administrative Procedures[318] shall recognize, without further scrutiny, a diploma of an EU citizen obtained in the health sector if it meets the requirements of applicable directives.[319] Moreover, it can be recognized with the involvement of proper expert in diplomas and the practice of non-EU citizens in health sector, or it can direct the applicant to take specific examination.

450. The AdminA plays a key role in the authorization of the recognition of qualification from the procedural point of view, because its provisions shall not be derogated in the QualA. Minimum deviation implies that the appeal on the decision issued by an academic or public education institution may be submitted to the Minister of Education. Whereas, if the application is aimed at the recognition of partial studies, the appeal on the first instance decision issued by a public education institution may be submitted to the sustaining organ of the institution.

451. Otherwise, AdminA shall be implemented together with its guarantees, as follows:

(a) The respect for personal data protection of the client and the lawful basis of data processing, storage and transmission to other authority is fully ensured in a procedure by law. In an appeal or a complaint to the Ombudsman, the client may enforce personal data protection as a fundamental right. In the FreeA and the ThirdA, there is an exhaustive list of the personal data of the client that shall be processed and transmitted to other competent authorities, and the period of storage of these data is also defined.
(b) The client or applicant has the right to be informed of the relevant data of the case; by reading the entire file in proceedings. This right to inspection covers personal data, evidences, expert opinion, protocols as well as confidential documents that established the authorization.
(c) The client or applicant is entitled to use electronic contacts with the authority in proceedings through an electronic identification code. Without personal application, through a downloadable format and an electronic letter he/she can obtain an appointment, pay the fee or acquire information.

318. Decree of the Minister of Health-care (EüM) No. 30 of 2008, 25 July on recognition of certificates in health care and issuance of documents related to recognition of Hungarian certificates abroad.
319. Directives 78/686/EEC, 78/687/EEC, 93/16/EEC and 2001/19/EC.

Part VIII. Access to Self-Employed Activities

Chapter 1. Overview of Applicable Legislation

452. Self-employment is based on fundamental rights ensured for all in the Fundamental Law. Freedom of undertaking, equal protection of right to property, free choice in occupation and profession, as well as fair competition in market and protection of consumers' rights are the main points of reference on self-employment activities or small entrepreneurship in a liberal market economy (Article M, XII, XIII and XV). However, these fundamental rights are limitable by law in a constitutional system taking into account the welfare, public policy or social boundaries and obligations of property. Market economy and autonomy of each actor in the economy is a principle[320] without individual rights itself, but both are strongly connected to numerous fundamental rights under the institutional protection of the state accomplishing its own tasks through them. Dynamics of liberal market economy are provided by the freedom in undertaking and competition without discrimination (Drinóczi, 2006).

453. Terms of *self-employment* in EU law and ILO documents are different, and no universally accepted definition exists. The former separates employment on the contractual basis under the supervision of another person as employer, while self-employment means an independent actor in the economy including agricultural producer, freelance professional, occasional trader in streets, and other agent of tourism who is working or servicing for a mutually negotiated price.[321] The definition of 'self-employed' by the ILO is wider, including the owner of a company without legal personality who is personally taking part in its economic activities; the working member of a cooperative, the facilitator family member, their employed trainee and the seasonal, temporary labourers.[322] There is no binding interpretation of 'self-employment' in the EU that could be transposed to the national law of Member States (Pap, 2009). As a result, there is diversity in legal regulation inside the EU on the common basis of independently managed economic activities by self-employed persons. Nowadays, a stronger social protection of self-employed

320. Constitutional Court decisions (21/1994. (IV.16.) AB határozat, 144/B/1990/4. AB határozat).
321. Council Directive 92/57/EEC.
322. International labour standards. A workers' educational manual. Fourth (revised) edition. International Labour Office, Geneva, 1998.

persons and action against misrepresented contracts for tax-deductions has been urged, even in Hungary. In sum, self-employment is internationally determined not as a specific, atypical legal relationship, but much more as a *collective term* including all remunerated works made by an independent and self-responsible person (Tóth, 2011).

454. Hungary is not a party state to the UN and the Council of Europe conventions protecting labour and social rights of migrant workers and their family members, including self-employed persons. However, due to the basic principle of non-discrimination in ILO conventions, Hungary as a party state since 1920[323] has been obliged to ensure labour laws equally *mutatis mutandis* for self-employed persons. For instance, health safety and security measures in the building industry shall be applied to self-employed entrepreneurs and their workers '*in accordance with national legislation and provisions*'.[324]

455. The meaning of self-employed person can be outlined by numerous provisions and legal sources in Hungary. In accordance with this, it includes economic activities of persons operating as owners of working instruments and other equipment without the control of another person, independently, regularly for one's own business responsibility. This gainful work is often based on the required qualification and special licenses issued by the authorities (e.g., public health, fire and environment protection permit for opening a workshop, etc.). Whereas, self-employment is a registered category in tax, unemployment, social insurance and health care contribution systems. Its main forms are available to migrants, too: individual entrepreneurship, agricultural (small) producer, personally working part-owner in a company and freelance professional implementing flat rate revenue provisions (e.g., artist, journalist, editor and interpreter). Due to the economy being in transit, with growing unemployment rates, thousands of previously employed labourers became self-employed persons in the early 1990s, surviving privatization and harsh competition in the building of the market economy. While the ratio of part-time jobs, labourers with fixed-time contracts and self-employed persons in Hungary is below the average in the EU,[325] a great extent of micro-entrepreneurships together with facilitator family members are considered to be '*self-employed under pressure* (of economic changes)' or '*forced entrepreneurs*' by unemployment and economic recession.[326]

---

323. Promulgation of the Statute of the International Labour Organization, Act XXXIII of 1921.
324. Act LXXX of 2000 on publishing the 167th Convention of the ILO (1988) concerning safety and health security conditions in building, Art.1 (3).
325. For instance, in 2013 the rate of part-time jobs in Hungary was 6.7%, in the EU it was 20.3%, labourers with fixed-time contract was 10.8% but in the EU it was 13.8% and the rate of self-employed persons in Hungary was 9.2% inside the active workforce while in the EU it was 12.5%. (Eurostat: 'Employment in Europe, 2002-2013').
326. In 2014, the number of registered individual entrepreneurs was 1,087,823 including agricultural entrepreneurs (444,992), entrepreneur license holders (376,285) and free-lance and other entrepreneurs together with working family members. Moreover, 52% of license holders operate in main job, 37% in additional job and 11% as retired persons. (Central Statistical Office, Labour-force Survey 2006–2014Q1).

456. A short discussion was initiated by the Government on how and why the laws should be modified, or whether a general, comprehensive act on self-employment should be prepared.[327] It proves that a unified regulation is not applicable, but a stronger social protection (against abusive multinational companies, unpaid, refused work or termination of contracts) of self-employed persons is necessary. Furthermore, the lower rate of public revenues (personal income tax and social contributions) paid by micro-entrepreneurs in comparison to stringent, regulated and controlled employment[328] incites the unlawful renaming of regular or genuine employment contracts as undertakings, self-employment contracts, although the independent and reliable work of entrepreneurs is formal. These abusive actions have been screened out by the tax authority and labour inspectors with limited success. Thus, a more effective authority controlling the system on real entrepreneurship profiles is urged, but without submission to a sweeping bill on self-employment. These debates have not involved foreign labourers, service providers or migratory movements, because the role of non-nationals in this economic sector is marginal (Hajduk, 2008).

457. In the absence of a comprehensive act on self-employment, the following legal sources shall be implemented in this field:

(a) EC law dividing provisions on regular employment and self-employment, service providing (across the borders);
(b) International, regional agreements including bilateral treaties, for instance, on facilitated training, social protection of migrant workers and access to labour market of party states;
(c) National regulation. It includes the Civil Code (in particular on concluding contract, indemnity bond, liability for damage and rules on business associations that were regulated in a separate act in 1988–March 2014); the UnemplA, its executive decrees,[329] the ExD, and the PermitD (including exceptional authorization in remunerated work and unemployment benefit); rules on taxation and social insurance (such as PensionA, SocInA; TaxA and TaxPA, EkhoA, SeTax); provisions on recognition of qualification and occupations (e.g., in the health care sector[330] respecting the general conditions of the QualA); substantive and

327. In May 2003, the Ministry of Employment and Labour issued a discussion paper on regulative principles. Summary of public debate is given by the State Secretary L. Garzo (29 Jun. 2003, MTI/ National Press Agency).

328. A short example of differences: the rate of personal income tax (of employed person) was 40% if the income was over 1,350,000 HUF, while a micro-entrepreneur is eligible for reduction the income with own costs related to economic activity and 18% of the clear earnings shall be paid as personal income tax. Since 2003, a simplified revenue act has offered 15% flat rate tax of micro-entrepreneur if yearly income does not reach 15,000,000 HUF. At the same time, the employer has to pay 32% of the salary of the employed person to the social and unemployment fund that is not charged if the same work is done by an entrepreneur.

329. For instance, Decree of the Minister of Labour No. 6 of 1996, 16 July regulates how unemployed person may apply for financial support (up to EUR 10,000) to become self-employed person or individual entrepreneur financed from the European Social Fund (EU).

330. Decree of the Health care Minister No. 30 of 2006, 25 July on recognition procedure of foreign qualification and diploma required to public health care.

procedural rules concerning preconditions for certain economic, service providing activities, including how to obtain real estate (LandA). The general framework for micro/small-entrepreneurship is determined in the PrivA.

458. The freedom in service provision inside the unified market of the EU[331] without the national administrative barriers required modification of numerous legal sources in Hungary, implementing the following principles and terms of establishment:

(a) the service providers can establish their own economic activity freely in a Member State including the service provision across the borders by a settled service provider in another Member State;
(b) settlement or establishment means a regular, open-ended economic activity in fact creating the services in own or rental property for a defined period (e.g., its license is issued for a defined period); registered office for establishment would be an affiliate, branch office or representation of a foreign company, as well as an office led by the service provider's staff or an independent person with full entitlement for managing and acting regularly on behalf of the entrepreneurship;
(c) in the state of service provision, authorization to the establishment and the economic activity shall be simplified (e.g., in a unified one-stop permission procedure, in personal hearing, easy accession to e-administration and information portal) taking into account the equivalent requirements that are already met by the service provider in another Member State;
(d) the freedom in service provision shall be based on equal treatment, prohibition of direct or covert discrimination (e.g., nationality or domicile of his/her service claimants shall not be required, the advantage provided for local service providers with reference on their social contacts, limited access to credits, rented workshops);
(e) in accordance with Articles 43 and 49 of the EC Treaty (now Articles 49 and 56 of the TFEU), all operations that are made without subordination of another person shall be considered to constitute an independent undertaking activity.

331. Directive of the European Parliament and the Council 2006/123/EC.

Chapter 2. Conditions for Entitlement to Work in Hungary as a Self-Employed Person

§1. General Conditions

459. Transposition of *service providers' freedom* ensures a general legal framework for independent undertakings including service provision across the borders (inside the EEA) through amendments.[332] In accordance with this, the settlement and investment of a foreign entrepreneur is accompanied by the term of self-employment.[333] At the end of this transposition process, the Parliament passed a new Act on Private Entrepreneurs and Sole Proprietorships (PrivA) replacing Act V of 1990 on private entrepreneurs. Moreover, the Act LXXVI of 2009 determines the freedom of settlement of service providers and free services across the borders giving general rules on their providing activities, with references on sectoral specificities.[334] The PrivA enters into force gradually (in 2010–2015), as follows:

(a) 'foreigners' establishment for economic purpose' means an independently managed, regular, profit-making, genuine economic activity with assumption of risk in a registered office, workshop or depot with localized equipment or instruments;
(b) economic service provision across the borders would be operated independently, for profit with assumption of economic risk but settlement of foreign entrepreneur is not required for it;
(c) 'self-employment' includes all independently conducted economic activities in accordance with social insurance and health care law regardless of the scope of the PrivA that is obliged to pay social contribution on the grounds of individual contract with health care and pension funds;
(d) regular business activity for profit-making with assumption of economic risk within the freedom of establishment may be engaged by a non-national in the form of private entrepreneurship, as a sole proprietorship in the register of companies that has no legal personality or as self-employment, or through a branch office, commercial representation, or as a part-owner in a business company or through a cooperative seated in Hungary. However, these options are not applicable if there are no employees of the non-national (including posting of foreigners) or his/her activity belongs to the public/tertiary education and research institute, artistic performance or professional sport;
(e) a non-national undertaking settled in an EEA Member State can engage in business activity in Hungary as a service provider across the borders according to the law defined, while another venture can do so if an international agreement or law directly entitles it for this activity;

332. Act LVI of 2009 entered into force gradually in 2009 and 2010.
333. Act XXIV of 1988 was amended by the Act LVI of 2009.
334. It transposes the Directive of the European Parliament and the Council 2006/123/EC and Council Decision 2008/49/EC that was replaced by the European Parliament and Council Regulation 1024/2012/EU. This act also provides equal treatment and mutual recognition of guarantees, documents for EEA-seated service providers.

(f) a non-national person as a private entrepreneur is eligible for starting and engaging regularly for profit-making business activity with assumption of economic risk within an establishment on the same conditions as nationals if he/she is the owner of a venture in an EEA Member State or this national treatment is ensured in a law or an international agreement. All legal requirements of qualification and business activity shall be met by this private entrepreneurship as local nationals (e.g., obtaining permissions from competent authorities). Furthermore, an independent non-national undertaking in acquisition of real estate (land, housing) shall be considered as a foreign natural person;
(g) business activity conducted by a branch office of a foreign venture registered in an EEA Member State would be conducted in a real estate (e.g., in a workshop, shop, depot), and there is no need for permission from competent authority (county/capital governmental office) to acquire it if it is provided by an international agreement or if there is a reciprocity in fact between Hungary and the state of the venture's seat. Labourers in branch office are employed by the foreign venture and rights of the employer are implemented through the branch office.[335]

460. According to the PrivA, natural persons shall have the *right to pursue an economic activity* – normally provided for remuneration – on their own account, in the territory of Hungary, under the right of establishment according to the Act on the general provisions relating to the start and pursuit of the business of service activities, on a regular basis under economic exposure with a view to making a profit. This can be elaborated as follows:

(a) private entrepreneur shall be subject to unlimited liability for any and all obligations arising out of or in connection with his activities to the extent of his personal resources;
(b) he/she is authorized to pursue different activities, and pursue them in any number of permanent establishments and branches;
(c) where authorization by the competent authority is prescribed as mandatory by law, to engage in a certain economic activity, the private entrepreneur may only start and pursue the activity in question when in possession of such authorization;
(d) he/she may employ people under contract, outworkers specified in other legislation, contributing family members and students of special schools and vocational schools;
(e) where an activity is subject to professional qualification, the private entrepreneur or at least one of his employees may engage in such activity if he/she is able to meet such qualification requirements unless an exemption is provided by law. If he/she operates several permanent establishments or branches, the qualification requirement must be satisfied for all permanent establishments or branches;

335. Act CXXXII of 1997 on Hungarian branch offices and commercial representatives of foreign companies seated abroad as modified by Act LVI of 2009.

(f) he/she must indicate the designation of private entrepreneurship (p.e.) and the register number next to his/her name (signature);
(g) in the event of the private entrepreneur's death, the widow of the heir – under the widow's consent – may take over the private entrepreneur's business operations (successor entrepreneur), subject to notification of such private entrepreneurial activities in accordance with the PrivA;
(h) taking into account sectorial specifications, the PrivA shall not apply to existing rules on sub-groups of entrepreneurship, such as the activities of small-scale agricultural producers as defined in the Personal Income Tax Act; private veterinary practices; legal practices; the activities of independent patent agents; the activities of notaries public; and the activities of independent court bailiffs.

The PrivA does not directly mention it, but it arises from the other (changing and incoherent) parts of the law that private entrepreneurs must indicate a place for management (registered office) that would be the address of a self-employed person, unless he/she has to set up a special business space (workshop, compartment, kiosk, shop, garden, etc.) depending on economic activities. Its operation basically requires, by law, various permits from local (municipal or district governmental) authorities (fire, sanitation, building and environment) and a lawful entitlement in connection with the office (rental contract and purchase of property).

461. The following *may pursue the activities of private entrepreneurs*: Hungarian nationals; EEA nationals and family members, persons within the ambit of the FreeA, third-country nationals who are long-term migrants (immigrant or permanent resident status) by the ThirdA, persons holding a residence permit for the purpose of gainful employment, family reunification or for the pursuit of studies, as well as refugees and stateless persons holding a residence permit granted on humanitarian grounds, if they meet the following conditions:

(a) they have full legal capacity,
(b) they have not been sentenced to imprisonment by a final court judgment for Penal Code crimes against public justice, international justice, crimes against property, and they have been relieved from the detrimental consequences attached to prior convictions; after July 2013 the exclusion closure covers on corruption, crimes against property, consumer's rights, data protection and money laundering;
(c) they have not been sentenced to imprisonment for a term of over one year for a premeditated crime, and they have been relieved from the detrimental consequences attached to prior convictions; and
(d) they are not members of sole proprietorship or a business association subject to unlimited liability.

462. Private entrepreneurs *may suspend their private entrepreneurial activities* for a minimum period of one month and a maximum period of five years that shall be notified to the authority maintaining the registry of private entrepreneurs using the standard electronic form. The authority in charge of the register shall forthwith notify the tax authority (NAV), the pension insurance agency empowered to manage the National Pension Insurance Fund concerning the suspension by way of electronic means. Following the notification of suspension, the private entrepreneur shall not engage in private entrepreneurial activities during the period of suspension, and may not obtain any rights or undertake any commitment relating to private entrepreneurial activities. The private entrepreneur is liable to honour any payment obligation arising out of his activities prior to the suspension and due in period of suspension. If he/she has a certificate, it shall be delivered to the issuing authority that notifies the registry authority on withdrawal of the certificate.

463. Right for the pursuit of the activities of private entrepreneurs *shall terminate* under the following circumstances:

(a) upon the private entrepreneur's own decision notifying the authority maintaining the registry using the standard electronic form prescribed for this purpose, on the day of notification;
(b) if the private entrepreneur has established a sole proprietorship, on the day preceding the operative date of the resolution of registration at court, or if the private entrepreneur has obtained the sole proprietorship's capital stock by way of transfer, on the day of transfer;
(c) on the day of the private entrepreneur's death;
(d) on the day of loss of the full legal capacity by a final court judgment on its statement;
(e) if the tax authority has withdrawn the private entrepreneur's tax number, on the day when the resolution becomes final;
(f) the authority issuing the certificate prohibits by a final decision the entrepreneurial activities for reasons of exclusion;
(g) after five years from the time of suspension, if he/she has not taken steps to reinstate his/her own activities; or
(h) his/her main entrepreneurial activities are engaged unlawfully.

The termination is indicated in the registry, the authority in charge of the register removes the data and this fact shall be forwarded to the tax authority, and the pension insurance agency empowered to manage the National Pension Insurance Fund electronically.

464. With a view to starting the activities of private entrepreneurs, the applicant natural person is required to *submit a notification to the authority* of nationwide jurisdiction appointed to control and monitor the activities of private entrepreneurs by the Government. It is the Central Office for Electronic Administration but the local administration is managed by the district governmental offices. The notification shall be submitted using the prescribed standard electronic form (notification form) containing all required information, including the personal data of the entrepreneur, his nationality, the main economic activities, any other activities planned to be performed with reference on the Nomenclature for Codes of Professions,[336]

336. In accordance with Regulation 1893/2006/EC establishing the statistical classification of economic activities NACE Revision 2.

and other data based on the TaxA. Through this electronic communication, the entrepreneur will obtain – if he/she is not in possession of the same – the taxation and social insurance registration number.

The register of private entrepreneurs improves the transparency of the activities of private entrepreneurs and promotes their lawful operation making available for the public the most relevant data for actors in the market and information for authorities' control *in situ* (e.g., the activities are suspended, the taxation number is withdrawn). Private entrepreneurs shall report any changes in their particulars contained in the register – including when planning to terminate their private entrepreneurial activities – within fifteen days from the effect of the change to the registering authority using the standard electronic form. The format that is forwarded to the private entrepreneurs' registry (notification before pursuit of the activities, notification on changes, suspended activities, etc.) is also regulated.[337] In absence of notification on change (e.g., the economic activity of the entrepreneur is extended or the Nomenclature is changing) the tax authority may impose a fine (EUR 100).

465. Upon request, after the notification to the authority the *private entrepreneur will get a certificate*[338] mentioning his name, license number, the major data of economic activity, address (seat, branches), the place and date of issue, and the name of the issuing authority. It is an authentic proof of the data contained in the register of private entrepreneurs on the date of issue. In the event of change in data of registry, the modification of the certificate is required. However, the certificate is not necessarily required for the start and pursuit of private entrepreneurial activities. This certificate is protected against falsification issued as securitized document[339] that is void if any of the following conditions are met:

(a) the holder's right for the pursuit of the activities of private entrepreneurship is terminated; hence it has to be withdrawn by the district governmental office;
(b) the entrepreneurial activities are suspended,
(c) data in the certificate has changed;
(d) it has been delivered to the district governmental office, or
(e) it was lost, stolen or destroyed. In such a case, a new certificate will be issued immediately by the district governmental office upon request.

466. Sole proprietorship is an entity without legal personality established *by a natural person (regardless of nationality)* listed in the register of private entrepreneurs; it is brought into existence when entered into the register of companies (business associations). Participating in the economy it has a legal capacity, obtaining rights and undertaking commitments under its own corporate name (e.g., it may acquire property, conclude contracts, and may sue and be sued). Similar to other business associations within the scope of the PrivA, the sole proprietorship also shall be registered at the court of registry as Act V of 2006 on Public Company

337. Ministerial Decree (IRM) No. 65 of 2009, 17 December on format to private entrepreneurs' register.
338. Ministerial Decree (IRM) No. 66 of 2009, 17 December on certificate of private entrepreneurs.
339. Similar to identity cards or passports, the security signs and method of issuance are regulated in Government Decree No. 86 of 1996, 14 June.

Information, Company Registration and Winding-up Proceedings determines with certain exceptions. For instance, the sole proprietorship shall have only one principal (founder), or one natural person may only has one sole proprietorship in the capacity of principal (founder), and some additional rules to the PrivA arise from the Civil Code.

467. The principal shall undertake unlimited liability for fulfilling commitments made in excess of the sole proprietorship's capital; this shall be indicated in the sole proprietorship's charter document. The sole proprietorship shall be primarily liable for its obligations with its assets. If its assets do not cover an obligation, the principal shall bear unlimited liability with his personal resources. Its abbreviation in public documents and in the registry is 'ec'. A sole proprietorship operating under unlimited subsidiary liability and its principal may not be a member with unlimited liability in a business association. Up to 2013 limited subsidiary liability could be opted for a sole proprietorship that was ceased, and those entities had to change the charter document unless they were deleted from the court registry. The new provisions on business associations decrease the dispositive power of parties in business law.

468. Sole proprietorships may be founded as follows:

(a) by transformation from private entrepreneurship. Wherein the right to the pursuit of private entrepreneurial activities ceases for reasons of foundation of a sole proprietorship, up to the time of termination of the entitlement, the amount of registered capital and economic activities would be determined in wider circle than as private entrepreneur; or
(b) as a new actor in the market.

Regardless of the manner of foundation, sole proprietorships may not commence operations before being admitted into the register of companies. The charter document for the formation shall be drawn up in an authentic instrument by a notary public, or in a private document countersigned by an attorney-at-law and signed by the principal (founder). If it uses the standard form of which a model is contained in the Act on Public Company Information, Company Registration and Winding-up Proceedings (in the Appendix), the procedure is quick at the court of registry. The charter document shall specify the name and address of the sole proprietorship, the founder's data including home address and register number assigned in the register of private entrepreneurs, and the sole proprietorship's gathering term of business/ economic activities regardless the Nomenclature of Codes on services: all activities are acceptable that are not prohibited or limited by law. A sole proprietorship may pursue any economic activity – of the ones indicated in the charter document – that is notified to the state tax authority as the sole proprietorship's main or other business activity. Furthermore, if the subscribed capital indicated in the charter document exceeds EUR 660, it may comprise contributions in cash and in kind, and if it does not exceed the said monetary amount, it must be provided in cash. The founder shall indicate the amount of capital stock in the application for registration, and contributions are to be made available at the time of foundation.

469. The main rules on operation of a sole proprietorship are as follows:

(a) Its principal shall have decision-making powers in all matters conferred under the competence of the supreme body by any legislation pertaining to sole proprietorships.
(b) The management shall be entrusted to an executive employee, or may be carried out by the principal under his membership in the sole proprietorship. If the sole proprietorship is managed by its principal, the principal shall function as the company's legal representative vis-à-vis third parties, and in front of the court and other authorities. In this case, the principal shall represent the sole proprietorship in writing.
(c) If the founder of the sole proprietorship failed to meet the conditions prescribed for private entrepreneurs, the company shall be considered to have failed to operate in compliance with regulations pertaining to the company's structure and operations.
(d) Where authorization by the competent authority is prescribed as mandatory by law to engage in a certain economic activity, the sole proprietorship may only begin and pursue such activity when in possession of such authorization, required professional qualification (at least one employee) and a management office (workshop, etc.).
(e) The principal shall have the right to alter the charter document including the business activities.
(f) In the event of the principal's death, the widow of the principal, or his heir if there is no widow or under the widow's consent, acting in his name and on his behalf may take over the sole proprietorship by replacing the principal, provided that he/she meets all requirements prescribed by the PrivA and that the competent court of registry is notified accordingly within thirty days from the date of occurrence of the underlying reason.

470. A *sole proprietorship shall terminate* if any of the following conditions are met:

(a) the period of time specified in the charter document expires or any other condition of termination is realized;
(b) the principal has adopted a decision for the company's termination without succession;
(c) the principal has adopted a decision for the company's termination with succession (transformation); it may be transferred into a business association under the relevant provisions laid down in the Civil Code properly implementing the rules of the Accounting Act pertaining to transformations;
(d) it is declared terminated by the court of registry;
(e) the court of registry orders its cancellation ex officio; or
(f) the court decides to terminate it in the course of liquidation.

The provisions governing liquidation, winding-up and bankruptcy proceedings shall also apply to sole proprietorships.

471. When an activity is subject to professional qualification, the private entrepreneur or principal of sole proprietorship (or its potential employee) establishing a business activity within the freedom of establishment or provision of services across the borders within the EEA may engage in such activity in conformity with such qualification requirements, or if any of his employees or participating family members have the required qualification. If the private entrepreneur operates at several places of business or branches, the qualification requirements must be satisfied for all places of business and branches. The QualA regulates the recognition of degrees obtained at foreign higher education institutions in three main procedures: automatic recognition and recognition with conditions of EEA diplomas of EEA nationals, and recognition process for non-EEA nationals or non-EEA diplomas. During the recognition process, the authority declares the legal force of the foreign degree equivalent to the legal force of a degree obtainable in Hungary. The resolution on the recognition of the level of qualification determines which Hungarian qualification is equivalent to the given foreign degree; thus, whether the foreign degree is equivalent to a Hungarian university degree or college degree, or to a degree obtainable at postgraduate training following a college or university degree. The QualA defines that the EEA national and family member applicant is only entitled to exercise a regulated profession (doctor, dentist, etc.) in Hungary if he/she disposes of the language skills necessary for the pursuit of the concrete profession. In accordance with this, regulated professionals can be engaged if the applicant (candidate) proves that he/she was working as a private entrepreneur or key official of a company for at least six/four consecutive years or for only three/two years but he/she had been trained before it for three/two years in an accredited education, or he/she was employed at least for six years in the regulated profession prior to application in a Member State, and previously he/she participated on an accredited education at least for two years. Moreover, work experience in the regulated profession must not be taken into account if the applicant had no practice within the period of ten years prior to the application for recognition of qualification (e.g., as a hair-dresser).

472. If a lawfully settled service provider (private entrepreneur) intends to supply his/her own services across the borders in the EEA, it must not be limited with reference to his/her improper qualification. If this service belongs to a regulated profession, he/she is eligible for service supply even in Hungary after two years of his/her own practice in the Member State of establishment within the previous ten years. This freedom of service supply is subject to all other provisions (e.g., implementation of name under which entrepreneur, professional is working, rules on safety of consumers) in close relation with the qualification of the service provider, with certain exceptions. For instance, a license from the chamber and registry at social insurance in order to account fees in the context of clients shall not be required from these service providers. However, the applicant meeting all legal requirements is eligible for membership or registry in the professional organization (chamber). Furthermore, he/she has to notify the competent authority and social insurance directorate of his/her activity that belongs to a regulated profession before the start of service supply in Hungary, his/her notice authority check may be managed *ex ante* or during the servicing period. In the absence of the necessary preconditions, the competent authority may prohibit the operation of the service provider in the territory of the country.

473. Self-employed persons are bound to *pay social insurance contributions*. Personal scope of the SocInA includes private entrepreneur certificate holder, licensed veterinary, pharmacist, social service provider, health care provider, attorney-at-law, patent attorney, notary public, judicial executive, member personally taking part in business activity in company, driving trainer and facilitator family member of these persons contributing to the business activity for remuneration. These persons, regardless of their legal status or nationality, shall be eligible for all social insurance (pension and health-care) benefits. Furthermore, self-employment is subject to Personal Income and VAT payment.

474. Self-employed persons have to pay an unemployment contribution to the Labour Fund (1.5% from earnings per month). As consideration, the private entrepreneur is entitled to use free of charge labour services (labour exchange, counselling and legal aid) at state labour offices. The Labour Fund finances private entrepreneur allowance if he/she is actively seeking work. It requires cooperation with the labour office and that previously unemployment contribution was paid at least for six months. The labour office offers jobs suited to his/her experiences and qualification. The maximum allowance is 65% of prior taxable income per month up to ninety days, if other social benefits or allowances are not granted. Finally, the UnemplA also provides financial support to establish self-employment engaging private entrepreneurship or to join as a working member (part-owner) to a company. Upon individual business plan, a non-reimbursed contribution up to EUR 10,000 and/or a deducted social insurance contribution for twelve months are available.

475. The Civil Code (Chapter III) ensures the right of *natural persons to set up companies* with legal personality (private limited-liability company, public or private limited company) or without legal personality (general partnership, limited partnership). Certain specific economic activities may be restricted by law to be pursued only in specific company forms. Business associations may be founded also by *non-resident and resident natural persons*, and such persons may join these business associations as a member, or acquire participation (shares) therein. With the exception of private limited-liability companies and public or private limited companies, at least two members are required for the foundation of a business association. According to the Civil Code, a natural person may be a member with unlimited liability in only one business association at any given point in time. A minor may not be a member with unlimited liability in a business association. A general partnership or limited partnership may not be a member with unlimited liability in a business association. Unless otherwise provided by law, a sole proprietorship (single-member business association) may establish another single-member company, and may be the sole member (shareholder) of a business association.

476. Business associations may also be created by way of transformation (converting from one company form to another, merger and de-merger). International treaties may contain regulations in derogation from the provisions of the Civil Code in respect of the participation of non-residents in business associations. Moreover, business associations may be established to engage in joint business operations for objectives other than profit (non-profit business associations) that may be established and operated in any corporate form.

477. Where authorization by the competent authority is prescribed as mandatory by law, to engage in a certain economic activity, the business association may only begin and pursue the activity in question when in possession of such authorization. If the activities are subject to professional qualification, those may be pursued by business associations only if there is at least one person among its participating members, employees, or among the persons working towards the benefit of the company under a long-term civil relationship concluded with the business association, who satisfies the qualification requirements set out in legal regulations.

478. Depending on the profile of self-employment and private undertakings, acquisition of real estate would be vital in establishing entrepreneurship. According to the LandA, restrictions on acquisition of property comprised of arable-land (including cultivable land, forest, meadow, reed, fishing-lake, etc.) are universally strong in Hungary. The Fundamental Law (Article P(2)) requires qualified majority of votes in passing the act on acquisition of arable land and forest. Subject to the exceptions set out in law, non-EEA citizen natural persons and legal entities may not acquire title of ownership of arable land. Consequently, the resident national, the EEA-citizen and other person whose legal status is preferential on the grounds of international treaty is entitled to acquire arable land and forest property, as follows:

(a) a parcel of arable land exceeding 3 million square metres – including the entire territory of arable lands on the grounds of his or her right to use it – may be acquired as property by an agricultural producer; or
(b) a parcel of arable land exceeding 10,000 square metres may be acquired as property by a person that is not an agricultural producer;
(c) an EEA national wishing to settle in Hungary to independently engage in agricultural production, and who has been legitimately using the arable land or forest in Hungary for at least five years without authority notice on unlawful usage or other illegal action;
(d) it is undertaken that within five years from the acquisition the usage shall not be transferred for other purposes that are determined in law;
(e) the young agricultural producer undertakes to settle and reside next to the property (in adjacent village or town) within one year from the acquisition starting agricultural activities or funding an agricultural centre on his/her property; and
(f) the authentic documentation is required to acquisition that is valid if it is registered by the competent authority.

Any contract violating the restrictions on the acquisition of title shall be null and void. If a real estate registration procedure is for the acquisition of title of ownership of arable land or forest area in excess of the permissible limits or in violation of the restrictions on the acquisition of title, the real estate supervisory authority maintaining the land registry (under subordination of the ministry of agriculture and natural resources) shall proceed according to the provisions applicable for the case of obvious invalidation of the document. The real estate supervisory authority shall be authorized to check the real estate register to determine whether the ownership statement is true. The public prosecutor may file a lawsuit for the annulment of a contract or contract clause pertaining to the acquisition of title of ownership of arable land. In such a case, the entire contract shall be null and void. This provision shall apply if the parties stipulated the effective date of conveyance of title by the aforementioned contract or contract clause contingent upon some condition or a future date, or upon a legal statement made by either party or a third person. Moreover, the acquisition of property shall be approved by the county agricultural authority within fifteen days from the submission of all documents. Without this approval the land and property registry refuses the notice on acquisition of the new owner.

However, the land usage may be provided with contract. The term of leasehold contracts concluded by foreign private persons and foreign legal entities shall not exceed twenty years.

479. The *non-arable land* (housing, office, workshop, etc.) property may be acquired by foreigners with permission issued by the county/capital governmental office by reference to the location of the property. LandD provides exemptions the authorization as follows:

(a) the acquisition of ownership through inheritance;
(b) the acquisition of EEA nationals, legal or non-legal entity corporates that are registered in any EEA state;
(c) persons/entities enjoy national treatment on the grounds of international treaty;
(d) long-term migrant with immigration permit who is a third-country national;
(e) recognized refugee;
(f) non-resident nationals; or
(g) dual or multiple nationals.

The LandD determines the cases in which permit shall be issued if applicant meets any condition as follows:

(a) acquisition of ownership does not violate public interest or municipal interest (it is enigmatic and LandD contains no further explanation;
(b) acquisition of ownership is based on property exchange;
(c) the purpose of acquisition of title is to cease common ownership;
(d) the foreign person has verifiably been residing and living in Hungary for a period of no less than five years for the purpose of employment; or
(e) a foreign natural person settling in Hungary as an independent entrepreneur needs this property for pursing the business activities for which the foreign natural person settled. No property intended to be acquired for the purpose of a real estate transaction (sale, exchange or lease) shall be construed as essential for business activities. If the entrepreneurship is terminated the property shall be alienated within one year unless the county/capital governmental office authorizes maintenance of ownership.

480. The interpretation of the 'necessity for business activities' is narrow in the practice of tax and land authority, for example, a travelling agency does not need to own property for conducting its business activity. A sole proprietorship that is deleted from the registry of the court or a private entrepreneur who does not have a registration number in the registry, or if his chamber of commerce membership is terminated, shall alienate the real ownership within one year.

481. Authorization may be refused if the state of which the foreign person is a national does not provide equal treatment to Hungarian citizens or Hungarian legal persons as to its residents under international convention or reciprocity.[340] The Ministry of Foreign Affairs shall be consulted as to whether an international convention or reciprocity applies.

§2. Administrative Rules and Procedures

482. The notification of the start of private entrepreneurial activities, the notification of changes, and the notification of suspension and termination of private entrepreneurial activities is exempt from fees and duties by the PrivA. The certificate may be requested at the time of notification of private entrepreneurial activities, or at any time during the pursuit of such activities (including when a license is requested on account of changes in the relevant data). Where a license is requested in person, it shall be made available to the private entrepreneur without delay at the district governmental office. In other cases, the private entrepreneur's license shall be delivered to the private entrepreneur without delay but within eight days from the day following the date of receipt. The authority shall adopt a resolution for the withdrawal of the certificate on the day the license is received, and shall communicate this resolution to the body in charge of the register as well. The authority authorizing or supervising the activity shall communicate its final and enforceable resolution adopted to prohibit the pursuit of activities to the registry authority and the body in charge of the register. The body in charge of the register shall, upon receipt of such resolution, ex officio erase the activity from the register.

483. The transaction price in establishing a business association as a sole proprietorship using an electronic and charter format implies a reduction of costs. Taking into account the honoraria of the legal representative or the costs relating to the authentication of fundamental documents by the notary public and the publication of the establishment in the Business Company Gazette, the company's registration at court costs approximately EUR 3,000.

484. The majority of the other possible required authorizations belong to the competence of the local municipal or district governmental office (e.g., license to open a shop, a workshop) based on the consent or conditions determined by locally or regionally managed partner-authorities, such as fire-prevention, health care, sanitation services or environment protection. In these procedures, the AdminA is

340. See for instance Announcement No. 8001 of 2002, 26 February by KüM-GM-IM-PM.

applicable, implementing the regular twenty-one day deadline. The recognition of a qualification or diploma is out of the municipal's purview. It belongs to the (regional) chamber of the given occupation, universities or national offices (for instance, the HEIC). The general procedural deadline is between thirty and ninety days, but its prolongation is possible in the absence of an authentic translation of the attached documents (from non-EU states) or if supplementary information is required.

485. The self-employed person is obliged to announce his/her own employment as well as the employment of other persons as regular employees by his/her entrepreneurship at the latest on the first day of employment (economic activity) to the competent county/capital labour office and the Central Labour Registry (EMMA operated by the National Employment Service). Furthermore, a notice of employment and economic activity shall be submitted before start to the competent county/capital pension and health care insurance directorates as well as to the tax office on a determined format or on the internet. According to the announcement and notice, the individual codes of self-employed persons and employees are confirmed, and the legality of economic activities can be proved during authority checks. The termination of employment or private entrepreneurship activity shall also be communicated to these organs within eight days from the termination. Occasional or employment on simplified labour contract shall not be notified strictly before the start of the work to these authorities.

486. As is evident, there is a 'total registration system' of entrepreneurs, employed and self-employed persons in Hungary, regardless of their nationality or other legal status. As a result, if there is a change in any registered data of persons or entrepreneurship concerned, it shall be notified or announced within eight days to the authority maintaining the registry.

487. EEA nationals shall be required to provide proof of eligibility for acquiring title of ownership in the form of official certificates. They are also required to provide guarantees for future commitments fixed in a private document of full probative force or in a public document as follows:

(a) an official certificate issued by the Regional Directorate of the OIN to verify that he/she has been legitimately residing in Hungary for three or more consecutive years;
(b) an authorization to reside, or a certificate in proof of having submitted an application for such authorization for any EU national who does not have a permanent residence permit;
(c) an official certificate issued by the agricultural county authority, verifying that the applicant had been engaged in agricultural activities in Hungary lawfully prior to the acquisition of ownership. It shall be supported by an environmental study consisting of the examination of the agricultural activities;
These certificates are applicable if they were issued within sixty days prior to the submission to prove his/her eligibility for ownership arable land.

(d) the applicant is being established in Hungary in the capacity of an independent agricultural producer and to refrain from using the land for purposes other than agriculture, not including the construction of buildings and edifices for residential and farming purposes, and to allow use of the arable land by others limited to an extent where the proceeds originating from such use shall not exceed 25% of his income from agricultural activities.

488. These documents shall be enclosed with the application for the registration of the transfer of title of the arable land in the real estate register. The real estate supervisory authority shall send a copy of its resolution for the registration of title transfer to the competent agricultural administration body along with a copy of the document submitted in evidence of the conveyance.

489. The agricultural county authority shall have powers to monitor compliance with the provisions on the EU national's commitment in the ownership of arable-land in conjunction with the real estate supervisory authority. If, following thorough deliberation of all prevailing circumstances, the agricultural county authority finds that the owner did not abide by the commitments, the private entrepreneur has terminated his activities or is no longer eligible to operate in a self-employed capacity, the owner's lawful and continuous residence in Hungary has terminated for any reason, the owner affected will be advised concerning the infringement and shall be instructed in writing to restore compliance within the time limit prescribed. Otherwise, the agricultural county authority shall impose a fine on the owner in question, wherein the amount of penalty is determined by the size of productiveness of the arable land at the time of acquisition. If the owner proves that all activities in which he is engaged in Hungary are agricultural, or that at least 50% of his income originates from agricultural activities, or that he is not a party to any relationship that requires personal participation, the fine will not be imposed.

490. The county/capital governmental office shall request the opinion of the mayor of the municipal government of the community (district of Budapest or the Capital) where the non-agricultural land (real estate property) is located, to determine whether the acquisition of the real estate property constitutes any injury to the interests of the municipal government. In the aforesaid request, the office shall inform the mayor regarding the time limit within which to convey his opinion with a view to taking it into consideration in the decision-making process. This time limit may not be less than fifteen days from the time the request was delivered. The following shall be attached with the application: document(s) evidencing the nationality of the applicant; the contract on the conveyance of title to the real estate in question, or the document evidencing grounds for the acquisition. The office shall be liable to obtain the authentic information relating to the property designated for purchase from the real estate register. The deadline for authorization is twenty-one days without the period of mayor's opinion giving. The fee is EUR 160, All required documents shall be submitted in an authentic Hungarian translation. The decision of governmental office may not be appealed but its judicial review is allowed. The approval of the minister in charge of foreign policies is required for the acquisition of real property by diplomatic and consular representations and similar international organizations. The minister in charge of foreign policies shall grant the above permission on the basis of an international convention or reciprocity.

§3. CONDITIONS FOR SPECIAL CATEGORIES OF SELF-EMPLOYED PERSONS

491. As mentioned above, there are certain specific requirements in various sectors of economic activities that shall be met by private entrepreneurs or business companies regardless of nationality. In fact, conditions regarding work experience, professional qualification, facilities or space of the economic activity are seen in all sectors and branches. Here are some examples, illustrating the logic of the regulation. The general conditions of service providers including their settlement in Hungary and trans-border servicing are determined in the Act LXXXVI of 2009 on how to start and operate their economic activities. Accordingly, the freedom in service providing for EEA entrepreneurs is ensured but notification of the service provider to the competent authority or/and authorization to start the operation of social services by the non-state and non-church entity may be required in law. Requirements for the provision of social services by private and other entrepreneurs are decreed by the Government.[341] It means that *social services* as determined in the SocialA may be provided not only by municipally established and owned institutes, but also on equal footing by companies, NGOs or self-employed (private entrepreneur) persons with certain exceptions (e.g., an integrated child or elderly and mental health care institutional service for inmates). The social service entrepreneur registration (license) shall be issued by the county social and guardian authority for the applicant who is eligible for the private entrepreneur certificate and who has at least three years of professional experience in social service or health care (in the EU), proved with an authentic document. Furthermore, the social institution maintained by the entrepreneur shall be granted a permit for operation meeting various legally determined requirements, depending on the kind of services (e.g., nursery, daily child care and elderly home are the most frequent services, but each of them has their own system of conditions). The registration shall be deleted if the requirements are not ensured or paying-off to the Treasury concerning the obtained subvention from the budget is not fulfilled. If a service is provided by an entrepreneur without registration the social and guardian authority shall impose a fine.

492. Certain occupations that are subject to diploma and have a high social prestige (regulated professions in the EU) are typically professed as self-employment facing a stringent self-control of the given branch of professionals through chambers, bars, public associations or bodies. For instance, a veterinary service provider may be, irrespective of his/her nationality, in possession of a license granted by the Hungarian Veterinary Chamber.[342] It is entitled to give the opinion on recognition of a foreign veterinary diploma, and it is entitled to participate in preparatory of the

341. Government Decree No. 369 of 2013, 24 October on registration, authorization and control of personal social services, child care and child protection services provided also by entrepreneurs.
342. Act CXXVII of 2012 on Hungarian Veterinary Chamber and veterinary service.

relevant legal rules. The public register of veterinaries led by the Chamber contains data about the nationality and language skills of its members. A veterinary service provider – differing from state tasks – can operate in Hungary, either as a self-employed person, as an employee or as a part-owner in an animal health business company, if he/she meets the following conditions:

(a) he/she is a member of the Chamber that issues a membership certificate including the properly paid fee and participation in mandatory training;
(b) he/she as an EEA national has a recognized or as a third-country-national has an equivalent diploma of veterinary, and he/she has at least five years practice as vet; if the last three years practice prior to the application was made out of Hungary, its ethical and professional acceptance is properly proved;
(c) he/she is in possession of all required facilitations, equipment and office/rooms as determined by the Government Decree and sanitary provisions required (the upgraded requirements that were introduced in 2012 shall be totally ensured within ten years);
(d) he/she has a proper liability insurance;
(e) his/her service is registered by the Chamber that issues a veterinary license; and
(f) he/she is not excluded for ethical reasons from the Chamber (exclusion may take two years).

It means that without license of praxis, membership in the Chamber and registry of vets the veterinary service provider must not operate in Hungary. If it is released the nutrition security authority shall impose a fine up to EUR 33,500.

493. Private labour exchange and lending service by entrepreneurship can be operated in possession of a registration (license) issued by the county/capital labour centre inside of the governmental office for the applicant who is eligible for a private entrepreneur certificate, proves the knowledge of the labour conditions and rules in target countries (labour exchange/recruitment abroad), provides the coverage as determined by the Decree of the Government,[343] has a proper office receiving clients and he/she undertakes to supply information and exchange services for employees free of charge.[344] The National Labour Office has a national registry of registered labour exchange and lending entrepreneurs. Registration of the entrepreneur shall be deleted and the name of the private entrepreneur shall not be put to the registry within one year if the requirements mentioned above are not met, or any violation of (labour) law in service supply has happened (e.g., false, unlawful or

343. Government Decree No. 118 of 2001, 30 June on authorization and conditions of manpower and labour exchange services. The deposit shall be at least EUR 1,700 and maximum EUR 6,700 depending on whether lending/placement of manpower is forwarded to inland EEA states or non-EEA states.

344. Fee paid by unemployed persons seeking job *expressis verbis* is forbidden by the ILO Convention No. 181. Hungary is a party state in this Convention, and the Decree also openly refers on this ban but the UnemplA does not exclude payment, compensation or remuneration from job seekers in foreign labour exchange. However, the job placement data basis of the EU (EURES system) provides free data on vacancies and relevant information from contact points within the entire EU.

invalid job offers were given and clients have severe losses and legal consequences abroad, such as expulsion and custody for irregular work).

494. Due to the high number of micro-entrepreneurships, a flat rate system is available if the annual income (without VAT) is below the threshold determined by law (approximately EUR 83,000 or EUR 334,000 for professional athletes). Freelance professionals may choose a lump sum payment and also a simplified method in paying public revenues. According to Act CXX of 2005 on simplified contribution to public revenues (hereinafter EkhoA), the payment of public dues under this act on the income legitimately comprising the income-base shall discharge: the obligation of payment and deduction of social security contributions payable by the employers; the obligation of pension contributions (private pension fund membership fees) payable by the insured persons, and the personal income tax liability conferred upon the payer and the private individual. Private individuals engaged in activities under the professions specified in EkhoA under contract – inter alia – for professional services or agency contracts, upon their declaration may satisfy their taxation obligations on the payments, if they obtain any income during the tax year in connection with any activity in possession of a private entrepreneur certificate. The above-mentioned declaration of the taxpayer shall be submitted to the local taxation authority. The flat rate means 15% from the annual income of the payer,[345] and upon payment of this sum the private individual gains eligibility to receive health care services, emergency medical services, accident compensations and pension benefits.

495. The EkhoA offers this opportunity for certain professionals, such as professional athletes, sport experts, editors, journalists, authors and writers, translators, sculptors, painters and related artists, composers, photographers, camera and video equipment operators, actors, entertainers, performing artists, puppeteers, musicians and singers, choreographers and dancers, folk musicians, clowns, magicians, acrobats and related associate professionals, scene-men, decorators, artistic directors, sound engineers or theatre dressers.

It is worth mentioning that only EEA nationals – including persons that are ensured in another EEA state – are eligible to apply for the benefits in the EkhoA; however, their family members are excluded.

496. According to the Act on Personal Income Tax (hereinafter: TaxA), the *small/agricultural producer* together with the facilitator family members may engage in economic activities as a self-employed person, if he/she is over the age of sixteen, he/she has his/her own facilities and arable land (in his/her own property or on the grounds of other civil law contract) that is required to produce agricultural products as determined in the appendix of the TaxA (e.g., honey, vegetable, breeding swine or poultry, brandy) and the annual earnings from this activity does not exceed approximately EUR 27,000). The small/agricultural producer certificate[346]

345. The regular dues together with transaction costs would be higher, particularly the progressive personal income taxation.

346. Government Decree No. 228 of 1996, 26 December on agricultural producer license.

shall be issued within eight days from its submission by the local representative of the Agricultural Chamber, while its legality and registry is controlled by the county agricultural authority. The family members of the producer and family farmers may also request family certificate. Small/family agricultural producers enjoy personal income tax deduction[347] (EUR 350) taking into account agricultural risks, and they have to pay social insurance contribution (17%) on the grounds of their minimum lawful monthly salary. However, a private entrepreneurship as well as business companies may be established by agricultural producers, but the small/agricultural producer license and registry are more simple and practical for less educated self-employed persons in rural areas (in 2014 the number of issued licences was 340,000).

497. The private entrepreneurs – under the ambit of the PrivA or in specific forms regulated in laws – and sole proprietors are eligible to pay the simplified entrepreneurial tax as per Act XLIII of 2002 (hereinafter SeTax) in order to reduce the administrative and transaction burdens in dues. Payers in SeTax shall satisfy the tax obligations pertaining to value-added tax, personal income tax, corporate tax and vocational training contribution, as well as in connection with the requirements specified in the rules of accounting and the said act, if the following conditions are met:

(a) in the preceding calendar year and the preceding tax year they had been continuously engaged in business operations as a private entrepreneur, or, if a legal person, unincorporated business association or sole proprietorship;
(b) they were not penalized by a final decision of the tax authority for any repeated violation of the obligation to issue receipts or invoices;
(c) they not subject to a dissolution procedure or a liquidation procedure by court order;
(d) they have generated, as a private entrepreneur, business revenue by supplying goods and services or, as a legal person, unincorporated business association or sole proprietorship, claimed any sales revenue (or similar income) lawfully;
(e) they have a current account in Hungary; and
(f) his/her total annual revenue in the tax year (financial year) immediately preceding the previous year – or in the tax year when functioning as a pre-company if the first day of this period falls on the tax year immediately preceding the previous year and the last day falls on the previous tax year – is below the threshold determined by law (approximately EUR 100,000). The eligibility of a taxpayer shall effectively terminate as of the day preceding the date of the last accounting document issued for advances received if such accounting document was issued for amounts exceeding this threshold in the calendar year.

498. The flat rate shall be 37% of the positive tax base but if income is over the threshold the rate is 50% concerning the income over the threshold. Tax-payers

347. It fits the *de minimis* principle in the EU, while the main issue for agricultural producers is how they can avoid giving an account on marketing. Tax deduction and preferences are secondary for them.

wishing to enter the simplified taxation system shall notify the state tax authority, on or before the twentieth day of December, using the prescribed form, of their intention to satisfy their tax liabilities for the following tax year. Taxpayers shall have until the same deadline to withdraw such notification. No application for extension shall be accepted upon the taxpayer's failure to meet the above deadline for notification or withdrawal.

499. Eligibility of a sole proprietorship shall not terminate upon the owner's death, if his widow, or his heir – under the widow's consent – takes over the company's ownership and enters the taxation scheme governed in the SeTax, provided that he is able to meet all of the relevant conditions prescribed by this Act. The competent court of registry shall be notified accordingly within thirty days of the time of occurrence of the underlying reason. If there are more inheritors, the maximal deadline is three months.

Chapter 3. Sanctions against Illegal Exercise of Self-Employment

500. The question arises as to what the *legal consequences of irregular or illegal self-employment* would be. First, it has to be clarified that public administrative, civil and criminal law sanctions are parallel and need not take each other into account. Moreover, numerous abusive manners have no specific legal consequence, or the legal practice has been limited, due to the low capacity of controllers or publicity. However, the major outcomes of illicit operation are as follows:

(a) fines imposed by the tax, labour and consumer protection or other sectoral (e.g., social and child care) authorities;
(b) withdrawal of the permit and refused renewal of authorization;
(c) exclusion from the chamber and deletion from the registry;
(d) ban from occupation by the Court;
(e) taxation and/or trial for economic offence;
(f) ethical procedure;
(g) expulsion order; entry and residence can be prohibited taking into account the weight of the committed offence (See paragraphs 309-312 and 328-329). In practical terms, it is the only way that is applicable in migration context, while others are universal, regardless of nationality or legal status of persons concerned.

501. The most effective sanction against illicit self-employment activities is connected to tax office control determined in the Act on Tax Procedure (hereinafter: TaxPA), such as the following:

(a) substitute for delay or incomplete action, announcement and documentation;
(b) a tax fine that suits the released shortfall in revenue (50%–200% of unpaid tax or amount of irregularly requested deduction or reimbursement);
(c) fine for failure in tax procedure is up to EUR 670;
(d) imposed fine for failure is frequently accompanied by measures against the entrepreneur that reach earnings in the absence of tax code, private entrepreneur certificate or Court registry of company. In such a case, the instruments and products of illegal economic activity can be confiscated, withheld or closed in order to enforce the payment of the fine by the entrepreneur within fifteen days;
(e) withdrawal of taxation registration number of private entrepreneur;
(f) imposed fine for failure shall be connected to the close-down of the place of the illegal activity (workshop, office or shop) up to twelve days or to the suspension of the economic activity (e.g., for unlawful employment or for failure to provide receipt). The close-down shall be notified on the entrance of the shop.

502. A private entrepreneur and a sole proprietorship are not eligible for rights or benefits that relate to operation and business life. Beyond the above-mentioned conditions of establishment and termination, two examples on legal consequences for trespassing provisions are as follows:

(a) the eligibility of a taxpayer in the SeTax shall effectively terminate as of the operative date of the tax authority's formal decision to impose a penalty for any violation of the obligation to issue receipts or invoices or for obstructing or hindering an inspection;
(b) Nine per cent of the income treated as the tax base in the EkhoA shall be declared as extra tax in the tax return and shall be paid before the deadline for filing the tax return. Moreover, the private entrepreneur, professional shall pay 18% extra tax if his/her yearly income is over the threshold or he/she has made the statement for entering the EkhoA system without eligibility with respect to the gainful activity in question.

503. The Penal Code is applicable as an exception in the context of unlawful entrepreneurship or self-employment. However, the provision on charlatanry (Article 187) would represent this exception. Any person who engages in activities under the pretence of a medical practice without proper authorization for compensation or on a regular basis, is guilty of a delinquency of quackery punishable by imprisonment for up to one year. The punishment for a felony shall be imprisonment for up to three years, if the charlatanry is committed by feigning the entitlement to practice medicine. For the purposes of this Article, 'authorized medical practitioner' shall mean the person who has a medical degree received at a domestic university or acquired at a foreign university and adopted (provided with a certificate of equivalence), or a non-national who has been authorized by the responsible authority to engage in medical activities without the adoption of his degree, provided in all cases that he has not been restrained by any court order from practicing medicine. Moreover, the Penal Code punishes the artifice of consumers (Article 417), trade of products in poor quality (Article 415) that would cover on private entrepreneurs. In practice, the relevance of minor offences is stronger while combating unlawful economic activities of non-nationals. The MinofA prohibits the unlawful, unauthorized trade of food, abuse in sale violating the consumers' right (e.g., using false notice on prices, amount of product, falsified quality in trade) and imitation of trade competitor (Articles 231–238). If it is committed by a private person – entrepreneur or petty trader – with intent, the tax authority, the regional customer protection authority, the public health authority, the agricultural authority and nutrition and sanitation authority are entitled to impose a fine up to EUR 500. The production in unlawful, unauthorized trade may be confiscated.

504. Ethical procedure can be launched at the Chamber against (private entrepreneurs) members for violation of professional rules and ethics. For instance, the Hungarian Veterinary Chamber may scrutinize whether its own member respects the requirements of a private veterinary operation, and finally it may initiate a procedure at the competent authorities (tax, social insurance, municipal, etc.) or suspend membership or exclude from the Chamber taking into account laws and judicial sanctions (e.g., judgment of executable imprisonment for at least a year implies exclusion from the membership in the Chamber).

Chapter 4. Legal Remedies and Procedural Safeguards

505. Rules on entry and residence authorization of migrants are within the ambit of the ThirdA, the FreeA and its executive decrees. Their common principle is a wide discretionary power of the immigration authority concerning the public welfare and public policy, while the applications shall be perfectly documented based on a prescribed format attaching numerous documents. For instance, the length of the validity period of the visa depends on the submitted documents proving purpose, conditions of travel and planned time of residence.

506. The ThirdA and the ThirdD regulate the verification of the applicant, whether his intended gainful economic activity is genuine or not, as follows:

(a) If the purpose of entry and residence is to engage in gainful employment, the applicant shall supply its proof, such as a document verifying the employment relationship; a business plan for the economic activities; a private entrepreneurial card (license/registration), or failing this, a private entrepreneur register number; a small-scale agricultural producer's license; a personal service contract, a contract for professional services or an exploitation contract entered into as a private individual.
(b) If the purpose of entry and residence is any gainful activity in the capacity of being the owner or director of a business association, cooperative or some other legal entity formed to engage in gainful employment, or being a member of the executive, representative or supervisory board of such entity shall be considered verified if: the business association, cooperative society or other legal entity established to engage in gainful operations (business association) employs at least three Hungarian citizens or persons with the right to free movement and residence in full-time employment for at least six consecutive months, legitimately, without any interruption; or the stay of the applicant third-country national in Hungary is essential for the business association, and the business plan enclosed with the application contains sufficient information to ascertain that the business association will prosper to ensure the applicant's subsistence. The contents of the business plan must be verified by credible means, such as, in particular, by supplying a contract for professional services, a personal services contract, an agreement, or a supply or sales contract.

507. Similar to third-country nationals, persons within the ambit of the FreeA and the FreeD shall verify the purpose and basis of residence. If the purpose of stay is to engage in gainful employment, the applicant shall supply proof, for instance, a document verifying the commencement of a relationship for the performance of work; a valid contract or an official copy of company records, a certificate of incorporation or a company certificate to verify that the applicant is engaged in any gainful activity in the capacity of being the owner or director of a business association, cooperative or some other legal entity formed to engage in gainful employment, or is a member of the executive, representative or supervisory board of such entity; a valid private entrepreneur's license or similar authorization – issued by the competent authority of another Member State – to engage in business activities, or a private entrepreneur register number in the absence of a private entrepreneurial certificate (license). For persons seeking employment, documents shall be applied to evidence that he/she is actively seeking employment, and that there is a probability of entering into gainful employment. For EEA nationals to whom the treatment afforded by Hungary is different from what is required under Articles 1–6 of Council Regulation 1612/68/EEC on the freedom of movement for workers within the EC, a work permit shall be enclosed.

508. The up-to-date registry of business associations and sole proprietorship belongs to the court of registry. The foundation of a sole proprietorship shall be notified to the competent Court of Registry (in each seat of county and in Budapest) for registration and publication within thirty days from the signature of the charter document. The sole proprietorship shall be considered established when admitted into the register of companies, effective as on the day of admission. The court of registry shall implement not only the PrivA but the rules of the Act on Public Company Information, Company Registration and Winding-up Proceedings including the procedure of judicial supervisory competence. The rights, facts and data constituting a part of the register which relate to the sole proprietorship and the principal of the sole proprietorship are considered public information. The principal shall be responsible for notifying the court of registry – by way of electronic means – concerning the foundation of the sole proprietorship, any amendment of the charter document, the rights, facts and data contained in the register of companies and the changes therein, as well as any other data required by law. The principal shall bear liability toward the sole proprietorship for any damage resulting from the incorrectness of the data, rights or facts notified, or from any delay in filing or failure to file the notification.

509. For the period of time till the sole proprietorship is registered by a final decision of the court of registry, the provisions of the Civil Code shall apply as to the nullity of the charter document. Once the sole proprietorship is registered, the charter document may not be contested, and it may be annulled only by a court in a lawsuit (e.g., if the document was not countersigned by a lawyer, the founder lacked legal capacity or the sole proprietorship's scope of activities is unlawful). Wherein a court of law has annulled the charter document, the court shall advise the principal – if possible – to eliminate the reasons for nullity. If this is not possible, the court shall declare the charter document valid for the period indicated in its decision, and shall order the court of registry, if necessary, to initiate judicial oversight proceedings. Where nullity of the charter document is pronounced after the sole proprietorship's registration, it shall not affect the commitments undertaken to the benefit or detriment of the sole proprietorship before the pronouncement of nullity.

510. The AdminA is a general codex in almost each administrative procedure – with the exception of taxation issues – that provides legal remedy in all substantial decisions of the authority, such as refusal of application, withdrawal of the permit, refused prolongation of the certificate or imposition of a fine. In accordance with this, within eight to fifteen days of the substantial decision's notice to the client, an appeal may be submitted to the higher administrative organ of the proceedings authority. The appeal has a suspensive effect unless the execution of the issued decision has to be immediately ordered on the ground of public policy, protection of life, property or national security. Regardless of the reasons for legal remedy, the second instance of administrative procedure involves checking the legality, formality and functionality of the first instance decision and finally it may modify, supplement, annul or confirm the first decision. A controlling mechanism on first instance decisions is ensured through the public prosecutor's review and regular supervision by the second instance authority as well. The final administrative decision may be reviewed at the County/Capital Administrative Court exclusively on the ground of violation of law that shall be indicated by the client.

511. The Court review is available not only in connection with the final administrative decision, but also in connection with the first instance decision if administrative remedy is excluded by law. For instance, the first instance decision belongs to the competence of the Minister or a central (national) office. According to the CivPA, the application for judicial review may be submitted to the County/Capital Administrative Court within thirty days of notice of the administrative decision to the client. It has no suspensive effect unless the judge, as a preparatory measure, orders suspension upon a verified, reasonable request of the client (e.g., protecting safety, property or sanitation). The Court reviews only the legality of the administrative decision in a non-litigation procedure (e.g., personal hearing is conducted as an exception) if fact-finding is not necessary or the opponent actor (respondent) has no intervention within a deadline. Judgment of the Court means abrogation of the decision, abrogation and order of repetition of the entire administrative procedure or as an exception – if law entitles the Court in certain issues – amendment of the administrative decision. Further appeal against this judgment is excluded. However, if the judicial review is based on the administrative decision in which administrative remedy is excluded, and the Court is entitled in law to amend the administrative decision – an appeal to the Regional Court is eligible. It is also justified in a non-litigation procedure, but upon the request of any client a judicial negotiation shall be appointed. The second instance judicial review may adopt the same types of judgment as adopted by the Court of first instance.

512. The AdminA shall be implemented in procedures relating to membership (entry, exclusion), registry issues (inclusion, deletion) in chambers or other public bodies that are entitled for decision-making in professionals' business activities unless law regulates otherwise. For instance, a refused application for membership in the Hungarian Veterinary Chamber shall be communicated to the applicant within thirty days that may be appealed also within thirty days. The Presidium of the Chamber shall decide it within thirty days. It may be reviewed by the County/Capital Administrative Court that may modify the final decision of the Chamber.[348]

513. The AdminA ensures numerous guarantees to fair procedure requirements, such as the following:

348. Act CXXVII of 2012 on Hungarian Veterinary Chamber and practice of private veterinaries.

(a) Right of the applicant to communicate in his/her mother tongue or other language or other applicable language upon his/her request. If the public official cannot understand the chosen language, an interpreter shall be involved, but the latter's fee is paid by the state if the administrative procedure relates to immediate protection of fundamental rights or the procedure is launched by the administrative organ (e.g., imposing a fine after an authority check *in situ*). In practice, a non-native client is accompanied by an assisting person in private entrepreneur and other self-employment authorization procedures.
(b) The client is entitled to delegate a representative in the administrative procedure. This person would be a friend, a family member or even a professional legal representative based on his/her option.
(c) The respect for personal data protection of the client and lawful basis of data processing, storage and transmission to other authorities is fully ensured in the procedure by law. In an appeal or a complaint to the National Authority of Data protection and Freedom of Information, the client may enforce personal data protection as a fundamental right. For instance, in the PrivA – as in other branches of law – there is an exhaustive list of the personal data of the client that shall be processed and transmitted to other competent authorities, and the period of storage of these data is also defined.
(d) Client or applicant has the right to be informed of relevant data of the case through reading the entire file in proceedings. This right to inspection covers personal data, evidences, expert opinion, protocols as well as confidential documents that established the authorization.
(e) The client or applicant is entitled to use electronic contact with the authority in proceedings through an electronic identification code. Without applying in person, through downloadable format and an electronic mail, he/she can obtain the authorization of a lot of requests, and at least one appointment, pay the fee or acquire information.

514. Procedure on membership, license and registry in a Chamber – as a precondition to engage in many activities in self-employment, private entrepreneurship or certain professions – belong to the scope of the AdminA. Chambers and other public bodies providing public services by law or decree shall be considered as public administrative organs. It means that they have to implement the AdminA together with all procedural safeguards and remedies. Two examples of the Court's entitlement to substantially modify the final administrative decision – including the Chamber's decision – determined by law, are as follows:

(a) The refusal of application for membership (and together with the license for private veterinary) by the Chamber of Pharmacists or of Medical Doctors[349] Chamber shall be notified to the applicant within thirty days. The same act provides inside appeal to the presidency of the Chamber if the county unit of the Chamber rejects the entry registration of the applicant (e.g., because he/she has not equivalent or recognized diploma that is required to the professional activity in

349. Act XCVII of 2006 on Professional Chambers in Health Care.

Hungary). The Court is entitled to amend the Chamber's decision in judicial review.

(b) According to the TaxPA, the final decision of the tax authority may be modified at the judicial review for legality.

Selected Bibliography

Adelman, Howard, Sik, Endre & Tessényi, Geza (eds.). 'Genesis of a Refugee Regime, The Case of Hungary' York Lane Press, Toronto, 1994.

Berke, Barna, Gyulavári, Tams & Kiss, György (Szerk.). *'Külföldiek foglalkoztatása Magyarországon'* [Employment of Foreigners in Hungary] KJK-Kerszöv, Budapest, 2002.

Carlier, Jean-Yves. *'The status of persons in the European Union. Casebook of Judgements'* Bruylant, Brussels, 2008.

Demeter, Judit. *'Az egyenlő bánásmód sérelme miatt indult hatósági eljárások tapasztalatai'* In: Majtényi Balázs (szerk.) Lejtős pálya. Antidiszkrimináció esesélyegyenlőség [The Practice of Procedures by ETA] L'Harmattan Kiadó, Budapest, 2009, 67–88.

Drinóczi, Timea. 'A piacgazdaság és a versenyszabadság.' In Chronowski et al. (eds.) *Magyaralkotmányjog III. Alapvető jogok.* Hungarian Constitutional Law – Fundamental Rights, Vol. 3. Dialóg Campus, Pécs 2006, 463–465.

Feischmidt Margit & Nyíri Pél (szerk.). *'Nem kívánt gyerekek. Külföldi gyerekek magyariskolákban'* [Not Desired Children in Public Schools in Hungary: Migrants] MTA Kisebbségkutató Intézet, Budapest, 2006.

Finszter, Géza. *'A rendészeti funkciók és a határőrség integrációja'* [Functions of Law Enforcement and Institutional Changes] In: Hautzinger, Zoltán (szerk.) Tanulmányok a Határőrség és rendőrség – az integrált rendvédelem című tudományos konferenciáról. Pécsi Határőr Tudományos Közleménye, Pécs, 2007, 13–27.

Fleck, Zoltán. *'Jogállam és igazságszolgáltatás a változó világban'* [Rule of Law and Justice in a Changing World] Pallas Páholy – Gondolat Kladó, Budapest, 2008.

Forgács, Imre. *'The Dilemmas of Public Administration in the Age of Integration'* Presentation Given at the Public Administration Conference *'Administration in the 21st Century'* Organised by HAS Public Administration Committee on 29 November 2006. It is summarised in *Európai Tükör*, Special Issues 2006. August, 39–46.

Groenendijk, Kees, Fernhout, Roel, Van Dam, Dominique, Van Oers, Ricky & Strik Tineke. 'The Family Reunification Directive in EU Member States. The first year of implementation' Comparative study. Centre for Migration Law, Nijmegen, 2007.

de Groot, René. 'A Clarification of the Fundamental Rights Implications of Stateless and Persons Erased from the Register of Residents' Briefing paper, European Parliament. December, 2007.

Guild Elspeth. 'Security of Residence and Expulsion of Foreigners: European Community Law'. In Guild E. & Minderhoud, P. (eds.) Security of Residence and Expulsion. Protection of Aliens in Europe. Kluwer Law International, 2001, 59–80.

Gyeney, Laura. *'Legális bevándorlás az Európai Unióba, különös tekintettel a családi élet tiszteletben tartásának jogára'* [Legal Immigration to the EU in the Context of the Right to Family Life] Pázmány Press, Budapest, 2014.

Gyulai, Gábor. 'Forgotten without Reason – Protection of Non-refugee Stateless Persons in Central Europe' Hungarian Helsinki Committee, Budapest, 2007.

Gyulai, Gábor. *'Hontalanság Magyarországon. Jelentés a hontalanok védelméről, a hontalanság megelőzéséről és csökkentéséről'* [Magyar Helsinki Bizottság Statelessness in Hungary – Report on Protection, Prevention and Reduction of Statelessness by the Hungarian Helsinki Committee], Budapest, 2010 December.

Gyulavári, Tamás. *'Három évvel az antidiszkriminációs szabályozás reformja után'* [Three Year Results in Practice of Act on Equal Treatment]. *Esély*, 2007/3: 3–35.

Haász, Veronika & Szappanyos, Melinda. *'Az ENSZ tagállamok emberi jogi helyzetét értékelő egyetemes időszakos felülvizsgálat (UPR)'* [The UN UPR System for Member States] Föld-rász 2011/1: 71–83.

Hajduk, Annamária (Szerk.). *'Esély vagy veszély? Bevándorlás Magyarországra'* [Immigration to Hungary: A Chance or a Threat?]. DEMOS, 2008.október.

Halmai, Gábor & Tóth, Attila Gábor (Szerk.). *'Emberi jogok'* [Human rights] Osiris Kiadó, Budapest, 2003.

Harvey, Colin. 'Promoting Insecurity: Public Order, Expulsion and the European Convention on Human Rights'. In: Security of Residence and Expulsion. Protection of Aliens in Europe. Guild, E. and Minderhoud, P. (eds.), Kluwer Law International, 2001. 41–57.

Hoványi, Gábor. *'A tudás és a nemzetközi tudásháló szerepe egy régió iparának fejlődésében'* [Knowledge and Role of Networks in the Industrial Development of our Region] *Európai Tükör* 2008/5: 47–57.

Hudák, Annamária, Gellér, Balázs, Kiss, László & Lukács, Éva. *'A diplomák ésszakképesítések kölcsönös elismerése az Euróoai Unióban és Magyarországon'* [Mutual Recognition of Qualifications and Diplomas in the EU] Egészségügyi, Szociális és Családügyi Minisztérium, Budapest, 2003.

Illés Sándor & Lukács, Éva Gellérné. 'Towards Researcher Mobility' *Európai Tükör*, Special Issue 2007/8: 139–155.

Illés, Sándor & Melegh, Attila. 'Hungary in the Schengen System: Bastion or Gateway? Qualitative and Quantitative Analysis of the Schengen-based Visa-system and Visa Issuance Practice in Hungary' Budapest, 2009 Hungarian Europe Society.

Inzelt, Annamária. *'Közvetlen tőkebefektetések és a vezetői tudás áramlása az átmenet idején'* [Direct Investment and Influx of Leaders' Knowledge in Transition Period] *Európai Tükör* 2008/1: 46–72.

Kádár, András. *'A bőség zavara? A magyar antidiszkriminációs rendszer vázlata'* In: Majtényi Balázs (szerk.) Lejtős pálya. Antidiszkrimináció és esélyegyenlőség

[The Structure of Counter-discrimination System in Hungary] L'Harmattan Kiadó, Budapest, 2009. 27–49.

Kovács, M. Mária & Tóth, Judit. '*Kin-state responsibility and ethnic citizenship*: The Hungarian case' In: *Citizenship Policies in the New Europe*. Rainer Bauböck, Bernhard Perchinig and Wiebke Sievers (eds.). Amsterdam University Press, 2007, 135–159.

Kovách, Imre, Nagy, Éva, Tibori, Timea & Tóth, Ágnes (szerk.). '*Európai Magyarország 2007*' [Hungary in Europe, 2007. It contains summary in English]. Budapest, MTA 2007, pp. 346–369.

Kováts, András (szerk.). '*Magyarrá válni. Bevándorlók honosítási és integrációs stratégiái*' [How to Become Hungarian – Immigrants' Strategy of Naturalisation and Integration] MTA Etnikai-nemzeti Kisebbségkutató Intézet, Budapest 2011, pp. 274.

Lukács, Éva Gellérné. '*Munkaerőszűrés a minőségért*' [How to Select the Best in the Labourmarket], OFA – KSH Kutatási Jelentések, Budapest 2007. 1–40.

Lukács, Éva Gellérné. '*Munkavállalók szabad mozgása az Európai Unióban – Gondolatok egy 40 éves évfordulóra*' [Free Movement of Workers in the European Union – to the 40th Anniversary]. *Föld-rész*, 2009/1: 9–23.

Lukács, Éva Gellérné & Gyulavári, Tamás. '*Szociálpolitika és foglalkoztatás*' [Social Rights and Employment] 199–215. *Európai Tükör*, Magyarország 5 éve az Európai Unióban. Special Issue, 2009 March, 199–215.

Mink, András. '*Alperes: az állam. A Magyar Helsinki Bizottság története*' [Defender: The State – The History of the Hungarian Helsinki Committee]. Budapest, 2005 MHB.

Nemes, Andras & Tóth, Judit. '*European Sportlaw (Textbook on Basics of Legal Studies – for Human Kinesiologists, Trainers and P.E. Teachers)*' Semmelweis University Budapest, Faculty of Physical Education and Sport Sciences. Revised edition, Budapest, 2002.

Nicholson, Frances, 'Challenges to Forging a Common European Asylum System in Line with International Obligations' In: *EU Immigration and Asylum Law. Text and Commentary*. Peers, Steve and Rogers, Nicola (eds.) Martinus Nijhoff Publishers, Leiden 2006, 505–537.

Pap, András László. '*Mozgásszabadság. Alkotmányjogi és nemzetkozi jogi alapok*' [Freedom of Movement – Its Constitutional and International Legal Basis]. L'Harmattan, Budapest, 2009.

Peers, Steve & Rogers, Nicola (eds.). *EU Immigration and Asylum Law. Text and Commentary*. Martinus Nijhoff Publishers, Leiden 2006, 1–1025.

Puskás, Julianna (ed.). 'Overseas Migration from East-Central and Southeastern Europe 1880–1940' Akadémiai Kiadó, 1990.

Rácz, István. '*A paraszti migráció és politikai megítélése Magyarországon 1849-1914*' [Emigration from Rural Area and its Political Assessment in Hungary 1849-1914]. Akadémia Könyvkiadó, Budapest 1980.

Sárosi, Annamária. '*Az állampolgárságot kapott külföldiek jellemzése Magyarországon és az Európai Unióban*' [The Socio-demographic Features of Re/naturalised Persons in Hungary and in the EU] In 'Magyarrá válni. Bevándorlók honosítási és integrációs stratégiái' Szerk. Kováts, A. MTA ENKI, Budapest, 2011, 101–126.

Szarka, László (ed.). 'Hungary and the Hungarian Minorities (Trends int he Past and in Our Time)' East European Monographs No. DCLVII, Columbia University Press, New York, 2004.

Takács, Albert. *'Szociális jogok' – A munkához való jog'* [Social Rights – Right to Work] In: Emberi jogok (Szerk: Halmai Gábor – Tóth Gábor Attila). Osiris, Budapest, 2003: 837–853.

Tóth, Judit. *'Menedékjog – kérdőjelekkel'* [Asylum Law with Burning Questions]. Közgazdasági és Jogi Könyvkiadó, Budapest, 1994. In its Appendix the author translated the UNHCR Handbook on refugee determination and some EEC documents pp. 272.

Tóth Judit. *'Átlépés a határon és a szállító társaságok felelőssége'* [Crossing the Borders and Sanctions against Carriers]. *Acta Humana* (1997) No. 27. pp. 52–66.

Tóth Judit (2000a). 'Diaspora Politics: Programs and Prospects' In: *New Diasporas in Hungary, Russia and Ukraine: Legal Regulations and Current Politics.* Kiss, I. and McGovern, C. (eds.) Open Society Institute/COLPI, Budapest, 2000, pp. 96–141.

Tóth Judit (2000b). 'Diaspora in Legal Regulations: 1989-1999' In: New Diasporas in Hungary, Russia and Ukraine: Legal Regulations and Current Politics) Kiss, I. and McGovern, C. (eds.) Open Society Institute/COLPI, Budapest, 2000, pp. 42–95.

Tóth Judit (2001a). 'Security of Residence and Expulsion: Protection of Aliens in Hungary. In Guild, E. & Minderhoud, P. (eds.) Security of Residence and Expulsion. Protection of Aliens in Europe. Kluwer Law International, 2001a, 165–174.

Tóth Judit (2001b). The Impact of the EU Migration Policies on Central-Eastern European Countries. *Refugee Survey Quarterly* (Oxford University Press) Vol.20, No.2 (2001b) pp. 102–114.

Tóth, Judit (2001c). *'A menedék anyagi jogi szabályai'* [The Substantive Rules on Asylum] In: Menedékjog a magyar gyakorlatban. Kézikönyv a menekültügyi eljárás résztvevői számára. Szerk: Kőszeg F. Kossuth Egyetemi Kiadó, Debrecen 2001, 47–85.

Tóth, Judit (2001d). *'A nemzetközi migráció jogi alapjai'*. In: Migráció és Európai Unió. (Szerk: Lukács Éva–Király Miklós) AduPrint, Budapest, 2001, pp. 81–123.

Tóth Judit (2002a). 'Pulling the Wool over Hungarians' Eyes. *Regio* (A review of studies on minorities, politics and society) 2002, Budapest, pp. 129–150.

Tóth, Judit (2002b). *'Világméretű párbeszéd a menedékjogról'* [Universal Dialogue in the UN on the Enganced Protection of Refugees]. *Acta Humana* 2002/48: 3–37.

Tóth Judit (2004a). *'Menekültek Magyarországon a jogi szabályozás tükrében'* [Refugees in the Hungarian Legal System] *Pannonhalmi Szemle,* 2004/3: 53–70.

Tóth, Judit (2004b). *'Státusjogok'* [Legal Standing of Nationals and Migrants in the Hungarian Legal System] Kisebbségkutatás Könyvek, Lucidus Kiadó, Budapest, 2004.

Tóth Judit. 'Principles and Practice of Nationality Law in Hungary' *Regio* (Minorities, Politics, Society) Vol. 8; 2005, pp. 21–39.

Tóth, Judit (2006a). *'Az európai menedékjogi és migrációs térség létrehozása. Oktatási anyag – Bírákképzése'* [Towards a Common Asylum and Migration Area in the EU – Training Material to Judges]. Országos Igazságszolgáltatási Hivatal, Budapest – Perfect Rt. 2006. január pp. 1–50.

Tóth, Judit (2006b). *'Migrant workers and free movement in Hungary'* In: *A Regional Approach to Free Movement of Workers: Labour Migration between Hungary and its Neighbouring Countries.* Julia Traser (ed.) European Studies Centre No.1, Szeged 2006, 25–32.

Tóth, Judit (2006c). *'Mit ér az állampolgárság, ha magyar?'* [What is the Legal Substance of the Hungarian National Status?] In: Közjogi tanulmányok Lőrincz Lajos 70. születésnapja tiszteletére. Szerk: Imre Miklós – Lamm Vanda – Máthé Gábor, Corvinus Egyetem – Károli Gáspár Református Egyetem – MTA Jogtudományi Intézet, Budapest, 2006. 419–426.

Tóth, Judit (2007a). *'Közérdek az Európai Bíróság előtt'* [Public Interest in the Case Law of European Court of Justice] *Európai Tükör,* 2007/1: 31–58.

Tóth, Judit (2007b). 'Is it Possible to Regulate Citizenship by Referendum?' *Minorities Research* (A Selection of Studies by Hungarian Authors) Budapest, Lucidus, No. 9, 2007, 88–121.

Tóth, Judit (2008a). *'Is there a Strategy on the Foreign Labour Force in Hungary?' Minorities Research* (A Selection of Studies by Hungarian Authors), Budapest, Lucidus, 2008, No. 10: 9–24.

Tóth, Judit (2008b). *'Munkaerőmozgás és az Európai Unió bővítése az átmeneti rendelkezésektükrében'* [Movement of Workers and Transitional Provisons in the Enlarged EU] *Romániai Magyar Jogtudományi Közlöny,* 2008/12: 5–10.

Tóth, Judit (2008c). 'When an Emergency has Come to Stay – The Birth of the Refugee Administration in 1988–89'. *Regio (Minorities, Politics, Society)* 2008/11: 96–145.

Tóth, Judit. 'Acquiring Nationality: Is it a Goal, a Tool, or an Assessment of Integration?' In: Legal Frameworks for the Integration of Third-Country Nationals. Niessen, Jan and Huddleston, Thomas (eds.). Martinus Nijhoff Publishers, Vol.18 'Immigration and Asylum Law and Policy in Europe', Leiden –Boston, 2009: 159-193.

Tóth Judit: Az uniós munkavállalók mozgása és annak néhány akadálya [Certain objections in free movement of workers]. *Föld-rész,* 2011/1: 47–69.

Tóth, Judit & Sik, Endre. 'Joining an EU Identity. Integration of Hungary or the Hungarians?' In: *Europeanization, National Identities and Migration. Changes in Boundary Constructions between Western and Eastern Europe.* Spohn, W. and Triandafyllidou, A. (eds.), Routledge Advances in Sociology. Routledge, 2003: 223–244.

Tóth, Judit & Sik, Endre. 'Hungary. In: European Immigration. A Sourcebook', Second edition. Tiandafyllidou, A. & Gropas, R. (eds.). Ashgate, Research in Migration and Ethnic Relations Series, England, 2014, pp. 173–184.

Varga, Réka. *'A Római Statútum jelentősége a nemzetközi jogban és a nemzetközi-büntetőjogban'* [The Relevance of the Rome Statute to the International Public and Penal Law] *Iustum Aequum Salutare* 2006/1-2: 95–98.

Váradi, Luca. 'Immigration Business in Hungary' *Central European Political Science Review* 2005/20: 117–139.

Selected Bibliography

Váradi, Luca. 'The Visa in Practice at the Serbian and at the Ukrainian Borders'. *Regio Minorities, Politics, Society)* 2006/9:150–178.
Zsoldos, Attila. 'The Legacy of Saint Stephen'. Lucidus, Budapest 2004.

Appendix

List of authority competences in migration relevant issues

Name	*Competence and tasks*			*Vertical units*		*Remark*
Ministry of the Interior	Migration policy and integration policy of migrants	Second instance decision in equity (national residence and asylum request)	Second instance decision in certain visa and humanitarian admission request	Responsibility for OIN, Police and civil security services	Directing the Central Registration Office	The name of the ministry was changed (2006–2011: Justice and Law Enforcement)
Ministry of Foreign Affairs	Representation in COREPER, formation of common external policy of the EU and in international organization (UNHCR EXCOM, UN HRC …)	Admission of diplomats and family members	Second instance decision in certain visa issues	Directing embassies and consular offices worldwide		

Name	*Competence and tasks*			*Vertical units*		*Remark*
Ministry of Justice	Legal harmonization and transposition of EU law, responsible for codification (preparatory to legislation and decree-making)	Co-operation with governmental agencies, ministries for a better governance	Responsible for free legal aid and legal assistance for protection seekers, expelled migrants	Directing the Office of Justice and its county/ capital units (20) that are inserted into the governmental offices		The name of Office of Justice was changed and formally inserted some units to the County/Capital offices of the public administration (Government Window)
Secretariat of the Prime Minister	Responsible for civil intelligence service	Responsible for governmental agenda		Directing the Civil Intelligence Service	Directing the county/capital governmental offices (20)	
Ministry of Human Resources	Public education policy also for migrants Health care policy	High-education and research policy providing invitation, scholarships for non-nationals	International co-operation in recognition of qualifications	Directing the Educational Office and National Equivalence Centre		

Ministry of National Economy	Employment policy	Public revenue and taxation policy	State budget and state household policy	Directing the county (19), capital and city (150) labour offices that are inserted into the governmental offices		
Office for Immigration and Naturalization (OIN)	First instance decision in certain admission and international protection, stateless status	Preparatory of naturalization	National contact-point in Eurodac, VIS, SIS, Prüm Agreement and re-admission, surrender issues	Second instance in entry, residence and removal authorization and expert opinion to other law enforcement organizations	Directing the Regional Directorate (7) and refugee centres (3)	
Police	Enforcement of migrants' removal	Expert opinion in admission and residence authorization, naturalization	Public hostels and compulsory confinements are managed	Border control, in-depth control and street checking	Headquarters, County (19), Capital and local (150) police units Anti-corruption and Counter-terror units	The Centre of Counter-terrorism was set up and the anti-corruption unit was extended in 2011

Name	*Competence and tasks*			*Vertical units*		*Remark*
Security services	Protection of sovereignty and constitutional order of the country	Expert opinion in admission and residence authorization, naturalization	Co-operation with partner authorities (in SIS, VIS … .)	NSO, Intelligence Service and Service Centre		NSO was renamed as Office for Constituional Protection
Consular offices	First instance decision in short-term visa (joint visa issuance on behalf of another Member State of the EU), small border traffic certificate issues	Consular protection of nationals	Co-operation with partners in Member States of the EU, emergency documents, evacuation …	Inside embassies and separate consular offices (approximately 70)		
National Employment Service	First instance decision in labour authorization Imposing fine	Conditions of employment and legality of employment is controlled	Registry of employed persons and manpower agencies Co-operation with law-enforcement	Unemployment and labour services at county/capital (20) and district governmental offices (170)	Labour inspection directorates at county/capital labour services (20)	

National Equivalence Centre	Decision in recognition of qualifications (diploma, scientific degree)	Co-operation with partners (e.g., Vocational Training Centre and Chambers of professionals) in equivalence issues	International co-operation (e.g., NARIC)	–		System of recognition is decentralised by sectors
National Tax and Customs Office (NAV)	Tax authorization (e.g., on private entrepreneurs)	Co-operation with law enforcement and labour inspectors	Customs and other public revenues authorization (e.g., social insurance contribution)	National Office directs country (19), Capital units		Customs Office and Tax Office was unified in 2011
National Innovation Office	Registry of accredited research institutes	Registry of hosting contract with third-country national researchers	–			Its name was changed more times in past

Name	*Competence and tasks*			*Vertical units*		*Remark*
Municipals	Public services for inhabitants in each settlement including migrants	3200 settlements at county (19) and capital, city and village level	Implementation of integration contract between the OIN and refugees, subsidiary protected persons residing in the settlement	Family care services		Tasks are reformed in 2012
Central Registration Office	Registry of address of inhabitants and registry of population	Identity card of nationals, long-term migrants, refugees	Passport for nationals	Directing 170 units that are inserted into district governmental offices		This entire system in this form will operate since 2012
Central Statistical Office	Migration statistics	Co-operation with EUROSTAT, UN, OECD on migration statistics	Directing the county units (20)			

Central Public Health Service	Medical screening of protection seekers, age control	Medical warrant of public health risk of migrants in residence authorization (notification to immigration authority)	Health condition certificate to labour contract	Capital/County Sanitary Authority that are inserted to governmental offices (20)	District and City (150) Sanitary Authority that are inserted to governmental offices and PHS institutes	
State President Office	Decision in naturalization and loss of nationality		–			
Public Prosecutors Office	Control on legality of deprivation of liberty	Public charge authority in trial	Control on legality of actions in public administration	Chief prosecutor directs county (19) and capital offices		
Courts	Judicial review on final administrative decisions	Remedy (second instance decisions by higher courts)	Registration and legal control on business associations and sole proprietorship by the Courts of Registry (20)	No hierarchy –		Supreme Court, Superior Courts (5), Capital/County Administrative Courts (20),L Local Courts (170)

Appendix

Name	*Competence and tasks*			*Vertical units*		*Remark*
Ombudsman	Remedy in maladministration cases					Ceasing the specific ombudsmen a universal ombudsman will set up in 2012

Index

The numbers here refer to paragraph numbers

Index

Index

Made in the USA
Monee, IL
18 October 2026

66037575R10201